BLOODLINES

Recovering Hitler's Nuremberg Laws,
From Patton's Trophy to Public Memorial

Anthony M. Platt

with Cecilia E. O'Leary

Paradigm Publishers
Boulder • London

Copyright © 2006 Paradigm Publishers

Published in the United States by Paradigm Publishers,
3360 Mitchell Lane, Suite E, Boulder, CO 80301 USA

Paradigm Publishers is the trade name of Birkenkamp & Company, LLC, Dean Birkenkamp, President and Publisher.

ISBN 1-59451-139-X (hardcover)
ISBN 1-59451-140-3 (paperback)

Library of Congress Cataloging-in-Publication Data

Platt, Anthony M.
  Bloodlines : recovering Hitler's Nuremberg Laws, from Patton's trophy to public memorial / Anthony M. Platt with Cecilia E. O'Leary.
    p. cm.
  Includes bibliographical references and index.
  ISBN 1-59451-139-X (hc) — ISBN 1-59451-140-3 (pbk) 1. Jews—Legal status, laws, etc.—Germany—History—20th century. 2.
Race defilement (Nuremberg Laws of 1935) 3.
Citizenship—Germany—History—20th century. 4. Germany—Politics and government—1933-1945. 5. Germany—Ethnic relations. 6. Henry E.
Huntington Library and Art Gallery. I. O'Leary, Cecilia Elizabeth, 1949- II. Title.
  DS135.G3315P63 2005
  943.086—dc22

                                2005027187

Printed and bound in the United States of America on acid-free paper that meets the standards of the American National Standard for Permanence of Paper for Printed Library Materials.

Designed, copyedited, and typeset by Gregory Shank, San Francisco.

10 09 08 07 06 1 2 3 4 5

For W. G. Sebald (1944–2001),
who complicated journeys past.
For Cassie, David, Joaquin, Jonah, Mila, and Nathan,
who face journeys ahead.

Contents

List of Illustrations	*vii*
Acknowledgments	*ix*
Definitions	*xi*
Quotations	*xii*

1 Origins Stories   1
Paradise for Humanists   1
The Closest You Come   5
The Last Word   12
A Suitable Past   15
Old Wounds   22

2 Present Absences   25
Almost-Jews   25
The Liberator   32
A Bolt out of the Blue   36
Oasis in the City   38

3 Tall Like Germans   42
Singing Germany   42
Postpone and Postpone   50

4 Human Betterment   55
Racial Hygiene   55
Eugenic Science   58
Nordic Internationalism   63

5 Blood and Honor   72
City of the Reich Party Rallies   72
The Jewish Question   75
Sentenced Without Guilt   80
Nazi Icon   82

6 Hitler's Signature   84
Refuge   84
American Citizen   86
Problem Child   89
Discovery at Eichstätt   91

7 Patton's Trophy   98
The Irony of Fate   98
War's End   100
The Important One   103

8 Outpost of Civilization   109
Company Village   109
To Hell with the People   115
In Their Proper Place   118

9 White Man's Burden   121
Too Much Democracy   121
Anglo-Saxon State   127
White City   129

10 Loot   132
Semitic Revenge   132
Evil Curiosities   136
Discipline in Peace   137
Public Presentation   138
Provenance   140

11 In Limbo   145
Quietly Ignored   145
Economics of Change   147
Public Face   149
Détente   151

12 History Lessons   160
Story of the Objects   160
Objects of the Story   165
Reframing   169
Mining the Past   171

13 Past and Present   175
In the Eyes of Others   175
Public History   179

Abbreviations   185
Chronology   186
End Notes   192
Sources and Bibliography   242
Index   257
About the Authors   268

Illustrations

1.1–3 The Nuremberg Laws, 1935. Reproduced by permission of *The Huntington Library, San Marino, California*. MSS Uncat. 6–9

1.4 Statement Dictated by General George S. Patton, Jr. Regarding Document Taken in Nuremberg, June 11, 1945. Reproduced by permission of *The Huntington Library, San Marino, California*. MSS Uncat. 16

1.5 *Mein Kampf*, 1941, signed by G. S. Patton, Jr., April 14, 1945. Reproduced by permission of *The Huntington Library, San Marino, California*. RB 258170. 17

1.6 General Patton presenting Huntington Trustee Robert Millikan with the packet of Nuremberg Laws, June 11, 1945. Reproduced by permission of *The Huntington Library, San Marino, California*. MSS Uncat. 18

1.7 George S. Patton, Jr., and Maurice Phillips as standard bearers at Pasadena Tournament of Roses, January 1, 1901. Reproduced by permission of *The Huntington Library, San Marino, California*. PhotCL 282 (210). 20

1.8 Mr. and Mrs. Patton with George Patton, Jr., Susan Patton, Henry Edwards Huntington, and Hancock Banning on porch of Lake Vineyard ranch, November 1903. Reproduced by permission of *The Huntington Library, San Marino, California*. PhotCL 282 (378). 21

2.1 Cecilia O'Leary and Martin Dannenberg in Baltimore, October 3, 1999. 37

2.2 Display Case of Nuremberg Laws and *Mein Kampf* at Skirball Cultural Center, Los Angeles, 1999. Copyright © Grant Mudford. 41

3.1 Frank Perls and Pablo Picasso, France, 1955. Courtesy of Marianne Perls. 49

4.1 Charles M. Goethe as a young man. Permission of California State University, Sacramento. Charles M. Goethe Collection. Department of Special Collections and University Archives. The Library. California State University, Sacramento. 66

5.1   Nuremberg, *ca.* April 1945. Courtesy of Martin Dannenberg.   73

6.1   Master Sergeant Martin Dannenberg in Germany, *ca.* April   93
1945. Courtesy of Martin Dannenberg.

6.2   Eichstätt, Germany, *ca.* April 1945. Courtesy of Martin   95
Dannenberg.

6.3–4   Martin Dannenberg and Frank Perls with Nuremberg Laws   96–97
in Eichstätt, Germany, April 27, 1945. Courtesy of Martin
Dannenberg.

7.1   General George S. Patton, Jr., with copy of *Mein Kampf* at   105
Huntington Library, June 11, 1945. Reproduced by permission
of *The Huntington Library, San Marino, California.* PhotPF
21100.

7.2   Huntington Library Board of Trustees luncheon, July 9, 1945.   107
Photo by Wendland/courtesy of the Archives, California
Institute of Technology. Robert Andrews Millikan Collection
89.8.

12.1   General Patton presenting Huntington Trustee Robert Millikan   161
with the packet of Nuremberg Laws, June 11, 1945. Reproduced
by permission of *The Huntington Library, San Marino,
California.* MSS Uncat.

12.2   Display Case of Nuremberg Laws and *Mein Kampf* at Skirball   164
Cultural Center, Los Angeles, 1999. Photograph by Ron
Eisenberg. Copyright © 1999, Skirball Cultural Center.

12.3   Martin Dannenberg's Visit to Skirball Cultural Center,   164
December 12, 1999. Photograph by Ron Eisenberg. Copyright
© 1999, Skirball Cultural Center.

12.4   Master Sergeant Martin Dannenberg in Germany, *ca.* April   170
1945. Courtesy of Martin Dannenberg.

Acknowledgments

This book was conceived as a joint project in the summer of 1999 when Cecilia O'Leary and I were visiting fellows at the Huntington Library. We developed the framework together and shared research tasks. For health reasons, Cecilia was not able to participate in the writing of the book, but she remained actively involved throughout the whole process, from first outline to last draft.

We would like to acknowledge the support and advice of many people, who guided us through a maze of research from San Marino to Nuremberg.

Special thanks to:

Martin Dannenberg, without whose memory and enthusiastic participation this project would not have been possible. Marianne Perls, who opened up her family's past to our investigation. Robert Patton, who welcomed an honest appraisal of his grandfather.

The Huntington Library: Robert Skotheim for facilitating access to internal documents; Dan Lewis for searching the archives; Alan Jutzi for encouraging leads; Susi Krasnoo for making us feel welcome; Maria Lepowsky for collegiality beyond the call of duty; Jennifer Watts and Erin Chase for help with photographs and documents; Lisa Blackburn for responding to many queries; and many other staff members, and past and present researchers, some of whom shared experiences with us on condition of anonymity. We recognize that Robert Skotheim and other members of his administration inherited many problems associated with the mishandling of the Nuremberg Laws by previous Huntington administrations.

The Skirball Cultural Center: Uri Herscher for his generosity of spirit and information; Pat Burdette for making our visits run smoothly; Robert Kirschner and Grace Cohen Grossman for sharing their curatorial insights; and Mia Cariño for documents and photographs.

The California Institute of Technology: Judith Goodstein for advice on sources; Bonnie Ludt for facilitating our research.

California State University, Sacramento: Jena Cooreman, Ethan Evans, Alaina Fasano, Becky Gieck, and Aleah Kiley for research assistance; Betty Moulds for help navigating the bureaucracy; and Lynn Cooper for steady friendship and support.

Gerhard Jochem at the Nuremberg City Archives for advice, interest, and practical help; Michael Berenbaum for insights about the Nuremberg Laws; Eric Chaim Kline for expertise on rare books and documents; Dick Walker and Kerwin Klein for guidance on California history; Lonnie Bunch for advice about the ethical responsibilities of museums; Walter Hill for facilitating access to documents and curators at the National Archives; Martin Blumenson, Richard Boylan, Greg Bradsher, Hugh Cole, Carlo D'Este, Harold Langley, and Ed Linenthal for introducing us to the inner world of the military; and Alex Stern for generously sharing her research on eugenics.

The numerous librarians, curators, archivists, and journalists who helped us to find the evidence: Jill Cogen (Huntington Library), Fred Bauman and Bruce Kirby (Library of Congress), Kurt Kuss, Sheila O'Neill, Julie Thomas (California State University, Sacramento), Charles Lemons (Patton Museum), Dale Mayer (Herbert Hoover Presidential Library), Dan McLaughlin (Pasadena Public Library), Mary Osielski (State University of New York at Albany), Karla Pearce (American Public Health Association), Tania Rizzo (Pasadena Historical Museum), Jessica Silver (Japanese American National Museum), Judy Throm (Smithsonian Archives of American Art), Alycia Vivona (Franklin D. Roosevelt Library), Viola Voss (Leo Baeck Institute), Steve Wasserman (*Los Angeles Times*), and Sharon Waxman (*Washington Post*).

The translators who made it possible for us to understand documents in German: Eva Ackerman, John Englander, Eva Englander, Clara Lato, and Greg Shank.

Friends and colleagues who over the years have encouraged me to blend my academic and creative writing voices: Frances Payne Adler, David Edgar, Betita Martínez, Mark Rabine, Dennis Sherman, and Janet Wolff.

Paradigm Publishers and its president Dean Birkenkamp for taking a chance on this project, especially my editor Leslie Lomas who imagined a book long before it became one; Alison Sullenberger, who got out the word; and Greg Shank, long-time friend and colleague, who turned words into a publication.

Those best of friends who closely and critically read too many proposals, drafts, and chapters: Lydia Chavez, Maria Lepowsky, Ed McCaughan, Janelle Reinelt, Dennis Sherman, Alex Stern, Dick Walker, and Janet Wolff. I wanted to hear those magic words, "Do not change one word," but fortunately they disregarded my request.

Tony Platt
Berkeley, August 2005

Definitions

Blood: A vital or animating force; national or racial ancestry.

Bloodline: Direct line of descendants; pedigree.

Cover: (verb) To place something upon or over, so as to protect or conceal; to be responsible for reporting the details of; to protect by occupying a strategic position.

Cover: (noun) A protective overlay; something that provides shelter; something, such as darkness, that screens, conceals, or disguises.

Coverage: The extent or degree to which something is observed, analyzed, and reported.

Covering: Something that covers so as to protect or conceal.

Memorial: Serving as a remembrance of a person or an event; of, relating to, or being in memory.

Recover: To get back; to restore to a normal state; to bring back under observation again; to get back something lost or taken away; to cover anew.

Recovery: Something gained or restored in recovering.

Trophy: A prize or memento received as a symbol of victory; a memento, as of one's personal achievements; the spoils of war.

Definitions have been selected from *The American College Dictionary*, Third Edition (Boston: Houghton Mifflin Company, 1997).

Pile the bodies high at Austerlitz and Waterloo.
Shovel them under and let me work—
I am the grass; I cover all.

Carl Sandburg, *Grass* (1918)

Doing history means building bridges between the past and present, ob-
serving both banks of the river, taking an active part on both sides.... The
tectonic layers of our lives rest so tightly one on top of the other that we
always come up against earlier events in later ones, not as matter that
has been fully formed and pushed aside, but absolutely present and alive.

Bernhard Schlink, *The Reader* (1995)

I have kept asking myself ... what the invisible connections that
determine our lives are, and how the threads run.

W. G. Sebald, *An Attempt at Restitution* (2001)

◙ Chapter 1 ◙

Origins Stories

We, the survivors, see everything from above, see everything at once, and still we do not know how it was.

(W. G. Sebald, 1999)

PARADISE FOR HUMANISTS

During the summer of 1999, Cecilia O'Leary and I were awarded fellowships to study California's cultural history at the prestigious Henry E. Huntington Library and Art Gallery in Southern California.[1] We expected our stay in secluded San Marino to be a leisurely break from preparing classes and our everyday lives as politically active intellectuals. Instead, we soon found ourselves in the middle of a passionate controversy about public history. Little did we imagine that a scholarly project on nineteenth-century Western history would lead us to an exploration of modern European history, Nazi legislation, the relationship between anti-Semitism and racism, fascist sympathies among California's elite, and the cultural politics of libraries and museums. And I certainly had no idea that this comfortable sabbatical in a sylvan retreat would trigger an exploration of contradictions in my own Jewish identity.

The Huntington, as it is known, is one of the oldest and most distinguished private institutions in the United States, globally recognized for its extraordinary library of rare books, exclusive collection of fine art, and elegant gardens. "Outside I have found a Garden of Eden for botanists," reported a visiting scholar in the 1940s, "and inside a paradise for humanists."[2] For almost eighty years, since it opened its doors on a full-time basis to visitors in 1928, the "breathtaking" Huntington has been on every tourist list as "one of the real jewels of Southern California."[3] Architecturally, its Beaux Arts buildings and palatial grounds evoke the imposing grandeur and gravitas of a European estate. Today, the half million annual visitors come primarily to stroll through one hundred and thirty acres of gardens; to visit the galleries in order to see Thomas Gainsborough's "Blue Boy" and other well-known examples of eighteenth and nineteenth century British

1

and French art; and to attend special events, such as the popular Lincoln and Washington exhibitions mounted in the 1990s.

Most visitors, however, are oblivious to the fact that at the center of the Huntington is its library, which by the 1940s had achieved a worldwide reputation as a "Research Shangri-La" among scholars interested in its specialized collections on "the intellectual development of the English-speaking peoples."[4] The Huntington now houses close to eight hundred thousand rare books and reference books, almost half a million photographs, more than half a million prints, maps, and ephemera, and four and one-half million manuscripts on British and American history, literature, art, and science.[5] Treasured items include the Ellsemere manuscript of Chaucer's *The Canterbury Tales* (*ca.* 1410), the Gutenberg Bible (*ca.* 1455), original letters of Washington, Jefferson, Franklin, and Lincoln, a collection of early editions of Shakespeare, and first editions of Wordsworth, Shelley, and Thoreau.[6]

Cecilia and I found ourselves in the middle of this exclusive establishment, two of only two thousand researchers a year with access to the library's resources. We were there with a handful of other fellows, competitively selected, for the summer 1999 program. As professors in a state university system, with a demanding teaching load and few opportunities for research, we looked forward to steeping ourselves in the Huntington's unique collection, with time off to stroll through acres of manicured gardens and take afternoon tea in the Rose Garden Room. At the end of May we turned in our grades for the spring semester, closed down our home in Berkeley, and loaded up the car with our bikes and beach equipment, ready for the good life in the sun. We planned to do research on weekdays, but not make work into an obsession, especially since Cecilia was recovering from a serious illness. We had rented a house with a large pool in nearby Pasadena and invited family and friends to join us at the weekends for barbeques, hiking the Mt. Wilson trail, and workouts at the local health club. On June 1, the Huntington's staff welcomed us into the inner sanctum, briefed us on an extensive list of dos and don'ts, and assigned us our own desks in the library's clubby reading room.

Our proposed project focused on public amnesia: how California's violent origins have been largely forgotten and replaced by "invented traditions."[7] Our aim was to understand how the state's preoccupation with utopian visions has obscured the bloody tragedies and atrocities that accompanied the rise of the Golden State. "Nowhere else were we Americans more affected than here, in our lives and conduct," wrote philosopher Josiah Royce in 1886, "by the feeling that we stood in the position of conquerors in a new land."[8] More than a century later, myths of progress have obscured the state's genesis in militarism and conquest. In California, says Joan Didion reflecting upon her own upbringing, "we did not believe that history could bloody the land, or even touch it."[9] Our research would illuminate, we hoped, the processes by which a variety of narratives became tapered into official history and embedded in everyday life—shaping the way we teach history in our schools and colleges; commemorating significant dates, people, and events; and enshrining historical significance in statues, symbols, and public holidays.

Cecilia had just completed a book on American patriotism that focused on how the nation battled over cultural definitions of loyalty and citizenship in the aftermath of the Civil War.[10] Drawn to this topic by her experience in the anti-war movement, she wanted to understand why the Right has so effectively monopolized the symbols of nationalism.[11] Now she intended to examine how the Mexican-American War, the Gold Rush and settler vigilantism, the Indian Wars, and the Spanish-American War in the Philippines shaped cultural rituals of patriotism in the West. My research would focus on how textbooks, travel guides, and the popular press glorified, justified, or minimized California's long history of violence and warfare.

We could not have found a better place than the Huntington to study the narrative of California: the stories, images, and symbols perceived as standing for the cultural essence of the state. Its collection of Western Americana includes diaries, correspondence, magazines, photographs, advertisements, and the personal papers of the men and women who created influential images of the Golden State. The Huntington's collections, we hoped, would enable us to understand the making and remaking of "the California story." We did not realize at the time that our investigation would take us across unanticipated historical and geographical borders, revealing "invisible connections that determine our lives ... and how the threads run."[12]

Eating breakfast on the patio by the pool on the last Saturday of June, I opened up the *Los Angeles Times* to read a front-page story that caught and retained my attention for the next five years. "Hitler Papers, Held Since '45 by Huntington, to Go on Display," read the headline.[13] It was a surprise to me and most of the world that the Huntington had stored an original copy of the Nuremberg Laws, including Hitler's "Blood Law," in its most secure, bombproof vault for the previous fifty-four years.

Over the weekend, I looked for more information about this unexpected announcement and found it everywhere: in the *New York Times*, on the Internet, and on television and radio talk shows. The last time anything this important had had happened to the Huntington was in 1991 when it provided access for scholars to its photographic archive of the Dead Sea Scrolls, an event that enhanced the Library's public-spirited reputation.[14] The Huntington is accustomed to routinely receiving flattering publicity about its world-famous acquisitions, popular exhibits, and breathtaking gardens.[15]

Once again, Huntington officials expected to draw favorable worldwide attention to its announcement on June 26, 1999, of its ownership of a rare original copy of Hitler's Nuremberg Laws, which it had possessed since 1945.[16] Three days later, for the first time in the United States, the documents would be put on public display in Los Angeles at the Skirball, a shimmering, new Jewish cultural center that is prominently located in the Sepulveda Pass. What caught my attention in the story was that the Huntington had kept the Nuremberg materials off the books since 1945, without disclosing their presence to scholars or the public — preserved but not accessioned.

The Huntington, it was reported, would continue to own the documents, but would loan them to the Skirball for an indefinite period. In addition, the Huntington announced its loan to the Skirball of a "deluxe edition of Hitler's *Mein Kampf* whose nightmarish vision was realized by the Nuremberg decrees." The Nuremberg Laws and the book, claimed the Huntington, "were both presented to General George S. Patton, Jr. by his troops in 1945, and were later given to the Huntington by the general, along with correspondence from the general to the Huntington concerning all of these materials."[17]

The Huntington's announcement that it owned the original Nuremberg Laws struck a note of incongruity. Perhaps it was the revelation of an icon that evoked one of Europe's most notorious tragedies in juxtaposition to a stately library that had been imagined in the early twentieth century as a "Parthenon in Pasadena."[18] The Huntington was the personal vision of Henry Edwards Huntington, who made a small fortune through development of the Pacific Electric Railway Company and other shrewd real estate speculation in and around Los Angeles. In 1913, Edward Huntington — as family and friends knew him — married his uncle's widow, Arabella, thereby combining the family's grand fortune amassed by railroad tycoon Collis Huntington of "Big Four" fame.[19] After ruthlessly buying up the contents of more than two hundred libraries, Huntington moved his nationally acclaimed collection from New York to the West Coast, much to the grumbling of the national guardians of cultural taste who regarded Southern California as the "hinterlands."[20]

When the Nuremberg Laws surfaced in the exclusive residential enclave of San Marino in the summer of 1999, thousands of miles from their birthplace sixty-four years earlier, there was an extraordinary flurry of media activity. The Huntington's announcement drew more publicity than its public relations department could handle. The event was covered around the world in one thousand print and six hundred television stories.[21] Beyond the *Los Angeles Times*, it was a front-page story in the *Washington Post*. CNN reported the event, as did the *Sunday Herald* in Scotland, *Agence France Presse*, and the *International Herald Tribune*. The *New York Times* reported the story on June 26 and again with translations of the Nuremberg Laws in its July 4 "Week in Review." Robert Skotheim and Uri Herscher, the presidents of the Huntington and Skirball respectively, were interviewed together on National Public Radio and NBC's "Today" show.[22] "The Nuremberg Laws of Hitler's Germany," observed the *New York Times*, "surely ranks among the most chilling documents of the 20th century." For the *Washington Post*, the 1935 legislation was "a landmark, chilling moment in the official persecution of the Jews." The Nuremberg Laws were described as "a document of immense historical moment" by the *International Herald Tribune*, as "emblematic of evil" by National Public Radio, and as "the most ignominious documents in the Jews' 4,000-year history" by the *Christian Science Monitor*.

The Nuremberg Laws—so called because Hitler ordered their passage in Nuremberg during the Nazi party's 1935 rally—consisted of three separate pieces of legislation that were approved unanimously by the Reichstag on September 15, 1935, and put into effect the following day. The Reich Flag Law replaced the colors of the Weimar Republic with the swastika. The Reich Citizenship Law established a distinction between "citizens of the Reich," namely, those of German or related blood, who were entitled to full political and civil rights, and "subjects," who were excluded from those rights. "From that moment on," observes historian Saul Friedländer, Jews in Germany had "a status similar to that of foreigners."[23]

However, the third statute—the Law for the Protection of German Blood and Honor, typically described as the Blood Law—is widely regarded as synonymous with the Nuremberg Laws. It legislated the subordinate status of Jews by prohibiting marriage or sexual relations between Jews and German citizens and specified that Jews were not allowed to employ female German citizens under forty-five years old as servants, or to fly the German flag. All three laws carried Hitler's personal signature.[24]

THE CLOSEST YOU COME

I was initially surprised that the Huntington's announcement generated such a commotion. After all, historians have long recognized that the Nuremberg Laws neither initiated Nazi policies of anti-Semitism, nor were they the inevitable precursor to the gas chambers. One of the first serious histories of the Third Reich, which I remember reading in the 1960s while a graduate student at Berkeley, hardly even mentioned the Nuremberg Laws.[25] More recently, as historians such as Ian Kershaw have documented, it is generally recognized that Hitler built his political career out of his long-time "vitriolic hatred" of Jews, going back at least to 1919 when he produced his first political tracts.[26] "The mightiest counterpart to the Aryan is represented by the Jew," Hitler wrote in *Mein Kampf*, published in 1925.[27] In 1933, the first year of the Third Reich, Jews were barred from public office, the civil service, journalism, and the legal profession; in 1934, they were removed from the Stock Exchange.[28] As Raul Hilberg observed, "When in the early days of 1933 the first civil servant wrote the first definition of 'non-Aryan' into a civil service ordinance, the fate of European Jewry was sealed."[29] Adopted by the Reichstag without discussion or debate in 1935, the Nuremberg Laws articulated and confirmed nationalist and racist policies that were already well under way. Moreover, there was nothing secret about the process: the day after the laws were passed on September 15, they were printed and distributed throughout Germany.

TA 9861/4013

Reichsflaggengesetz.

Vom 15.September 1935.

Der Reichstag hat einstimmig das folgende Gesetz beschlossen, das hiermit verkündet wird:

Artikel 1

Die Reichsfarben sind schwarz-weiß-rot.

Artikel 2

Reichs- und Nationalflagge ist die Hakenkreuzflagge. Sie ist zugleich Handelsflagge.

Artikel 3

Der Führer und Reichskanzler bestimmt die Form der Reichskriegsflagge und der Reichsdienstflagge.

Artikel 4

Der Reichsminister des Jnnern erläßt, soweit nicht die Zuständigkeit des Reichskriegsministers gegeben ist, die zur Durchführung und Ergänzung dieses Gesetzes erforderlichen Rechts- und Verwaltungsvorschriften.

Artikel 5

Dieses Gesetz tritt am Tage nach der Verkündung in Kraft.

Nürnberg, den 15.September 1935,
am Reichsparteitag der Freiheit.

Der Führer und Reichskanzler.

Der Reichsminister des Jnnern.

Der Reichskriegsminister und Oberbefehlshaber der Wehrmacht.

1.1 The Reich Flag Law, enacted in Nuremberg, September 15, 1935, signed by Adolf Hitler, Wilhelm Frick (Minister of the Interior), and General Werner von Blomberg (Minister of War). This law made the swastika the national symbol. "No Jew may be allowed to hoist this sacred insignia," said Hermann Göring.

T/A 9862./5016

Reichsbürgergesetz

Vom 15.September 1935.

Der Reichstag hat einstimmig das folgende Gesetz beschlossen, das hiermit verkündet wird:

§ 1

(1) Staatsangehöriger ist, wer dem Schutzverband des Deutschen Reiches angehört und ihm dafür besonders verpflichtet ist.

(2) Die Staatsangehörigkeit wird nach den Vorschriften des Reichs- und Staatsangehörigkeitsgesetzes erworben.

§ 2

(1) Reichsbürger ist nur der Staatsangehörige deutschen oder artverwandten Blutes, der durch sein Verhalten beweist, daß er gewillt und geeignet ist, in Treue dem Deutschen Volk und Reich zu dienen.

(2) Das Reichsbürgerrecht wird durch Verleihung des Reichsbürgerbriefes erworben.

(3) Der Reichsbürger ist der alleinige Träger der vollen politischen Rechte nach Maßgabe der Gesetze.

§ 3

Der Reichsminister des Jnnern erläßt im Einvernehmen mit dem Stellvertreter des Führers die zur Durchführung und Ergänzung des Gesetzes erforderlichen Rechts- und Verwaltungsvorschriften.

Nürnberg, den 15.September 1935,
am Reichsparteitag der Freiheit.

Der Führer und Reichskanzler

[signature]

Der Reichsminister des Jnnern

Frick

[signature]

1.2 The Citizenship Law, enacted in Nuremberg, September 15, 1935, signed by Adolf Hitler and Wilhelm Frick. This law gave full political and civil rights only to citizens of German or related blood. Jews became noncitizens in their own land.

TA 9863/5012

Gesetz zum Schutze des deutschen Blutes
und der deutschen Ehre.

Vom 15.September 1935.

Durchdrungen von der Erkenntnis, daß die Reinheit des
deutschen Blutes die Voraussetzung für den Fortbestand des
Deutschen Volkes ist, und beseelt von dem unbeugsamen Willen,
die Deutsche Nation für alle Zukunft zu sichern, hat der
Reichstag einstimmig das folgende Gesetz beschlossen, das
hiermit verkündet wird:

§ 1

(1) Eheschließungen zwischen Juden und Staatsangehörigen deutschen oder artverwandten Blutes sind verboten. Trotzdem
geschlossene Ehen sind nichtig, auch wenn sie zur Umgehung
dieses Gesetzes im Ausland geschlossen sind.
(2) Die Nichtigkeitsklage kann nur der Staatsanwalt erheben.

§ 2

Außerehelicher ~~Geschlechts~~verkehr zwischen Juden und
Staatsangehörigen deutschen oder artverwandten Blutes ist verboten.

§ 3

Juden dürfen weibliche Staatsangehörige deutschen oder artverwandten Blutes unter 45 Jahren in ihrem Haushalt nicht be-
schäftigen.

§ 4

(1) Juden ist das Hissen der Reichs- und Nationalflagge und
das Zeigen der Reichsfarben verboten.
(2) Dagegen ist ihnen das Zeigen der jüdischen Farben gestat-
tet. Die Ausübung dieser Befugnis steht unter staatlichem
Schutz.

./.

Anfng 2248.

1.3 The Law for the Protection of German Blood and Honor, enacted in Nuremberg, September 15, 1935, signed by Adolf Hitler, Wilhelm Frick, Franz Gürtner (Minister of Justice), and Rudolf Hess (Hitler's deputy). The Blood Law, as it is known, prohibited marriage and sexuality between Germans and Jews, employment by Jews of Germans under forty-five years old as servants, and flying of the German flag by Jews. The Blood Law is widely regarded as a decisive moment in the escalating persecution of European Jews.

§ 5

(1) Wer dem Verbot des § 1 zuwiderhandelt, wird mit Zuchthaus
bestraft.
(2) Der Mann, der dem Verbot des § 2 zuwiderhandelt, wird mit
Gefängnis oder mit Zuchthaus bestraft.
(3) Wer den Bestimmungen der §§ 3 oder 4 zuwiderhandelt, wird
mit Gefängnis bis zu einem Jahr und mit Geldstrafe oder mit
einer dieser Strafen bestraft.

§ 6

Der Reichsminister des Jnnern erläßt im Einvernehmen mit
dem Stellvertreter des Führers und dem Reichsminister der Justiz die zur Durchführung und Ergänzung des Gesetzes erforderlichen Rechts- und Verwaltungsvorschriften.

§ 7

Das Gesetz tritt am Tage nach der Verkündung, § 3 jedoch
erst am 1.Januar 1936 in Kraft.

Nürnberg, den 15.September 1935,
am Reichsparteitag der Freiheit.

Der Führer und Reichskanzler.

Der Reichsminister des Jnnern.

Der Reichsminister der Justiz.

Der Stellvertreter des Führers.

1.3 The Law for the Protection of German Blood and Honor, page 2.

When I first saw press photographs of the original Nuremberg Laws held by the Huntington, I was struck by their ordinariness, unable to grasp why they figured so prominently as decisive markers on the journey by Europe's Jews from second-class citizenship to exile and death. The three laws are certainly not much to look at: typewritten on four nondescript pages, they include handmade corrections. The infamous Blood Law consists of seven brief paragraphs, fewer than two hundred and twenty-five words. It begins with the familiar cadence of Nazi hyperbole—"certain in the knowledge that the purity of the German blood is the fundamental necessity for the continuation of the German people, and endowed with unflinching will to secure the German nation for all times to come"—but continues in the straightforward language of technocratic legalism, without any rhetorical flourishes. "The Reichstag has unanimously approved the following law, which is herewith made public:

Paragraph 1.

(1) Marriages between Jews and citizens of German or German-related blood are forbidden. Marriages which have been performed in spite of this law, even if they have been performed in a foreign country, are void.

(2) Complaints declaring them void can originate only with the District Attorney.

Paragraph 2.

Extramarital sexual intercourse between Jews and citizens of German or German-related blood is forbidden.

Paragraph 3.

Jews are not allowed to employ female citizens of German or German-related blood under 45 years in their household.

Paragraph 4.

(1) Jews are forbidden to raise the Reich and National flag and they cannot show the National colors.

(2) However, they are allowed to display the Jewish colors. The exercise of this disposition is under the state's protection.

Paragraph 5.

(1) Whoever acts against Paragraph 1 will be punished with forced labor.

(2) The man who acts against Paragraph 2 will be punished with prison or forced labor.

(3) Whoever acts against Paragraph 3 or 4 will be punished with prison not exceeding one year and with a fine, or with one of these punishments.

Paragraph 6.

The Secretary of the Interior will, together with the Deputy Führer and the Attorney General, issue the necessary law and administrative ordinances.

Paragraph 7.

The law is valid on the date of its publication, but Paragraph 3 will be valid only as of 1 January 1936."[30]

It is not so much the content of the Nuremberg Laws, I quickly realized, as their symbolic value that makes them so weighty. "Uncovering them is like finding an original copy of the U.S. Constitution—but, unfortunately, a very evil one signed by the man who instigated it," says Saul Friedländer, an expert on Nazi Germany.[31] "The document is very important, possibly the last draft that Hitler saw before signing."[32] Maybe their legislative origins in the fascist pomp of Nuremberg give them more significance than, for example, Hitler's signed memo authorizing doctors to carry out "mercy killings," namely, the murder of five thousand disabled children, followed by two hundred thousand adults.[33] In the absence of documents signed by Hitler ordering the mass murder of Jews, the Blood Law has become in popular memory a physical relic of genocide, typically considered "Hitler's blueprint for the Holocaust," "the foundation for the Holocaust," "a crucial ... first step in Nazi racial laws that ultimately led to the Holocaust," and "a decisive step on the bitter road to Auschwitz."[34]

This interpretation is also shared by widely read histories of the holocaust. "The Nuremberg Laws, which rescinded the civil rights of Germany's six hundred thousand Jews (and later the millions of Jews in countries occupied by Germany)," notes an illustrated history of the twentieth century, "represented the first stage of Hitler's 'final solution' to rid Europe of all its Jews."[35] Though the Laws "may seem innocuous and merely the work of bureaucrats," writes Michael Berenbaum, "categorization had deadly consequences. Definition was the first step toward destruction."[36] Historian Peter Loewenberg similarly takes the view that "the Nuremberg Laws represent a major step in the increasing marginalization of Jews from German life. In order to carry out the program of The Final Solution, the target group first has to be marginalized, dehumanized, and removed from the code of citizenship. This is a critical moment. This legally excludes them. The next step is humiliation—*Kristallnacht*, 1938—then the wearing of yellow stars, then deportation, and finally the death camps."[37]

When asked by the Huntington to appraise the Huntington's copy of the Nuremberg Laws, Eric Klein, an expert on rare Judaica and Nazi memorabilia, reported: "I view these works as both original and unique historical documents.... [They] became the fundamental laws which served to sever Jews from the fabric of the German State." Moreover, he explained, "by extension [they] laid the groundwork for the eventual expulsion and extermination of the Jewish people as a doctrine, and policy of the Nazi state, later to be known as 'the final solution.'"[38] Klein estimated the value of the documents at about three million dollars, though it is difficult, he said, to establish a fair market value because no comparable works have been available for purchase.[39] "Hitler signed lots of stuff and his signature is not all that rare. But there's nothing with his signature on a law or document ordering the extinction of Jews. This is the closest you come."[40]

THE LAST WORD

During the last weekend of June 1999, I paid close attention to every news item, partly because it was entertaining to be in the center of media hoopla. I also wondered why the Huntington had been involved with a flamboyant war hero like General Patton and why such an important icon had remained hidden in the Huntington's basement for fifty-four years.

Robert Skotheim expected the Huntington's act of inter-institutional generosity to widen the opening in the Pasadena Wall and to be greeted as a sign of détente between the traditionally separate worlds of east and west Los Angeles. "There is a democratization taking place within the museum community," Skotheim observed. "We now feel we have a broader obligation to serve the public."[41] He hoped that media coverage would emphasize the "positive aspects of what we did, loaning it to the Skirball" and how the loan represented an important development by the traditionally insular Huntington to reach out to other museums.[42] "In a fragmented Los Angeles environment," said Skotheim, "we have become concerned with what the Huntington can do in collaboration with other cultural institutions to build a sense of community."[43] Or as Catherine Babcock, the Huntington's director of communications, framed the transaction, "Two cultural institutions came together to do the right thing."[44] The Huntington, I imagined, wanted the headlines to read, "Huntington Generously Donates Nuremberg Laws to Jewish Center."

As a relatively new and eclectic Jewish cultural center, it was a coup for the Skirball to acquire an important icon of "the Nazi catastrophe." The Nuremberg Laws immediately became "the most historically significant documents" in the Skirball's collection.[45] "I would have given my right arm to get the Nuremberg Laws for the U.S. Holocaust Museum when we opened in 1993," said its first director, Michael Berenbaum.[46] For Rabbi Uri Herscher, the Skirball's president, acquisition of the Nuremberg Laws was a redemptive parable about "the answer democracy enables us to give genocide." The Laws that were "meant to destroy the Jewish people and all hope of democracy," Herscher asserted, "will be displayed at the Skirball to encourage visitors to remember that Hitler did not have the last word. The democratic faith has the last word."[47]

As it turned out, at least in the short run, the last word on the matter belonged to the media. Aside from the *New York Times*—which took its cue from the Huntington and Skirball's joint press release—the reported story emphasized not so much the Huntington's philanthropy, Jewish endurance in the face of unprecedented persecution, or Patton's liberation of a Nazi icon, but in the words of the *Washington Post*'s front-page headline, the "Hidden History of the Nazi Laws."[48] This theme echoed through press coverage around the world. "A Key Nazi Document Surfaces" was the story in the *International Herald Tribune*.[49] The "controversy" for the *Christian Science Monitor* was "the fact that [the Laws] languished for five decades out of the public eye."[50] In its follow-up story to the June

28 press conference, the *Los Angeles Times* joined the fray, noting inelegantly that the Huntington's president "did not fully explain why the library never revealed that it possessed the documents."[51] A few days later, the *Washington Post* weighed in with questions from one of its readers: "Is it legally and morally permissible for a member of the armed forces, even a highly decorated general, to take unique historic documents and do with them as he pleases? I can understand a soldier considering himself entitled to some wartime souvenir, such as an abandoned enemy helmet or weapon. But can he keep any work of art or historic document that the enemy has left behind?"[52]

Sharon Waxman, a Los Angeles-based reporter for the *Post* who broke the story, focused on how the Nuremberg Laws "had been buried—unknown and unseen—in the inner vault" of the Huntington.[53] David Zeidberg, Director of the Library, explained to Waxman that the Huntington had kept them secret for so long because Patton had said, "Here, put these in the vault." And, Zeidberg added, "There is some statement from a [Huntington] trustee in the early '50s saying, 'We were told not to say anything.'"[54] *Slate*, the on-line news service, found this response a "curiously weak reason that such important papers were buried without almost anybody's knowledge for 54 years." When Skotheim told the *Los Angeles Times* that the Huntington had never displayed the documents "because they do not fit into the library's focus," *Slate* was skeptical about this "equally mild primary explanation."[55] Jewish theologian Michael Berenbaum was more blunt: "I think we'll find it was a case of nobody really gave a damn," he told the Associated Press.[56]

Leslie Gersicoff, a Russian Jew visiting the Skirball Cultural Center, told a reporter, "It is ... a mystery why this," she said gesturing to the case displaying the Nuremberg Laws, "hasn't been made public before this. I cannot understand how a museum [the Huntington] that understands the importance of originality can say it was all right to keep these secret." The *Christian Science Monitor* concluded its story with a dagger to the Huntington's heart: "If these [Nuremberg Laws] had been made public sooner," observed Ms. Gersicoff, "I think many who lost loved ones in the Holocaust could have reached healing sooner."[57]

Doubts about the Huntington's explanations for the missing fifty-four years spread even to some of the participants in the Huntington-Skirball's joint press conference, at which everybody was supposed to radiate a united front of positive affirmation. "I wonder why they didn't give [the Nuremberg Laws] away or lend them out years ago," admitted MacArthur Fellow Saul Friedländer, who was begrudgingly on hand to lend his scholarly heft to the occasion.[58] "They have such importance for the community of victims and give more completeness to events that recede with time."[59] It was "puzzling" to Friedländer "why this was not made public sooner."[60] When a visitor to the Skirball asked a docent why the Huntington had concealed the Nuremberg Laws for so long, she replied, "Out of sight, out of mind. Well, you know," she said with a shrug, "it's San Marino."[61]

For obvious diplomatic reasons, as president of the Skirball and recipient of the Huntington's largesse, Uri Herscher tried to be more tactful, but his gratitude to the Huntington had a little sting in its tail. "It's easy to suspect [the Huntington of] a conspiracy or a special agenda," Herscher told the *Los Angeles Times*. "Quite simply, I believe that these documents were just not part of their day-to-day thinking."[62] To the *Jewish Journal of Greater Los Angeles*, which reaches many of the Skirball's supporters in West Los Angeles and the San Fernando Valley, Herscher was more candid: "They viewed the documents as artifacts that didn't relate to their collections. They weren't aware of their emotional impact."[63]

By the time the Nuremberg Laws story reached national radio and television, the issue of provenance loomed large. After an NBC staffer interviewed David Zeidberg as background for the upcoming press conference, the Huntington's librarian complained that the reporter "didn't know anything about the Huntington or Nuremberg Laws, but he knew what the story was: 'Why did you deliberately suppress the documents?'"[64]

During an interview on National Public Radio on June 27, Jacki Lyden asked Skotheim the question that was troubling many reporters: "I don't mean to put you on the spot,"—which, of course, she did—"but what does it say about our cultural division in America that these documents were for so long not transferred to a different museum, a Jewish museum; that it didn't occur to anyone in 54 years at the Huntington that they needed to be brought forward?" Lyden pointedly asked Skotheim if it was time for public institutions to now work in a more cooperative way. "Oh, I think so," he replied. "But institutions don't ordinarily lend things, historically, from one to another."[65]

Skotheim continued to bear the brunt of hostile questioning. The same day on NBC's "Today" show, anchor Jack Ford challenged the Huntington's president on national television: "Dr. Skotheim, as we've mentioned, the text of these laws has been available for some time now. But the question being asked by many is, 'Why did the Huntington Library simply hold these documents in a vault for more than fifty years rather than give the public access to them?'" Skotheim's defensive, flustered (and as I would later discover, inaccurate and unverified) response did not help the Huntington's cause: "Well, the Huntington Library is devoted to Anglo-American history, literature, and works of art. And it was a fluke that General Patton put those documents there.... And German historians did not come to the Huntington Library.... Most librarians do not wake up in the morning wondering what they have in their collections that they can give away."[66]

After they left the studio, Uri Herscher advised his colleague that the Huntington needed to come up with a more credible response to the question. Saul Friedländer shared the same opinion: "It's an unlikely story, it's silly," he said a few days later. "But it's their story and that's what they say."[67]

A SUITABLE PAST

As I followed the early coverage of the Huntington's announcement, I became increasingly curious why Huntington officials seemed so defensive about the missing fifty-four years. Like Saul Friedländer, I thought the Huntington's explanation seemed far-fetched and fabricated. "Huntington officials make no apologies" for withholding the Nuremberg Laws since 1945, said the *Los Angeles Times*, implying that an apology would have been in order.[68]

The Huntington's claim of ownership relied on the role played by Patton in their discovery in Germany and subsequent transfer to the Huntington. Patton, it was explained, "gave these captured Nazi items"—the Nuremberg Laws and *Mein Kampf*—to the Library in 1945. The Nuremberg Laws, said the Huntington's president, had never been exhibited at the Library in the previous fifty-four years because "they do not fall within the subject areas of scholarly research or public display of our institution." Instead, the Huntington had decided to "preserve them until they could be exhibited in an appropriate venue." That venue, noted Robert Skotheim, had finally materialized in the form of the Skirball, a bustling Jewish cultural center that opened to the public in 1996. "*This*," he said, "would be the appropriate venue in which to exhibit the Hitler-related materials given to the Huntington by General Patton." Here at the Skirball, he emphasized, "they can be viewed in context."[69] For Uri Herscher, who lost two-thirds of his relatives in concentration camps, the context was also personal. The Nuremberg Laws, he told a television audience, "represent the blueprint for the destruction of one-third of world Jewry," made all the more "real when you see it in Hitler's handwriting."[70]

On June 28, Skotheim, Herscher, David Zeidberg, and Saul Friedländer, who holds the UCLA Chair in the History of the Holocaust, gathered at the Skirball Cultural Center to release evidence and photographs to journalists hungry for detailed information. In the public relations packet was General Patton's marvelous, swashbuckling account of how the "Nazi materials" had been captured in 1945. "When the Third Army entered the city of Nuremberg there was quite a fight going on and the city was burning," said Patton in a statement dictated in San Marino to Huntington staff on June 11, 1945. "Some troops of the 90th Infantry Division fighting through the town came to a stairway which they went down with grenades, in case there were any Germans. There were no Germans. They found a vault, not open, and persuaded a German to open it for them. In it they found this thing." Patton said that his troops probably captured the Nuremberg Laws on March 14, 1945, but he was not sure about the date. "We captured so many towns I have forgotten just which day." But he recalled that the commanding officer of the 90th Division, General Van Fleet, gave him the Laws in "a great public presentation" about May 27, 1945. "So it is my property," concluded Patton for the record.[71]

STATEMENT DICTATED BY GENERAL GEORGE S. PATTON, JR.
regarding document taken in Nuremberg

When the Third Army entered the city of Nuremberg there was
quite a fight going on and the city was burning. Some troops
of the 90th Infantry Division fighting through the town came to
a stairway which they went down with grenades, in case there
were any Germans. There were no Germans. They found a vault,
not open, and persuaded a German to open it for them. In it
they found this thing. That was all that was in the vault.

These soldiers of the 90th Division were very fond of me and
I was very fond of them. They thought they would like to do
something for me, so they sent for me, and we had a great public
presentation. The former commanding general of the 90th Division,
now commander of the Third Corps, General Van Fleet, - he actually
made the presentation to me. So it is my property. They have
given me a lot of other things but this is the important one.
This [document] was taken the day we captured Nuremberg, about
the 14th of March. We captured so many towns I have forgotten
just which day. The presentation must have been about the 27th
of May.

in inner bomb vault

Regarding Mein Kampf

That book was alleged by a talkative German to be one of a
limited edition of the unexpurgated text. There were alleged to
have been one hundred copies. It was published by a man named
Emman. He is the No. 3 bad man in Germany. I have him in jail
now. We'll stretch him pretty quick!
- - - - - - -

Huntington Library
San Marino, Calif.
June 11, 1945
PH & EP

1.4 General George S. Patton's account of how the Nuremberg Laws and special edition of
Mein Kampf were retrieved in Germany in 1945 near the end of the war in Europe. The
Huntington Library relied on this statement, dictated on June 11, 1945, for provenance.

As for the special edition of *Mein Kampf* donated by Patton to the Huntington,
"a talkative German" reportedly told the general that it was "one of a limited
edition of the unexpurgated text. There were alleged to have been one hundred

copies. It was published by a man named Emman [*sic*]. He is the No. 3 bad man in Germany. I have him in jail now," recalled Patton. "We'll stretch him pretty quick!"[72] On the front cover of this huge, kitschy book, bound in leather with bronze clasps, and embossed with a gold swastika, Patton autographed his gift to the Huntington Library—the only inscription of its kind in the Huntington's vast collection.

In addition to documentation of the Nuremberg Laws, the Huntington also issued a previously unpublished photograph, taken on June 11, 1945, by the Huntington's staff photographer, Charles W. Wendland. In this image, General George S. Patton, in full military regalia, transfers a manila envelope—containing the Nuremberg Laws and secured with the wax seals of the Third Reich—to the

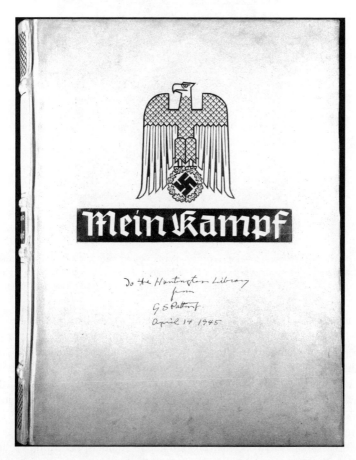

1.5 Cover of special edition of *Mein Kampf*, signed by General Patton as a gift to the Huntington Library, April 14, 1945.

1.6 General Patton delivers envelope containing the Nuremberg Laws to Huntington trustee Robert Millikan, under a portrait of George Washington. This photograph, taken by Huntington photographer Charles Wendland on June 11, 1945, was not released to the public until 1999.

chairman of the Huntington's board of trustees, Robert Millikan, attired in a double-breasted suit and characteristic bow tie. Behind them, looking down approvingly from a portrait attributed to Charles Peale, stands George Washington, also in uniform, his hand resting on a cannon. Patton must have especially appreciated this moment because he claimed "cousin George" as a distant relative.[73] All eyes are drawn down to the Nuremberg Laws, which Patton considered one of his prize trophies. My troops, he told Millikan, "have given me a lot of other things but this is the important one."[74]

Robert Millikan was a one-man powerhouse in Southern California's academia, the leading figure at the California Institute of Technology, whose science faculty ranked with the best in country. He had been recruited from the University of

Chicago in 1921 to take on his new job as chairman of the Executive Council of Caltech in Pasadena, an executive position that he held for twenty-four years.[75] With the financial backing of lumber tycoon Arthur Fleming and contributions from sixty California millionaires, including Edward Huntington, Millikan quickly transformed Caltech into a world-class institution.[76] Awarded the Nobel Prize in physics in 1923, Millikan had a knack for organization, fundraising, and publicity, skills that made Caltech the envy of scientists around the world.[77]

In 1925, Millikan also joined the board of trustees of the Huntington, a few miles away in neighboring San Marino, becoming its powerful and influential chairman from 1938 until his death in 1953. Millikan's views permeated the Huntington's cultural agenda, research priorities, and personnel policies for close to thirty years. After Albert Einstein, he was the country's "most public figure in science," writes one of his biographers. "When Millikan spoke, the country listened."[78] During his first visit to Caltech in 1930, Einstein observed that his host played "the role of God." In response to a companion at a dinner party who warned Einstein that a planned outing might be postponed due to bad weather, he replied, "Oh no, it won't rain; Millikan has arranged it."[79]

In 1945, General George Patton was one of the most celebrated public figures in the country. "His polished exterior glistened," noted historian Martin Blumenson. "He was always on display, his energy coiled like a cat's."[80] A popular magazine identified him as one of the West's "bright stars" long before he led armies through North Africa and Europe.[81] While crossing the Rhine in March 1945, the last stage in the campaign to defeat Hitler's armies, Patton still found time to pose for photojournalist Margaret Bourke White, who was covering the war for *Life* magazine. She was entranced by a "natty figure standing in the midst of the billowing red parachute silk." It was "the awesome General Patton," she wrote. "When he laughed his expression was lively and charming, and I took another picture." Patton admonished her, "And don't show the creases in my neck." She followed his orders: the photograph radiates staged heroism, his three stars glittering in the light. The next two pages of Bourke White's book include un-posed photographs of General Eisenhower, looking strained and war-weary.[82]

The Patton family name is central to the Huntington's historical memory and origins stories. "The close family friendship of the Huntingtons and the Pattons explains why General Patton gave these captured Nazi items to the Library in 1945," said Robert Skotheim.[83] It makes sense that General Patton chose the Huntington as a repository for his Nazi memorabilia, since the Huntington-Patton ties go back to the 1900s. Both families were members of Southern California's small, interconnected elite, the economic and political equivalent of local royalty. In 1903, when Edward Huntington bought the Shorb ranch and property on which the Huntington is now located, his new neighbor at the Lake Vineyard Ranch was George S. Patton, Sr., the son-in-law of Benjamin D. Wilson, an influential landowner and first mayor of Los Angeles under U.S. rule. Before he built his house in Southern California, Edward Huntington used to stay with the Pattons, next door to his future property. "It seems almost like home for me to be there," he wrote his daughter in 1905, "as I seem to be like one of the family."[84]

George S. Patton, the future general's father, became Huntington's close friend, confidante, and business partner in Southern California. The senior Patton made his wealth in land development, vineyards, and oil investments, and from 1903 to 1910 worked as the general manager of the Huntington Land and Improvement Company.[85] He served as vice-chairman of the Huntington Library's first board of trustees, established in 1919, and as its chairman from 1925 until his death in 1927.[86] Edward Huntington also had a personal relationship with his friend's son, Georgie, who grew up riding his pony on Huntington's estate and as a teenager attended society dances and picnics on Catalina Island, presided over by the Huntingtons. The World War II hero began his climb up the military hierarchy in 1904, when he was admitted to West Point with the help of Edward Huntington, who recommended his young neighbor as "the kind of timber that we want to train up for the future defense of our country."[87]

1.7 Georgie Patton, on left, as standard-bearer at Pasadena Tournament of Roses, January 1, 1901.

1.8 George Patton, Jr., standing on the porch of the family home with his mother (to his left), Edward Huntington, and his father, George Patton, Sr., November 1903.

The future general retained a fond and grateful association with the Huntingtons and the setting where he first developed his taste for war. In letters to his parents from military academy, he regularly inquired about "Mr. H."[88] When his father and Edward Huntington died within a few weeks of each other in 1927, Georgie lost two of the most significant influences on his life. On April 15, 1945, General Patton, Jr., recalled this youthful association when he shipped off the huge copy of *Mein Kampf* to the Huntington from Germany. He hoped that the book would be of historical interest to the Library, as well as a "tribute" to his father's role in the Huntington's development.[89]

When I visited the Huntington in the summer of 1999, the Patton name was still very much revered. A photo of Georgie as a young boy riding his pony hung in the president's conference room. "Pasadena and San Marino," observed General Patton's grandson, "is the cradle of the Patton fan club. They have the party line on him: 'great man, could do no wrong.'"[90] When the Huntington made its decision to loan the Nuremberg Laws to another institution, many long-time supporters agreed, "So long as we don't give up ownership or the long-term association between the Patton and Huntington families. The family relationship is important to us. You don't want to lose that association."[91]

The Huntington, confirmed Robert Skotheim, "is concerned with preserving the Patton-Huntington connection. We thought it would make sense to have the documents go to an institution in Los Angeles," rather than elsewhere in the country. The Skirball Cultural Center was particularly appealing to the Huntington's president as a place to locate the Nuremberg Laws, because it "is not a Holocaust museum, it is about telling the story of triumph, not victimization."[92] Here, Skotheim hoped, Patton and the Huntington would get credit for liberating the Nuremberg Laws. "Finally, I have to say 'good for old Patton!'" Skotheim wrote Herscher in celebration of the deal struck by the two presidents. "He must have had his heart in the right place after all."[93] But Uri Herscher, it would turn out, had serious concerns about the state of General Patton's heart.

OLD WOUNDS

When I returned to the library to continue my research after the weekend of publicity, the Huntington was abuzz with gossip. On Tuesday, June 29, the Huntington's president and leading administrators convened a special meeting of staff and visiting fellows to squelch rumors and brief us about the loan of "Hitler materials" to the Skirball.[94] For me it would have been over that day if the Huntington's president had said, "We realize that the Huntington should have made these documents available to the public long ago. We take responsibility for our institutional amnesia and while they are on loan to the Skirball Cultural Center, we have asked the National Archives to investigate provenance and title. We will abide by their determination."

But nothing of the kind was said. Instead, Huntington officials rebuked "the media" for questioning the Huntington's good faith. "No good deed goes unpunished," said a grim Robert Skotheim, for whom reporters' insensitivity was an example of East Coast chauvinism and condescension, comparable to how, early in the twentieth century, "Mr. Huntington was lampooned for putting his institution in California" instead of New York or Boston.[95]

Skotheim and David Zeidberg, who was in charge of overseeing the Huntington-Skirball transaction, expressed frustration with the media's coverage, in particular the *Washington Post*'s Sharon Waxman: "She seemed more interested in breaking her story first than getting much of it right," said Zeidberg,[96] who was also upset that the *Post* had caricatured Skotheim, unfairly and inaccurately, as a provincial rube from northern Washington.[97] "Strange as it may seen," wrote Waxman, "it never occurred to Skotheim or, probably, any of his predecessors in Pasadena— the very heart of Protestant, establishment Los Angeles—to seek out someone from the west side of Los Angeles, home to a wealthy, politically active Jewish population, much less a Holocaust institution elsewhere in the world."[98]

Contrasting images of the Huntington and Skirball played out as a subtext in the media, with Skotheim and Herscher predictably typecast in the Hollywood roles of the reserved, longtime, American patrician and the extroverted Israeli-born rabbi: the "old-line American of Norwegian descent" and "son of Jewish refugees from Germany."[99] And the lead actors occasionally followed this script. "We Norwegians are not very expressive," Skotheim wrote Herscher. "But I must confess my deep satisfaction at being in a position wherein I could make the transfer of documents happen."[100] Similarly, the Huntington's director of communications recognized that "we have very different styles. We're a 'Just the facts, ma'am' kind of institution, we don't wear our hearts on our sleeves."[101]

As I sat through the briefing at the Huntington, I became increasingly uncomfortable. I had expected a solemn and subdued ceremony, perhaps a moment of silence to commemorate a sorrowful past, not a circling of the wagons to defend the Huntington's honor. The meeting concluded with the presentation of a bouquet to the Huntington's publicist in gratitude for how she had handled the antagonistic media. As the bemused audience politely applauded, Catherine Babcock stood smiling on stage, cradling flowers in front of a huge blow-up, projected on a screen, of the Nazi law for the "Protection of German Blood and Honor."

In that moment I felt a "strange, emotional power," to use Saul Friedländer's phrase, in the visceral presence of Hitler's Blood Law. It is as though "some of the terror and horror is attached."[102] I was reminded of my experience a few years ago at the U.S. Holocaust Memorial Museum in Washington, D.C., when I came face-to-face with the "detritus of annihilation"—piles of suitcases, wedding rings, shoes, and other reminders of life in all their "vivid materiality."[103] I experienced the same sense of emotional dislocation that African Americans must feel when they witness exhibits of slave shackles, whipping posts, and lynching postcards.[104]

Looking around at the faces of the perhaps one hundred people in the room, I saw several colleagues with heads lowered, eyes tearing up. After the briefing, I sought out others in the audience who were similarly troubled. To one curator, the Huntington's failure to acknowledge possession of the Nuremberg Laws for so long was an "insidious omission." Another was upset by the "silence and lack of public responsibility." A visiting scholar was furious and saddened by the institution's incapacity to recognize the hunger for discussion among staff and researchers.[105] But the Huntington's leadership was so preoccupied with its public reputation that it did not pick up any signs of internal discontent.[106] After the briefing ended, I was flooded with incoherent images of the holocaust from my childhood and unanswered questions: Why did Patton stash the Nuremberg Laws at the Huntington in 1945? How reliable was his account of how they became his "property"? Why had the Huntington kept such an important icon hidden from history for fifty-four years?

Later that day, I walked to my favorite place in the gardens, a graceful colonnade surrounded by an effusion of summer roses. The surreal tableau on stage had churned up issues in my own identity that I thought were long resolved. This encounter with the past left me surprised by "the power of old wounds to leak into the present" and vulnerable to exploring my own origins stories.[107]

🔲 Chapter 2 🔲

Present Absences

The suppressed past will rankle and return.

(Eva Hoffman, 2004)

ALMOST-JEWS

The extermination of Jews in the 1940s loomed silently large during my youth. I grew up in northern England in the wake of World War II, in the declining capital of industrialization, its chimneys belching out sooty gray fumes around the clock. "Manchester reminded me of everything I was trying to forget," commented artist Max Ferber when he arrived in 1942, the year of my birth and his exile from nazism; his parents disappeared into the camps.[1] For generations, Manchester had been home to one of the oldest gatherings of Jewish immigrants in England. Jobs in the cotton industry attracted the first Jews in the late eighteenth century and by 1850 there were enough, mostly Germans, to fill two congregations. Manchester was more influenced by German Jews than was any other city in Europe.[2] Twenty years later, Sephardic Jews also opened up their own synagogue.[3]

My Romanian and Polish grandparents arrived at the turn of the new century, tinkers and dealers, trying to get a foot inside the smokestacks before the 1905 Aliens Act closed the door. Grandpa Daniels was one of eighty-nine hawkers, and Grandpa Platt one of 1,122 tailors in North Manchester's Jewish mosh pit of Lithuanians, Romanians, Russians, Poles, Africans, Turks, and Middle Easterners, united only by fear of the pogrom and the lure of commerce.[4] My illiterate paternal grandfather insisted on a name that resonated with the English gentry, but likely he had been born a prosaic Plat or Blatt.

The Daniels and Platt families clung for a while to their diminishing Yiddish and struggled with the mysteries of English, which they learned to speak and read, but barely write. My paternal grandmother, Annie, always had trouble with her *v*'s and, unfortunately, liked to wear "a welvet hat with a weil." They all stayed close to home and trusted only their own. "One of ours?" they would ask each other when trying to verify a stranger's provenance. By American standards, Manchester's ghetto was a very small world: maybe twenty-five thousand by

1900, and not much larger some fifty-five years later when I came of age.[5] But one big happy family it wasn't. My mother's class-savvy parents, convinced that Romanian Jews topped the new immigrant pecking order, were stunned when their Eileen fell in love with my dad Monty, a Polish *dripki* who seemed destined for a life of poverty.[6]

My parents, born in 1915 and 1920 in the city where Frederick Engels's family lived, were materialists who worshipped no icons other than Bertrand Russell's science for peace and progress, and Havelock Ellis's sex manuals. They were the prototypical post–World War I modernists, the New Man and New Woman who never had any doubt that nature is spelled with a small *n*. Anything vaguely spiritual was regarded with suspicion as some kind of atavistic magic. As close students of encyclopedias and dictionaries, they believed every mystery had an answer. They abandoned Yiddish, except for a few phrases, named me after a Catholic saint (Anthony, followed by my brother, Stephen, and sister, Susan, names for looking forward, not back), and as good young communists subordinated the Jewish Question to the proletarian struggle. But they did not follow (nor were they given the space to follow) the example of some of their secular counterparts in Germany, who in the early twentieth century had converted to Christianity or baptized their children as they moved, so they thought, into the mainstream.

My dad decided the big issues in our household. He made my siblings and me go through the motions "for the grandparents"—bar mitzvahs for the boys, synagogue on the high holidays, a traditional Friday night dinner. But he also made it clear to us that the religious piece of Judaism was all mumbo jumbo, the leftover rituals of backward peasants. My mother, following Monty's step at every turn, including the one that eventually took her down a blind alley, also abandoned any kind of religious practice. They both remained atheists all their lives, even during the last months of miserable deaths from lung cancer, when, against all odds, they persisted in looking to doctors, not rabbis, for a miracle.

In the household of my childhood, Eileen, doing what she knew best and had learned from her mother, maintained a space for traditional Ashkenazi recipes alongside the haute cuisine imported from the Continent. Throughout her life, but especially as she moved into the upper middle class, she did good works for Jewish and Zionist charities. She read the *Jewish Chronicle* and was attentive to the successes of Jewish actors, Jewish athletes, and Jewish politicians. All her close and not-so-close friends were Jewish, every one of them. Near the end of her life, she moved into the same Jewish old age home in which her mother, the Romanian immigrant, had lived for many years and died.

My dad, who scoffed at Eileen's philanthropic Zionism, also retained a strong Jewish identity rooted in his everyday life. His three oldest friends, his second wife, and his last girlfriend were all Jewish. And of my brother, sister, and me, he was closest to Sue, whom he regularly visited in Israel, long after he had given up any hope that a Jewish state could create a better human society than any other place on earth. "Just as fucked up as everywhere else," he would report after a visit. But he kept going back.

My dad's Jewish identity was shaped not so much by an active desire for cultural preservation, as by an appreciation for the necessities of self-preservation. England has a long history of active anti-Semitism, which encouraged Jews — especially ones as successful as my dad was in the rag trade — to stay on their toes and be watchful: keep a getaway suitcase packed and an accessible account. As a teen, Monty went to a mixed, working-class high school in Salford, where the lads divided themselves into teams of "yids versus yoks" for pickup football games at lunchtime. Later, his practical paranoia was fuelled by the concentration camps, which he witnessed in 1945 when he was in the British Army, but never discussed with his children, and honed in the mid-1950s by the post-Khrushchev revelations of Jew-hating in his once beloved Soviet Union.[7] Like my Puerto Rican friend Piri, who always sniffs the air for the *caca* of racial insult, my extended family had their antennae permanently circling the atmosphere, searching for enemy signals.

My parents were not unlike Henry Selwyn, one of the German émigrés profiled by W. G. Sebald, for whom World War II was a "blinding, bad time," about which "I could not say a thing even if I wanted to."[8] I can remember my parents' response in the 1950s when images of the concentration camps appeared on television: my mother, her lips pursed, rhythmically clicked her tongue; my father, who always had something to say about everything, sat silent and sank into his chair. As Eva Hoffman observed about her own parents' "huddled hiding" from the holocaust, "the whole wretched, shameful, unspeakable business went underground."[9] And when the silence was broken, there was a vocabulary of psychopathology to fill the void: nazism as aberration, as non-rationality running wild, as reversion to barbarism. Zygmunt Bauman had not yet qualified the holocaust as "a legitimate resident in the house of modernity; indeed, one who would not be at home in any other house."[10]

I grew up in the 1940s and 1950s, before the experiences of Jews during the war became framed in apocalyptic terms. In my youth, there were references to "atrocities" and "crimes against humanity," even "genocide," following enactment of the United Nations treaty in 1951.[11] And although "holocaust" (from the Greek word meaning "that which is completely burnt") was applied to the mass murder of Jews as early as 1942, its common usage in this way was not established until the late 1950s.[12] My earliest impressions of what happened to "my people" were formed before the holocaust became "The Holocaust"; before NBC televised its "Holocaust" mini-series in 1978; before the President's Commission on the Victims of the Holocaust recommended in 1979 the creation of the United States Holocaust Memorial Museum;[13] before scholars in the 1990s debated "intentionalist" versus "functionalist" theories of nazism;[14] before arguments broke out about whether the holocaust was "uniquely dreadful" or dreadfully common;[15] before Steven Spielberg (in *Schindler's List,* 1993) popularized the holocaust into a story of good versus evil; before there were, in Eva Hoffman's words, "eruptions of near-obsessive interest," marked by the proliferation of survivors' memoirs, holocaust exhibits, holocaust centers, holocaust museums, and holocaust memorials;[16] before public depictions of the holocaust became the exclusive domain of government agencies and "professional museology";[17] and before the opening of the Yad Vashem Holocaust History Museum in Israel (1973), the Museum of Tolerance in Los Angeles (February 1993), the national Holocaust Museum in Washington, D.C. (April 1993), and the Skirball Cultural Center (including its Holocaust memorial) in Los Angeles (April 1996).[18]

Back in England in the 1950s, I grew up in an atmosphere of cautious assimilation and double messages. "How odd of God/to choose the Jews," as Hilaire Belloc put it. When my mum and dad quickly climbed the class ladder, they moved us out of the Salford ghetto and leapfrogged over middle-class Didsbury into village life in the country, with its faux Elizabethan pubs, horsey set, and ever-so-polite anti-Semitism. We were among the first Jews to infiltrate the rural, Protestant suburbs of Cheshire. Though many others soon followed, my parents and their friends were forced to set up their own club for aspiring Jewish golfers. Later, the club opened its doors to aspiring Indian and Pakistani golfers, and other outcasts from suburban gentility.

When I was on the edge of puberty, my parents took me on a trip to Oxford University, which then seemed far away, in the hope that I would begin to channel my raging hormones into a purposeful goal. My family placed a great deal of emphasis on meritocratic achievement: one of my dad's proudest accomplishments was being acknowledged in a popular guide to success in business for his "efficient and tightly controlled beehive of activity."[19] For a year or so, now aged nine, I crammed at a private prep school. One of a handful of Jews, I was polished for speeding along the fast track into the meritocracy: first the prestigious Manchester Grammar School (MGS) in 1953, then Oxford in 1960. I benefited from the postwar decline in anti-Semitism in the same way that Jews in the United States "moved closer to the comforts available to [the] white middle-class," especially after the Supreme Court in 1948 invalidated restrictive covenants in neighborhoods excluding Jewish buyers, and New York State made it illegal to discriminate against Jews in university admissions.[20]

At MGS, my high school, there was such a sizable minority of Jewish students, mostly "scholarship boys," that we had our own assembly every morning and were exempted from singing "Onward Christian Soldiers." My maternal grandmother continued to worry about my safety, even though it was no longer justified. After I broke my shoulder at age thirteen playing rugby, she sniffed the air. "Wasn't Jewish?" she asked about the kid who had tackled me, already suspecting the answer.

A few years later, Grandma Daniels would warn me about the danger of *shiksas* on the prowl for Jewish husbands. "Who can blame them?" she would say: You do not hear about Jewish men being taken to court by frustrated wives for financial negligence or loss of consortium. But my brother and I were no match for those wily Christian gold-diggers. My first wife was respectably Protestant, and the second a lapsed Catholic who still crosses herself before the plane takes off. For health as much as cultural reasons, I made sure that my son Daniel was circumcised, unlike my brother Steve, who left his Tom's peter intact. There was some rejoicing in the family when our sister Sue migrated to Israel, albeit in search of high jinks, not the Messiah. Her marriage to a divorced, dark-skinned Iraqi Jew was welcomed as slight improvement on her older brothers' track record of marrying out.

By the 1960s, with British racial anxieties shifting to rebellions in the colonies and the specter of Caribbean, African, and Asian immigration to the core, I rarely encountered anti-Semitism in high school and college, and then only from individuals, not institutions.[21] Now that there were bigger and better demons to trump the Hebrews, we were given the opportunity to prove our loyalty to the Crown. My grandmother grew up a staunch racist, hating all *schwartzes* but never knowing one, until the Caribbean staff at her fancy Jewish retirement home adopted her recipe for chicken soup. The last time I visited her, on her ninety-ninth birthday, she called out a cook to meet me and there they stood, the Jamaican and the Jew, arms around each other. On the other hand, my Uncle Phil, who moved from Manchester to New York as a young man, stood firm in his hatred of "niggers" and died a bitter old man with his bigotry unblemished.

My parents did not buy into this double standard because they understood that Hitler hated Blacks as much as he hated Jews. When political exiles from Africa sought refuge in Manchester in the 1940s, Monty and Eileen showed their solidarity with the Kenyan Mau Maus by attending a cocktail party for Jomo Kenyatta. I was brought up to believe that apartheid was as morally wrong as anti-Semitism, even if it meant giving up the family's season ticket to the Lancashire Cricket Club when it invited South Africa to play in violation of the boycott. Among my mother's collection of antiques, now displayed on a shelf in my office, was an eighteenth-century abolitionist snuffbox, decorated with a slave breaking his shackles and the inscription, "Am I not your brother?"

But there were limits to my family's anti-racism. The further away the injustice—Africans terrorized by the Boers, Negroes facing dogs and water hoses in the U.S. South—the stronger my parents' indignation. Meanwhile, twenty miles from our suburban village was the laager of Moss Side, where immigrants from the Caribbean and Africa huddled in the rooming houses of absentee landlords, waiting for work. My dad hired black men in his textile factory only to do the most menial work and their kids did not receive scholarships to MGS. The closest I got to people in that community was through the grime-streaked windows of a double-decker bus as it made its way past the crumbling terraced houses non-stop to Manchester.

By the time I moved to Berkeley, California, in 1963 to rise with the crème de la crème up through graduate school, anti-Semitism had receded into the background in the United States and Jews were out in academia. The battleground for me shifted to racism and civil rights, free speech and Marxism, the war in Vietnam, feminism, and gay rights. "Everyone else," I can hear my Israeli brother-in-law saying. "The problem with Jews is that they care about everyone else but themselves." Yossi never has this problem. For him, Jewish identity and the struggle for justice are intertwined. He left Iraq with his parents under the gun and with only one possible destination. Mine was a different immigrant story. I left England to escape an overbearing father, not racial persecution, and to get far away from the provinces, not pogroms. I could choose my journey and, wisely, I chose California as my Promised Land.

When I joined the New Left, anti-Semitism was our lowest priority. "Never again" was not exactly a slogan that resonated in our lives. My heart was not with Judah Benjamin, the Jewish senator from Louisiana who served the Confederate government as Secretary of War, and whose portrait hangs in honor at the Skirball Cultural Center.[22] Neither was it with the Jews of New York who generally supported the teachers' unions against Black community control of schools. Nor with the Jews of Miami who rejected the godless Cuban Revolution. Nor with the Jews of Beverly Hills fearful of Mexicans swamping the Golden State. My models were the Jewish Marxists, lefties, and activists who fought for more than ethnic or national liberation. In the mid-1970s, I would lose my plum job at Berkeley for being a lefty, not a Jew.

When the Palestinian *intifada* erupted, I worried about my sister and her family's safety and sanity. Yet I neither felt torn by divided cultural loyalties, nor did I abandon political analysis. I see the world in the same way Phillip Lopate does, and maybe I, too, am "lacking in tribal feeling. When it comes to mass murder, I can see no difference between their casualties and ours."[23] And after September 11, I thought it was even more necessary to speak out against American unilateralism and Israeli militarism. "Jews, of all people," observes playwright Tony Kushner, "with our history of suffering," should know better than to acquiesce in the "dreadful suffering of the Palestinian people."[24] How can silence be good for the Jews? Like my grandmother, you may have noticed, I have started to make statements posing as questions.

I admit that I felt a twinge of unease when my daughter Rebecca decided some fifteen years ago to embrace Catholicism and give her wedding bouquet to the Virgin Mary when she married her Mexican boyfriend. But I was bothered more by the religiosity of her decision than by any sense of cultural betrayal. I would have felt worse if she had married an Orthodox Jew and been destined to walk behind him with eight kids in tow. Also, it was fine with me when my son Daniel followed his sister by marrying Anna, a Catholic Chicana. He did not convert but, like the rest of us, is trying to figure out how to live in a hybrid family that celebrates multiple gods. I do not think of my four grandchildren as diluting the race, but rather as getting all these unexpected bonuses in their cultural genes. I hope they will never feel obliged or compelled to choose only one true identity.[25]

"Almost-Jews" is how Howard Zinn describes the straddled identities of people like us, for whom ethnicity is not destiny.[26] My children's names reverberate with the Old Testament, yet many of my closest friends are, as my parents' generation used to say, non-Jews. I love Jewish humor and hanging out with people who have a similar Jewish past to mine. Occasionally I'll even go to a Passover celebration. But I am not interested in accompanying Lynn, my atheistic friend, to an inspirational synagogue for the high holidays. And I politely turned down an old comrade when she tried to recruit me to a group of hip, feminist Jews, who mix mysticism with stretching. She had mistaken my recent interest in yoga as a sign that I was searching for my Jewish roots.

To be truthful, I had not given any serious attention to the history of my development as a Jew until the Huntington briefing on June 29, 1999. Then, increasingly, I began to explore the making and remaking of my Jewishness. I did not know at the beginning of my research that a detective story about an iconic document would also turn into an exploration of the complexities of identity.

Located on Oxford and Stratford streets in San Marino, the Huntington triggered a flashback to my undergraduate days in England in the early 1960s. As the grandson of East European, immigrant Jews and the son of nouveau riche entrepreneurs from the provinces, I felt out of place at Oxford University among so many Protestant toffs and gentlemen scholars. My experience was not unlike Jewish intellectuals in Germany in the 1920s who, in Joseph Roth's memorable phrase, felt like "immigrants on home ground."[27] More than thirty years later, despite my long tenure in academia and the encroaching post-modernity of greater Los Angeles, I again felt de-centered. Maybe I was reminded of being an inside outsider by the Huntington's tendency to emulate the imagined solidity of a British Edwardian past. I was certain that I had entered the world of period costume dramas, so beloved by public television, when the Huntington invited its junior fellows to an evening of croquet and cocktails: "White attire is suggested, Pimm's Cups will be served," read the invitation.

My initial search of the Huntington's public collections for data on California's historiography broadened into a quest for evidence that I hoped would come from the Huntington's internal archives about its own origins. Did Huntington officials know in 1945 that they possessed an important icon? If they knew, what did they do with this knowledge? If they did not know, was this from choice or ignorance or calculated amnesia? Why did it take so long for the Huntington to acknowledge that it owned the Nuremberg Laws, and on what basis did it assert ownership?

Later, my visit to the Skirball Cultural Center would raise a very different set of problematic issues. The exhibition of an object such as the Nuremberg Laws is clearly designed to embed memory of the holocaust inside the grand narratives of history. But, as Zygmunt Bauman has observed, the contents of remembrance are by no means self-evident. The people who design memorials must make difficult decisions about "what is to be learned from the Holocaust, who is to learn it and to what effect."[28] How, I wondered, would the Skirball, a Jewish cultural center, deal with a display of the Nuremberg Laws in which General Patton, according to the Huntington's account, figures so heroically as an agent of liberation. What history lessons would the Skirball teach?

I decided to take off what I thought would be a few days from my research project to see if there were any answers to these unanswered questions. But to my surprise, it took three years to complete an investigation that, rare for me, I had neither anticipated nor planned.

THE LIBERATOR

Old Blood and Guts. Our blood, his guts.
(World War II saying)

As a Jew born during World War II, of course I knew about the Nuremberg Laws because they figure so prominently in the story of the holocaust. I was also aware of General George Patton's iconoclastic reputation. Since his unexpected, mundane death in a car accident in Germany in December 1945, his larger-than-life persona has been aggrandized in war memoirs, documentaries, museums, children's books, motivational manuals, and cyberspace.[29] Patton consistently dominated any scene in which he was included, both during his life and after his death: his reincarnation is omnipresent, just as he predicted.[30]

Popular memory of George S. Patton, Jr., or "Old Blood and Guts" as military men fondly recall him, is overwhelmingly adulatory: he was on the right side in the "Good War." The prevailing assessment is that Patton was a courageous and innovative military tactician with a "daring, freewheeling approach to modern warfare."[31] After his death, the Army claimed him as a favorite son. In a documentary narrated by Ronald Reagan and introduced by a serious, pipe-smoking Walter Matthau, Patton is sanctified for military prowess that "will live as long as courage is honored as a human virtue."[32] More recently, a Home Box Office documentary projects him as "rolling thunder, a man who grabbed fate by the throat and made himself a winner.... One of America's greatest soldiers, a genuine hero."[33] In a Time-Life book on World War II, Patton is depicted as "larger than life" and compared to Babe Ruth coming up to the plate: "Here's a big guy who's going to kick hell out of something."[34]

Patton remains a populist figure. When I went online in 2000, *eBay.com* posted several pages of Patton memorabilia for sale, including a 1950s chrome plastic tank ($13.25); the July 7, 1941, issue of *Life*, with a helmeted Patton on its front cover—the pose Michael Dukakis failed to emulate in his 1988 effort to project presidential toughness ($25.49); a GI General Patton ($26); a picture of Patton "pissing in the Rhine" before leading the Third Army across Germany ($10); and an original signature ($350) and a signed letter ($1,225). When I was outbid for a first edition of Patton's *War As I Knew It*, another seller offered me a hardback copy, twenty-second printing, for $19.99 plus shipping.

The scholarly and popular literature on Patton could fill a small library, with the Patton Museum offering a six-page bibliography on the topic. There are some fifty books in which he is the main subject matter, mostly biographies and accounts of battles and military strategy. Several books are available for young readers, typically in the mold of Alden Hatch's portrait of "that stern, spare figure with the ice-gray eyes, the six-guns swinging at his hips and the stars glittering on his helmet."[35] This genre celebrates militarism and treats Patton's life as a be-all-that-you-can-be example of self-determination. "Even at an early age, George Patton knew exactly what he wanted to do with his life," so goes a typical potboiler. Patton is promoted as a "romantic vision for other young people so they, too, can fashion their own destinies and color the pages of history."[36]

Another important category of Patton literature involves motivational and inspirational themes, applied to techniques of organizational leadership. A small book of instructional guidance à la Patton sold one hundred thousand copies between 1979 and 1991.[37] To firm up your character, take lessons from Patton.[38] "What can your business learn from the toughest, shrewdest military leader who ever went to war?" asks an advertisement for a recent book, *Patton on Leadership*.[39]

Patton is often remembered as "the liberator" who pushed U.S. troops to victory and forced his own soldiers and local Nazi collaborators to witness the concentration camps.[40] He is also typically depicted as a great but troubled man of history, as portrayed in the 1970 movie *Patton*. In 1999, my own views about Patton were based not so much on historical knowledge as on populist tales and George C. Scott's performance. I shared the sense of a contemporary movie critic that I had witnessed a documentary about "the real general and not the gifted actor."[41] This is not surprising, given the script was based on a military historian's biography of Patton and the movie was produced by Frank McCarthy, who knew Patton well during the war.[42] In 1971, the movie was nominated for ten Oscars and won seven, including best picture, best director, and best actor. "It will not soothe your memories," wrote one critic, "but it will re-create a time before young men thought it amusing to burn their country's flag."[43] To Rex Reed, *Patton* was an "absorbing testament to the life of a unique human being, and a war movie for people who hate war movies."[44]

Some critics have suggested that *Patton* had an anti-war slant because Scott depicted the general as a loony eccentric, bloated with self-importance, perhaps an echo of his earlier role as General Turgidson in *Dr. Strangelove*.[45] But George C. Scott actually admired Patton because "he was a professional, and I admire professionalism. And for whatever else he was, good or bad, he was an individual. That's what's most important to me today, when everybody around seems to be some kind of damn ostrich."[46] Moreover, compared to the edgy anti-war messages of *Mash* and *Catch 22*, both released between 1969 and 1970, *Patton* glorified militarism and evoked the righteousness of a popular war at a time when the American war in Vietnam was facing growing resistance back home. Richard Nixon, who identified with Patton as a leader hanging tough against the odds, became a booster for the film and watched it twice just before he ordered troops into Cambodia. Nixon was "a walking ad for the movie," observed Darryl Zanuck, chairman of Twentieth Century-Fox.[47]

I went down into the Huntington's basement library to read up on Patton, curious to see how scholars parse the mythic general. I quickly found Martin Blumenson's definitive editions of *The Patton Papers*. Volume one, published in 1972, covers the period from 1885, the year of Patton's birth, to 1940. Two years later, Blumenson published a second volume, which continues through Patton's death in 1945. Both books are based on the author's unrestricted access to Patton's personal papers, diaries, and correspondence. Blumenson had served under Patton in the Third Army during World War II and was trusted by the Army and Patton's family to be thorough and fair. Blumenson reproduces Patton's own words in great detail and in their historical contexts. Patton's views about the world did not require much deciphering because he was a prolific correspondent, maintained a daily diary, and liked to publicize his views. "Patton didn't give a damn about keeping anything secret," says Hugh Cole, the Third Army's historian.[48]

I sat down with volume two and looked up "Jews, Patton's attitude toward" in the index. I was not surprised to learn about Patton's anti-Semitism, which is to be expected of a leading upper-class figure of the early twentieth century. What shocked me, however, was how much venomous hatred Patton directed at the Jewish survivors he encountered in the concentration camps in 1945: "The Jewish type of DP [displaced person] is, in the majority of cases, a sub-human species without any of the cultural or social refinements of our time," Patton wrote in his diary. "Practically all of them had the flat brownish gray eye common among the Hawaiians which, to my mind, indicates very low intelligence."[49] He reluctantly complied with General Eisenhower's order to "give the Jews special accommodation ... in spite of my personal feelings against them" and his sympathy for German survivors — "the only decent people left in Europe," he confided to his wife.[50]

Martin Blumenson, who is Jewish, was also distraught on first discovering the level of Patton's bigotry, and even told his editor that he did not know if he would be able to complete *The Patton Papers*.[51] He resolved his dilemma by concluding that Patton's "absurd ravings" were the likely result of a lifetime of physical injuries, aggravated by stress at the end of the war. "Clearly, he had become delusional."[52] Another biographer suggests that Patton's "gratuitous bigotry" may have been "contaminated by the plague with which Hitler infected Germany."[53] Whether you agree that Patton's behavior at the end of the war was the result of "a severe case of burnout," as Carlo D'Este suggests,[54] it is still unnerving to discover that the "liberator" was "frankly opposed" to the Nuremberg war crimes tribunal and that he considered Jewish survivors "lost to all decency."[55]

How well known is Patton's hatred of Jews? During his lifetime, I discovered, he shared his prejudices with a wide circle of family and friends. After his death, Patton's anti-Semitism was recognized in public long before the release of his diaries in the 1970s revealed the depth of his bigotry. General Eisenhower's senior Jewish chaplain, for example, complained to his boss at the end of the war that Patton was treating Jewish survivors as though they were perpetrators.[56] "There are quite a number of indications," recalled a rabbi in 1962, "that his attitude toward Jews was not the most friendly."[57] Patton's nephew, who idolized his godfather, recalled in the early 1960s that Patton thought the U.S. government was too punitive toward Germany at the end of the war. "They can't even understand the German," Patton told Fred Ayer in 1945. "It is either that or they're too much influenced by the Jews who understandably want revenge."[58]

Patton scholars are not alone in being well aware of the general's views about Jews. When historian Hasia Diner went to see the movie *Patton* in 1970, "I and my friends all knew that Patton was anti-Semitic," she recalls. How did she know this? "Oh, it was common knowledge among Jews."[59] To Rabbi Abraham Cooper, Associate Dean of the Simon Wiesenthal Center in Los Angeles, Patton was a "world-class anti-Semite."[60] When I interviewed Michael Berenbaum, then director of the Shoah Foundation, he was similarly well informed about Patton's reputation for Jew-hating.[61]

I also suspected that the comments of Uri Herscher, the Skirball's president, to the press on June 26, 1999, were hedged with ambivalence:

> No memory rooted in the twentieth century is more potent than the Nazi Holocaust. The Skirball is not alone in recognizing that the memory of the Holocaust imposes a moral obligation to caution us against the possibility of genocide, to be grateful for the answer democracy enables us to give genocide— and to preserve the record. General Patton no doubt had something of the sort in mind when he accepted some basic Nazi documents removed from Germany by U.S. soldiers and deposited them at the Huntington Library. Given the state of our world as this century nears its end, the General might well have agreed that the time has come to bring these materials to public attention, in the hope of attaching ourselves ever more firmly to our democratic promise.[62]

Phrases such as "no doubt," "something of the sort in mind," and "might well have" hardly suggest a ringing endorsement of Patton's commitment to the "democratic promise." I would later find out that Uri Herscher was well informed about Patton's anti-Semitism, and even suspected him of fascist leanings.[63]

A BOLT OUT OF THE BLUE

My other reason for conducting research in the Huntington's basement was to see what Patton had to say in his diary about the discovery of the Nuremberg Laws, about the "great public presentation" of the Laws to him by General Van Fleet, and about his visit to the Huntington on June 11, 1945, when he turned them over to Robert Millikan.[64] In *The Patton Papers,* Blumenson reports that Patton returned to the United States in June 1945, and that he "stopped in at the Huntington Library" during his visit to the Los Angeles area.[65] But there are no details about the visit. Moreover, Blumenson's book does not include any of Patton's diary entries for this period. The *Los Angeles Times,* I would later discover, reported every moment of Patton's tumultuous return to Southern California—including the route of his daily motorcade and his participation in the singing of "Onward Christian Soldiers" at his childhood church—but did not make even a single reference to the Huntington Library.[66] Why this sudden antipathy to publicity?

Cecilia made a call to an archivist at the Manuscript Division of the Library of Congress, where the George S. Patton, Jr. Papers are held. He confirmed that Patton had apparently not maintained his personal diary during his visit to the United States.[67] Regarding the "great public presentation" of the Nuremberg Laws to Patton "about the 27th of May," there were also, surprisingly, no records. We were referred to the Holocaust-Era Assets Records Project at the National Archives for possible information about the provenance of the Nuremberg Laws. Its director, Greg Bradsher, could not find any records that documented the seizure of the Nuremberg Laws or the presentation by General Fleet to General Patton, but he mentioned that he had seen a letter to the *Washington Post* that might be a useful lead.[68]

At about the same time as we were embarking on our revised project, some three thousand miles away in Baltimore eighty-three-year-old Martin Dannenberg experienced a flashback. A front-page story by Sharon Waxman in the *Washington Post* had reminded him of what happened in Germany near the end of World War II, some fifty-four years earlier.[69] But he had a different memory of how the Nuremberg Laws had been discovered, one that challenged the accuracy of Patton's account. Dannenberg politely informed the *Washington Post* that Waxman's story "needs some revision." According to Dannenberg, it was the 203d Counter-Intelligence Corps (CIC), of which he was special agent in charge, and not "troops of the 90th Infantry Division" that had retrieved the Nuremberg Laws. Patton's version contained other errors, wrote Dannenberg: the Nuremberg Laws had been found in Eichstätt, not Nuremberg; the CIC had been led to the documents by an informant, so there was no need to go "fighting through the town

... with grenades"; and Dannenberg did not recall any ceremonial presentation to Patton. The 203d CIC turned over the Nuremberg Laws to Patton's intelligence chief with the understanding that they would be forwarded to the "SHAEF (Supreme Headquarters, Allied Expeditionary Force) document people [based in Paris], who were collecting evidence for the expected trial of war criminals.... It is evident," concluded Dannenberg's letter to the editor, "that Gen. Patton never sent them on to Paris but retained them as a personal souvenir that made its way into the Huntington Library." Dannenberg's letter also mentioned that his three-man CIC team included Agent Maxwell Pickens of Bessemer, Alabama, and Military Intelligence Interpreter Frank R. Perls of Los Angeles.[70]

Soon after we read Dannenberg's account, Cecilia contacted him by phone to begin the process of vetting his story. He clearly had direct, personal knowledge of how the Nuremberg Laws were acquired in 1945. Yet, would the account of a man in his mid-80s be credible on events that took place more than fifty years earlier? Cecilia, who is trained in oral history and regularly includes autobiographical voices in her syllabi, met with Dannenberg in his home in Baltimore.

She quickly discovered that he has a sharp mind and solid information to back up his vivid memories. "I had often wondered what happened to the document. It was a bolt out of the blue when I read about its rediscovery at the Huntington Library," said Dannenberg. Moreover, he had copies of photographs that he had taken "with my Minox spy camera" to document his discovery of the Nuremberg

2.1 Cecilia O'Leary and Martin Dannenberg share memories and evidence about what happened in Eichstätt, Germany, in 1945. The conversation took place in Baltimore, October 3, 1999.

Laws. "I have a shot of Frank Perls and me holding the documents," he claimed. "There were three of us involved," said Martin Dannenberg. "Two Jewish boys and a Southern Baptist, who I'm sure hadn't the foggiest idea of the importance of what we had uncovered." But Dannenberg was well aware that the Nuremberg Laws had "doomed Jews to the nightmare of the Holocaust," as was Perls, who, according to Dannenberg, had fled Nazi Germany in the early 1930s.[71]

OASIS IN THE CITY

When Cecilia and I assembled our data and compared notes, we realized not only that Patton had fabricated his account, but also that we could now reconstruct the history of the original Nuremberg Laws, from their passage in 1935 in the city of the Reich Party rallies, to their disappearance ten years later into the Huntington's vault. For the first time in my academic career, I was now doing research on the history of Jews and anti-Semitism. I began reading up on Nazi propaganda. "Excuse me," I asked a clerk at the local Barnes and Noble in Pasadena, "do you have anything by Hitler?" "Would that be Adolf?" he asked politely. When my research *at* the Huntington turned into research *on* the Huntington, the atmosphere quickly turned chilly. "You're acting more like a journalist than a scholar," an administrator accused me, as if there could not be a worse insult.[72] All of a sudden certain files were off limits and our presence was suspect to some administrators, even as several staff members supported our investigation. As has often been the case in my career, my research was turning into an activist project.

Though I was meeting resistance from guardians of the Huntington's reputation, my Jewish credentials were opening doors that otherwise would have been shut. It was as if I had discovered the Jewish equivalent of the Masons' secret handshake. As word got out that I was investigating L'Affaire Nuremberg at the Huntington, several people approached me with their ex-officio stories. "When I first started working here in the 1970s," a curator recalled, "I would get at least one inquiry every year from somebody who wanted to know whether we had any books made from human skin." A researcher told me that she was never invited to lunch with administrators in the 1970s "because of my husband's Jewish accent." Another researcher stopped doing research there in the 1980s "because the place was so anti-Semitic." A local librarian told me that he did not like to visit the Huntington: "It's too WASP." A curator led me to a photograph of General Patton holding his donated copy of *Mein Kampf* that hung in the corridor of the Rare Book Department. "We pass it every day," she said.[73]

The more I heard these confessions, the more I felt like the protagonist in Nathaniel West's (née Nathan Weinstein) 1933 novel, who begins his job as the cynical Agony Aunt columnist for a newspaper and ends up inseparable from the desperate people who send their cries for help to *Miss Lonelyhearts*. "You're becoming really Jewish," observed my partner Cecilia, the Irish Catholic redhead who likes to put a potpourri of saintly tchotchkes over my desk to ward off evil spirits. "Really Jewish?" I shot back, hunting for innuendo, but I knew she was on to something. I was beginning to vicariously experience my ethnicity as an imposed racial category rather than as a voluntary, highly elastic, cultural identity.[74]

My newfound curiosity about the Nuremberg Laws took me away from secluded San Marino to the other world of West Los Angeles, to a three-year-old institution nestled at the foot of the Santa Monica Mountains. The Skirball's striking complex of steel, glass, and stone covers fifteen acres of hillside. Its Israeli-Canadian architect, Moshe Safdie, imagined the center as "an oasis in the city," with a sense of transparency and an effect that is "soft, almost silky." He sought "to make a place that seeks serenity and calm ... a place to uplift the spirit—a place that stimulates and provokes, but without losing its essential optimism."[75] As a visitor at the Huntington, you feel that you have been invited into a fabulous mansion where, if you watch your manners, you will be exposed to refinement, knowledge, and arts that are uplifting and enlightening. At the Skirball, you are invited to make the center into your surrogate home. "It is not a place that demands reverence," says Uri Herscher. "If someone wants to come here just to read a newspaper in the fresh air, drink a cup of coffee, hold a conversation ... the architecture tells you it's fine."[76]

The Skirball Cultural Center was conceived in the 1980s with a public persona and educational mission as its primary goals, but its roots are in the reformist tradition of American Judaism, going back to the Hebrew Union College (HUC), founded in 1875 in Cincinnati by Isaac Mayer Wise, who prior to the Civil War had shaken up Jewish orthodoxy by eliminating sex segregation in his synagogue. Wise established HUC as an academic center for modernist Judaism in North America and as a college to train rabbis, cantors, and teachers.[77]

By 1965, when its Board of Governors decided to move the campus to Los Angeles, the HUC had also acquired a twenty-five-thousand-piece collection of Jewish artifacts, documents, and memorabilia. HUC opened to the public in 1971 on its new campus adjacent to the University of Southern California. The Skirball Museum, established by HUC in 1972, began its road to independence when Rabbi Uri Herscher came to Los Angeles in 1979 as Executive Vice-President of HUC with a vision of the museum as a cultural center that would reach the city's growing Jewish population, particularly those without any religious affiliations. In 1995, the Skirball Cultural Center was incorporated as an independent, nonprofit institution, headed by Herscher. A year later, on April 21, it opened to the public.[78]

The Skirball was constructed between 1989 and 1995 in a central location, at the bottom of a hillside in the Sepulveda Pass, just off the San Diego Freeway. It is only a few miles away from the newly built J. Paul Getty Museum, which opened to the public in December 1997 and quickly became one of the most popular tourist attractions in Los Angeles. The Skirball's broad family programming has made it such a popular destination for locals and tourists that it even outdraws the Getty.[79] In terms of support, financing, and public interest, the center has been a phenomenal success, with a quickly made reputation as "perhaps the world's largest Jewish cultural institution of its kind." By September 2003, only seven years after it opened, the Skirball was operating with a sixty million dollar endowment, an annual budget of $11.6 million, 117 full-time employees, and three hundred volunteers.[80] It has attracted more than three million visitors, at about the same annual rate as the well-established Huntington.

Similar to the Huntington, the Skirball presents exhibitions and maintains a collection of artworks and artifacts. Unlike the Huntington, however, the Skirball's utopian and hopeful message is presented Hollywood-style in events, videos, teleconferencing, and star-studded performances. "There will be concerts, performances, lectures, readings, symposia, classes for adults and for children, conferences that can be broadcast by satellite or cable, art exhibitions, even food fairs," predicted its president Uri Herscher in 1996. "That's what will make this a cultural center, rather than a museum."[81] The Skirball's programming, which attracts more visitors than its exhibits draw, is eclectically multicultural. Events in early 2002, for example, included a demonstration of Israeli dance techniques, a concert by the Los Angeles Philharmonic, a world music concert, a lecture on women and religious minorities in Islam, an Arthur Miller play, and a conversation with Elmore Leonard. Whereas the Huntington's mission is to "preserve and display" cultural treasures of the past, the Skirball takes "seriously the inheritance of the past, but that doesn't mean we remain in the past."[82] Visitors to the Huntington expect to witness sacred artifacts. At the Skirball, they could just as easily take in a play, have a discussion with a media star, or meet friends for lunch.

I visited the Skirball early in July 1999. The center may be a "multicultural, eclectic entity," in the words of the *Los Angeles Times* art critic,[83] but its core is Judaism, and it had been a long time since I spent several hours in an institution organized around themes of Jews in the New World. I appreciated the sensual ambience and warm welcome, but I felt uneasy in the main permanent exhibit on "Jewish Life from Antiquity to America."[84] As a child in England, I had fidgeted through pious accounts of heroic tenacity against all odds. The linear story line of an epic journey by The Jewish People from the wilderness of Egypt to the Golden Land (*goldene medineh*) of West Los Angeles grates on my analytical sensibilities. I prefer my identity politics to be much more porous.

After quickly walking past the upbeat story of Jewish progress, I came to the case displaying the Nuremberg Laws, finally on public display after fifty-four years in the Huntington's nuclear-proof basement. The few sheets of typewritten decrees, banal indeed, were dwarfed by the huge vanity copy of *Mein Kampf,* which Patton had claimed as a war trophy in April 1945. As I watched elderly visitors linger before the exhibit and peer into the gloomy cabinet, I too became immersed in present absences: my father's silence about his impressions of the concentration camps, my grandparents' nose for whiffs of danger, my brother-in-law's chiding about my ambivalent identity.[85] I stopped to chat with volunteers and docents, middle-aged Jewish women with strong opinions and a rooted presence, so much like my mother before her zest turned bitter. The familiarity took me by surprise.

2.2 The Nuremberg Laws and *Mein Kampf* on display at the Skirball Cultural Center in late 1999. To the left and reflected in the glass of the Nuremberg case are three portraits of victims of the holocaust. Above these portraits is a collage of images from the next room's exhibit on Israel.

▣ Chapter 3 ▣

Tall Like Germans

Never mind to whom he prays,
The rotten mess is in the race.
(German jingle, late nineteenth century)

SINGING GERMANY

While Cecilia flew back east to debrief Martin Dannenberg and reconstruct his experience of retrieving the Nuremberg Laws in Eichstätt, Germany, in April 1945, I tried to track down the other two members of his counterintelligence team. All I could find out about Special Agent J. Maxwell "Easy" Pickens was that he had worked for a steel company in Birmingham, Alabama, prior to the war and had died many years ago. Frank Perls was also unavailable to confirm Dannenberg's memory because he had died back in 1975. But a search of the Los Angeles telephone directory brought me to his niece, Marianne Perls, who told me that she had inherited some of her uncle's personal papers.

It was easy for me to make personal connections with Martin Dannenberg, even though we are from different countries and different generations—he was born in 1915, the same year as my father's birth. When the war in Europe ended, I was three years old, living with my mother and grandparents in a predominantly Jewish neighborhood of north Manchester, a comfortable ghetto, but a ghetto nevertheless. My dad would return from his stint in the army to find doors opening to Jews that were shut tight in the 1930s. As a beneficiary of the decline of organized anti-Semitism, I was the first in my family to make it to college, not any college, but Oxford, which guaranteed me an academic or professional career if that is what I wanted.

As with my family's trajectory in England, Martin Dannenberg found the United States increasingly hospitable to Jewish upward mobility in the mid-twentieth century; he went from the bottom to the top rung of an insurance company in his lifetime, just as my father went from an impoverished youth to company executive in forty years. I was very familiar with Dannenberg's journey, unlike that of Frank Perls, whose diasporic experiences were very different. He came of age in Germany when history unfolded in the opposite direction. As he zigzagged to eventual success in California, his mother would run into dead ends.

From information provided by Dannenberg I knew that Frank Perls was Jewish and had grown up in Germany; an obituary in the *New York Times* notes that he had died a prominent art dealer in Los Angeles in 1975.[1] At first I had trouble finding common ground with Frank Perls, which was surprising given that we shared some important life experiences: we were both born in Europe and were the first in our families to immigrate to California, where Perls struck it rich in the booming Los Angeles economy, while I discovered gold in the state's expanding system of higher education. Until I dug into research on Perls's background, he remained a cipher. I knew very little about the European Jews of Perls's generation who had escaped the holocaust; what I did know was one-dimensional. From my youth I had inherited compressed images of reified victims—such as Rod Steiger's portrayal of Sol Nazerman, a broken shell of a man in the wrenching 1964 movie, *The Pawnbroker*—rather than flesh-and-blood people who acted out their lives, albeit under the most repressive conditions.

Frank Perls, it would turn out, came from a family of sufficient distinction to leave its personal records to various collections around the country, including the Smithsonian Art Archives in Washington, D.C., and the Leo Baeck Institute in New York. This material would enable us to track the personal journey of an exiled German Jew as he returned to his homeland to capture the documents that symbolized his family's uprooting. At the same time, the history of the Perls family offered an opportunity to look closely at the underbelly of assimilation and to understand how the 1935 Nuremberg Laws emerged in a country that a decade earlier had seemed as welcoming to Jews as California had been to me in the 1960s.

Franz "Frank" Perls grew up between the world wars in the material comfort and cultural stimulation of a cosmopolitan German household.[2] During a period in which Martin Dannenberg was becoming accustomed to seeing signs that announced "No Jews or Dogs" and to finding certain areas of Baltimore "restricted to refined gentiles only,"[3] Franz's father Hugo was employed at the German Foreign Office, "clipping French, English, Swiss and American newspapers for the Kaiser's consumption."[4] Germany was much more hospitable than was the rest of Europe to Jews fleeing Russian persecution at the turn of the century. England, for example, was rife with "anti-alien, anti-Semitic prejudice," while German Jews discovered entrées to intermarriage and religious conversion.[5]

In 1910, Hugo Perls and Käte Kolker—whose parents were, respectively, "synagogue-going Jews" and "strict Jews"—converted to Christianity. "Everyone really thought that one can *become* a Christian," reminisced Frank some sixty years later. Käte's parents disinherited her when she married Hugo in a church wedding in Berlin. Hugo's mother rejected her new daughter-in-law. Confirming their rupture with the past, the newlyweds decided not to circumcise Franz, born eight months later in October 1910, and had him baptized a Lutheran the following month.[6] In recognition of his first spoken word and his parents' artistic interests, Franz was nicknamed Dada, a name he retained among family and friends even after Franz assimilated into Frank to mark his U.S. citizenship in April 1943.[7] In 1910, Hugo and Käte could not imagine in their worst nightmares that twenty-five years later, at a Nuremberg Rally, Hitler would associate their son's name with Jewish decadence. "Dadaists, futurists, and impressionists forget that the task of Art is not to promote degeneracy but to fight degeneracy," ranted Hitler. "Those who affect the primitive style are either swindlers or maniacs."[8]

The birth of Franz signaled a hopeful time for the Perls family. "Long before the Weimar Republic put the finishing touches to the long process of Jewish emancipation," observes Zygmunt Bauman, "Germany was widely conceived by international Jewry as the haven of religious and national equality and tolerance. Germany entered this century with many more Jewish academics and professionals than contemporary America or Britain. Popular resentment of Jews was neither deep-seated nor widespread."[9] Religious conversion and mixed marriages were quite common, with almost one of every ten Jews married to a non-Jewish partner. By the early 1930s, "Jews were almost completely emancipated and almost completely integrated into the German community."[10]

When the Nazis enacted the Nuremberg Laws in 1935, they initially had a great deal of trouble sorting out Aryans from Jews: determining whether a Jew who converted to Christianity remained a Jew, figuring out what to do about Protestant women married to Jewish men, and scientifically deciding how much ancestral blood constituted Jewishness.[11] In the end, of course, it would make no difference: one drop of Jewish blood in your household could get you killed. But in the mid-1930s, industrious bureaucrats, physicians, anthropologists, ministers, and judges put a great deal of effort into the fine legalisms of racial categorization. A new profession of licensed "family researchers" emerged to help government agencies, employers, and applicants document the purity or impurities of Aryan blood.[12] The need for this kind of biological sleuthing indicates the degree to which Jews had become integrated into German society in the 1920s and early 1930s.[13]

The lives and work of Hugo and Käte Perls testify to this post–World War I cultural opening. Hugo, born in Poland, moved to Berlin with his mother, where he grew up in comfort.[14] As a child he learned Hebrew and attended religious services, but as he got older, his family lost interest in Jewish rituals.[15] His father, who died before Hugo was born, was a dealer in leather, his mother a "well-to-do cultured woman." She played the piano, spoke several languages, and required Hugo to take violin lessons. Among his close teenage friends was the future pianist Artur Rubinstein.

Hugo's early career benefited from all the perks offered to upwardly mobile

Weimar professionals. He studied philosophy and art history at Freiberg and Berlin universities, and later received his law degree. An accomplished linguist who could read and write Greek, Latin, French, and English, he joined the German Civil Service and worked in the Ministry of the Interior until World War I, when he was transferred to the Ministry of Foreign Affairs. In 1921, he left the government and went into business as an art dealer, drawing upon the "ample means that he inherited from his family."[16] A decade before Hitler's rise to power, he could share the exultation of writer Joseph Roth: "We have sung Germany, the real Germany!"[17]

By the time of Hugo's marriage to Käte Kolker in 1910, they were already business partners. As collectors and dealers they helped to shape a growing international market for avant-garde art. "Picasso likes to say," Frank Perls recalled in 1971, "that he has known me since eight months before my birth, referring to meeting my parents when they bought their first picture by Picasso."[18] Franz's parents prospered in Berlin, which was home to more than eighty thousand Jews.[19] Hugo got to know Picasso, "the most human of humans," while Käte sat for several portraits by Edvard Munch.[20] One of Mies van der Rohe's first projects was the Perls House, which the architectural visionary designed for Käte and Hugo in 1911. "Mies and my parents were the best of friends. They let Mies do what he wanted to do. They even let him paint the outside a rosy-ochre and plant pine trees in the grey sandy garden. My parents commissioned Max Pechstein to paint enormous canvasses to be put into the dining room as quasi-murals."[21] When the Perls sold their house in the early 1920s, they donated Pechstein's Matisse-inspired "Bathing Girls" to the National Gallery in Berlin. Some twenty years later, it would be destroyed in a bonfire of degenerate art, the museum itself reduced to a "torso."[22]

Franz's childhood of secular, comfortable privilege and stimulation was not unlike my own adolescence in England one generation later. He was protected from "all ugliness, tragedy, life, death, poverty, war, and murder"—with a tutor at home in his early years, summers at a spa resort, and private schooling in Pully, Switzerland. But his parents also propelled him into a world of ideas and cultural engagement: attending dinner parties with celebrities such as Thomas Mann and Bruno Walter, visiting new galleries and radical exhibitions, and shopping for luxury items in Berlin's fashionable district. Käte Perls wanted her three sons to feel that they had a rightful place in the new Germany. "We, the children," recalled Frank, "must grow to look like those Germans, we must be strong, stand up straight, swim, have straight legs, must not talk unless spoken to, must be seen but not heard, must walk, walk, walk, eat, eat, eat to grow, grow, grow, to be tall like Germans. In one big swoop, in one generation, these German Protestant Jews grew some six inches taller than their parents were."[23]

Käte and Hugo may have felt secure about converting to the Christian mainstream, but they remained on the political and cultural edge of German respectability. They were close to Karl Liebknecht, convicted in 1916 for his opposition to World War I. Hugo had never met anybody like Liebknecht, with his "flowing black hair, fiery black eyes, and energetic confidence." The revolutionary activist, Hugo recalled later in his life, was "an unusual man with a passion for the idea of socialism to the point that he saw things social and antisocial even in a match." Hugo disagreed with his friend about the philosophical merits of Marxism, but shared his assessment that only a social revolution could improve the conditions of the "starving proletariat who had bled for their so-called achievements, but ended up empty-handed."[24]

When Liebknecht was imprisoned, Käte brought him food, clothing, and cigarettes, receiving in return "a political education."[25] On his release, Hugo warned him about rumors of assassination plots that he had heard at the Foreign Office, but it was too late.[26] In 1919, along with Rosa Luxemburg and other leaders of Spartakist Rising, Liebknecht was executed without trial. "The new party of Karl Liebknecht [the Spartakusbund]," as Hugo bluntly observed, "was quickly annihilated through mere murder."[27] In the 1930s, Major George S. Patton, Jr.— then executive officer of the Third Cavalry at Fort Myer, Virginia—acknowledged this coup d'état as a highlight of modern political history. The lesson he learned was that "a loyal and well led Army destroyed the course of Communism ere it could raise its ugly head above the ruins of a war weary nation."[28] According to Frank Perls, when Käte tried to flee nazism in the early 1940s, her socialist political past "kept her from getting into the United States."[29]

Always a free spirit and rebel, Käte was a powerful influence on her son's development. An independent feminist who had studied acting in Berlin before become a leading art dealer, she moved in leftist circles, instilling in her son an obligation to be an informed activist. When Hugo took eight-year-old Franz to a parade in 1918 celebrating the end of World War I, Käte berated her husband. "My children hate the Kaiser," she screamed at him. Franz remembered standing at his bedroom window, "looking out on a rainy day, out over the roofs of Berlin where smokestacks and horizon became a hazy line, thinking I could see the soldiers at Verdun dying in the rain."[30]

As a young man, aged seventeen, Franz Perls was befriended by the poet and writer, Ernst Toller, then in his mid-thirties. By 1928, when they first met, Toller had already written several popular plays. Some were written during his five years in prison for "high treason," namely, supporting the revolutionary movement of 1919 and speaking out against World War I: "The air poisoned by the stink of corpses / A single awful cry of madness."[31] Toller, the son of a successful Jewish merchant, "became a hero" to Franz because of "his enormous involvement with Marx, God, Nature, Humanity; his unshakeable belief in a socialist regime for Germany, his fear of German militarism becoming powerful again through the armament barons of the Ruhr and Rhineland." Ernst Toller "opened my mind," said Frank.[32] In 1933, Joseph Goebbels denounced "the Jew Toller" and added him to a long list of banned authors.[33]

By about 1928, Käte Perls began to sniff danger in the air. She had a "constant fear of a rebirth of the ugly spirit" of war and her familiarity with German history triggered warnings about German militarism. "She was the female Jeremiah in my life," recalled Frank, "more a prophet than a grumbler." At the "pinnacle of family fortune"—his family getting rich on sales of Picassos, Matisses, and Cézannes—Hugo returned home one day from a business trip to Munich and reported that he had seen a large sign outside a beer hall: "NO DOGS, NO JEWS." From that day on, Frank's mother made plans to leave Germany. "Let's get out, let's get out," she urged Hugo, who was reluctant to leave a thriving business. It was Käte, recalled Frank, who saved the family from extermination, nearly losing her own life in the process.

With the National Socialist German Workers' Party (NSDAP) on the rise, Franz Perls also began to notice the ominous swagger of their cadres on campus. As a student at Frankfurt University in 1929, Franz was threatened by a Nazi activist brandishing a sword and yelling, "*Juden Raus*. This *Judenjunge* will get my saber into his fat belly." A friend intervened to save him, disarming his antagonist, Baldur von Schirach. A few days later, Franz and his friend Ludwig von Hessen were having lunch in a local vegetarian restaurant when they ran into von Schirach. "There in a corner, the curtains drawn, at a wooden table sat the spinach and noodle man: Adolf Hitler with my enemy." When von Schirach made a little speech for his mentor about Jews "running around our university," von Hessen put him right: "Franz Perls is a Protestant," he announced.[34]

Franz Perls was lucky to get away with this challenge to von Schirach in Hitler's presence. His would-be-slayer was not an ordinary thug. The son of an aristocratic German father and American mother, from a very early age Baldur von Schirach was a "convinced anti-Semite," who joined the Nazis in 1924 and was quickly recruited into Hitler's innermost circle. In 1929, the party put him in charge of the National Socialist German Students' League and two years later, appointed him Reich Youth Leader of the NSDAP. In 1933, at the age of twenty-six, and now in charge of the six million members of the Hitler Youth organization, "his cult seemed second only to that of Hitler himself." That same year, Wilhelm Frick appointed him to the Ministry of Interior's committee that was established to develop the country's racial policies. In 1940, he was promoted to *Gauleiter* (regional chief) and Governor of Vienna, where he supervised the transportation of one hundred and eighty-five thousand Jews to Polish concentration camps. Two years later, he defended his role in deporting "tens of thousands upon tens of thousands of Jews into the ghetto of the East" as a policy "contributing to European culture." For these crimes against humanity, von Schirach was convicted at the Nuremberg War Crimes Tribunal and sentenced—along with Rudolf Hess and Albert Speer—to twenty years at Spandau. His denunciation from the dock of Hitler as a "millionfold murderer" probably saved his life.[35]

In 1929, Franz Perls dismissed Hitler as "not much more than a rabble-rouser." He remained in college, taking mostly art history classes, at the University of Vienna in 1929, University of Berlin in 1930, the University of Freiburg in 1931, and University of Frankfurt in 1932–1933, including a class on the origins and evolution of World War I.[36] He shared the view of some progressive intellectuals that Hitler would be unable to seize and hold power. "Just let him take the Government for a week, a month," thought Franz. "He'll see. He cannot do anything without the Social Democrats."[37] Two years later, Franz was still in Germany, while Hugo had taken his wife's advice and followed Käte to Paris. "In 1931," recalled Hugo, "I definitely left Germany."[38]

Even after the Reichstag fire in February 1933, Franz was of two minds about leaving. He even considered joining the Communist Party, and his hesitation probably saved his life. One of the first acts of the Nazi regime after it came to power in March was to round up and imprison some ten thousand communists and socialists in its first concentration camp at Dachau, about twelve miles outside Munich.[39] As a child, Franz had gone to the "adorable mud-spa town of Dachau" to get treatment for his nerve-damaged arm. "Suddenly Dachau represented not the healing mud any more, but just mud." Meanwhile, he still could not imagine that Nazi nationalism would lead to the destruction of "some fifteen million people," to a war that would make "one big heap of rubble out of Dresden, Hamburg, and Berlin." He was furious at the Nazis, "but who can say [in 1933] that he saw more, saw the grim twelve years that were ahead, who can say that he was more than furious, deeply shocked, seriously hurt by single incidents."[40]

By spring 1933, "the beginning of the twelve-year-long thousand year Reich," Franz was ready to follow the lead of his parents—now amicably divorced since October 1931—and on March 23 bought a one-way rail ticket to Paris, where Käte had started up her new art gallery and joined the émigré cultural scene. Another twelve years would pass before Frank returned to Germany. Meanwhile, now twenty-three years old, in exile and unemployed, Franz worked for his mother in her new Paris gallery, scouring the auction houses for paintings that other dealers missed or ignored. Käte held court at the Café du Dome, where Franz was introduced to Billy Wilder (née Samuel Wilder, a Polish Jew), Peter Lorre, and the whole Parisian film scene until it moved to Hollywood. Dada was hired on the set of Wilder's *Mauvaise Graine* (1934), claiming to have played a small role in discovering its ingénue star, Danielle Darrieux. For the next two years, he worked for the British film company, Gaumont, moving back and forth between Paris and London.[41] Years later, Billy Wilder would get his star-struck friend a bit role as an art dealer in Vincente Minnelli's 1956 movie *Lust for Life* (starring Kirk Douglas as Vincent van Gogh and Anthony Quinn as Paul Gauguin); and Pablo Picasso commemorated the event with a sketch of Perls as "Père Tanguy" during production in France.[42]

3.1 Frank Perls and Pablo Picasso in France, 1955. Frank's parents, Hugo and Käte Perls, were close friends of Picasso from the 1920s through the war.

Before the outbreak of war in 1939, the transplanted Perls family prospered in France. Käte, with the help of Franz and advice of Hugo, made the Käte Perls Galerie into a flourishing enterprise. While Franz traveled all over Europe for the business, Hugo reinvented himself as a philosopher, lecturing occasionally at the Sorbonne and publishing, in 1938, a book on Plato's aesthetics, while retaining an economic foothold in the art world.[43] On a trip to Vienna in 1937, one of his backstreet contacts tried to interest him in some paintings. "'That you have to buy,'" he told Hugo Perls. "'In ten years you will be a millionaire.' He had thrown on the table a dozen of Hitler's water colors, mostly sights of Vienna, a bit like Utrillo, but more exact." Hugo turned down the offer.[44]

POSTPONE AND POSTPONE

The Perls's sons were the first to get out of Europe. Franz arrived in New York in October 1937 to join his brother Klaus. A month later, they opened Perls Galleries at the corner of East 58th Street and Madison Avenue, an event reported in the *New York Post, New York Times, New York Sun, World Telegram*, and other media. Promoted as a gallery "for the young collector," one magazine welcomed its debut as "the final step" from its genesis in Berlin and Paris "in an interesting evolution which might be called the 'democratization of an art gallery,' in bringing moderately priced French moderns to the American public." Franz and Klaus, reported *The Spur*, "are young, themselves, and are in sympathy with the young collector. As they were brought up to run an art gallery, they have a shrewd sense of art values based on their wide experience in the field."[45]

As Klaus and Franz quickly established themselves in the United States, their parents and aunt Elise Flatow, Hugo's sister, were trapped back in France, trying to stay one step ahead of the Nazis. With the German armies threatening invasion, they traveled to the Riviera, strategically locating themselves in Cagnes-sur-Mer, close to the American consulate in Marseille and escape routes by sea and land. In April 1940, some two months before its defeat, the French government set up a special prison for political refugees, French leftists, and "enemy aliens" in the Gurs concentration camp, located in the foothills of the Pyrenees in the Basque region of southwestern France. By May 12, Käte and some four thousand Jews, including Elise, had been rounded up and imprisoned at Gurs. Hugo somehow managed to avoid the dragnet.[46]

When the German army entered Paris on June 14, 1940—followed one week later by the armistice—Käte was even more at risk because the pact between Germany and France required French authorities to "surrender on demand" any German nationals being hunted by the Nazis; moreover, Gurs was now under the administration of the anti-Semitic, collaborationist Vichy regime. Käte was released on June 20, perhaps in the confusion of the transition to the new regime or as a result of bribing her guards. Whatever the reason, she was lucky, at least for the moment. Of the twenty-two thousand prisoners (over eighty percent Jews) interned at Gurs during its three-year operation, eleven hundred died in prison, many from contagious diseases, and another 3,907 were turned over to the NSDAP for transportation to the concentration camps in occupied Poland, primarily Auschwitz.[47]

Käte headed to Marseille, where she reconnected with Hugo. Both of them were frantically trying to get visas to travel to the United States. It was a chaotic, dangerous scene. Back in New York, Klaus Perls coordinated efforts to get his parents out of Europe. On paper, it appeared that the odds favored Hugo and Käte because their three sons were settled in the United States—two businessmen and an aspiring physicist—and there was plenty of money to support the whole family through the successful Perls Galleries, a subsidiary of the Käte Perls Galerie in Paris.[48] Frank sought advice from the State Department about how to get money to his mother in "unoccupied French territory."[49] But Klaus and Frank were unaware of the battles taking place within the Roosevelt administration over the refugee issue, and in particular of how supporters of a very restrictive policy had gained the upper hand in the early 1940s.

On September 23, 1940, Käte sent a cable to her son Klaus in New York, urging him to enlist the help of the Emergency Rescue Committee (ERC) in getting "tourist visas for intellectuals father mother."[50] Formed in New York in the summer of 1940, the ERC's main purpose was to help German refugees escape Nazi Europe. During its thirteen-month existence, it managed to get some fifteen hundred people—mostly well-known political dissidents, intellectuals, and cultural workers—out of France, with the help of the black market, false passports, and grudgingly doled out American visas.[51] Käte was at risk, Klaus told the ERC, because she was "identified with the 'clique' around Picasso [and] of course, always used her influence against the 'fifth column' in France, and I fear this is only too well known by the German authorities. Furthermore, both my parents are Jewish."[52]

Klaus's fear was well placed; his mother's freedom was short-lived. She was picked up in Marseille and imprisoned at the Hotel Bompard, which had been turned into an unofficial detention center for as many as seventy women. The father of Georges Barellet, who worked at Marseille's Department of Aliens (*Bureau des Étrangers*), owned the hotel. Barellet profiteered from the Bompard's operation by charging the German authorities a per capita fee to detain women and gouging the prisoners through inflated prices for food. For a few thousand francs, Barellet was known to bribe local authorities to release a detainee. He may have been a "shameless opportunist," writes historian Andy Marino, but he was "a friend of anybody with money, and was well disposed to help refugees."[53]

Käte managed to get word to New York about her new situation. "She is in grave danger," Klaus wrote the ERC on October 3.[54] "The close association of Käte Perls with Picasso and the other progressive and politically active artists of Paris has had the result that after she had found a temporary haven in Marseille, the French have now interned her—obviously under pressure from the Nazi government. Käte Perls is a very outspoken woman, and it is to be feared that she will go on campaigning even in her concentration camp, and she is therefore in immediate danger of being treated as a 'traitor,' and it seems superfluous to say what that would mean."[55] On October 21, Käte managed to smuggle out a letter from Bompard, reported Klaus. "It tells in hair-raising words of the immense suffering to which the poor innocent inmates are continuously subjected."[56]

Klaus in New York and Frank, now settled in Los Angeles, asked their influential friends to lobby the State Department for visas that would allow Käte and Hugo entry into the United States. Klaus provided affidavits from sponsors and records of bank accounts showing that Käte could earn a living with her art import business, while Frank enlisted the help of Hollywood celebrities, including Thomas Mitchell, a character actor who in 1939 appeared in *Gone with the Wind*, *Mr. Smith Goes to Washington*, and *Stagecoach* (for which he won an Oscar in 1940). Frank later claimed that another movie star, Walter Huston, successfully influenced Eleanor Roosevelt to send a cable to the U.S. consul in Marseille: "Story about Mrs. Käte Perls poppycock, try to liberate her."[57] Frank's account was embroidered for dramatic effect, but it was basically accurate.

Walter Huston, who had played the title role in D. W. Griffith's *Abraham Lincoln* (1930) and would win an Oscar in 1948 for best supporting actor in *The Treasure of the Sierra Madre*, did in fact know Eleanor Roosevelt and had campaigned for her husband. On December 15, he sent her a handwritten note from his residence at the Beverly Hills Hotel. It was a "privilege," he wrote Mrs. Roosevelt, "to have a small part in the re-election of the one man who can lead us out of difficulties." He enclosed Frank Perls's account of his mother's situation. "I don't know whether anything can be done about it or not, but if without too much trouble to you, it could be placed in proper channels, it would be greatly appreciated by me, and the son of this unfortunate woman."[58]

Frank's affidavit included information about Käte's reputation in the art world, her sons' respectability, and her imprisonment at the Hotel Bompard. "Mrs. Käte Perls is very ill," wrote Frank, "and in an unimaginable way suffering from her internment. French authorities should be advised immediately to release Mrs. Käte PERLS as her internment cannot be attributed to anything else but misunderstandings. Klaus G. Perls has asked for his second papers (citizenship) and is scheduled to get same in a very short time and will then be able to ask for a preference visa for his mother. IMPORTANT it is however to get Mrs. Käte Perls out of the horrible Camp Hotel Bompard where she is interned. Mrs. Perls receives monthly funds from her sons through the American Express Company and has always enough money on her to cover living expenses and hotel charges. ALL INCURRING EXPENSES WILL BE REIMBURSED BY ME."[59]

Eleanor Roosevelt responded to Huston ten days later through her secretary, promising to ask the State Department to investigate Käte Perls's situation.[60] She also wrote to her main ally in the State Department, Sumner Welles, saying she "would appreciate your doing what you can in the enclosed case" and "letting her have a report on it as soon as you are able to get one."[61] Eleanor Roosevelt had been involved since 1935 in international efforts to open up the United States to refugees from Europe. Among her many activities on this issue was public support for the Emergency Rescue Committee. But she was hedged in by her husband's more cautious position on the refugee question, widespread anti-immigrant attitudes, and the generally hostile attitude of the State Department.[62]

Eleanor Roosevelt's nemesis in the State Department was Breckinridge Long, "an extreme nativist with a particular suspicion of Eastern Europeans." A career diplomat, who had served as assistant secretary of state under Woodrow Wilson and as ambassador to Italy in 1933, Long was put in charge of the State Department's Visa Division in 1940, a position that he used to obstruct efforts to facilitate the entry of refugees into the United States. He spread rumors, for example, that Nazi spies were posing as refugees. In June 1940, when Käte Perls was in Gurs, Long circulated a memo within the State Department. "We can delay and effectively stop for a temporary period of indefinite length the number of immigrants into the United States," wrote Long. "We could do this by simply advising our consuls to put every obstacle in the way and to require additional evidence and to resort to various administrative devices which would postpone and postpone and postpone the granting of the visas." Long's tactics were effective: during the war, about ninety percent of the quota reserved for refugees from fascism remained unfilled.[63]

Eleanor Roosevelt did what she could to maneuver around these roadblocks, especially through her ties to Undersecretary of State Sumner Welles, a member of Franklin Roosevelt's foreign policy inner circle and a long-time personal friend. Until he was forced to resign from the State Department in August 1943 over allegations of homosexuality, Welles acted on requests he received from Eleanor Roosevelt, including Käte Perls's case.[64] "I have called upon our consular office at Marseille for a telegraphic report on this case. Immediately upon the receipt of reply, I shall let you know about the matter."[65] A few days later, Walter Huston received an ecstatic message that he passed on to Eleanor Roosevelt. "This is to tell you," Frank wrote, "that my mother has been liberated from the camp and I will never forget what you did for us." Huston added his own appreciation: "Let me add thanks for the magic you performed. This is one more instance of your profound kindness. Please give my love to the President."[66]

Eleanor Roosevelt's intervention succeeded in getting Käte out of a concentration camp, but not into the United States.[67] In February 1941, the Emergency Rescue Committee informed Klaus Perls that his mother had not qualified for an emergency visa from the State Department because her "biography does not give any evidence of danger."[68] Klaus sought help from the World Jewish Congress and kept up pressure on the State Department. Later in 1941, he was successful in getting his father a visa into the United States,[69] but not his mother.[70] If Käte had stayed in Germany, there is no doubt that she would be dead, her religious conversion trumped by her Jewish blood. Now, presumably due to her leftist politics, she was also *persona non grata* in Nazi-occupied France and apparently blacklisted in the United States.

Meanwhile, in April 1940 Frank had moved to Los Angeles, where he opened up his own business, Frank Perls Gallery, on Sunset Boulevard. In April 1943, a few weeks after he volunteered for the army, Franz would officially become Frank, an American citizen ready to fight for a country that would not admit his mother. His experience was comparable to the Japanese-American soldiers who helped to liberate Dachau while their families back in the United States remained imprisoned, not as convicted criminals, but on the presumption of disloyalty based on their racial identity.[71]

回 Chapter 4 回

Human Betterment

Good blood will tell.
(Charles M. Goethe, 1936)

RACIAL HYGIENE

As the Perls family was plotting its getaway from a regime that aspired to make Europe *Judenfrei*, a group of influential policymakers based in Pasadena—not far from where Frank Perls would set up his new gallery—were touting Germany's "determination to take every possible step to insure Nordic race purity."[1] It has been widely recognized that the Third Reich embraced biological theories of race as a foundational ideology; and that leading German intellectuals and professionals did their part to demonstrate that "biology is destiny" long before the concentration camps were turned into efficient killing machines.[2] Only in recent years, however, have we begun to learn how Nazi race experts consulted their American counterparts for inspiration and advice.[3]

What surprised me as I researched the background of the Nuremberg Laws was the extent of reciprocity between German and American researchers, and how actively the California eugenics circle boosted the glories of Nazi "racial science." I also discovered that the respectable supporters of the booming field of eugenics in the 1930s included Robert Millikan, chairman of the Huntington's board of trustees, and Charles M. Goethe, a leading Sacramento philanthropist who achieved the informal status of a founding father on my own campus in the 1950s. With this serendipitous stumble into a connection with Sacramento State University, my research became even more personal and compelling, another piece in an increasingly complex puzzle.

Everywhere I turned, it seemed, I ran into issues that struck close to home. Now, there were ghosts to be exorcised not only in a venerable, private institution such as the Huntington, with roots in nineteenth-century *noblesse oblige*, but also in a modern state university that did not begin to invent its traditions until after World War II.

The eugenics movement, which emerged at the turn of the last century, was designed, in the words of one of its founders, Francis Galton, to give "the more suitable races or strains of blood a better chance of prevailing speedily over the less suitable."[4] Influenced by new developments in genetics, medicine, and public health, at the core of eugenics was an assumption about "the central role of heredity in determining physical and mental traits and in the innate inequality of individuals and groups."[5] Belief in the role of genetic inheritance as a determining cause of social inequality was by no means unique to the Third Reich. Social Darwinism, as it was known, had a long, respectable history in the West.[6]

But eugenics was "all over the political map,"[7] with enormous variation in policies and practices from country to country: it was endorsed by Fabian socialists in England and by Nazis in Germany; linked to birth control and progressive economic reforms in Denmark, and to racial policies against itinerant *tattare* (Roma) in Sweden; an expression of fascist ideology in Argentina and of cultural hybridity in Mexico; and closely associated with the sterilization of those defined as "feeble-minded" in Germany, the United States, Sweden, and Denmark, but not in Holland, England, and Mexico.[8]

In the United States, eugenics was dominated by hard-line tendencies. Its right-wing supporters promoted "Anglo-Saxon" societies as the engine of modern civilization and advocated policies of apartheid to protect the "well born" from contamination by the poor, mentally ill, and "socially inadequate." Its leaders believed that a variety of social successes (wealth, political leadership, and intellectual discoveries), as well as social problems (poverty, illegitimacy, crime, mental illness, and unemployment), could be traced to inherited biological attributes associated with "racial temperament." They advocated "positive eugenics" to increase the birthrate of privileged families and "negative eugenics" to reduce the birthrate of the "socially inadequate."[9]

Eugenics was also a cultural vehicle for expressing anxiety about the "degeneration" of middle-class "Aryans." For many American eugenicists, sterilization was not so much a technical, medical procedure to enhance physical and mental health, as it was a way to cleanse the body politic of racial and sexual impurities that were the result of the declining birthrate of the well-to-do and the "evil of crossbreeding."[10] Eugenics organizations hoped that their research would demonstrate the biological basis of white supremacy, thus bolstering restrictions on welfare benefits to poor families, bans on interracial marriage or "miscegenation," and limits on immigration from non-European countries, as well as campaigns for compulsory sterilization.

In the early 1930s, when the Nazis were developing racial policies and struggling to find a scientific rationale for their vision of Aryan citizenship, they looked for practical models and endorsement from the American eugenics movement. On the East Coast, they appreciated the work of the Eugenics Record Office (ERO) at Cold Spring Harbor, Long Island, a prestigious data-gathering operation funded by corporate philanthropy. In 1936, the University of Heidelberg awarded the ERO's director, Harry Laughlin, an honorary doctorate in medicine for his contributions to eugenics. Laughlin informed the dean of the university's medical school that he was "greatly honored to accept [a] degree from the University of Heidelberg which stands for the highest ideals of scholarship and research achieved by those racial stocks which have contributed so much to the foundation blood of the American people."[11]

The West Coast also had its racial visionaries, who, like their Nazi counterparts, were preoccupied with protecting Aryan progress from degeneracy. The center for this activity was a eugenics think tank in Pasadena with the Orwellian title of the Human Betterment Foundation (HBF).[12] The foundation, established in 1929 as a nonprofit organization, was created and initially funded by Ezra S. Gosney, an activist reformer with a penchant for social engineering and conservative politics. Born in Kentucky in 1855, Gosney practiced law in Arizona and made his fortune there in sheep and cattle breeding. In 1905, he moved to Pasadena and invested in citrus farming and real estate. "Perhaps," observed the editors of *Eugenics*, "his association with the livestock industry" gave him the idea that people "were just as capable of improvement as were their species of domesticated animals and cultivated plants."[13]

The proponents of eugenics were not obscure cranks, but the best and brightest representatives of a small elite that dominated Southern California until the 1950s. In Pasadena, Gosney linked up with Paul Popenoe, director of the Institute of Family Relations in Los Angeles. By 1929, the self-made expert on biology had already achieved a national reputation in eugenics.[14] With co-author Roswell Hill Johnson, Popenoe wrote one of the most widely read textbooks, *Applied Eugenics*, published by Macmillan in 1918, reprinted in 1926, and revised in 1933. Gosney hired Popenoe as the HBF's executive director and recruited a board of California luminaries, including Sacramento banker Charles M. Goethe, Stanford's chancellor David Starr Jordan and psychologist Lewis Terman, publisher Harry Chandler, and professors from Berkeley, the University of Southern California, and Caltech.

Four members of the Huntington's board of trustees also were actively involved with the Human Betterment Foundation. Three trustees were charter members of the foundation: banker Henry Robinson, Huntington trustee from 1922 to 1937; social scientist William Munro, trustee from 1937 to 1957; and Caltech physicist Robert Millikan, trustee from 1925 to 1953. Millikan and Munro were actively involved in day-to-day operations and personnel matters, and well informed about the HBF's publications and outreach. Millikan joined the foundation in 1937, partly in unity with its vision, and partly with an eye to fundraising contacts.[15] Munro served as the foundation's vice-president in the early 1940s. When the foundation was dissolved in 1942, Millikan staked Caltech's claim to its files and resources. Utilities executive and banker James Page, a Huntington trustee from 1945 to 1962, was involved as chairman of Caltech's board of trustees in overseeing the transfer of the foundation's assets to Caltech, where a research fund was set up in the biology department in memory of the HBF's founder, Ezra Gosney.[16]

For a small think tank with few full-time staff members, the foundation exerted considerable influence over public opinion through its network of patrons, political allies, and academic supporters. Its close ties to Caltech and the Huntington Library enhanced its prestige. It had two main functions: to lobby governments in support of sterilization policies and to promote eugenics in public discourse. The foundation was involved more in distributing and publicizing the results of research than in carrying out scientific investigations.[17] In 1933, the HBF claimed to have sent out one of its pamphlets to nearly half a million contacts in universities and government agencies around the world.[18]

Before the Nazis came to power in 1933, the German eugenics movement had been impressed by research compiled by the HBF. One of the foundation's first studies, *Sterilization for Human Betterment*, published in Pasadena in 1929, appeared in a German edition the following year. An article written by Paul Popenoe that summarized California's experiences with sterilization was published in Germany in 1931. The foundation's publications caught the attention of Dr. Arthur Gütt and Dr. Herbert Linden, prominent experts on "racial hygiene" in the Nazi government's Ministry of the Interior, which in 1935 would be responsible for drafting the Nuremberg Laws. In 1933, Gütt, a leader of the eugenics movement, was appointed Ministerial Adviser for Racial Culture and Heredity, and Linden was put in charge of Eugenics and Race. Gütt and Linden wanted to make use of research done by the HBF for propaganda purposes; and California's eugenic think tank was glad to bask in the serious attention it was finally receiving from a powerful government. It was a relationship of mutual admiration, as well as convenience.[19]

EUGENIC SCIENCE

In Germany prior to 1933, the idea of sterilizing certain categories of "degenerates" had support in medical circles long before Hitler's rise to power and before eugenics was inevitably wedded to anti-Semitism.[20] The new Nazi government seized the moment, making eugenics the ideological centerpiece of a political philosophy that "conceptualized and practiced racial hygiene as an integral part of its overall racism."[21] For this initiative they engaged the enthusiastic support of a cadre of intellectuals and professionals. "Nazi rule relied not only on repression but also on an appeal to communal ideals of civic improvement," notes historian Claudia Koonz. "The road to Auschwitz was paved with righteousness."[22] The "German professor," journalist Joseph Roth caustically observed in 1933, is "the inventor of the philological equivalent of poison gas, who is paid to disseminate the idea of Prussian superiority, the non-commissioned officer of the university."[23]

In a speech to the newly created Committee of Experts on Population and Racial Policy, Interior Minister Wilhelm Frick proposed a "law for the prevention of defective progeny" and linked the problem of "hereditary defectives" with the menace of "race-mixing." Frick drew attention to the problems posed by four thousand recently naturalized immigrants living in Berlin, "mostly of foreign stock and to a great extent eastern Jews." By the end of Frick's speech, his comments on the need to increase the birthrate of healthy Germans and return "the woman back to the hearth" segued into a defense of "race-purity" and the dangers of "miscegenation." Frick was explicit about the racial assumptions guiding his reproductive policies: "We must carefully watch the progressive race-mixture and race-deterioration of our people, since the German man and the German woman no longer are conscious of their blood and their race…. Miscegenation must be labeled what it is: namely, the foundation for mental and spiritual degeneration and alienation from the native stock."[24]

Two weeks after Frick's speech, the Reich government introduced a Law for the Prevention of Genetically Diseased Offspring (also known as the Sterilization Law), enacted on July 14, 1933, and implemented on January 1, 1934.[25] When the new law was published in the government's legal journal, it included flattering references to the Human Betterment Foundation, including the HBF's assertion that sterilization "is a practical and essential step to prevent racial degeneration."[26] German historian Stefan Kühl regards the work of the Human Betterment Foundation as the "basis for the development of the German sterilization law."[27]

George Dock, a Pasadena physician and founding supporter of the HBF, was so impressed with the German Sterilization Law that he suggested to Gosney that the foundation could benefit from its influence on the Nazi regime. "I think the reference to the California work, and the work of the Foundation," wrote Dock, "is a very significant thing. The matter has given me a better opinion of Mr. Hitler than I had before. He may be too impulsive in some matters, but he is sound on the theory and practice of eugenic sterilization."[28] The foundation let its supporters know in 1933 that the Reich Minister of Justice "has recently sent out a copy of the German [Sterilization] law for general distribution, to which is appended a German translation of one of the pamphlets of the Human Betterment Foundation."[29]

When Charles Goethe returned from a fact-finding visit to Germany in 1934, he commended the HBF for its influence on Nazi eugenics. "You will be interested to know," Goethe wrote Gosney, "that your work has played a powerful part in shaping the opinions of the group of intellectuals who are behind Hitler in this epoch-making program. Everywhere I sensed that their opinions have been tremendously stimulated by American thought, and particularly by the work of the Human Betterment Foundation. I want you, my dear friend, to carry this thought with you for the rest of your life, that you have really jolted into action a great government of 60 million people."[30]

Prior to the Nazi regime, the leader in eugenic sterilizations was the United States, where tens of thousands mostly poor women were subjected to involuntary sterilization between 1907 and 1940.[31] As a result of California's sterilization laws, at least twenty thousand women and men in state hospitals and prisons had been involuntarily sterilized by 1964. California "consistently outdistanced every other state" in terms of the number of eugenic sterilizations, notes a recent study.[32] In comparison with Germany's record, however, the eugenics program in the United States looked paltry and ineffective, a cause for envy among its American counterparts. Paul Popenoe, executive director of the Human Betterment Foundation, looked to Hitler's Sterilization Law as a model for "all civilized countries."[33] Charles Goethe was similarly impressed that Hitler's government was committed to putting into action "the modern world's first eugenic program, having behind it the tremendously powerful force of sixty two millions welded into an efficient unit under a dictatorship."[34]

The new law, according to Nazi officials, was designed to "eradicate biologically inferior hereditary taints" and to "promote a gradual cleansing of the nation's ethnic body."[35] At first, officials targeted for sterilization adults suffering from a variety of diseases that were alleged to be genetically transmitted, such as feeblemindedness, schizophrenia, epilepsy, blindness, deafness, and alcoholism. An elaborate medical and legal infrastructure was established to create and enforce regulations associated with the Sterilization Law: more than two hundred Hereditary Health Courts—staffed by a mixture of judges, doctors, and so-called racial experts—heard evidence and handed down decisions, inevitably in favor of the government; by 1936, there were one hundred and eight hospitals designated to process speedy sterilizations.[36] Back in the United States, C. M. Goethe assured an audience in Sacramento that "eugenics trials proceed with fully as much caution as if they were held in the United States. Germany has cross-card-indexed her people until she has located all her probable weaklings.... Her plan is: Eliminate all low-powers to make room for high-powers. And thereby also save taxes."[37]

Within three years, two hundred thousand people had been sterilized, almost ten times as many as in the United States in the previous thirty years.[38] The Nazi government originally set a target of 1.2 million, but settled for four hundred thousand: three hundred thousand by 1939, another sixty thousand after 1939 in Germany, and forty thousand in annexed countries.[39] The specially created courts paid lip service to scientific evidence, substituting instead political expediency and their own cultural biases. The term "feeblemindedness" was expanded to incorporate beggars, vagrants, prostitutes, and "antisocials."[40] Health court judges were also receptive to requests to sterilize East European Jews, gypsies, and the families of African Germans.[41]

Back in the United States, the Human Betterment Foundation enthusiastically defended Nazi sterilization policies. When Paul Popenoe submitted an article on the 1933 law to the *Journal of Heredity*, he enclosed a large photograph of Hitler to illustrate the text, which included several favorable quotations from *Mein Kampf*.[42] It was welcome news to Popenoe that Hitler's "hopes of national regeneration [rested] solidly on the application of biological principles to human society" and that Germany's policy "will accord with the best thought of eugenicists in all civilized countries." He reassured his colleagues that reports in the press of four hundred thousand anticipated sterilizations were "unfounded"; that the Nazi government was "avoiding the misplaced emphasis on their earlier pronouncements on questions of race" and increasingly relying on the expert opinion of "scientific leadership," such as that provided by Dr. Arthur Gütt.[43] But Popenoe failed to mention that Gütt, a staunch advocate of "racial hygiene," had been active in Hitler's *völkisch* movement in East Prussia in the mid-1920s, joining the Nazi party in September 1932. Gütt ingratiated himself with the new government through a document on "State Population Policy" that framed his eugenics proposal in racist imagery. For this he was rewarded with an appointment to a senior post in the medical department of the Reich Ministry of the Interior in May 1933.[44]

Gütt also chaired the Ministry of the Interior's Committee of Experts on Population and Racial Policy, a twelve-member commission that was praised by the Human Betterment Foundation for its scientific credentials. But the committee included only one person who had any genuine expertise on the topic. The rest of the "recognized leaders of the eugenics movement," to use Popenoe's ingenuous description,[45] were Nazi hacks, including Hans Günther, professor of "Racial Science" at the University of Jena, and Gerhard Wagner, leader of the Nazi doctors' association and "one of the most rabid Jew-baiters in Hitler's entourage," who would become a key architect of the Nuremberg Laws.[46] The Nazis widely cited Günther's research to illustrate the "Nordic race" as a creative historical force and Jews as "ferments of disintegration."[47] Yet Popenoe could reassure a colleague early in 1934 that "not even Hitler proposes to sterilize anyone on the grounds of racial origin."[48] Two years later, he wrote to Otmar Freiherr von Verschuer, a leading Nazi eugenicist, asking for statistics to rebut what he considered negative propaganda in the United States about Germany's sterilization program. "We are always anxious to see that conditions in Germany are not misunderstood or misrepresented."[49]

When Nazi eugenicists asked for help in publicizing their achievements around the world, their American colleagues readily obliged. In 1934, Dr. Bruno Gebhard, director of the Racial Hygiene Museum in Munich, was invited by the American Public Health Association to attend its annual convention in Pasadena.[50] On August 24, 1934, the same day that the Reich Commission of National Health advised Germans to "choose only a wife of the same or of Nordic blood [and] keep away from aliens of non-European racial origin," public health officials in New

York organized a reception for Gebhard before he departed for the West Coast.[51] At the Pasadena conference, Gebhard's display on "Public Health and Eugenics in New Germany," side by side with the Human Betterment Foundation's display on "Eugenic Sterilization," was the "chief attraction" in the civic auditorium's exhibit hall. It was "suggested and approved by Adolf Hitler himself," said Gebhard, "and comes to Pasadena as an illustration of the method by which Der Führer hopes to build up the health and strength of the German people."[52]

It is true, as Daniel Kevles observed, that American supporters of Nazi eugenics in the mid-1930s "could not know—and likely did not want to imagine—that a river of blood would eventually run from the sterilization law of 1933 to Auschwitz and Buchenwald."[53] But they did know a great deal about the racist underpinnings of Nazi eugenics, about the abuse of medical ethics and violations of patients' rights in the sterilization program, about the increasing attacks on and vilification of Jews, and about the Nazi affiliations of German "racial scientists." That they chose to say nothing about these matters cannot be attributed to ignorance. The press was filled with references to the racial uses of sterilization policies. Moreover, members of the Human Betterment Foundation were in regular, direct contact with advocates of racial science in Germany.

In February 1934, for example, the *New York Times* reported that German eugenicists were advocating the sterilization of all "Negroid children in the Rhineland and Ruhr districts," irrespective of their mental and emotional abilities. "We have enough non-Aryans in Germany already," said a Nazi spokesman.[54] The following year, the *Los Angeles Times* published a long defense of Nazi sterilization policies, in which the author blamed communists and Marxists for equating sterilization with anti-Semitism. The Nazis "had to resort to the teachings of eugenic science," argued Dr. Burchardi, because Germany had been "deprived of her colonies, blessed with many hundreds of defective racial hybrids as a lasting memory of the colored army of occupation, and dismembered all around."[55] This was a reference to the estimated five hundred so-called *Rheinlandbastarde*—the children of French-African soldiers who had settled in Germany after World War I. Hitler had them all sterilized in 1937.[56]

If members of the Human Betterment Foundation somehow missed these articles, they only had to read documents sent to them by colleagues in Germany, conveniently translated into English, such as Wilhelm Frick's "The Race Law of the Third Reich," published in February 1934. Frick's speech contained fourteen disparaging references to Jews. The main goal of the German Revolution, noted Frick, was "Germany for the Germans and under German leadership." The only internal threat to this goal came from "a race which was foreign to the German people [who] obtained power through the party and parliamentary system and, above all, with the aid of their money: the Jews." The world needed to recognize that the German people are "specifically Nordic" and "do not include ... the negroid race which is hardly represented in Germany and, above all, not the Jews."

"Germans," continued Frick, "are not prepared to bend the knee permanently to the power of an alien race that is scattered all over the world, and hence adopts an international standpoint, but, at the same time, holds together in all the countries of the world, and pursues its own interests at the cost of all peoples in the world with extreme tenacity, at all costs and with complete ruthlessness."[57]

NORDIC INTERNATIONALISM

Perhaps the best example of what members of the Human Betterment Foundation knew exactly about internal conditions in Germany after 1933 can be found in the diaries, memos, and reports of its long-time patron, Charles M. Goethe, who closely followed developments in Europe and was in regular contact with Nazi racial scientists.[58] Goethe was a public ideologue, proud to let everybody know in his 1936 presidential address to the Eugenics Research Association that he respected Nazi Germany's "honest yearnings for a better population."[59]

Before I started doing research for this book, I was vaguely aware that California State University at Sacramento (CSUS), where I have taught since 1977, had honored Charles M. Goethe during the campus's formative years in the 1940s and 1950s. Driving onto campus, I typically park my car close to the centrally located C. M. Goethe Arboretum, whose two large signs announced the university's ties to its first major benefactor until campus protests forced their removal in the summer of 2005. I had heard stories that Goethe was something of a crank with bizarre ideas about nature and race, but I did not realize that he was an aficionado of Nazi racial science. My interest in Goethe became more serious when I discovered that before World War II he was an important leader of the American eugenics movement and had ties to the Huntington via the Human Betterment Foundation.

Based in Sacramento throughout his long life, Goethe was bred for success. He completed high school in Sacramento in 1891 and passed the bar in 1900, but never practiced law. Instead, he worked in his father's bank and real estate business, leading a self-disciplined life, and observing his family's conventional Lutheran religiosity. In 1903, he married Mary Glide and into one of the wealthiest families in Sacramento. Through shrewd investments and real estate deals, his wealth steadily accumulated to $24 million by the time of his death in 1966.[60]

In the late 1940s, my university cultivated a close relationship with the aging Goethe, courting him for his money and prestige. He was appointed to the university's advisory board in the 1950s; the campus arboretum and science building were named after him; and in 1965, the university organized a "national recognition day" to celebrate his ninetieth birthday. "Would that there were more men like Dr. Goethe," noted Guy West, CSUS's first president (1947 to 1965), about the man he described as "Sacramento's most remarkable citizen."[61] In the end, all this groveling paid off. Goethe changed his will to make CSUS his primary beneficiary, bequeathing his residence, library, papers, and an estimated $653,000 to Sacramento State. If the university's motivation for honoring Goethe was essentially pecuniary, it did not hurt that he also gave the young college an invented pedigree, with ties to old Sacramento and mythic roots in nineteenth-century pioneer California.

Sacramento State University was not the only institution to shower Goethe with kudos. The University of the Pacific awarded him an honorary doctorate in 1955, the National Park Service made him an "Honorary Chief Naturalist," and a plaque acknowledges the "central role" of the Goethes in the development of the naturalist program at Fallen Leaf Lake near Lake Tahoe. There is also a Goethe room at the California Academy of Sciences, in San Francisco's Golden Gate Park, a tribute to Goethe's financial support of the Morrison planetarium.[62] In 1976, the Save-the-Redwoods League posthumously honored one of their earliest benefactors by naming a forty-acre grove after Goethe in the Prairie Creek Redwoods State Park in Humboldt County.[63]

When Sacramento State University feted Goethe in 1965, President Lyndon Johnson sent a telegram commending "an American whose life has been so richly dedicated to the service of humanity" and describing Goethe as a leader of "distinction, integrity and unceasing energy." From Earl Warren, chief justice of the Supreme Court, came recognition of a "remarkable career of public service." Stewart Udall, Secretary of the Interior, acknowledged Goethe's "contributions to conservation and particularly to the interpretation of America's natural, historic and scenic wonders in the national parks," while Governor Edmund Brown sent birthday greetings to "our number one citizen."[64]

What my university, as well as other recipients of his philanthropy, chose to strategically ignore and later erase from memory was Goethe's appreciation of Nazi eugenics, his full-blown bigotry, and his discriminatory business practices that helped to shape racial boundaries in Sacramento. In the 1920s, Goethe had stopped selling real estate to Mexican immigrants and Mexican Americans because they were "a very undesirable class of installment purchasers."[65] He instructed his brokers "to make no more sales to them. They cannot grasp the theory of contracts, as do even the negroes who are coming in to California from the South in considerable numbers."[66] He also refused to sell homes to Japanese immigrants and issued warnings about the "Chinafication of our country."[67] In the 1940s, he bankrolled racist, anti-Japanese campaigns;[68] and in the 1950s, he railed against the "Oriental penetration" of the United States.[69]

Goethe's ideas were widely known during his lifetime, in large part because he was a shameless, self-promoting huckster. One of the first serious studies of American eugenics, published in 1963, singled out Goethe for his unremitting "racist point of view."[70] Now that I have spent several months delving into the details of Goethe's ideas, my stomach clenches whenever I park on campus. I have joined a campaign urging the university community to reflect on how and why it honored a self-professed racist with an honorary degree in 1955, the year that Emmett Till was lynched in Mississippi and Rosa Parks took her seat on a bus in Montgomery.[71]

Goethe was a public activist in the tradition of Progressive philanthropists who used their wealth for hands-on projects of significant social consequences. He was interested in conventional politics, but it was not his passion. He regularly supported candidates and politicians who had a reputation for right-wing views on race and communism. He was an early supporter of Richard Nixon, even giving him advice on how to maintain good relations with the press.[72] In the late 1950s, when Goethe lobbied Congress to maintain racial restrictions on immigration, Strom Thurmond let him know that "I appreciate your comments, as I am also opposed to opening up our immigration floodgates."[73] Goethe was also on the mailing list of Georgia Governor Marvin Griffin, a fierce opponent of integration who was convinced that communists had highjacked the Civil Rights movement and that "the white race are the only people able to perpetuate the Christian religion."[74]

But it was to a variety of civic rather than political causes that Goethe was primarily devoted—protecting wilderness areas and supporting research in genetics and plant biology—all of which were framed within his passion for eugenics, in particular a sense of urgency about the need to protect pure stocks from mongrelization and extinction, whether Nordic Americans or redwood forests.[75] Goethe was an influential member of the most important eugenics associations and invested at least one million dollars of his own money in writing about and promoting tracts on eugenics, conservation, race, and immigration.[76] In the early 1920s, he formed the Immigration Study Commission in order to lobby the government to prevent an influx of "low-powers," especially from Mexico, into California. In 1924, he successfully pressed the Commonwealth Club of California, an elite fraternal society based in San Francisco, to create a eugenics section. In Sacramento in 1933, he organized, funded, and led the Eugenics Society of Northern California, which he administered out of his office, and in 1936 he served as president of the national Eugenics Research Association.[77]

Goethe stayed in touch with the eugenics movement in Europe, the East Coast, and Southern California, steadily doling out grants to promote his favorite researchers and projects, including the Human Betterment Foundation. Through a prolific outpouring of correspondence and personal newsletters, he kept his colleagues in Pasadena well informed about eugenic accomplishments in Nazi Germany. Goethe retained strong cultural ties to Germany throughout his life, in part through his paternal origins, and in part as a matter of cultural preference. Goethe's German grandfather moved to Sacramento in 1867 to establish the Evangelical Lutheran Church, ministering primarily to German immigrant families. His father Henry, who made money in real estate, a bank, and other business ventures, also taught at the German Lutheran School. Charles grew up speaking German and as a young adult confessed, "I am a true American and yet I am false to the land of my birth when I feel a thrill of emotion and there is an intensely German feeling comes over me when I sing in the tongue of the Fatherland the old war songs."[78]

4.1 Eugenics advocate Charles M. Goethe (1875–1966) as a young man. A strong supporter of Nazi racial science, Goethe received many honors for his philanthropic projects. Among his admirers were Sacramento State University, the National Park Service, and the Save-the-Redwoods League.

During his travels around the world, Goethe visited Germany at least four times.[79] During the spring of 1934, he traveled through France and Germany to find out first-hand about new developments in European eugenics, and to report back to his colleagues in the United States. He welcomed the Nazi government's determination to restore Germany's international stature. In May 1934, while he was traveling in France, it was clear to Goethe that Hitler was now "as permanent as Mussolini" and that "Jews are being eradicated."[80] A few weeks later, crossing into Germany, Hitler's ideas about nutrition caught his attention. "There is an atmosphere of idealism about these shops that is fascinating," he wrote in his diary. "They have something of the admirable Seventh-Day Adventist spirit. They aim to reform [through] diet and claim [Hitler's] clarity is due to his vegetarianism."[81] In June 1934, Goethe returned to Berlin for the first time since 1912, where he "received the Hitlerian salute" and saw "Brown shirts" and "Nazi bands everywhere, trucks of Nazis singing hymns." To Goethe, "Hitlerism [was] a surging forward of idealism. It is amazing that a vegetarian should have consolidated behind him the public opinion of what were overweight, corpulent Germans of a [one quarter] century ago." He looked closely at "the faces of the Nazi. One is impressed with their idealism."[82]

Goethe also paid close attention to the faces of the Jew. On the one hand, he observed that claims of anti-Semitic hounding were exaggerated. He saw "Jews everywhere, no signs of persecution, at big hotels, conspicuous spenders."[83] Some had made their fortunes, he was told, running brothels throughout Poland, Russia, and Germany. One Jewish entrepreneur had "made five million marks here [through] commercialized vice" and "maintained expensive quarters in our hotel." German confidantes confirmed his view that "Jews are cosmopolites knowing no allegiance to nation but to money." On the other hand, he was glad to hear that "Hitler has eliminated from population-mass about one-tenth of the wealthiest [Jews], who, at commencement of the Nazi movement, were removing their capital to other lands."[84]

On his return to Europe in the summer of 1939—four years after passage of the Nuremberg Laws and a few months after *Kristallnacht*—his anti-Semitism remained intact, unshakeable. Goethe noted in his diary a French professor's disdain for "Melting Pot propaganda and our allowing the Hebrews to control our anthropological thought."[85] His visit to France convinced Goethe that French anti-Semitism was "based upon the tragic failure of the Jewish Premier Leon Blum," the leader of the Socialist Party, who became the first Jewish Prime Minister of France in May 1936.[86] Blum, Goethe believed, was responsible "for the enormous accumulation of debt during his administration" and "a real loss of the French empire in Africa."[87]

Goethe's interest in the Nazi government was not simply a nostalgic yearning for his biological and cultural roots. He was neither a sentimentalist nor a fifth columnist, as suggested by Edwin Black,[88] but rather a long-time defender of "that sense of scrupulous business honor of the Nordic race dating back to the time of the Crusades." Goethe was preoccupied with the fear that the Nordic tradition of "unique contributions to all mankind" was being diminished worldwide as a result of "the coming of heterogeneity." What was required, noted Goethe in 1928, was a "movement of Nordic internationalism."[89] Goethe admired Hitler's regime only because it had the courage to carry out its eugenics agenda. "The sterilization statutes, electrified into action by the Hitlerian signature," Goethe observed in 1934, "are a force to be reckoned with."[90] He wanted the United States to emulate Nazi eugenics in order to maintain its global supremacy over Germany.

On his return in 1935 from what he grandiosely described as "another six months' European study of Population Pressure and of Immigration Control," Goethe sent out one of his many briefings. "However much one abhors dictatorship, one is also impressed that Germany, by sterilization, and by stimulating birthrates among the eugenically high-powered, is gaining an advantage over us as to future leadership." Goethe was persuaded that the United States needed to "pass a Quota Act against Latin America, register all aliens, and deport, like France, aliens to make jobs for the old American stock." He had little patience for "melting pot foolishness" in the United States, which he regarded as an effort by "the hyphenate lobby" to dilute the purity of "Nordic homogeneity."[91]

Some time in 1934, Goethe sent his views about Hitler's eugenics program to Harry Laughlin, director of the Eugenics Research Office in Cold Spring Harbor, New York. Goethe recognized in Germany "the determination to take every possible step to insure Nordic race purity," an effort comparable to, but much more impressive than, legislation in the 1920s in the United States to stop "the menace of a colossal migration from war-weary Europe." To stay competitive with Germany in the world, Goethe advocated "speeding up the high-powers' birth rate" and "sterilization of those undoubtedly socially inadequate." The Nazi government had the right idea. "Seldom has any propaganda ever been released more convincing than the Nazi pictures of the imbecile, the moron compared with the flower of German youth. The contrasts are dramatic." Germany had set an example for how to deal with the problem of the declining birthrate in the United States of "Harvard graduates and Mayflower descendants," and the growing birthrate of "our negro group" and other "non-Nordics," observed Goethe. "The Germans are at least in action about it."

Evoking an apocalyptic vision of racial degeneracy, accelerated by "moves toward hybridization," Goethe lamented that "much cannot be undone" in the United States. "If however, we study Hitler's methods, accept what is gold, reject the dross, we may make America Germany's successful rival. Germany plans sterilization of 400,000 low-powers soon. We will not proceed with such speed. We can, however, commence to think of positive eugenics, of multiplying our high-power strains, while we consider working out a common-sense sterilization program."[92]

Through the 1930s, Goethe remained a firm and steadfast supporter of Nazi eugenics. As the media began to sound the alarm about Hitler's racial policies and reputable scientists withdrew their support, Goethe stuck to his initial impressions, writing off criticism as the propaganda of liberals and Jews. In a letter to a fellow eugenicist, written eleven days after the Nuremberg Laws were rubber-stamped by Hitler's Reichstag, Goethe noted: "Contact with the eugenic movement in Germany, particularly in 1934, convinced me that, like them, we should try to be intensely practical." Goethe believed that if the United States followed similar policies with respect to sterilization and immigration restrictions, "we would then have the manpower and public opinion to proceed to clean up our own population mess." Goethe was impressed by "the sane and cautious manner in which the German sterilization program is proceeding."[93]

In his 1936 presidential address to the Eugenics Research Association, Goethe defended the Nazi sterilization program as "administered wisely, and without racial cruelty." He dismissed as misinformation reports that "German sterilization is used to hound one group [Jews]." Until Hitler came to power, Goethe told the audience, California "had led all the world in sterilization operations. Today even California's quarter-century record has, in two years, been outdistanced by Germany."[94] Privately, he noted in his diary that Latin American governments had much to learn from Nazi Germany. Brazil, for example, needed a "dictator" such as "a Hitler who understands sterilization! Why when the 21st century opens Brazil will have as many Negroids as Africa."[95]

In 1936, Goethe was one of only three delegates from the United States to attend and participate in the annual meeting of the International Federation of Eugenic Organizations, held in Scheveningen, the Netherlands. Fifteen delegates from Germany, who reported on the latest development in "racial hygiene" campaigns, dominated the conference.[96] A few years later, he recalled that he had been "amazed at their profound research."[97] Throughout 1937, Goethe remained an enthusiastic booster of Nazi eugenics, warning one of his many correspondents, "If we don't adopt their methods, they will run away from us with world leaders."[98] To learn more about Germany's programs, he contacted Ottmar Freiherr von Verschuer, founder of Frankfurt University's Institute for Hereditary Biology and Racial Hygiene, and a steadfast supporter of Hitler's racial policies.[99] Goethe introduced himself to von Verschuer in April 1937 as the president of the U.S. Eugenics Research Association, asking if it would be possible to visit the Frankfurt Institute. "I feel, because of the violent anti-German propaganda in the United States, our people know almost nothing of what is happening in Germany."[100]

In December 1937, Goethe sent von Verschuer apologies for his inability to visit Germany, praising him for his "marvelous work.... I feel passionately that you are leading all mankind herein. One must exercise herein the greatest tact. America is flooded with anti-German propaganda. It is abundantly financed and originates from a quarter [Jews], which you know only too well.... However, this ought to not blind us to the fact that Germany is advancing more rapidly in *Erbbiologie* than all the rest of mankind."[101] Goethe continued to lavish praise on von Verschuer's program into 1938, again commending "the marvelous progress you and your German associates are making."[102] A few days after the pogroms of *Kristallnacht*, Goethe commiserated with von Verschuer: "I regret that my fellow countrymen are so blinded by propaganda just at present that they are not reasoning out regarding the very fine work which the splendid eugenicists of Germany are doing.... I am a loyal American in every way," continued Goethe. "This does not, however, lessen my respect for the great scientists of Germany."[103]

Charles Goethe was atypical of most eugenics activists in the sense that he was not restrained by professional and scientific obligations. He remained a supreme individualist, preferring to stay removed from the everyday operations of organizations such as the Human Betterment Foundation. But Goethe was an effective organizer, shrewdly influencing the direction of the eugenics movement through financial support, and helping to create a network of communication through a barrage of newsletters, reports, and correspondence. He was more forthright than most eugenicists in promoting his right-wing ideology because his wealth exempted him from observing academic and professional etiquette. His colleague Robert Millikan, as we shall see, shared Goethe's racial worldview, but was much more discrete and diplomatic in his public pronouncements. Goethe and Popenoe's efforts to actively promote ties with Nazi racial scientists during the 1930s put the Human Betterment Foundation in the international spotlight. It was only when the United States joined the war against Germany that the foundation's supporters felt uneasy center stage.

The failure of the Human Betterment Foundation to maintain their independence from Hitler's racial scientists can be attributed in part to the seduction of fame and power. Yet a more persuasive explanation for their collaboration is that they shared the same cultural and political assumptions as their Nazi counterparts: belief in the genetic superiority of Nordic or Aryan civilizations over "backward" peoples; anxiety about the degeneration of the white population through miscegenation; and concern over the growing disparity between the high birthrate of the "socially inadequate" and low birthrate of the "Northern European type of family."[104] For Interior Minister Wilhelm Frick, "typically Nordic peoples" were the bedrock of modernity: "In addition to ourselves, [they] are the Scandinavians, the Dutch, the English and the North Americans, all of whom we can describe collectively as Germanic."[105] Paul Popenoe, the Human Betterment Foundation's executive director, similarly looked to the history of countries such as Scotland, Switzerland, and Holland for "abundant proof that a superior people will wrest from the most hostile environment a worth-while destiny and civilization."[106]

While eugenicists associated with the Human Betterment Foundation projected their anxieties south, alarmed by the high birthrate of "peon type" families, the

Nazis worried about the pollution of Aryans by "foreign eastern stock." When Frick talked in 1934 about the need to remove "obnoxious excrescences" from the "national body corporate," it was clear whom he had in mind.[107] Five years later, the Third Reich's veneer of legal propriety and medical professionalism associated with the Sterilization Law had been abandoned for fascist expediency and "a policy of mass murder."[108] In September 1939, after Hitler signed a personal note authorizing "mercy killings," nurses and doctors in specially selected "pediatric wards" murdered some five thousand children born with physical deformities. In 1940 to 1941, gas chambers were first used to kill seventy thousand mentally and physically disabled adults who had been judged "life unworthy of life." An estimated two hundred thousand adults were eventually killed in the Nazi euthanasia program, a prelude to the mass-produced butchery of millions.[109]

Jews were included in campaigns to purge the "national body corporate" of "useless and unhealthy parts" through sterilization and euthanasia, but they were not disproportionately targeted.[110] It was not their future children or disabled relatives, but they themselves who would be primarily marked for extinction.[111] Before extermination, though, came the Nuremberg Laws.

🔳 Chapter 5 🔳

Blood and Honor

The German destruction of the European Jews was a tour de force.

(Raul Hilberg, 1985)

CITY OF THE REICH PARTY RALLIES

Before I started my research for this book, I had a tendency to mix, or sometimes even to blend the Nuremberg of 1935 with the Nuremberg of 1945. It was all a blur—goose-stepping parades, the Blood Law, fascist architectural grandeur, and Nazi officials just following orders. My confusion was to be expected, given that I grew up in a literate household that bypassed the study of modern German history and discouraged family members from visiting Germany. My decision to buy a Volkswagen in the late 1960s—by which time I was now well settled across the pond, married, and a parent—was greeted with censorious clucking by my parents. My father, meanwhile, cherished his German camera and bought German machinery for his factory. When I pointed out this contradiction, I quickly realized that I had stepped across the line into non-rational territory.

For most Jews, Nuremberg is synonymous with the laws passed in 1935. The city does not take "any pride" in this association, says a local German archivist. "The Nazis triggered the worst crime that ever happened to mankind and spoiled the name of the German people and of our city forever."[1] But there are also other Nurembergs: city of medieval treasures, city of Nazi rallies, and city of war-crimes trials, to name the most obvious. After British planes finished bombing on the night of January 2, 1945, Nuremberg also became a city of rubble, second only to Dresden in the scope of destruction. The German survivors of this "catastrophe"—the word used by W. G. Sebald—became silent and forgetful in its wake, not unlike survivors everywhere.[2] Sebald's mother "saw Nürnberg in flames, / but cannot recall now / what the burning town looked like / or what her feelings were / at this sight."[3]

When General Patton flew triumphantly over Nuremberg on April 27, 1945, the "appalling sight" shocked him.[4] The city was "the most completely destroyed

72

place I have ever seen. It is really rather pathetic to see such a historical monument so completely destroyed."[5] His previous memory of Nuremberg was as a tourist with his father and wife in 1912, when the city was an obligatory stopover for early-twentieth-century visitors seeking an authentic site of pre-modern Germany.[6] Long before Nuremberg was destroyed in 1945 and resurrected in the era of postwar prosperity, it had been a center of medieval trade, high culture, and imperial splendor.

For hundreds of years, going back to the mid-twelfth century, Nuremberg has a record of welcoming and expelling, incorporating and exterminating Jews. Driven out in the late fifteenth century, they were back again at the end of the seventeenth century. A silver Torah crown, rescued at the end of World War II and now on display in the holocaust case of the Jewish Museum in New York, was made in Nuremberg in the early eighteenth century. A small Jewish community began to form in 1857, a Reform synagogue was consecrated in 1874, and an Orthodox synagogue completed in 1902. By 1900, there were some six thousand Jews in Nuremberg, and up to nine thousand by 1933.[7]

The nineteenth-century Jews who settled in Nuremberg found a niche within the city's industrial growth—dominating the hop trade, producing toys and bicycles, and entering the professions as lawyers and doctors.[8] When a German-American Jewish salesman from San Diego visited Nuremberg in 1873, he was

5.1 Martin Dannenberg finds Nuremberg reduced to rubble at the end of the war in Europe, April 1945.

impressed by the "wonderful old city," with its ancient masonry, art treasures, and cobble-stoned squares. "The Jewish burying ground," Abraham Rothschild wrote home, "is also one of the great sights of the city; you think indeed you are in a garden of flowers." And of the modern buildings in the city, "the greatest is the new Jewish synagogue."[9]

By World War I, Nuremberg's Jewish community was smaller than in most other German cities, but it felt secure and relatively privileged.[10] Nuremberg was receptive to distinguished Jews like Walter Berlin, prosperous Jews like Leo (Lehmann) Katzenberger, and working-class Jews like Bernhard Kolb. Walter Berlin's family tree was rooted in seventeenth-century Germany. He followed in the tradition of his grandfather—the Royal Bavarian Advocate in Ansbach— by becoming a lawyer in 1913, with mostly industrial and commercial firms as clients. He was made a captain in the German army, and was awarded an Iron Cross and Bavarian Order of Military Merit for his service during World War I.[11]

Leo Katzenberger and his two brothers, David and Max, were the thriving owners of twenty-five stores throughout Germany, with the headquarters and warehouse based in Nuremberg, where Leo's family lived in a villa. In the late 1930s, he served as president and leader of the Jewish congregation in the city.[12] Bernhard Kolb grew up in an orphanage near Nuremberg, worked as a traveling salesman before getting married and settling in the city in 1920. He was injured in the trenches during the war, lost two brothers in 1914, and another in 1916 at Verdun. By 1923, he was a family man with two children, employed as general director of the Jewish congregation.[13] In the mid-1920s, Walter Berlin, Bernhard Kolb, and Leo Katzenberger were pillars of the local community, as secure as Hugo and Käte Perls were in Berlin. A decade later, they would all be running for their lives.

There may have been practical reasons to stage the International Military Tribunal in Nuremberg in November 1945—such as the availability of the surprisingly intact Palace of Justice and a large prison—but the victors must have appreciated the symbolism: Democracy whips fascism in its home town, the rule of law prevails over the rule of man.[14] If Munich was the birthplace of the Nazi movement, Nuremberg was its shrine to "the delirious days of the annual rallies."[15] It was here that Julius Streicher made his name with the publication in 1923 of *Der Stürmer* (*The Stormtrooper* or *Attacker*), a vicious piece of anti-Semitic propaganda. Here, too, he would be executed in 1946 for crimes against humanity. By 1922, Streicher had sworn his loyalty to Hitler and helped to double the Nazi party's membership in the city. The surrounding countryside, according to Ian Kershaw, was "piously Protestant, fervently nationalist, and stridently antisemitic." Nuremberg provided the Nazis with "a stronghold far greater than was offered by its home city of Munich in the Catholic south of Bavaria, and a symbolic capital," which was later designated as the "City of the Reich Party Rallies."[16] Nuremberg also represented a link to the glory days of the German

Empire, to visions of Pan-Germanism, and to epic Wagnerian operas—all-important cultural trappings of nazism.

The NSDAP, or Nazi party, held its first rally in Nuremberg in August 1927. The Nazis returned in 1929 for a congress that was much larger than its predecessor, with thirty to forty thousand party members in attendance. With Hitler paying close attention to the rally as a propaganda performance, the massive Zeppelinfeld amphitheatre had been constructed to showcase "the glamour of fascism."[17] The titanic Congress Hall, modeled after Rome's Coliseum and other grandiose tributes to the Nazi aesthetic, was also imagined, but never completed in Nuremberg. When the party returned for the fourth time in September 1934, it had become a government in power and a Hitler personality cult was in full bloom, creating an "entire industry of kitsch." William Shirer recalled street sellers hawking postcards featuring portraits of Frederick the Great, Bismarck, Hindenburg, and Hitler.[18] Although Hitler generally did not allow long-standing historic sites to be renamed after him, he made an exception for the Hauptmarkt in Nuremberg, which became Adolf-Hitler-Platz.[19]

The 1934 Rally, according to historian Ian Kershaw, was "consciously devised as a vehicle for the Führer cult. Hitler now towered above his movement, which had assembled to pay him homage." Leni Riefenstahl's *Triumph of the Will*—a title selected by Hitler—captured the event in a film that subsequently played to packed houses in Germany and confirmed his unchallenged personification of the nation.[20] An emboldened Hitler proclaimed, "The German form of life is definitely determined for the next thousand years. The Age of Nerves of the nineteenth century has found its close with us."[21] The following year, 1935, the Party Congress returned to Nuremberg for one of its most triumphant productions.

THE JEWISH QUESTION

The "Reich Party Congress of Freedom"—ironically named to signal Germany's ability to rearm itself—began on September 10.[22] Hundreds of thousands of the party faithful gathered to hear Hitler give seventeen speeches at "the High Mass of our party," as Joseph Goebbels called it.[23] In the evening of September 15, after several hours of parades across the Nuremberg Market Place, the Reichstag met in the hall of the Nuremberg Cultural Association to pass the Flag, Citizenship, and Blood laws. It was the first and last time that a Reichstag session would be convened outside Berlin.[24]

The Nazi regime never formally repealed the Weimar Constitution, even though the Third Reich destroyed the Weimar Republic. Hitler typically ruled by fiat, on the basis of an emergency presidential decree of February 28, 1933, for the Protection of the People and the State, which Hindenburg had been tricked into signing after the Reichstag fire. The decree enabled the Führer "to rule by a sort of continual martial law," observed Shirer. Hitler preserved the Reichstag as an automatic endorsement of his dictatorship. It met only a dozen times until war was declared in 1939. It held no debates, heard speeches only from Hitler or his deputies, and did not enact any legislation, other than the three Nuremberg Laws and the Enabling Act of March 24, 1933, by which the Reichstag transferred its legislative functions to the Nazi government.[25]

If the Nazis ruled by fiat and the Third Reich dismantled democratic institutions, why was it important for Hitler to convene the Reichstag to endorse widespread, longstanding practices of anti-Semitism? This topic has engaged historians from three analytical perspectives that constitute not so much an irreconcilable argument as different vantage points. Passage of the Nuremberg Laws is variously understood as a propaganda spectacle for international and domestic consumption; as Hitler's political finesse in resolving differences between party radicals and state bureaucrats about how to manage the Jewish Question; and as a mobilization of functionaries into the practical work of detaching Jews from Germany.[26] These interpretations are not mutually exclusive.

"The severance of Jew from German," says Raul Hilberg, was a "very complex operation," given how integrated Jews had become into the larger society during the 1920s.[27] By 1941, the whole process was pared down to the mechanics of repression and annihilation, but in the early days of the Third Reich the focus was on political persuasion and reorganization of governing institutions. The Nuremberg Laws figured prominently in this transformation. To historian Gisela Bock, the Blood Law was one of "three core laws of National Socialist hereditary and racial policy," the others being the 1933 Sterilization Law and the 1935 Marital Health Law that banned marriage between "superior" and "inferior" members of the "German-blooded" population.[28] Similarly, Henry Friedlander regards the Sterilization Law as "the cornerstone of the regime's eugenic and racial legislation," and the Nuremberg Laws as its "centerpiece."[29]

Prior to September 1935, Hitler had not taken any decisive political actions regarding Jews. This inactivity, observes Ian Kershaw, was "tactical, not temperamental."[30] Mainly owing to foreign policy considerations and economic instabilities during 1934, the regime had reined in the more barbaric aspects of anti-Semitic terrorism, while giving the green light to discrimination and intimidation.[31] Early in 1935, "the brakes on antisemitic violence began to be loosened," with Streicher and other Nazi militants pushing hard for full implementation of the party's program on racial purity.[32] By spring, the view from the grass-roots Right was that if anti-Semitic violence were "set in motion by us from below," then "the government would ... have to follow."[33] The state bureaucracy was also under pressure to produce "retrospective legal sanction" for the Gestapo's anti-Jewish measures, such as its February 1935 ban on Jews raising the swastika flag.[34]

Some Nazi officials were concerned that "unlawful" activities against Jews could be bad for the economy. On August 20, 1935, Wilhelm Frick was also counseling his colleagues that "wild single actions" were politically counter-productive. As Hilberg shrewdly makes the point, the opposition to anti-Jewish vigilantism, expressed by party functionaries such as Hjalmar Schacht, president of the Reichsbank, was not motivated by any concern for Jews. "Schacht did *not* oppose anti-Jewish action. He opposed 'wild' party measures. He preferred the 'legal' way, that is, certainty instead of uncertainty. It was uncertainty that hurt business."[35]

By the late summer, Hitler was forced to take action. He had tried to juggle the radicals, who supported unregulated terrorism against Jews, and the party conservatives, who advocated legislative regulation. It was a disagreement over tactics, not goals. "Out of the need to reconcile these conflicting positions," suggests Kershaw, "the Nuremberg laws emerged."[36] Throughout the spring and summer, the demand for anti-Jewish legislation had increased within the party. In April, the Reich Minister of the Interior signaled that new legislation was in the works. In June, party organs stepped up the demand for the exclusion of Jews from citizenship and for the "total physical apartheid" of Aryans and Jews. Streicher and other radicals especially focused on the need to ban all sexual intercourse between the "races." This was not a new demand. As early as 1930, Frick had proposed a draft bill in the Reichstag "for the Protection of the German Nation," advocating drastic punishment for sex with Jews and "colored races."[37] By 1935, Jews had been barred from public office, the civil service, journalism, the stock exchange, and various other professions.[38] Since 1933, under the leadership of Gerhard Wagner, the Nazi Physicians' League also had actively lobbied the government for blood legislation. And Wagner had Hitler's ear on this topic.[39]

When Hitler left for the Rally on September 10, he had already decided to use the Reichstag to endorse the swastika as the national flag, but he had not made a decision about citizenship and blood laws.[40] Two days later, he made up his mind. He was under pressure to solve the political rift within the party, but he also needed an event of sufficient dramatic power to justify reconvening the Reichstag outside Berlin. At his opening address to the Party Rally on September 11, Hitler identified "Jewish Marxism" at the top of a list of international enemies responsible for "the ferment of decomposition, the elements of dissolution" in the world surrounding Germany. "Rootless Jewish-international wandering scholars are infiltrating the nations, agitating against all healthy common sense and whipping up hostility among the people."[41] Two days later, on September 13, having decided that he wanted the Reichstag also to pass race legislation, Hitler instructed the Interior Ministry that they had two days to draft laws for his approval.[42]

That evening, Bernhard Lösener, who was in charge of race and Jewish affairs in the Reich Ministry of the Interior, was summoned to Nuremberg and given twenty-four hours to draft the Blood Law. Lösener and a colleague, Ministerialrat Franz Medicus, flew into Nuremberg the next day and were briefed by their superiors, State Secretaries Hans Pfundtner and Wilhelm Stuckart, both of whom reported to Wilhelm Frick.[43] It was typical, recalled Lösener after the war, that "even laws of great consequences had to be produced at short notice, without thorough preparation," but nothing was comparable to this situation.

Lösener was not given any written instructions and had no direct contact with Hitler. "The atmosphere for our work was the worst possible because the whole town was filled with the commotion of the Reich Party Rally, the marchings and the meetings." Drafts of the legislation had to be submitted to Frick, who had not participated in any discussions with Lösener or his staff, as well as to Stuckart and the well-connected Gerhard Wagner. At midnight on Saturday, some twenty hours before the Reichstag session, Frick brought instructions from Hitler that Lösener should draft four different versions of the Blood Law—varying in severity of punishments—and, additionally, to complete the legislative program, a Reich Citizenship Law.

Lösener's team worked through the night and next day, "physically and mentally very exhausted," writing drafts of legislation and press releases on the back of menus in their hotel's bar, getting Hitler's approval of the citizenship law in the middle of the night, and lobbying "associates who could influence Hitler to decide on the choice of the wording of the [Blood] law." But it was not until the Reichstag convened that Lösener was informed which draft Hitler had authorized. The whole affair, he later complained, was "extremely undignified."[44]

The Blood Law, as enacted on September 15, banned sexual relations between "Jews and citizens of German or German-related blood," but did not specify or define the meaning of Jew. Party activists wanted the definition to include a single drop of Jewish blood and converts to Judaism, while legal bureaucrats preferred a more flexible interpretation. As Hilberg suggests, "the party 'combated' the part-Jew as a carrier of 'Jewish influence,' whereas the civil service wanted to protect in the part-Jew 'that part which is German.' The final definition was written in the Interior Ministry, and so it is not surprising that the party view did not prevail," at least not in 1935.[45]

Lösener, who had worked for many years in the customs administration before being transferred to the Ministry of Interior, would claim after the war that he had tried to save *Mischlinge* in 1935, that he was working from the inside to protect as many part-Jews as possible. But Lösener was the kind of flexible technocrat who readily adapted to circumstances. He was involved in the drafting of twenty-seven Jewish edicts, including the September 1941 decree that required Jews to appear in public only when wearing the sign *Jude* centered in the Star of David, displayed prominently on their clothing. Lösener busily worked out details of the new logo: size (as large as a hand), colors (black on yellow), and location (left front).[46]

Hitler's speech to the Reichstag on September 15 was the first time that he had focused on the "Jewish Question" in a major public speech since becoming chancellor.[47] He welcomed the opportunity to introduce the legislation in Nuremberg, which "by virtue of the National Socialist Movement ... is closely connected with the laws which will be presented to you today for passage."[48]

Hitler went on to blame "the Bolshevist International of Moscow" for spreading disorder throughout the world.[49] "It is almost exclusively Jewish elements," he observed, "which are at work as instigators of this campaign to spread animosity and confusion among the peoples.... The international unrest in the world unfortunately appears to have given rise to the opinion among Jews in Germany that now perhaps the time has come to set Jewish interests up in clear opposition to the German national interests in the Reich." This is the moment, concluded Hitler, to attempt to "establish tolerable relations with the Jewish people." If the Blood Law fails and the problem proves "insoluble" through legislation, he warned, then the matter "would have to be assigned to the National Socialist Party for a final solution by law."[50]

Hermann Göring, in his capacity as Reichstag President, followed Hitler with a call to adopt the swastika as a national symbol. "If this flag is to fly over Germany in the future, no Jew may be allowed to hoist this sacred insignia." At the close of his speech, Göring read the texts of the three laws. When he came to the section of the Blood Law that prohibited Jews from flying the swastika but permitted them to fly the "Jewish colors," the whole assembly erupted in hoots of derisive laughter.[51]

After the three Laws were approved by a unanimous vote of the delegates, Hitler called for party discipline and spoke out against "independent action against Jews."[52] Later, original copies of the Laws were produced for signatures. Hitler, Interior Minister Frick, and General Werner von Blomberg, Minister of War and Commander-in-Chief of the Wehrmacht, signed the Flag Law; Hitler and Frick signed the Citizenship Law; and Hitler, Frick, Justice Minister Franz Gürtner, and Rudolf Hess, Hitler's deputy, signed the Blood Law.

According to some commentators, the Nuremberg Laws were primarily a sop to international diplomatic opinion. "The session of the Reichstag at Nuremberg," says Gerhard Jochem, a curator at the Nuremberg City Archives, "was a propagandistic event to show the world unanimous approval of the Nazis' anti-Semitism by the German people."[53] But if this was a purpose of the legislation, it certainly was not persuasive in the United States, where public opinion was indignantly critical.[54] The New York Times, in a front-page story on September 16, described the Nuremberg Laws as "a series of laws that put Jews beyond the legal and social pale of the German nation."[55] The Associated Press reported that Hitler had "hurled defiance to Jews throughout the world."[56] Time magazine included a description of the atmosphere in the Reichstag when Göring, "in menacing tones," read out the wording of the three decrees, including the ban on Jews employing German servants under the age of forty-five years old. "The implications of this proviso struck the German Reichstag so forcibly that Deputies clutched their quaking midriffs and the whole chamber roared with Homeric laughter until tears of mirth glistened on many a cheek. Banging down his gavel President Göring boomed: 'No Jew can insult Germany!'"[57]

Passage of the Nuremberg Laws was more effective as a propaganda device inside Germany than outside its borders. Understood as an advertising campaign, "akin to a corporate logo or brand name," the three Nuremberg Laws, not just the Blood Law, communicated a clear, interlocking message: the swastika (flag) stood for Reich citizens (Aryans) and against non-citizens (Jews).[58] To elevate the political significance of the Blood Law over that of the Flag and Citizenship Laws misses their symbolic interrelationship. Moreover, as of September 15, 1935, the state and party now had a common legal and political framework for solving the Jewish Question. By early 1936, according to a report issued by the Social Democrats in Berlin, "the feeling that the Jews are another race is today a general one."[59]

The Nuremberg Laws served as the prototype for the racial classification of "Aryans" as German citizens. The Ministry of Interior came up with elaborate guidelines for the taxonomy of Jews to determine compliance and, more important, lack of compliance with the Blood Law. After September 15, 1935, it was a violation of the law if a person of "German blood" had sex with a Jew (four Jewish grandparents or a member of a Jewish religious organization), or with a *Mischling* (descended from two Jewish grandparents and a practicing Jew). *Mischlinge* of the second degree (one Jewish grandparent), or of the first degree (two Jewish grandparents, but not a practicing Jew or married to a Jew), were theoretically exempt from the Blood Law. But "Jews" could not marry *Mischlinge* of the second degree, and *Mischlinge* of the second degree could not marry each other. In addition, there were all kinds of exemptions, known as "liberations," for those who could show "positive merit" or had friends in high places.[60]

This Byzantine elaboration of the Blood Law confirms Zygmunt Bauman's insight that the space between the idea and practice of purging Jews from Germany was "filled wall-to-wall with bureaucratic action." He states that "however vivid was Hitler's imagination, it would have accomplished little if it had not been taken over, and translated into a routine process of problem-solving, by a huge and rational bureaucratic apparatus.... True, bureaucracy did not hatch the fear of racial contamination and the obsession with racial hygiene. For that it needed visionaries, as bureaucracy picks up where visionaries stop. But bureaucracy made the holocaust. And it made it in its own image."[61] By 1939, more than four hundred additional decrees, regulations, and amendments had consigned Jews and other "non-Aryan" groups "to the outer fringes of society, prisoners in their own land."[62]

SENTENCED WITHOUT GUILT

Meanwhile, conditions on the ground for Jews in Germany quickly deteriorated. Many families, such as Käte and Hugo Perls and their children, chose to emigrate, others were forced out, and some stayed until the bitter end. In Nuremberg, after 1922 Jewish graves were regularly desecrated. Yet even as Julius Streicher's gang increased its attacks on Jews, Walter Berlin was still able to use his clout as a lawyer and representative of Jewish organizations with Benno Martin, Nuremberg's police chief. "Martin often gave warning when individual Jews were in imminent danger and was, within the limits of his possibilities," Berlin told his son, "ready with practical help, such as the immediate issue of passports which allowed travel abroad."[63] But when Streicher was put in charge of a boycott of the city's Jewish stores on April 1, 1933, the exodus began. In July of that year, four hundred prominent Jews were rounded up and humiliated, some forced to trim lawns with their teeth.[64] Between 1933 and 1939, an estimated 5,638 Jews left Nuremberg, 2,539 of them for other countries.[65]

The nationally coordinated attacks on Jews, known as *Reichskristallnacht*, that took place on November 9–10, 1938, were particularly brutal in Nuremberg. Of the ninety-one Jews who died throughout Germany, Nuremberg had twenty-six victims.[66] The synagogues were burned, Jewish-owned stores were smashed, and dead bodies lay in the streets. "These were people," recalled a fifteen-year-old eyewitness, "who were killed the night before or had committed suicide in desperation. This is where I came face to face with death for the first time in my life."[67] Walter Berlin's apartment was broken into and trashed; the next day he was arrested and beaten, causing the loss of an eye. After his lawyer's license was revoked, he and his wife were lucky to get to England in April 1939. Meanwhile, in November 1938, Bernhard Kolb was sent to Dachau and then released back to Nuremberg. He and wife Reta somehow physically survived the war and emigrated to the United States in 1947, but the rest of his family was murdered: his sister and members of her family in Auschwitz; his brother Hugo—the only brother to survive World War I—along with his family somewhere in Poland; and his daughter Erna and family in Bergen-Belsen.[68]

Of the three Katzenberger brothers who lived in Nuremberg, only David survived the holocaust, lucky to be among the twelve hundred prisoners from Theresienstadt in Czechoslovakia that were shipped to Switzerland in February 1945. Max had visited Palestine in 1936, but returned to Germany, telling his family that they would be safe. He and his wife disappeared into the camps in March 1942.[69] That same year, Leo became a defendant in a show trial—"the most flagrant example" of the abuse of the Blood Law "to break friendly relations between Jews and Germans." An aging Katzenberger was accused of *Rassenschande* (extramarital sexual relations) with a young married woman, Irene Seiler, whom he had helped—at her father's request—to start up a photography business. The charges were trumped up and unproven, but Katzenberger was convicted and, even to the surprise of the prosecutor, sentenced to death. Mrs. Seiler was sent to prison for perjury, but released after six months, perhaps as a result of Hitler's personal intervention. The Führer always maintained the chivalrous notion that Christian women should not be blamed for the sexual debauchery of Jewish men.[70] On June 3, 1942, at the age of sixty-nine, Leo Katzenberger was executed in Munich. In 1946, the verdict was annulled; and in 1999, the Council of Nuremberg named a street in his memory. A plaque, unveiled in November 2001, reads: "In memoriam of Leo Katzenberger, head of Nuremberg's Jewish community, arrested and indicted because of the 'Nuremberg racial laws' in a propaganda trial at Nuremberg Special Court, sentenced without guilt and executed as a victim of the Nazis' racist 'justice.'"[71]

By the time of Katzenberger's death, the 2,611 Jews still living in Nuremberg were on their way to concentration camps. Deported in seven transports (from November 29, 1941, to January 17, 1944), they left the city from the March Field railroad station, located outside town and out of public view, supervised by Benno Martin, Nuremberg's police chief and now a member of the SS (*Schutzstaffel* or Protection Squad) who, years earlier, had tried to save individual Jews from Streicher's mob. By war's end, only sixty-five Nuremberg Jews survived the concentration camps, reducing the Jewish presence in the city to its size in medieval times. Today, the city's memorial book lists 2,374 Jewish "victims of the Shoah," or catastrophe, including those who died through murder, so-called euthanasia, suicide, or in a state of shock.[72]

NAZI ICON

The Nuremberg Laws of 1935 were an important policy document and catalyst for unleashing bureaucratic initiative, but they also quickly assumed iconic importance. To Jews, the Nuremberg Laws represented defeat: a signpost pointing to the dead end ahead. "We stood in the front row of the defenders of Europe," wrote Joseph Roth about the role of Jewish intellectuals in Weimar Germany, "and we were the first to be defeated."[73]

For Hitler's regime, the Nuremberg Laws were a decisive marker on the triumphant journey to the thousand-year Reich, and a celebration of a joyous occasion—the purging of a deadly microbe from the political body of a resurrected Germany. The Nazi regime polished its propaganda until it gleamed. "Every word pronounced in Germany between 1933 and 1945 was weighed as on gold-scales," observed Hugo Perls. "Thus Germany became the land of the lie."[74]

According to Hans Heinrich Lammers, the head of the Reich Chancellery, the original Nuremberg Laws were "handed over to the Mayor of the city of Nuremberg in November 1935," in tribute to the honorary title it had garnered as the "City of the Reich Party Rallies."[75] The mayor kept the Laws in a "secret file" in a safe in his office.[76] This decision echoed, no doubt purposefully, Holy Roman Emperor Sigismund's decree in the early fifteenth century that made Nuremberg the repository of imperial jewels.

Important Nazi documents—including the Nuremberg Laws—were regularly put on display for educational and cultural purposes. "Applications from several places have been received to make original law documents available for the purpose of exhibition," Lammers observed early in 1937.[77] In April of that year, Alfred Rosenberg, Hitler's chief ideological functionary, requested the use of the Nuremberg Laws to display in an exhibit, "Give Me Four Years Time."[78] A few months later, Rosenberg again requested that the Laws be made available for an exhibition, this time on the topic of "Nuremberg: A German City," which was organized by Rudolf Hess in conjunction with the upcoming Reich Party Convention. "The basic idea of the exhibition," Rosenberg explained, "is to document ... the historical and politico-cultural development of the city of Nuremberg.... Given the framework of this exhibition, it would be relevant, if possible, to show the originals of the law on race, which the Reichstag has passed."[79]

Wilhelm Frick, Minister of the Interior, raised his concern with Lammers that "original law documents" were being "loaned out so often" that there was a danger of loss or damage, "even with careful handling." As one of the few people in Hitler's inner circle to have regular access to the Führer,[80] Lammers agreed with Frick and issued an order that the "Fundamental Laws of the State no longer be provided for the purposes of exhibition. In suitable cases, however, we have no reservation about allowing exhibitors to have photocopies [*Photokopie*] of the documents."[81] When Rosenberg asked that an exception be made in his case, he was turned down. "The Führer stands by his original decision," Lammers wrote Rosenberg, "by which original law documents will no longer be made available for purposes of exhibition, and believes that in the case before him, the granting of an exception is not appropriate.[82] Therefore, I am not in a position to place the original documents at your disposal. There would be no objections, however, to display the photocopies that we already sent to you."[83]

For security reasons during the war, almost all the holdings in Nuremberg's municipal archives were moved out of the city to nearby villages and castles.[84] The Nuremberg Laws remained in the mayor's safe until late in 1943, when the mayor turned them over to police chief Benno Martin.[85] Martin, in turn, entrusted them to Hans Rauch, an official of the German Finance Ministry and director of the Nuremberg office of the Reich Treasury. Rauch owned a family farm in nearby Eichstätt, where he was also a director of a local bank—the Bayerische Hypotheken- und Wechselbank. On October 9, 1943, together with another director, Rauch deposited the original Nuremberg Laws in a vault in the Eichstätt bank. Each director kept a key, both of which were required to get access to the vault.[86] Here the Nuremberg Laws remained until Hans Rauch led an American Army intelligence team to the bank in Eichstätt on April 27, 1945.

▣ Chapter 6 ▣

Hitler's Signature

Again we seek Thy counsel,
But not in cringing guise.
We whine not for Thy mercy—
To slay: God make us wise.

(General George S. Patton, Jr., 1943)

REFUGE

While Nazi officials were trying to find a secure place for the Nuremberg Laws, hundreds of thousands of European Jews searched for their own refuge. For Jews living in France, there were all kinds of escape routes, but it was risky to travel and there was no guarantee that the destination would be hospitable. By 1941, Käte Perls's ex-husband and three sons had reached the United States, but she was denied a visa to join them. Instead, she chose the nearest country to the United States and sought refuge in Cuba, following a route taken by generations of Jewish refugees: victims of the Spanish Inquisition, Brazilian merchants fleeing Portuguese persecution in the seventeenth century, and Eastern Europeans escaping pogroms in the early twentieth century.[1]

Käte Perls was part of the fourth wave of Jews who came to Cuba in the twentieth century. Immigrants from the United States settled there following their participation in the Spanish-American War. A group of Sephardic Jews (*Turcos*) arrived from Turkey, and others from Mexico in the 1900s. After World War I, thousands of Eastern European Jews arrived in Cuba, hoping to find a back door into Florida. After restrictive immigration laws were enacted in the United States in 1924, many refugees were forced to settle in Cuba at a time of economic recession and chronic unemployment; in 1925, there were more than eight hundred Jewish peddlers there.[2] In the 1920s, East European Jews followed the strategy in Cuba that had appeared successful for Jews in Germany: they minimized their Jewish roots and identified themselves as *Polacos* and *Alemanos* in order "to keep out of harm's way."[3]

But from 1933 until the United States entered World War II, Cuba was another risky destination for Jews. Before the 1930s, there had been no systematic anti-

Semitism on the island, but with Hitler's rise to power in 1933, a fascist movement emerged, with ties to German Nazis and Spanish Falangists, and "a Jew-baiting press flourished."[4] Käte Perls was fortunate not to be on board the S.S. *St. Louis*, which carried some nine hundred Jewish refugees across the Atlantic to Cuba in May 1939. Refused entry in Havana, the ship returned most of the passengers to their deaths in Europe.[5] With the consolidation of Cuban Jews into a united front of the *Comité Central* in 1939 and the Cuban government's support for the United States after the attack on Pearl Harbor on December 7, 1941, organized anti-Semitism was defeated in Cuba.

Between 1933 and 1944, perhaps as many as twelve thousand refugees landed in Cuba, the majority from Germany, Poland, and Austria. Käte Perls, her former sister-in-law, Elise Flatow, and others who had been in French concentration camps came by ship from France and Africa.[6] Only about fifteen percent of the European refugees settled in Cuba, the rest eventually moving on to other countries, primarily the United States. Some stayed by choice, others by necessity. Jews from Belgium established diamond-polishing operations, employing more than twelve hundred workers in 1943; others became successful in trade and small industries.[7] Elise Flatow made it to Cuba with half a truck full of luggage, including a chair and six cardboard boxes. She shared a room with two other people at the Savoy Hotel, scraping by on money sent by her brother. Some of her fellow residents also had been in Gurs, including a former judge and his wife. "I am feeling at home here," she told her brother in August 1944, while at the same time she urged him to get her a U.S. visa.[8]

Käte Perls was still involved in the family art business, but on the run in France she had few resources with her and had to depend on relatives in the United States for support. Frank Perls sold a Picasso painting to raise money for his mother's journey. She traveled first to Casablanca, finding time there to write to Picasso back in Paris, and then took a ship across the Atlantic.[9] When she arrived in Havana early in 1942, she relied on Hugo and her sons to send her money.[10] By now, she was ill with cancer. Still, she could afford to stay in grand hotels like the Nacional and Packard on the basis of her stake in her sons' galleries in New York and Los Angeles, and her own entrepreneurial knack. "She was successful," Klaus once said of his mother, "because I created the outlet."[11] To Käte, it was the other way around: "You have so much of value from me in your hands—Rafael, Bosch, Greco," she wrote Hugo from Cuba.[12]

Käte made the most of her time in Cuba—hanging out with some of the more socially prominent families, traveling all over the island in a friend's "glorious car," and getting to know Cuban artists, such as Mario Carreño. She organized exhibitions at the Lyceum Club and made "good connections," even though there were few buyers. "This way," she wrote Hugo, "I see all of Cuba. Everyone is trying to lift up my spirits, show their interest in me. You know how it always is."[13] She missed her lover, the Spanish poet and revolutionary Ventura Gassol, whom she had met in émigré circles in France. She feared for Gassol's life in the repressive climate of Pierre Laval's Vichy government. He sent her "many foolish letters" and she pined for him like a young girl. "Fate would be too cruel to destroy this love affair," she wrote her ex-husband. "It is really *le grand amour.* If Gassol is dead, then I must go to the USA, but I doubt that I will muster the strength to do so."[14]

In New York, Hugo, now a citizen, continued in his efforts to get visas for Käte and his sister. "According to the courts here," Elise wrote from Havana in April 1942, "German Jews are now considered friendly aliens and the chance exists of getting a visa." It might take a few months, she told him.[15] But it took years. This process did not become easier until January 1944, when the Roosevelt administration established the War Refugee Board to review visa applications from refugees. Before the creation of this board, the State Department, particularly under the influence of Assistant Secretary Breckinridge Long, had rejected most Jewish applicants. Treasury Secretary Henry Morgenthau's recently completed report, "On the Acquiescence of This Government to the Murder of the Jews"—which charged the State Department with using "government machinery to prevent the rescue of the Jews"—gave President Roosevelt the nerve, prodded by his wife Eleanor, to take on the State Department. As a result, tens of thousands of Jews, including Käte Perls and Elise Flatow, finally gained entry into the United States.[16]

Käte arrived in New York either in the late summer or fall of 1944.[17] By January 1945, she was living on West 57th Street, operating a small gallery out of her home, and squeezing the most out of life until she died a few months later.[18] Gassol survived the war in France and returned to Spain in the 1970s following the death of Franco. Hugo married for a third time—to Eugenie Söderberg, the Jewish, German-born, Swedish-American writer and journalist—and lived into his early 90s, surviving his son Frank, who died aged sixty-four in 1975 from too much of the good life and a bad heart.[19]

AMERICAN CITIZEN

Frank Perls made the most of the economic start and training that his parents had given him in Berlin and Paris. Cashing in his share of Perls Galleries in New York, he headed west in 1939 to set up shop in Southern California. He credited Billy Wilder with this smart decision, a recollection confirmed by the director in 1999. "I was great friends with Frank," the 94-year old Wilder told me, "very close to him. I knew his mother and father in Germany and in Paris. They were art dealers. I collected through them. I loved Frank's mother."[20] Here is the story that Frank Perls told about how he ended up in Los Angeles.[21]

"In 1939 Billy Wilder was living in a large clapboard house in Beverly Hills. Earlier he had come to New York. Billy said he could rent me a store on Sunset

Boulevard and I could sell a lot of pictures there to his friends. Billy Wilder became my first barker.... I first saw Sunset Boulevard in 1939. Billy picked me up in Pasadena at the railroad station.... El Capitan, a Santa Fe coach train, had brought me there in 39 hours.... The orange groves were on both sides of the tracks and Billy Wilder, whom I had known since 1928—disguised as the Hollywood writer he was, with sports jacket, hat and shirt and tie (dapper)—welcomed me. I got into his car with my bag, three packages of paintings, watercolors, and drawings, and soon we were on Sunset Boulevart [*sic*] driving west." It was the right move: he opened up the fashionable Frank Perls Gallery in the "cultural desert" of Los Angeles, and after the war made his fortune selling to Southern California's nouveau riche and curating important exhibitions on modern art, for which he was made a life fellow of the Los Angeles County Museum.[22]

The war, however, delayed his economic success. After the bombing of Pearl Harbor, Frank Perls was categorized as an "enemy alien" and subject to wartime restrictions, including a curfew that prevented him from keeping his business open in the evening. He tried to prove his loyalty by volunteering for the U.S. Army in March 1942 and working with the Office of War Information to organize a United Nations War Poster exhibition and a similar competition for the Los Angeles County Museum.[23] He also wanted to volunteer in the local fire department, but was turned down. In September of that year he applied for citizenship, but still was required to observe the curfew.

Frank then enlisted the support of Billy Wilder and painter George Biddle, whose brother was the U.S. attorney general. He had high hopes of being granted an "exemption from curfew and other restrictions applying to enemy aliens."[24] Frank asked Francis Biddle if he could "send me a little letter acknowledging my loyalty and the fact that you know me personally and that I am your brother's dealer. I am sure that this letter with the testimonies of local county and city officials will help me to get the exemption from the curfew."[25] The attorney general immediately sent a "very charming recommendation" for exemption and told his subordinate based in Los Angeles to intercede on Frank's behalf. "I am and always have been the best future American Citizen. I believe in Democracy and I have always in word and deed done my utmost to live and fight for Democracy," Frank wrote in his September 1942 application for exemption from curfew restrictions. But his connections in high places made no difference to the local military bureaucrat— privately dubbed by Frank as "Major Goebbels"—who sent a "completely negative reply." Frank forwarded this rejection to the attorney general, along with his concern that "stateless refugees" from Germany were being unfairly identified with "the Nazis." Francis Biddle was sympathetic, but unable to help him.[26]

With his induction into the army on October 1, 1942, Frank was now officially "exempted from observing curfew regulations."[27] He closed down his business, reported for duty on October 7, and was sent for basic training to Camp Barkeley, Texas, where he worked as a clerk in the records department. On April 14, 1943, he was at the Army Air Force base in Santa Maria, California, when he received official notification that he was now an American citizen. Private Perls was not unhappy with his "very nice post — it is only about two hours from the Biltmore Hotel" — but he thought he "could be of greater service to the government in the intelligence unit."[28]

Frank's fluency in English, French, and German made him a good candidate for Military Intelligence and eventually got him "a safe war with the not so safe 30th Infantry Division." He spent the second half of 1943 getting trained as an interpreter and interrogator at Camp Ritchie, Maryland, along with hundreds of other young immigrants from Germany and Austria, many of them Jews — professionals, academics, doctors, journalists, "and one art dealer, age 33."[29] After his training, Master Sergeant Perls was assigned to the G-2 (intelligence) section of the 30th Infantry Division; in April 1944, he was shipped to a Military Intelligence Training Center in England.[30] His unit, Military Intelligence Interpreter (MII) 421, was based in the village of Broadway in the Cotswolds, where in the 1950s my family would stay when attending performances of Shakespeare's plays in nearby Stratford-upon-Avon. Unknown to Perls, while he was being briefed on conditions in France and giving French lessons to fellow soldiers, General Patton had established the headquarters of an advance party of his Third Army in northwest England, preparing for the invasion of France.[31]

On June 13, 1944 — exactly one week after D-Day — Perls and his team shipped out for France, arriving the next day under heavy attack from German planes. They descended a rope ladder into a barge that took MII 421 to their Normandy landing at Saint-Laurent-sur-Mer, where the American Cemetery now contains the remains or records of almost eleven thousand soldiers. Two days after landing in France, Frank Perls did his first interrogation of German prisoners of war and started to gather intelligence from French civilians and the underground resistance movement.[32] By the summer, adjusted to life in France, he wrote to his Aunt Elise in Cuba about the "touching and hearty welcome of the French population." She hoped that he would soon be "sane and safe in liberated Paris."[33]

Beyond his challenging assignments as an interrogator and interpreter, Frank Perls was expected to carry out more mundane functions. In early January 1945, while on guard duty on a "lonely road" near the Bastogne war zone, he had his first and only direct contact with General Patton. The story Perls later told about this incident is consistent with what is known about Patton's whereabouts and raunchy language. Perls had "an encounter with an all-lights-on group of three jeeps, which I stopped with my Thompson ready to shoot (would I have done that?) and found in the second jeep an angry Patton standing up and screaming at me: 'What the fuck are you holding up the war for.' Reply: 'Standing Orders, General, no lights on this road.' Patton: 'Fuck your orders and get out of the way or I'll shoot you down like a Kraut.' Had he known that I once had been a kraut myself, what would he have done? I was far enough away, the jeeps were crackling and he fortunately did not hear my German accent. I did recognize the General, his gleaming helmet (fifteen coats of lacquer, against his own orders to keep helmets dirty)."[34] A few months later, Perls would have another encounter with Patton, this time indirectly.

Frank Perls's activities with the 30th Infantry Division between June and August 1944—helping to capture German soldiers, interrogating suspected Nazis, and recovering weapons and money—were acknowledged when he received a Bronze Star for his "outstanding courage, personal bravery, and professional skill ... in the performance of his duties" as a "military intelligence interpreter."[35] But Perls's most memorable accomplishment during his military service not only went unrewarded and unrecognized in the army's official records, it also involved General Patton, who once again was in violation of his own standing orders.

PROBLEM CHILD

On April 25, 1944, two days before my second birthday, General Patton showed up in the northern English village of Knutsford, about thirty miles from my home, to give his blessing to a Welcome Club for American soldiers. It was a low-key public relations event, presided over by local dignitaries, with improbable names like Mrs. Constantine Smith and Colonel Thomas Blatherwick. It was not the kind of place or gathering where Jews would be welcomed in 1944. At that time, several years before my parents were permitted to join the country set, my mother was living with her parents in Broughton Park, a Jewish enclave in north Manchester, and trying to keep me under control. My dad was off somewhere hush-hush, working in the psychological warfare department of British intelligence as personal assistant to Major Leo Long, who many years later, after the collapse of the Soviet Union, was revealed to be an important Soviet mole, codenamed Elli. In 1946, Long asked my father to work for him in military intelligence headquarters in Berlin, but Monty turned him down even though "he was very persuasive and phoned me to reconsider. Was I being recruited?" my dad later wondered when news broke in 1992 about Long's membership in the Cambridge spy group.

In April 1944, General Patton also had communists on his mind. In his informal speech in Knutsford, he noted that it was "the evident destiny of the British and Americans ... to rule the world." As an afterthought, he added "the Russians" to his list of postwar powers. Back home in the United States, some press reports omitted his reference to the Soviet Union, while others took offense at Patton's grandiosity. *Newsweek* called him a "ferocious fumbler" and an Illinois Congressman referred to his comments as "balmy as Hitler's."[36] Patton's slip-of-the-tongue revealed his long-held suspicions of Soviet ambitions. He shared J. Edgar Hoover's belief that "the most dangerous and possibly ultimate enemy was not Germany or Japan," he told his nephew, an FBI agent, "but Soviet Russia and her international network."[37]

Patton's fault lay not in having these views, but in expressing them too crudely, too publicly, too prematurely. If he had lived a few more years, his Cold War ideology would have been compatible with mainstream politics. Dwight D. Eisenhower appreciated Patton as "the most brilliant commander of an army in the open field that our or any other service has produced."[38] But Patton's arrogance, insubordination, impulsive behavior, and especially his undiplomatic mouth gave Eisenhower reasons to worry about him, as he would a "problem child."[39] As early as World War I, Patton's father had warned George that his "gift of gab" might be his undoing. "Unless restrained such a gift is always dangerous.... I hope in your speeches you will be very careful and self-restrained—for your own good and for your future."[40] His impetuousness was no less under control some twenty-four years later, in 1943, when Eisenhower warned him "to be more circumspect and less flip in conversation on military matters."[41]

Patton could not resist publicity, and in return the media lapped him up: *Life* magazine called him "the pet of all the newspapermen."[42] World War II made the now familiar image of him into a popular and emblematic icon of the American warrior: in military uniform, riding or standing by a tank, his "war face" set in grim determination.[43] By 1940, as one newspaper headline put it, his name was a "Synonym for Daring Action."[44] The flamboyance and insubordination that irritated his superiors made him "one of the Army's most fabulous characters."[45] Patton was a favorite of the press corps, observed Oscar Koch, Patton's chief intelligence officer, because "he filled the gap with news when good news was necessary for the morale of troops and the folks back home. Correspondents knew it, and they followed Patton when they could."[46] He was on the cover of *Life* in its 1941 "Defense Issue" and in a feature story the following year; he was featured on the cover of *Newsweek* and *Time* in the same week in 1943, of *Newsweek* in 1944, and *Time* again in 1945.[47] He was also profiled in *The Saturday Evening Post*, *Reader's Digest*, and *Collier's*, as well as on the radio and in newsreels.[48] "I went to a movie of myself in Tunisia," Patton noted in his diary.[49] His pompous, leaden poetry was published in women's magazines and set to music, while *Newsweek* reproduced his prayer for good weather.[50]

A few months before the "Knutsford incident," Patton was in trouble with Eisenhower, who considered relieving him of his command of the Seventh Army. During the invasion of Italy in August 1943, Patton visited injured soldiers in a field hospital. He slapped and yelled at two shell-shocked soldiers, calling one of them "a Goddamned coward, you yellow son of a bitch." In his diary the next day, he noted that "companies should deal with such men, and if they shirk their duty, they should be tried for cowardice and shot." When Eisenhower heard what had happened, he was furious. The need for "firm and drastic measures," he wrote Patton, "does not excuse brutality, abuse of the sick, nor exhibition of uncontrollable temper in front of subordinates."[51]

Eisenhower hoped that his private reprimand of Patton would curb the worst of Patton's impulsive behavior, "not only because of his great personal loyalty to you and me," he confided in General George Marshall, "but because fundamentally he is so avid for recognition as a great military commander that he will ruthlessly suppress any habit of his own that will tend to jeopardize it."[52] But Eisenhower's shrewd assessment was no match for Patton's capacity for self-destruction. After his unscripted comments a few months later in Knutsford, Eisenhower ordered him to submit any future speeches to his office for approval. "I am never to talk in public without first submitting what I am going to say to Ike and himself for censorship," Patton noted bitterly in his diary.[53]

DISCOVERY AT EICHSTÄTT

The two "incidents" evaporated from public view as Patton, now commanding the Third Army, led the charge through Europe.[54] "Patton's reported prophecy that 'Hitler had stuck his prick into my meat grinder' had come true," recalled Frank Perls, "and slowly but surely the Allied armies advanced into the Rhineland."[55] The infantry and armored divisions of III Corps—one of six Corps that served in General Patton's Third Army—were among the first to cross over the Rhine into Germany on March 19, 1945.[56] By April 15, German resistance in the Ruhr was broken, with over one hundred thousand troops surrendering to the III Corps, led by Major General James A. Van Fleet.[57] Five days later, on Hitler's birthday, III Corps gained control of Nuremberg after fierce resistance by "fanatical German troops" who, according to U.S. Army historians, tried "to prevent the fall of that great city whence had come the infamous Nazi racial laws. The city had become to them a symbol."[58]

On April 26, the 86th Infantry Division captured the city of Eichstätt, about thirty miles south of Nuremberg.[59] The next day—while Patton was at a press conference in nearby Erlangen, predicting that the war was almost over[60]—a three-man team from the 203d Detachment of the U.S. Army's Counter-Intelligence Corps arrived in Eichstätt with the nephew of a former official of the German Finance Ministry, on a tip that they would find important Nazi documents in a local bank.[61]

The overall mission of the Counter-Intelligence Corps (CIC) was the investigation of espionage, sabotage, treason, and breaches of military security. As the war drew to a close in Europe, its responsibilities expanded to include detecting and apprehending Nazi officials and others involved in war crimes, as well as securing the capture of Nazi documents and records.[62] By the time that Master Sergeant Martin Dannenberg shipped out from Boston for Normandy in August 1944, he was a Special Agent-in-Charge (SAC) with the 203d CIC Detachment, attached to the III Corps in General George S. Patton's Third Army. In April 1945, the eighteen-man 203d, led by Major H. P. Wardwell, had dual reporting responsibilities: to Colonel Bernard J. Horner, who was in charge of the III Corps's intelligence section (G-2), and to the top people in CIC at Supreme Headquarters Allied Expeditionary Force (SHAEF) in Paris.[63] When CIC headquarters in Paris had orders for the 203d, they were funneled via Colonel Horner. Major Wardwell was both chief of the 203d and a member of Horner's staff in connection with CIC's investigative operations. In short, the CIC had two masters, one military and one political, motivated by different interests.

Late in 1944, Master Sergeant Frank Perls was restless, trying to get a commission as an officer. After a run-in with an executive officer in October, he was demoted to private for "inefficiency and conduct unbecoming an officer." A month after his commanding officer, Captain David Speer, backed him up, however, he was promoted to technical sergeant and, by February 1945 his original rank had been restored. A special agent who interviewed Frank in January reported that he would be "an invaluable asset to any CIC detachment"—he scored "excellent" on initiative, resourcefulness, and "aggressiveness and interest."[64] His commanding officer on Team 421 tried to retain Frank, and another officer recommended him for promotion to second lieutenant in the Military Intelligence Service, but both requests were denied.[65] Martin Dannenberg needed somebody who could speak and translate German fluently, and he was assigned Frank Perls.[66]

In January, Perls was transferred to the 203d CIC Detachment; as of February, he was running its interrogation center.[67] "I have been working for the last few weeks for the Counter-Intelligence Corps," Frank wrote his friend, the painter George Biddle, "and the CO has asked me to join his Detachment. There is a good chance for a commission and it's very interesting work. Unfortunately it's nothing I can write about, but I'll try to remember a few good stories."[68] The 203d Detachment that entered Germany early in February 1945, after the Battle of the Bulge, included SAC Dannenberg and Master Sergeant Perls.

Dannenberg and Perls shared German Jewish origins, though from different centuries, and each received a Bronze Star. Beyond that, however, they had little in common. Perls came from a cosmopolitan background of privilege and had traveled far and wide. Dannenberg had lived most of his life in one city, his formative experiences shaped by the Depression. Dannenberg set his sights on doing intelligence work during the war, had little trouble finding an entrée, and was satisfied with his assignment; Perls was in several army units and was frustrated by his inability to get a commission. Perls was larger than life: flamboyant, gregarious, entrepreneurial, a bon vivant and wheeler and dealer. His "natural showmanship," observed a CIC special agent, made him "an interrogator of unusual ability."[69]

By contrast, Dannenberg was slim and dapper, a self-contained and modest man who played it by the book. His training in intelligence made him wary of the press, careful not to draw attention to himself. Perls was just as much a mover and shaker in the constricted world of the military as he was in civilian life. He made contact with war correspondents, feeding them dramatically colorful stories that were prone to exaggeration.[70] He also wrote his own pieces for the American press and *Stars and Stripes* about the art scene in France.[71] The two men made an incongruous but complementary team: Dannenberg a disciplined and meticulous investigator, Perls fluent in German and French, an expert on forgeries and deception. Perls was knowledgeable about the terrain, Dannenberg about the inner workings of the military.

6.1 Master Sergeant Martin Dannenberg in Germany near the war's end, 1945. Dannenberg was Special Agent-in-Charge of the Counter-Intelligence Corps unit that retrieved the Nuremberg Laws.

Martin Dannenberg has lived his whole life in Baltimore: he was born there in 1915 and attended its public schools; he worked days and went to college at night, first as an undergraduate at Johns Hopkins and then law school at the University of Baltimore, without getting degrees. "I was a prodigious reader and partly self-educated," he says. His family's business collapsed in the 1930s and jobs were scarce. When he started working as a clerk at Sun Life Insurance Company in 1932, there were neighborhoods of the city that effectively barred Jews and African Americans from owning homes through the use of restrictive covenants.[72] Except for the three years, 1942 to 1945, that he was in the army, Dannenberg spent his whole career at Sun Life, working his way up from the bottom rung to Chairman of the Board in 1979.

Before joining the military in 1942, Dannenberg did some voluntary investigative work for the Office of Naval Intelligence, in which he hoped to enlist, but was turned down because of a problem with his vision. Through the suggestion of a local contact, he enlisted in the army in August and, two months later, was recruited into the recently formed Counter-Intelligence Corps. In September 1944, he shipped out to France, making it past German U-boats and destroyed freighters into Cherbourg's bombed-out harbor; it was "a horrible sight at night to see burning, sinking ships."[73]

In the weeks before Germany's surrender on May 9, 1945, events moved with chaotic speed. The responsibilities of the Counter-Intelligence Corps multiplied as they were called upon to interrogate suspected Nazis, track down saboteurs, and preserve documents relating to the Third Reich. Back home in the United States, prior to being shipped out in August 1944, the 203d unit had plenty of time to write long reports with fourteen carbon copies. "Once we got overseas," recalls Martin Dannenberg, "we made one copy, if we even wrote a report, which often there was rarely time to do."

It was almost by accident that Dannenberg's team found the Nuremberg Laws on April 27. Dannenberg, Perls, and Easy Pickens had been in Regensburg on an investigation to track down the commandant of the concentration camp at Dachau. They picked up a low-level civilian Nazi official who was trying to get back to his home near Eichstätt. "He told us," recalls Dannenberg, "that he had information about some important government documents and if we took him to his hometown, he would lead us to them. You could say that he gave us this information as a bribe because there were travel restrictions and German civilians weren't typically allowed to travel in military vehicles."

The Nazi official took the 203d CIC team to a farm outside the town of Eichstätt, south of Nuremberg and southwest of Regensburg, where his uncle, Hans Rauch, lived. The former official of the Finance Ministry and director of the Nuremberg office of the Reich Treasury was nowhere to be found until his wife was persuaded to lead them to a barn. "She rapped on the floor, a signal, and then a trap-door opened and Uncle Hans appeared," says Dannenberg. "It was like the

Phantom of the Opera! He had been hiding from the Gestapo, not us, because he had made some remarks about the war being lost. The Nazis didn't allow anyone to say that Germany was defeated. When he heard our car, he had hidden under the floorboards because he thought it might be the Gestapo."

6.2 The town square in Eichstätt, April 1945.

Rauch agreed to help the 203d retrieve the Nuremberg Laws, not that he was given any choice. He told them that he was not a Nazi at heart. "This was the stock story we heard all over Germany," says Dannenberg. "We joked about it: there was only one Nazi in Germany, Hitler, all the others were under duress." It took two keys to open the room in which the bank vault was located. Dannenberg was reluctant to blow open the door because the documents might be damaged. Hans Rauch had one key, and the other was with a retired German officer, an injured veteran of the Battle of Stalingrad.[74] The 203d picked up the major from a nearby farm and, late in the afternoon of April 27, the group made its way to the Bayerische Hypotheken- und Wechselbank, just off the town square of Eichstätt, now occupied by American tanks.

In the bank's vault the 203d found the original Nuremberg Laws, a photocopy of the Laws, and various pieces of correspondence, all inside a sealed envelope, embossed with Nazi insignia. "I took a knife and slit open the top of the envelope," recalls Dannenberg. "The pages of the Nuremberg decrees were there. Hitler's signature looked authentic to me. I knew it was an important document, but I asked Perls for his opinion. He said they were authentic: 'They're the reason my family had to flee Germany.'" To document the discovery, Dannenberg asked Special Agent Pickens to take a roll of pictures with "a tiny Minox spy camera," lit only by flashlights and a lantern. A few gloomy but decipherable photographs remain. In one, Dannenberg and Perls hold the documents and in another are the two pages of the "Law for the Protection of German Blood and Honor."[75]

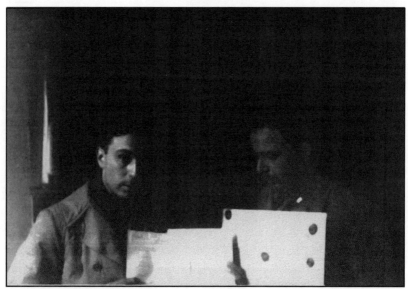

6.3 Martin Dannenberg and Frank Perls with Nuremberg Laws, retrieved from a bank in Eichstätt, April 27, 1945.

Also in the vault was a box wrapped in brown paper, which Rauch opened for the team. Inside were the family jewels of Count von Stauffenberg, who had been executed on July 20, 1944, for his part in the plot to assassinate Hitler.[76] According to Dannenberg, "None of the three of us actually touched the jewels. I suspected it might be booby-trapped. I told Perls to write a receipt statement that the jewels were replaced in the vault, and it named our three names. It was handwritten in German by Perls and signed by Rauch. I don't recall ever seeing it again." Perls claimed—no doubt a wild guess—that the jewels were worth two hundred and fifty thousand dollars.[77] Fifty-four years later, as they pondered whether to publicize their copy of the Nuremberg Laws, officials at the Huntington Library in Southern California would worry about the whereabouts of the jewels.

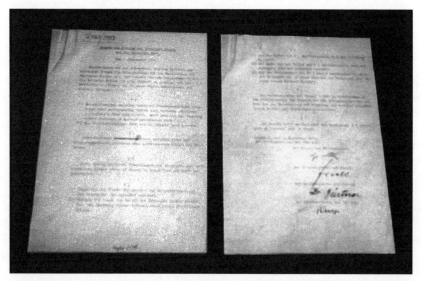

6.4 Photograph of Nuremberg Laws taken with "Minox spy camera," lit by flashlights and lantern.

▣ Chapter 7 ▣

Patton's Trophy

And so they are ever returning to us, the dead.

(W. G. Sebald, 1993)

THE IRONY OF FATE

Martin Dannenberg returned to Eichstätt that evening and kept the documents with him overnight in his room at the Hotel Traube, just across the town square from the CIC office in City Hall. On April 28, the day after the discovery, he took the packet down to breakfast to show to other members of the 203d who were stationed in Eichstätt. Later that morning, Dannenberg was in his office preparing to head over to the III Corps headquarters to transmit the Nuremberg Laws to Colonel Horner, Van Fleet's G-2. Major Wardwell came in with Joseph Driscoll, a correspondent for the *New York Herald Tribune*. "I remember this very clearly," says Dannenberg, "because normally intelligence personnel were forbidden to give interviews with the press." Given the significance of the discovery, Wardwell told Dannenberg that he was free to talk with Driscoll. The *Herald Tribune* reporter used the 203d's typewriter to write the story, sent it off to New York, and made a carbon copy for Dannenberg, which he kept. Dannenberg was not named for security reasons, but there was nothing to stop Perls from talking to the press.[1] When Frank's wife Sally read the story, she spread the word to the family about Dada's discovery. "Did you by any chance see this morning's N. Y. Herald Trib?" she wrote Frank's brother Tommy. "Your big brother has his name in the paper for a change, this time for 'capturing' the Nuernberg Code."[2]

There was no doubt in anybody's mind that this was an extraordinary discovery. "I've seen many things and have had a few interesting experiences which I wish I had the space to recount," Dannenberg wrote to his rabbi in Baltimore. "I have seen the products of Dachau and Buchenwald. I've talked to the head of the Polish extermination camp, who enthusiastically described the efficiency of this man-made inferno. I've visited many of the shrines of Nazism in Nürnberg and Munich. I've had in my hands the original draft and signed manifesto known as the Nürnberg Code. The irony of fate!" Rabbi Abraham Shusterman in turn spread

98

the "dramatic story" to his congregation that the former president of the Har Sinai Brotherhood in Baltimore had captured the "Nurnberg Code."[3]

When he returned home after the war, Dannenberg gave talks on his experiences in Germany, including his discovery of "this despicable document. Just six months ago in a little town near Munich, I saw with my own eyes the evil which derived from a document I had held in my hands just a few days prior. The town was Dachau, the exact place was the infamous concentration camp.... The document was the original paper signed by Adolf Hitler and other Nazi officials. We know it as the Nuremberg Laws," he told the Har Sinai congregation in October 1945. Dannenberg described the "debauchery of bestiality" that he had witnessed and asked, "How far from the age of savagery have we, the human race, really progressed? The greatest enemy of a decent world order," he concluded, "is in the minds and spirits of men—in their prejudice, their intolerance, their jingoism and bravado about their own nationalistic and racial virtues, their blindness to the world's interdependence, their failure to see that the welfare of any involves the welfare of all."[4]

Frank Perls was also eager to tell people back home about his exploits with the CIC. "Somehow a genial man this Eisenhower," he wrote George and Hélène Biddle. "Beat the German army to shreds, too. Beat the German Army. Period.... He abolished the Nurnberg laws in Germany. Perls found them.... Did you know that I found the original Nurnberg laws (Race, flag, citizen)? Patton got them."[5] Frank also let his former commanding officer know, "I found the original Nurnberg laws (in duplicate), signed by Adolf Hitler, Frick and Rudolf Hess and that Patton got them and I got nuttin ... as far as Army recognition goes."[6]

War correspondents covered the story in at least three countries. "General George S. Patton's army," reported the *New York Herald Tribune,* "which has swept up Reich art treasures, gold reserves and 600,000 German prisoners in its march across Hitlerland, collected today a real curio, 'The Law for the Safeguarding of German Blood and Honor,' the so-called Nuernberg Code, signed by Hitler to regularize Jewish persecutions. With fitting justice this remarkable document was uncovered by a German-born Jew, Sergeant Frank Perls, of Los Angeles, who joined the American Army after his father, said to have been the wealthiest art dealer in Germany, was compelled to flee from the Reich because of the Nuernberg laws of racial discrimination."[7]

A French magazine also wrote about the discovery. "As an art dealer and Jew, Frank Perls has two excellent reasons to concern himself with the existence of a document that caused the Israelites the strongest feelings since they learned about Moses' commandments."[8] And in England, "Original document discovered," reported the *Times.* "The original of the infamous anti-Jewish Nuremberg laws ... has fallen into the hands of the Third Army.... Appropriately, the document was handed over to a German-born Jew."[9]

After telling his story to the reporter from the *Herald Tribune* on April 28,

Dannenberg instructed Frank Perls to write a "memo of transmission" that would accompany the Nuremberg Laws up the chain of command. Perls wrote and signed a three-paragraph note that summarized the significance and provenance of the Nuremberg Laws, and commented on the discovery of a "sealed package" of the Stauffenberg family jewels.[10] Perls also made a quick, literal translation of the three laws. This memo and translation remained with the Nuremberg Laws on their journey to California and into the next century.

Later that day, accompanied by Major Wardwell, Dannenberg delivered the Nuremberg Laws to Colonel B. J. Horner, the G-2 of III Corps, whose offices at that time were located in an old beer hall in Beilngries, a few miles northeast of Eichstätt.[11] G-2's responsibilities included the seizure, examination, analysis, and disposal of captured enemy documents.[12] Master Sergeant Donald J. Johnson, who functioned as Horner's office manager and supervised administrative paperwork for G-2, remembers how excited Dannenberg was when he delivered the packet. "I recall vividly," Johnson wrote Dannenberg recently, "you telling me about the discovery of the Laws." Horner, however, says Dannenberg, "didn't seem to attach much importance to the find but nevertheless instructed me to report it to the document people in Paris," where SHAEF had its headquarters. "I don't believe Horner was too interested," confirms Don Johnson. "He was pretty wild those days and I am quite sure he was anti-Semitic. I had overheard some of his comments."[13]

Then on April 28, on Horner's orders Dannenberg took the Nuremberg packet over to the headquarters of III Corps and handed it to Colonel James Phillips, General Van Fleet's chief of staff. A day or two later—Dannenberg does not remember the exact date—Wardwell was ordered to take a sealed packet containing the Nuremberg Laws from Van Fleet to General Patton's headquarters. Dannenberg accompanied Wardwell to answer any possible questions about how the Laws were found. He waited outside while Wardwell gave them to a member of Patton's staff. "That was the last time I saw the documents," says Dannenberg. "I assumed that they were on their way to Paris where seized Nazi documents were being centralized for use in the expected trials of war criminals." Instead, they remained at Lucky Forward, Patton's headquarters in Erlangen, a few miles northwest of Nuremberg.[14]

WAR'S END

The war ended on a sour note for Frank Perls. He had gained a reputation in the CIC for getting SS troops and Nazi officials to talk, but his brash style put him at odds with some officers.[15] By June 1945, he was back as an interpreter with Military Intelligence, bored with "chasing after bloody Amtsleiters" (officials) and "screening factory workers," and resentful that he had been denied credit for his accomplishments. "After all the work I did for CIC, they did not even give me a letter of commendation," he wrote his former commanding officer.[16] He managed to get a CIC captain to give him a handwritten note that praised Perls's "unfailing enthusiasm and energy" and "fine work," but it did not do him any good.[17]

In July, citing his knowledge of art history and experience as an art dealer, and with the support of his commanding officer and the head of G-2, Perls put in his request for a promotion to second lieutenant and a transfer to the Arts and Monuments (A & M) Section of the Allied Military Government.[18] A month later, he received notice that his promotion had been provisionally approved on the merits, but was "on ice." He made one final effort to enlist the help of the officer who had encouraged his application several months earlier.[19] "CIC would like to keep me," he wrote his old boss, "but the work as an A & M man would certainly be of greater advantage to the Government at this stage of the game. After all, who wants to find Herr Hitler and write that complicated arrest report?"[20] When this plea failed, he left the army in September for the art world of Los Angeles.[21] He did not know then and never came to realize that three months earlier, General Patton had stashed the Nuremberg Laws at the Huntington in San Marino, a few miles away from Frank Perls's gallery on Sunset Boulevard.

At about the same time as Frank Perls was becoming frustrated by his inability to get a commission, General Patton was testing Eisenhower's patience for the last time. In early May, at war's end in Europe, Patton was put in charge of a huge section of Bavaria. There he was responsible for governing close to ten million people: seven million Germans, two million displaced persons, and the Third Army, a job for which he was emotionally, politically, and educationally unsuited.[22] Ladislas Farago argues that Eisenhower may have driven Patton over the edge by giving him an "impossible assignment.... He was set adrift in waters he could not possibly negotiate. It was a shabby payoff."[23]

Patton told a wide circle of friends that he was opposed to the demilitarization of Germany. He thought many Germans, even nominal Nazis, should be retained in important economic and political positions. "This non-fraternization is very stupid," he told his brother-in-law.[24] He was expected to be diplomatically cordial to his Russian counterparts, but he considered them "a scurvy race and simply savages. We could beat hell out of them," he wrote his wife on May 13, about one week into his new job.[25] In the complex postwar world of political realignment, Eisenhower regarded Patton as a liability and worried that his "crackpot actions" would generate bad publicity back home.[26] "SS means no more in Germany than being a Democrat in America," Patton told a press conference on May 8, as if to prove Eisenhower's point.[27]

Patton returned to the United States for a month's leave on June 4, ostensibly to whip up public support for war bonds. In reality, Truman and Eisenhower wanted him out of the limelight in Germany and were doing all they could to rein him in. Colonel Frank McCarthy, at that time General Marshall's executive officer—and many years later, the producer of *Patton*, which starred George C. Scott—warned his boss that Patton required "special attention" to make sure that his loose lips did not cause more trouble for the army.[28] In this atmosphere of uncertainty and tension about Patton's postwar role, Patton and General Jimmy Doolittle returned to Southern California to an extraordinary outpouring of public support.[29]

When the generals arrived in Los Angeles, a million "wildly cheering" people lined the streets and gave them a welcome "as genuine as it was tumultuous."[30] Patton was long used to this kind of adulation. "Never never never stop being ambitious," a young Georgie Patton had reminded himself in his diary. Patton was "compulsively driven," his grandson would later observe, "to exhibit visible personality in everything he did." As a cadet at the Virginia Military Institute in 1904, he was known to change his clothes more than ten times a day.[31] The conquering hero was in his element the evening of June 9, 1945, when he returned home: over one hundred thousand spectators crowded into the Memorial Coliseum for a spectacle that evoked the pomp, grandeur, and militarism of a Nuremberg Rally, but with Hollywood's razzmatazz. An explosion of aerial bombs greeted the generals' arrival. "I love that kind of war," Patton told the crowd after watching a mock tank battle, choreographed by Hollywood's Mervyn LeRoy, director of *Thirty Seconds over Tokyo*. With Jack Benny serving as master of ceremonies, Judy Garland sang "God Bless America," Carmen Miranda danced, Bette Davis recited a Patton poem ("God of Battles"), Edward G. Robinson delivered a Patton speech, and Margaret O'Brien read the Lord's Prayer, followed by the sounding of taps for fallen soldiers.[32]

The next day, Patton attended his childhood church in San Gabriel before leading a motorcade through the suburbs of Los Angeles. Everywhere he went, "the route was lined on both sides by cheering, expectant humanity," an expression of public gratitude for the end of the war in Europe. "If you don't know me," Patton told the crowd at City Hall in San Marino, "you're ignorant as hell. This is my part of the country."[33] Though he received some criticism for peppering his speeches with mild cursing and for urging young children at a Sunday school service to prepare for the next war, overall Patton was wary of the press and stuck to an uncontroversial script. "They are very fine fighting men," he responded when a reporter asked his opinion about the Russians.[34]

The day before he left Los Angeles, Patton made an unscheduled visit to the Huntington. There was no press entourage or publicity. Robert Millikan, Caltech's chairman and president of the Huntington's board of trustees, had sent Patton a polite letter inviting him to the Library "during your stay here, if you find the time and have the inclination to pay it a visit," but he was not expected to show up.[35] During Patton's visit to Los Angeles, Millikan and his wife "purred contentedly at home, having side-stepped all the big doings. All the big boys of the army have been showing off," Greta Millikan confided in her diary, "while Gen. Patton has been rushing our Southern Cal with sirens and motorcycles, Rose Bowl and

Coliseum blow-outs." On June 11, with little warning, Millikan and fellow trustee William Munro were "summoned to the Huntington" to host Patton's surprise visit.[36]

Patton was delighted to be back at the place where he had grown up. It reminded him of his close relationships with Edward Huntington and his father, the two men who shaped his military career. The general arrived with his wife Beatrice and sister Nita, with whom he had just stayed overnight in his childhood home. Patton walked around the Huntington's grounds, Millikan told his wife, "expansive, a little sentimental, confidential, protesting that he deserved little credit for his successes—that God used him to good purpose—the whole recital interlarded with profanity of a high order."[37] Confidential about what?

An important reason for Patton's visit to the Huntington was to hand over the Nuremberg Laws, which he had brought with him from Germany. It was the only item Patton deposited at the Huntington that he did not trust to the mail. Earlier in the year, Patton had been given an oversize, rococo copy of *Mein Kampf*, which he sent to the Huntington in memory of his father's association with the Library.[38] When he returned to Germany, he would send other materials to the Huntington by mail. But he made a point of personally delivering the Nuremberg Laws in their original envelope, which also included a photocopy of the Laws, supporting correspondence, and Frank Perls's transmittal memo and translations of the Laws into English.

THE IMPORTANT ONE

Is it possible that Patton and officials at the Huntington did not appreciate the historical significance of the Nuremberg Laws, as Huntington officials suggested in 1999? Robert Skotheim, the Huntington's president, was right to caution that we should not impose a contemporary sensibility on events of the 1940s, and that the framing of Nazi atrocities as "The Holocaust" did not take place until several years after World War II. "There was no holocaust history in 1945," said Skotheim, and the Nuremberg Laws had not yet achieved iconic status.[39] In general, this is reasonable advice, but in this specific case the evidence suggests that Patton, Millikan, and others at the Huntington on June 11, 1945, knew that they were participating in a momentous occasion. In the photograph documenting the transaction, the two great men—three if you include the portrait of George Washington—defer to the document as if in the presence of a holy relic.

As a self-made historian, Patton was knowledgeable about primary documents. "I have been a student of war since I was about seven years old," he told a reporter.[40] "Patton had a sense of the importance of the historical record," observes Hugh Cole.[41] By April 1945, word was out that Patton would appreciate receiving important Nazi documents and books. Joseph Stein, a lieutenant in the

Third Army, found a presentation tribute to the German Air Force, signed by Hermann Göring, which he forwarded to Patton's G-2 in the hope that "this might be a worthwhile addition to General Patton's Collection of Trophies."[42]

The original copy of the Nuremberg Laws was surely one of Patton's prized trophies. The media had widely and critically covered their passage in 1935, and the world press reported on their discovery in 1945 by Martin Dannenberg and his team. "This is the important one," Patton told Robert Millikan when they met at the Huntington on June 11.[43] Moreover, key members of the Huntington's board should have recognized the importance of these documents. Herbert Hoover, a Huntington trustee, was himself involved at that time in collecting Nazi documents for the Hoover War Library at Stanford. Later that year, he would receive direct reports about Patton's controversial status in the military from one of his assistants, Frank Mason.[44] Millikan read German (as did the Huntington's assistant secretary), had studied in Germany, was familiar with Nazi documents, and was well connected in Washington, D.C.[45]

Hoover and Millikan, in particular, were well informed about anti-Semitic policies under the Nazis. Hoover had gone on record in 1938 to express "my own indignation and to join in an expression of public protest at the treatment of the Jews in Germany.... It is still my belief that the German people if they could express themselves would not approve these acts against the Jews. But as they cannot express themselves it is the duty of men everywhere to express our indignation not alone at the suffering these men are imposing upon an innocent people but at the blow they are striking at civilization itself."[46] After the war, Hoover was actively involved in developing a plan for "settling the Palestine Question and providing ample Jewish refuge."[47] Robert Millikan also was finely attuned to issues involving German Jews. At Caltech in the 1920s, he had been enmeshed in the quota controversy regarding the appointment of Jewish scientists, and from 1933 to 1945 he served on the governing board of the General Committee of the Emergency Committee in Aid of Displaced Foreign Scholars.[48]

During the June 11 visit, presumably at Millikan's suggestion, Patton dictated an unsigned statement of two paragraphs "regarding document taken in Nuremberg." Millikan no doubt wanted a written account of how Patton came into possession of the Laws and an acknowledgement of ownership to protect the Huntington's interests, which as president of the board he carefully guarded. The statement was later transcribed by two Huntington secretaries and kept in the same packet as the Nuremberg Laws. The Huntington's photographer commemorated the event with images of Patton handing over the Nuremberg Laws to Millikan under General Washington's gaze; of Patton holding the ceremonial copy of *Mein Kampf* in front of a stone relief of his patron, Edward Huntington; and of Patton inspecting a display of *Mein Kampf* in the library.

The next day, Patton left for Washington, D.C., where he spent time with President Truman "as a couple of old soldiers reminiscing about the artillery and our men."[49] When he returned to Germany, he sent the Huntington a variety of documentary materials. He had told the Huntington on June 11 that he intended to use the Library as a temporary location for documents and books that he would ship to them from Germany. On July 31, for example, the Huntington's librarian informed Patton that two crates weighing one hundred and fifteen pounds had arrived. "When you were here recently," wrote Leslie Bliss, "you mentioned that you were sending to this Library two more boxes of captured German material but indicated that, at present at least, this material should be held in safe storage until you knew definitely what its ultimate destination would be. I can now report," Bliss wrote on July 31, "that the two boxes, one containing three important and interesting volumes of Nazi records, the other two ancient helmets, have arrived safely and are stored in our Rare Book Room pending further instructions from you."[50]

7.1 General Patton holds *Mein Kampf* in front of relief of his mentor, Edward Huntington, at Huntington Library, June 11, 1945.

Later in the summer, Patton decided to send materials to the Huntington concerning American military strategy in Europe, known as *After Action Reports*. "I do not wish to impose on your friendship, but I thought that perhaps the library might be interested in such documents," Patton wrote Bliss. "At the moment they are marked Top Secret by the War Department so that they could not be exhibited but this grading will be lowered so that within a year at most they will be available."[51] The Huntington, responded Bliss, "will be very happy indeed to receive and preserve for the future any of your manuscript material on World War II. We shall be honored to act as a depository for such interesting records of this great conflict, but even more glad to continue to receive material which adds to the personal history of such an old-time Californian as yourself."[52] When he forwarded the *After Action Reports* to the Huntington on September 11, Patton reminded Leslie Bliss "the books may not be put on display."[53]

The final communication between the Huntington and General Patton took place on October 31, when Leslie Bliss acknowledged receiving "the first copy of your *War as I Knew It* [Patton's war memoirs] and sundry other documents.... I am depositing all of this material in our Rare-Book Stack for safe keeping. We will scrupulously abide by your instructions," Bliss wrote, "not to make available any of this material for public inspection during your lifetime."[54]

As for the Nuremberg Laws, Patton for once decided to be prudent. Normally, he relished displaying his flamboyant persona and making unscripted comments in public. It must have been extraordinary difficult for him to resist showing off the Nuremberg Laws and authorizing release of the photographs taken at the Huntington. On this occasion, though, he did not talk to the media; he did not leave any official record; and he did not even comment in his personal diary. In June 1945, he was trying to avoid any kind of controversy that might get him into further trouble with Eisenhower.[55] The evidence is compelling, as we shall see, that he had looted the Nuremberg Laws in violation of explicit military orders. So he told Huntington officials, "it was his wish that these documents [Nuremberg Laws] should be preserved in the Huntington Library, but with no publicity about them," recalled trustee William Munro a few years later. Munro, along with Millikan, had met with Patton when he visited the Huntington on June 11, so he had direct information about Patton's intentions and instructions. "Accordingly," said Munro, "the papers were placed in our vault and no official record was made of the transaction."[56]

A few days after Patton's visit to the Huntington, Herbert Hoover, a member of the Huntington's five-person governing board, let Robert Millikan know that he was planning a visit to Pasadena early in July and would be available for a meeting of the trustees.[57] Millikan quickly convened a special meeting of the board to fit the ex-president's schedule. Hoover rarely attended meetings at the Huntington, but kept up a regular correspondence with Millikan, whose ideas on science and religion he appreciated.[58] On July 9, almost one month after Patton's visit to Los

Angeles, the Huntington's board of trustees met. Four out of five trustees were present: Hoover, Millikan, William Munro, and James Page—an ex-president, two academics, and a banker.[59] The budget for 1945–1946 was discussed and approved. A few other minor matters were on the agenda; an hour later, the formal meeting was over and lunch was served.[60]

7.2 Huntington board of trustees and Huntington staff break for lunch after meeting, July 9, 1945. Former President Herbert Hoover (third from the left) sits next to Robert Millikan (to his left).

The trustees had another opportunity to talk with Hoover that evening, when Greta Millikan hosted a dinner for the ex-president at Caltech's Athenaeum. "Mr. Hoover turned up rather unexpectedly for a trustees meeting," Mrs. Millikan noted in her diary. He was "pretty dour" and it took some maneuvering to bring him into the conversation. "He fears Russia but believes we must learn to get on with her. Our distinguished guest couldn't resist a feeble dig at the people who got us into this war, thereby reverting to his isolationism."[61] There was much for the Huntington trustees to discuss that day: What should be done about Patton's deposit of the Nuremberg Laws and other documents? How could it be established whether there was any proof of Patton's rightful ownership? Whatever was said about Patton's recent visit during the board meeting or at lunch and dinner, the participants left no formal or informal records of that discussion. The Huntington's only official documentation was a brief, four-line announcement in the 1944–1945 annual report, which acknowledged Patton's gift of *Mein Kampf*, but without reference to any other transactions or even to his visit on June 11.[62]

The trustees respected Patton's orders: they did not accession the Nuremberg Laws into the Huntington's collection or publicize their presence in the Library. Instead, they put the Nuremberg Laws, related materials, and the photograph of Patton and Millikan into storage, and waited for Patton's instructions regarding disposal of "certain documents" when he returned from his assignment in Europe.[63]

▣ Chapter 8 ▣

Outpost of Civilization

The heritage of fascist rule survives inside democracy as well as outside it.
(Paul Gilroy, 2000)

COMPANY VILLAGE

General Patton deposited the Nuremberg Laws at the Huntington out of sentimental loyalty to his father and patron, and because he could count on the board's discretion. In a small world built on connections and a personal style of leadership, trustees and administrators were trusted to be "tight-lipped" about internal matters, even with members of their own family.[1] Those who had direct knowledge about how the Huntington became guardian of the Nuremberg Laws in 1945 left a sparse paper trail. Also, it must have been reassuring for Patton to leave his trophy with a group of powerful men who shared similar views about the important issues of the day: the global threat of communism, the importance of close ties between government and the military, the dangerously liberal legacies of the New Deal, the need to keep a watchful eye on Jewish upward mobility, and the necessity of preserving Anglo-American society from racial contamination by African Americans, Mexicans, and Asians.

Between 1925, when it opened its doors to the public, and the 1970s, when institutional reforms finally occurred, the Huntington's governance, organizational milieu, and research program were conservative, isolationist, and proudly elitist. It was one of the last of Southern California's old-school ruling institutions to change. Central to its foundational assumptions was a racialized view of the world. When Edward Huntington started collecting in the grand manner in the latter part of the nineteenth century, he envisioned himself as a pioneer establishing a beachhead of "Anglo-American civilization" in the cultural wilderness of the West.[2] His generation of ruling families looked to the Old World, not to California's recent Mexican and Indian legacies, for models of aesthetic taste. The region's past had "little value," wrote John Hittell, a California booster, in 1882. "We have no ancient monuments or records." Before the Gold Rush, California was "beyond the thought and traffic of the refined and wealthy Caucasian communities," observed Hittell, but "suddenly a wonderful change occurred. Enlightenment took the place of savagism over a wide region."[3]

109

In the case of Edward Huntington, to be enlightened meant transplanting European treasures to Southern California, where they would mark the arrival of Civilization and anchor an origins myth in white supremacy. This fantasy of California as an outpost of Anglo-Saxon purity in the New World was contradicted by the realities of California's bloodlines, which, as Carey McWilliams pointed out, were a "triangular fusion" of Indian, Mexican-Spanish, and Anglo roots.[4] By the end of the nineteenth century—with the addition of ex-slaves from the South, Russians, Aleuts, Asians, and Southern Europeans, to name only a few of California's immigrants, and a long history of cross-cultural contact, intermarriage, and rape—there was little that remained of any biological purity, if it ever existed.

By the 1920s, the relatively diffuse and porous power structure of nineteenth-century Southern California had been "superseded by a long era of WASP exclusionism as once cosmopolitan Los Angeles became, culturally and demographically, the most nativist and fundamentalist of big cities."[5] Los Angeles was now predominantly white and Protestant, with a small but active Catholic presence. Out of a population of 1.2 million, thirty thousand Mexicans were second-class residents in their own city. Following the outbreak of bubonic plague in Los Angeles in 1924, government officials responded with a "ferocious campaign" of ethnic cleansing in Mexican neighborhoods.[6] The Jewish entrepreneurial pioneers of the previous generation—now barred from corporate boards, social clubs, and jobs in downtown law firms, banking, and insurance—were forced into their own segregated neighborhoods and economy for nearly thirty years until they eventually reemerged to compete for power.[7] Jews were not welcome in Pasadena, and Mexicans only as day laborers and servants.

Edward Huntington's vision of the West was shaped on the East Coast. His small-town roots went back to Oneonta in central New York State, where his parents owned a general store. On his mother's side, he was a descendant of theologian Jonathan Edwards, for whom he was named. On his father's side, he was related to Samuel Huntington, a signer of the Declaration of Independence and president of the Continental Congress for two years.[8] Perhaps Edward inherited his bookish and worldly predisposition from these ancestors, but his material ability to realize these interests came from his famous uncle, Collis Huntington, one of California's "Big Four." Together with Leland Stanford, Mark Hopkins, and Charles Crocker, Collis Huntington was the major entrepreneurial figure in the West's rapid economic development. In the 1860s, Collis was in the right place at the right time, quickly making his fortune as an owner of the Central Pacific and Southern Pacific railroads, and thus as a beneficiary of government land grants and subsidies.[9] Collis hired his favorite nephew, Edward, when he was a young man. By 1892, Edward was managing his uncle's financial interests in California; later he made his own fortune in street railroads and real estate.[10]

Edward benefited, economically and personally, from his uncle's death in

1900. Of Collis's fifty million dollar estate, his wife Arabella, known as Belle, received between twenty and twenty-five million dollars; his nephew's share was between twelve and fifteen million dollars.[11] Edward followed "the Huntington tradition," commented a popular historian: "he had continued to make money and to hold on to it. He had even surpassed his uncle and evolved a new method of accumulating capital: that of marrying it."[12] Divorced by his wife Mary in 1906 after six years without "marital relations," Edward went public with his relationship with Belle, his uncle's widow, with whom he was rumored to have had an affair for many years.[13] In 1913, Edward, now sixty-three, married Belle, "thereby reuniting the bulk of his uncle's fortune."[14]

In 1910, from his retirement at age sixty until his death in 1927, Edward Huntington devoted himself, purposefully and systematically, to buying up more than two hundred entire libraries, including some of the most important books and manuscripts in the world. "His agents," observed a popular historian, "made clean sweeps of the auction houses here and abroad."[15] It was, in the words of a Huntington scholar, "a carnival of extravagance."[16] In the early 1900s, Edward Huntington had bought some eight hundred acres of land in what is now San Marino, where he built a mansion conceived as "a residence around a library."[17] Edward wanted to live full-time in California, but Belle preferred their home in New York and their chateau near Versailles. Only upon her death in 1924 did she move permanently to the San Marino property, where she was interred—as was Edward three years later—in a huge mausoleum modeled after a Greek temple.[18]

Between 1911 and 1925, Huntington acquired several world-class trophies for the Library—medieval and Renaissance manuscripts, hand-written bibles, Shakespeare folios, presidential papers, and rare first editions of poetry and fiction.[19] "In fifteen years he had made his San Marino ranch one of the world's important storehouses of the literature and history of the English-speaking people," noted Oscar Lewis in 1938, "a magnet that draws scholars and research workers from every civilized country."[20]

Initially, Edward Huntington intended to leave his estate and collections to the County of Los Angeles, to be maintained as a public museum, park, and library. But his adviser George Ellery Hale, the well-known astronomer, was concerned that politicians lacking the necessary "judgment and taste" would take the Library in a leftist direction. Instead, he urged Huntington in 1914 to leave his collections to the Pasadena Music and Art Association, of which he was conveniently president.[21] The electoral gains of the Socialist Party in Los Angeles from 1909 to 1912 must have given Huntington cause to worry,[22] and by 1916 he had decided to set up a separate institution. Huntington's public-spiritedness had its limits. "I would discharge every agitator, and see to it that they never have another day's work with the Railway Company," he wrote his attorney William Dunn in 1918 when streetcar workers organized a strike.[23]

When Edward decided to incorporate San Marino in 1913—and thereby protect his property interests from Pasadena and other neighboring towns—George Patton, Sr., managed the deal and became the town's first mayor.[24] Huntington's decision in 1910 to import an oasis of highbrow civilization into the Golden State may have been based on the inspirational vision of the entrepreneurial Hale, but it was to George Patton, Sr. (and his other close friend, attorney Billy Dunn) that he looked for sensible advice.[25]

The Henry E. Huntington Library and Art Gallery was formally established in 1919 under the terms of a trust indenture, which established "a library, art gallery, museum and park." Its mission, citing an 1885 California statute, was to advance "learning, the arts and sciences, and to promote the public welfare."[26] Edward and Belle Huntington set up its first governing board of trustees in 1919, but public access was limited owing to Belle's bitter opposition to allowing outsiders onto the property.[27] The Huntington was eventually opened to the public in March 1925, after Belle's death. Edward lived long enough to see the California Senate pass a unanimous resolution expressing gratitude for "one of the most outstanding endowments of the century," and the appointment of historian Frederick Jackson Turner as the Huntington's first research associate.[28] By the time of his death in May 1927, Edward Huntington had invested about half his fortune in the land, buildings, collections, and endowment for his "monument" to art and learning. "No author in the future," commented a local journalist, "will dare to write English history until he has made the pilgrimage to the shrine on the hills of San Marino."[29]

The nonprofit status of the Huntington was later guaranteed in the state's constitution by a specific section that named the Library and Art Gallery as "exempt from taxation." Although it was bequeathed "to the people of the world for educational purposes," Huntington made sure that the private, nonprofit institution was firmly under the control of his family and friends, and would remain independent, insulated, and self-perpetuating.[30] He specified that the Library "shall not be merged or consolidated with any other institution."[31] The first board of trustees was composed of Edward's son Howard, his wife's son Archer Huntington, his two closest friends, Billy Dunn and George Patton, Sr., and George Hale. When Howard Huntington died in 1922, Edward replaced him with Henry Robinson, a director of Edison and president of the First National Bank, and an influential leader in the Los Angeles establishment.[32] In 1925, Dunn was replaced by Robert Millikan, the de facto president of the California Institute of Technology.

Millikan and Hale envisioned the Huntington not only as a repository of treasures, but also a world-class research institution devoted to demonstrating "the progress of our civilization." Museums of the late nineteenth and early twentieth century typically included displays that celebrated the contributions of industrial capitalism as evidence of the superiority of the West over "primitive peoples."[33] The Huntington also reflected the growing trend toward the "sacralization" of the arts—the sense, as Lawrence Levine observed, that "culture is something created by the few for the few, threatened by the many, and imperiled by democracy."[34] Hale recalled that de Tocqueville had once "described the American people as that portion of the British race whose duty it is to clear the forests of the New World, leaving the intellectual development of the race to be accomplished in Great Britain. The establishment in California of a research institution like the Huntington Library," continued Hale in a 1925 letter to George Patton, Sr., "shows how far America has encroached upon the duties of the Old World, but the long train of events leading up from colonial days to such great intellectual advances has never been recorded. The opportunity is unique."[35]

As a member of the first board of trustees, established in 1919, and its chairman from 1925 until his death in 1927, George Patton, Sr., shared this utopian vision. He was a Wilsonian Democrat with a romantic nostalgia for the "lost cause" of the Confederacy and a taste for antidemocratic politics. He brought up his son, the future general, in Lake Vineyard (now San Marino) with etchings of Robert E. Lee and Stonewall Jackson on the living room wall.[36] In his valedictory speech to the class of 1877 at the Virginia Military Institute, Patton, Sr., had decried the "ten years horror of Reconstruction" and longed for the days of "Old English Conservatism." Some twenty-five years later, as district attorney of Los Angeles he told the Sunset Club that he had never seen a slave in the South treated as badly as a plow horse in the North. "The immutable laws of Nature and God," he said, "as well as the monitory finger of history, all forbid any plan of reparation which shall in the slightest degree imperil the continued supremacy of our own race, or threaten the pollution of its Aryan blood."[37] In his unsuccessful race for the Senate in 1911, Patton affirmed that "here in California we occupy the position of the vanguard of Aryan civilization."[38]

Robert Millikan, who played a key role in the Huntington's formative years, was similarly attracted to California because it represented "the westernmost outpost of Nordic civilization." In 1924, he observed that "the present rapid growth of Southern California, the influx into it of a population which is twice as largely Anglo-Saxon as that existing in New York, Chicago, or any other great centers of this country, the preceding establishment of the Mount Wilson Observatory, the Huntington Library, and the California Institute, the geographical and climatic conditions all combine to make *this a time and this a place of exceptional opportunity*."[39]

Hale's blueprint for the Library as primarily a research institution was approved by Edward Huntington in October 1925 and incorporated into a revised trust indenture the following year.[40] There would be "a marked preference for British and American authors and artists" and "books, manuscripts, and pictures illustrating the intellectual development of the English-speaking peoples."[41] The collections should be reserved for use by "discriminating scholars, who alone are competent to use them for the advancement of knowledge," observed the Huntington's first research director in 1927. "However, public exhibitions in the Library and Art Gallery should be arranged as often as possible."[42] To protect the Huntington's independence, Hale included the provision that exhibits should be restricted to the Library. "In harmony with Mr. Huntington's wishes," books, manuscripts, and works of art should "never [be] loaned for use elsewhere."[43] Many years later, it would take considerable effort by reformers within the Huntington to change this no-loan clause.[44] "It was almost written into the California Constitution," says Anthony Bliss, whose father and grandfather worked at the Huntington, "that nothing could leave the grounds."[45]

The Huntington Library was a product of a highly centralized and monolithic municipal political system.[46] When Edward Huntington selected the Pasadena area in the 1900s to build his showcase palace, he could count on the support of Episcopalian bankers, volunteers from the Junior League, and a nepotistic ruling elite that knew how to preserve power. The white, Protestant enclave of San Marino, the site of the Library, was protected by racial covenants and buffered from Los Angeles by "sedate" Pasadena, where a mob burned down a Chinese laundry in 1885. It was a region known well into the twentieth century as the "paradise of the professional patriot and the red-baiter."[47]

Edward Huntington constructed his Library as a company village, with trusted confidantes on the board for life and carefully selected employees placed in positions of responsibility to guard institutional reputation. For most of its twentieth-century history, the Huntington was run like a private club: its founding members vetted new members on the basis of personal compatibility, a shared worldview, and institutional loyalty. In 1947, while searching for a new research director, Millikan looked for someone who would be a "good contact man for the Library." He was interested in one candidate who seemed "desirable from a personal standpoint," given his background as chief of counterespionage for the Office of Strategic Services in Europe. "He is said to have an attractive and also a wealthy wife."[48] High-level functionaries were expected to be discreet about internal matters, defend the Library's interests, and operate comfortably in the Huntington's rarified social milieu.

In the eighty-six years since the Huntington was incorporated in 1919, there have been only thirty-six trustees—in addition to Edward and Belle Huntington— serving on the five-member board. Until 1991, when the by-laws were amended to put limits on tenure, trustees served until death or resignation.[49] The five trustees who governed the Huntington at the time of Patton's visit spanned thirty-seven years of governance. Robert Millikan served on the board from 1925 to 1953; Herbert Hoover from 1936 to 1957; William Munro from 1937 to 1957; Edwin Hubble from 1938 to 1953; and James Page from 1945 to 1962.

The same kind of stability and continuity that marked the board was also characteristic of key staff members, even in recent years. In the seventy-eight years since Max Ferrand was hired to be in charge of research in 1927, the

Huntington has had only seven directors.[50] Leslie Bliss, the Huntington's first librarian, moved his whole family from New England to San Marino in 1920 when Edward Huntington decided to relocate his collection to the West Coast.[51] His son Carey Bliss was on staff for forty-six years, retiring in 1983 as curator of rare books.[52] Robert O. Schad, secretary of the board and curator of rare books, was with the Huntington for forty-four years until 1961.[53] When William Hertrich, superintendent of grounds, died in 1966, he had been associated with Edward Huntington, and then the Huntington, for over sixty years.[54] Mary Robertson, current chief curator of rare manuscripts, has worked at the Huntington for twenty-seven years since 1978, and Alan Jutzi, current chief curator of rare books, has been on staff for thirty-five years since 1970.

The Huntington's board was typical of Southern California's nepotistic and self-perpetuating elite during the first half of the twentieth century. Governed by a small clique that shared similar cultural tastes and politics, the board passed on the baton to their club buddies when an opening occurred. As Lewis Lapham observed of the American governing class in the 1950s, "everybody knew, more or less, everybody else."[55] Almost half of the Huntington's trustees have been corporate leaders, mostly executives in banking, oil, investment, utilities, and entertainment.[56] A significant number have been movers and shakers in the Republican Party, including a former president, Nixon's science advisor, the co-chairman of Nixon's Senate campaign committee, Reagan's attorney general and a member of his "kitchen cabinet," and friends of the Nixon family.[57] Even professionals on the board are well connected: five trustees were at one time associated with the most powerful law firm in Los Angeles—Gibson, Dunn and Crutcher;[58] and several academic trustees were power brokers, active in Washington, D.C., and military-related research.[59]

Influential, white, primarily Episcopalian and Presbyterian men dominated the board in the twentieth century. A woman was not appointed as trustee until 1991, ten years after the first Catholic, Robert Erburu, made it to the board.[60] There has never been an African American, Latino, American Indian, or Asian American either on the board or in any senior managerial or curatorial position. The first appointment of a woman to a top administrative position took place in 1989, and the first high-level administrator who is Jewish in 1996.[61]

TO HELL WITH THE PEOPLE

When General Patton visited the Huntington in June 1945 and strolled its gardens, chatting confidentially with Robert Millikan, he was no doubt comforted by nostalgic memories of his childhood. But the two men also saw eye to eye on many international and domestic issues.

The prevailing view of Patton shared by military historians is that he became psychologically derailed at the end of the war, his vitriolic outbursts against Jews rooted in "a severe case of burnout."[62] Martin Blumenson, for example, suggests that his increasingly bizarre behavior was the result of a lifetime of physical injuries, wartime stress, and disappointment at the end of the war.[63] The political positions Patton professed about world affairs in 1945, so it is argued, were at odds with his long career as a professional, apolitical soldier. He himself claimed that he had never even registered to vote, much less voted, and that a postwar political career did not interest him, despite efforts by right-wing supporters to float his name as Secretary of War and recruit him to run for Congress.[64]

This assessment, however, underestimates Patton's longstanding right-wing ideology and his self-identity as a public figure who regularly took strong positions on controversial issues. His hostile attitude to Jews—no doubt exacerbated by the war—was embedded in a lifetime of racial experiences, and went far beyond the genteel anti-Semitism of his social circle. If he had lived beyond the war, he would likely have followed the pattern of many former high-ranking officers who joined corporate boards, became cabinet members and ambassadors, and repositioned themselves as Cold War warriors.[65] Throughout his life, he consistently expressed white supremacist views, distrusted democratic institutions, and was attracted to fascist ideas.

Patton's personal bigotry was not simply an irrational psychological phenomenon, but an expression of a coherent set of beliefs. He identified with the South's perspective on the Civil War and shared his father's antipathy to Reconstruction. In the 1910s, he advocated imperialist ventures in Mexico. "If we take the country," he wrote his father, "we could settle it and these people would be happier and better off."[66] In the 1930s, concerned about the independence movement in Hawaii, he proposed imprisonment of leftists.[67] In 1942, in response to a letter from a childhood friend, who wanted to work in the internment camps with Japanese Americans, Patton replied: "I am unable to be of any assistance to you, because it is my firm conviction that I would be unpatriotic if I aided anyone in bringing aid and comfort to my country's enemies."[68]

Robert Patton comes close to the mark when he describes his grandfather's politics as "a sort of reactionary royalism."[69] By 1902, not yet seventeen years old, Georgie Patton, Jr., had already decided on a career in the military. The fastest track to success as an officer was the Military Academy at West Point, but access was difficult and highly competitive, with only one hundred and fifty cadets admitted each year. Georgie had trouble getting admitted due to his erratic academic record and ended up spending his first year at the Virginia Military Institute, which his father and grandfather had attended. Eventually, with Edward Huntington's help, George Patton, Sr., was successful in getting his son transferred to West Point as California Senator Thomas R. Bard's appointee for 1904.[70]

Georgie grew up with Mexican servants at home; black maids waited on him at the Virginia Military Institute. He was guaranteed a lifetime of luxury when he married Beatrice Banning Ayer in 1910: his considerably wealthier father-in-law, Frederick Ayer, put him on the family payroll and subsidized a coddled military career, complete with traveling servants, a stable of horses, and all the trappings of minor aristocracy.[71] A Chinese cook prepared his meals and a faithful Negro orderly pressed his uniforms and dressed him in the 1940s.[72]

To historian Edward Linenthal, Patton was "a modern warrior in the old berserker tradition, highly conscious of his role as a high priest of battle."[73] Patton's penchant for the Confederacy and his southern pedigree tend to underline this interpretation.[74] Yet Patton was very much a modern man of the twentieth century, as well as an ideologue with deeply felt and long-held convictions.[75] His politics were shaped by a variety of cultural and social forces: a romantic affinity with the "lost cause" and his father's legacy as a Wilsonian Democrat; the settler ideology of Southern California, with its emphasis on clearing a "wilderness" for "civilization"; the schooling and social status of a privileged elite; and a lifetime career as an officer in a segregated military.

Patton straddled both centuries as a nineteenth-century warrior and a twentieth-century strategist in a rising imperialist nation. From the past came his belief in a military code based on notions of honor and chivalry. From modernity came antidemocratic ideas about defending the race from degeneracy, reinforced by fascist interpretations of nationalism and the dangers of communism, all wrapped up in religious mysticism and prophecy. His stagecraft, profanity-laced speeches, and availability to the press were rooted in an appreciation of the visual uses of propaganda and twentieth-century advertising techniques.

By the time he was in his late twenties, Patton had articulated his own political views and what would become a lifelong hatred of the Left. "Only in epochs where the state is dominent has [sic] men advanced," he wrote his father in 1916. "Individual man has habitually failed to run himself for himself. He must be run. Germany has the only true idea. The few must run the many for the latters [sic] good. To Hell with the people."[76] He supported his father's run for the Senate as a Democrat, but despised Woodrow Wilson for delaying the country's involvement in World War I. The president, he advised his father, "has not the soul of a louse nor the mind of a worm. Or the back bone of a jelly fish."[77]

His first published poem derided the "cowards born of Fear and Greed," who had "crooned to the tigers of ethical right, / Or had begged of the wolves fair play." To Patton, pacifists "do not dare admit the truth, / Though writ in letters red, / That man shall triumph now as then / By blood, which man has shed."[78] While on his first tour of Hawaii in 1926, he lectured his troops on the dangers posed by "sexless" pacifists for whom "the history of the race from the fierce struggles in primordial slime to the present day is a blank."[79]

Patton had an opportunity to put his ideas into practice in 1932, when he showed Chief of Staff Douglas McArthur and President Hoover—soon to become a Huntington trustee—that he could be counted on to lead his cavalry regiment against fellow World War I veterans, encamped in Washington, D.C., to demand their benefits. Patton believed that the Bonus Marchers had been stirred up by communists and revolutionaries, and had crossed the line from protest to insurrection. He took pleasure in leading the charge and "had some nice work at close range" as he waded into the crowd—"sabers rose and fell with a comforting smack," he noted in his diary.[80] A few months later, he prepared a manual for "Federal Troops in Domestic Disturbances," based on his experiences against the Bonus Marchers. In this "savage document," to use Martin Blumenson's description, he advocates preemptive strikes. "If they are running, a few good wounds in the buttocks will encourage them. If they resist, they must be killed." If you hear that leaders are gathering for a meeting, "a night raid ... will be most useful—no prisoners should be taken." Military discipline, observed Patton, was the key to maintaining social order. "The success of the Bolsheviki in 1917 was due wholly to the hesitating and weak character of the Russian officers." In post–World War I Germany, on the other hand, a resolute army defeated a revolutionary insurrection.[81]

A year after Patton helped to rout the Bonus Marchers, the Nazis came to power in Germany. On his second tour of Hawaii in 1934, Patton bought his own English translation of *Mein Kampf*, which he annotated. He underlined Hitler's ridicule of Parliamentary rule: "a Majority can never be a substitute for the Man ... a hundred fools do not make one wise man, an heroic decision is not likely to come from a hundred cowards." And he marked Hitler's assertion that "it is not the aim of our present-day Democracy to form an assemblage of wise men but rather to collect ... a crowd of subservient nonentities who can easily be led."[82]

Patton's reputation as a soldier's soldier and man of the people derived from his management style and public relations image as a rough diamond, not from his politics, which were consistently authoritarian and antidemocratic. In the 1940s, he ridiculed the "just plain foolish liberals," who supported Roosevelt, and told his nephew that the country needed to be on guard against "subversive bastards" and the "low-class slime" that are trying to "wreck this country from the inside."[83]

IN THEIR PROPER PLACE

Issues of race formed the core of Patton's beliefs. During World War I, he was attended by a Dr. Greenbourg—"a nice little Jew who was careful not to hurt"— when Patton was injured and needed medical attention.[84] Years later, he hired a Jewish tutor to help his son prepare for West Point examinations, and Jews served on his staff in the military, including Oscar Koch, his intelligence officer.[85] He was very much at ease with African Americans, Asians, Mexicans, and Jews, as long as they were in their proper place, subordinate and loyal.[86]

On his father's side, Georgie's great-grandmother had lost two sons in the

Civil War and had a "relentless loathing for Yankees." His grandmother, who lived in Virginia with her husband and slaves, had been "raised to view blacks as furniture," notes Patton's grandson. His grandfather on his mother's side, Benjamin D. Wilson, also from the South, was a self-made man, making his fortune as a fur trapper and adventurer in the Indian wars and the war against Mexico. He married the daughter of a Mexican land baron, who died at age twenty-one, and reinvented himself as Don Benito, eventually owning some twenty thousand acres of land in and around Los Angeles. His second wife, Margaret Hereford, was Georgie Patton's mother. She, too, had strong ties to the Confederate South.[87]

Patton did not just passively receive Confederate values from his parents, but actively embraced and made them his own, reshaping them to meet the exigencies of manifest destiny. In 1915, he was so impressed by the racist movie *Birth of a Nation*—"it was finer than anything he had ever seen"—that he went back a second time with his wife and then read the book, *The Clansman*, on which it was based.[88] In 1920, Georgie and his father visited the Virginia grave of his Confederate relatives who had died during the Civil War. Years later, he would take his daughter Ruth Ellen to see Robert E. Lee's grave, where he bought her a small Confederate flag as a souvenir and proudly told her, "You're so unreconstructed."[89]

When he was assigned to the Eighth Cavalry Regiment under "Nigger Jack" Pershing in 1915, Patton readily accommodated to the rough-and-ready racism of the Texas border.[90] He was on good terms with Colonel Sterling of the Texas Rangers, who bragged to Georgie that he had killed thirty-five people, "not counting niggers and Mexicans."[91] He was taken with Dave Allison, a local marshal who "kills several mexicans each month," he wrote his wife.[92] He also took time to let his Aunt Nannie know about another Texan who told him, "Damn it, a fellow took me for a Mex and I had to shoot him three times before he believed I was white."[93] When Patton killed two Mexican soldiers in 1916, he celebrated by cutting notches in the grip of his ivory-handled revolver, strapped the dead men to the hoods of cars like deer, and drove back to camp. "You are probably wondering if my conscience hurts me for killing a man," he wrote his wife. "It does not. I feel about it just as I did when I got my [first] sword fish, surprised at my luck."[94]

Patton grew up in a family that used racial and ethnic epithets in everyday conversation.[95] When Georgie was a student at Virginia Military Institute, his sister Nita wrote him, "How do you like all the negras, they must be very funny?"[96] In a letter written to his mother in 1909, he described kissing Beatrice Ayer, his future wife, in New York and "shocking all the niggers at the hotel."[97] In 1927, he recalled a story his father told about "being approached by a nigger boy selling peaches."[98] Later in life, General Patton was more careful about what he said in public, but his attitudes did not change. In 1930, he told his younger daughter about a Jewish West Pointer who had fought bravely during World War I, thus proving that the Military Academy could make something of even "a dirty little Jew."[99] While stationed in Hawaii, he dismissed the locals as "brown-skinned inferiors there to serve drinks and mow the polo field." And when he got mean drunk, as he often did during his time in Hawaii, he would rant on about his wife's Polynesian "nigger" friends.[100] As late as 1943, he felt comfortable writing to his wife about a visit to the dentist, followed by an anecdote about a "nigger prisoner."[101] He remained convinced during the war that "a colored soldier cannot think fast enough to fight in armor."[102]

During the course of World War II, Patton sharpened his racial taxonomy. "The quiet dignity of the Arab" was the result of "pure dumbness."[103] The Arabs in Tunisia were "lower—if this is possible—than the Arabs in Morocco."[104] The Germans were a "good race" compared to the Russians, whom he regarded as "recently civilized Mongolian savages" with "devious Oriental minds."[105] These views were shared with and reciprocated by his wife and close friends. In a letter to her husband in 1943, Beatrice described an acquaintance as "an objectionable little Jew, with a strong accent."[106] Her half-brother Charles fuelled Patton's prejudices about Jews with his own belief in the *Protocols of the Elders of Zion*,[107] while her brother Fred, the FBI agent, swapped horror stories about communism with him.[108] "The more I see of Arabs the less I think of them," Patton wrote Fred in 1943. "By having studied them a great deal I have found out the trouble. They are a mixture of all the bad races on earth.... In addition, at all times, there has been a negro infiltration so that the Arab is really something. I am getting so that they have the same effect on me as a toad."[109]

回 Chapter 9 回

White Man's Burden

In conserving our Nordic blood, we are discharging a great world responsibility.

(C. M. Goethe, 1928)

TOO MUCH DEMOCRACY

I kept a book on my desk for several weeks, since I needed to read it for this project. I procrastinated, not because I was too busy with other tasks, but because I knew it would be a discomforting experience. It addresses painful issues of memory and public history. Finally, while working on the Patton chapter, I opened it up. The book is gorgeous in appearance — thick velvety paper, an elegant typeface based on a fifteenth-century design, and stunning sepia photographic reproductions. Its subject is lynching photographs. I find it difficult to look at for more than a few pages at a time. It is the work of James Allen, who started collecting these photographs when he realized that many of them are actually postcards that people bought to keep as a souvenir of a memorable day's outing or to send to their uncle Bill or girlfriend Sally with messages of the "wish you were here" variety. "In America," Allen comments, "everything is for sale, even a national shame."[1]

The murdered people in *Without Sanctuary* are mostly African Americans: their bludgeoned, burned, naked, castrated, lonely bodies on humiliating display, which is the point of a lynching. Here, too, is the "jew" Leo Frank, who was hung in 1915 by a mob in Marietta, Georgia, the site of his death and the resurrection of the Ku Klux Klan. Frank was convicted in a show trial for raping and murdering a young girl who worked in his factory. His case was not unlike that of Leo Katzenberger, arrested in 1942 in Nuremberg on trumped-up charges of sexual transgressions. Both of these men were accused of violating blood laws, both were executed after a sham trial, and both were posthumously pardoned.[2]

Reading Patton's racial ranting is like looking at postcards of lynching: his vitriolic honesty is unsettling. Maybe because he was writing in his diary and personal correspondence, he felt no compunction about spewing out his darkest fantasies like a man suffering from Tourette's syndrome. But it would be a mistake to regard his views about race as only a private matter. If there had been time during his visit to California to convene a seminar on the race question at the Huntington or Caltech, there would have been more agreement than disagreement around the table. Patton's crude style and bluster might have offended some academics, but not the content of his ideas.

He would have received a respectful hearing from Robert Millikan, the Huntington's top man and Caltech scientist; from philanthropist Charles Goethe, who helped to finance the Human Betterment Foundation; from its former executive director Paul Popenoe, who made a national name for himself in marriage counseling after World War II; and from well-known academic Robert Cleland, who was hired at the Huntington in the early 1940s to shape the study of California's history.

These men of influence did not agree on everything. Patton was suspicious of international bodies such as the United Nations, while Millikan was supportive. Goethe was so preoccupied with getting Nordics to worry more about "race consciousness" than about "race prejudice" that it became an obsession.[3] Patton supported internment of Japanese Americans; Millikan was initially opposed. But they shared similar beliefs about the inheritance of racial traits and the hierarchy of racial groups; similar concerns about the dangers of miscegenation, integration, and government efforts to rectify social inequality; and they would have agreed that too much democracy was a dangerous thing. I can also imagine them in 1934 shaking their heads in agreement as they read an item in the U.S.-published *Eugenical News*, reprinted from the Nazi press, about how "large German cities" were being "literally swamped by ... Jewish physicians."[4]

Robert Millikan left the University of Chicago and arrived in Pasadena in 1921 to become chairman of Caltech's Executive Council. Two years later, he received the Nobel Prize in physics. He joined the Huntington's board of trustees in 1925 and was its chairman from 1938 until his death in 1953. The last surviving member of a group of trustees appointed by Edward Huntington, Millikan was a hands-on executive, who busied himself in the day-to-day details of the Library. "Hardly a Saturday passed that did not see him counseling at the institution upon some current problem."[5] As a public intellectual involved in shaping national military policies and an indefatigable entrepreneur, he moved easily between the worlds of business, government, and academia.

Millikan's ideology was shaped by his father's conservative theology and the politics of Midwestern, conservative Republicanism. A Taft Republican in 1912 and later an informal adviser to Herbert Hoover, Millikan was scornful of government efforts to redistribute wealth. Social engineering, he told *Science* magazine in 1919, was better left to private philanthropy, while progress depended on the "creation of wealth," with "the scientist [as] merely the scout, the explorer, who is sent on ahead to discover and open up new leads to nature's gold."[6] Between 1913 and 1931, Millikan was on AT&T's payroll, with a consultant's annual retainer.[7]

On issues concerning welfare and economic redistribution, Millikan had much in common with Paul Popenoe, who claimed a federally guaranteed minimum wage and old-age pensions were "dysgenic," in the sense that they interfered with natural selection and cultivated "the increase of the inferior part of the population at the expense of the superior."[8] The circle around the Human Betterment Foundation typically linked welfare with immigration. "Relief," complained Charles Goethe in 1935, "goes overwhelmingly to alien morons."[9]

On important issues of the day, Millikan could count on the support of like-minded Huntington trustees, such as Archer Huntington and Herbert Hoover, who shared his concern about the "trend to the left" in the West.[10] Millikan campaigned against federal regulation of private enterprise, and was a fanatical opponent of federal funding of education, which he regarded as "the most ominous tendency toward totalitarianism in the United States that is now on the horizon." If unchecked, this trend, he told a representative of the National Association of Manufacturers in 1943, would lead the country into a "spectacle of indoctrination."[11]

Millikan's antipathy to federal funding did not extend to military research, which he pursued with extraordinary success. By 1919, he already had a track record of mobilizing scientists "in aid of the war."[12] Defense research, he told a military gathering in 1934, should be "a peace-time ... and not a war-time thing."[13] During World War II, Millikan secured government funding for Caltech's rocket project, which grew from a $200,000 grant in 1941 to an $80 million war industry three years later, with nearly five thousand people on the university's payroll. An assembly line plant just outside Pasadena produced over one million rockets. "Caltech literally became a branch of the Bureau of Ordnance," recalled physicist William Fowler.[14] Over in Europe, General Patton used Caltech's rockets against German battalions. "The new shell with the funny fuse is devastating," Patton observed in 1944,[15] a few months before he would meet Millikan for the first time during his visit to the Huntington. In 1945, the War Department thanked Millikan for the role that Caltech had played in the Manhattan Project. "No one outside the project," wrote Major General Groves, "can ever really know how much we depended on your people" to build the atomic bombs that were dropped on Hiroshima and Nagasaki.[16]

On international issues, Millikan opposed isolationist policies that were popular in conservative political circles and campaigned for an American presence in the world, including early intervention in World War II, measures to contain the spread of Soviet influence, and support for the United Nations.[17] On domestic issues, he lined up with the anticommunist Right. He kept his distance from Thomas Mann during the writer's visit to Los Angeles in 1938 because "his influence has all been cast on the communist side.... Of all the fundamentally fallacious reasoning," Millikan wrote the president of Occidental College, "that has been the most disastrous in turning back the wheels of our social progress."[18] Millikan resigned from the American Committee for Democracy and Intellectual Freedom because it was not sufficiently vigilant against Nazi and Communist agents who were "infiltrating into all the organizations which they think they can capture."[19] And he endorsed the Americanism Educational League's efforts to expose "the evils of communism."[20]

Millikan advocated reconciliation between religion and science, but preached against the dangers of modern literature, with its "emotional, destructive, over-sexed, neurotic influences."[21] To Millikan, the Roosevelt administration represented the slippery slope to communism. "We are now living under the most reactionary government this country has ever known," he told a gathering of the Los Angeles Bar Association in 1936.[22] He remained a staunch, right-wing Republican all his life: a crusader against social security and federally funded education;[23] an activist ideologue in the Cold War, lending his support to the Chiang Kai-shek regime in China;[24] and a public supporter of Richard Nixon's 1950 Senate campaign.[25]

With heroes that included George Westinghouse, Booker T. Washington, and Theodore Roosevelt, Millikan thought that democracy worked best when it was left in the hands of powerful, benevolent men.[26] In this respect he echoed the earlier views of Paul Popenoe who, with co-author Roswell Johnson, believed that good government is best served by an "aristo-democracy," administered by experts who recognize that "poverty is in many ways eugenic in its effect."[27]

Millikan's antidemocratic tendencies were most apparent around issues of race. He ideological assumptions were the same as those that guided the Nuremberg Laws: a belief in the existence of distinct biological races; a commitment to the superiority of "Anglo-Saxon" stock as the bedrock of modernity;[28] and a defense of policies of segregation and apartheid. "Look at the difference between our own civilization and the static civilizations of Asia," he observed in 1924, "where Nirvana is the goal of human life and a large fraction of the population reaches it quickly through starvation. Why is it that 'fifty years of Europe is better than a cycle of Cathay'? Is it not simply because in certain sections of the world, primarily those inhabited by the Nordic race, a certain set of ideas have [sic] got a start in men's minds, the ideas of progress and of responsibility."[29]

Although more careful in his public pronouncements than was Charles Goethe and more prudent than General Patton, Millikan maintained a belief in the inferiority of colonized peoples around the world and of African Americans at home. "I am sitting down in the Santa Fe station in Chicago," he wrote his wife and children in 1925, "surrounded with Coons and many other kinds of colored elegance."[30] Next year, traveling through the Panama Canal on his way to the Guggenheim mines in Bolivia, he credited the American presence with cleaning up "a hell hole of disease and filth…. In a word it's 'the white man's burden' with a vengeance."[31] A few days later, stopping in Peru, he was disgusted by the sight of "the filthiest indians you ever dreamed of," their degeneracy evident in the unwillingness of the women "to make themselves attractive even in crude ways."[32]

Millikan's personal views on race in the 1920s were quite consistent with the publicly expressed ideas of intellectuals such as Paul Popenoe, a frankly outspoken supporter of white supremacy. Differences in "racial temperament" between Negroes and whites, asserted Popenoe, are based on constitutional, inherited tendencies. How else can we explain why the "Negro race in Africa has never, by its own initiative, risen much above barbarism." Or why Negroes "when placed side by side with the white race … fails to come up to their standard, or indeed to come anywhere near it." Is there any other conclusion, asked Popenoe, other than "the Negro lacks in his germ-plasm excellence of some qualities which the white race possess, and which are essential for success in competition with the civilizations of the white races at the present day?"[33]

Popenoe's call for maintenance of "the color line" and legal sanctions against "miscegenation" was backed up by his belief that Negroes were not only "eugenically inferior," but also characterized by sexual impulsiveness and weak inhibitions.[34] He advocated a similar policing of the nation's borders against immigrants from eastern and southern Europe, who threatened to pollute the country with the "evil of crossbreeding."[35] Discussing the dangers posed by the unregulated birthrate of African Americans, Popenoe had a simple solution: use them as fodder in war. "One sees that in many nations there are certain races which are more valuable on the firing line than in industries at the rear; and it appears that they should play the part for which they are best fitted…. In the United States are millions of negroes who are of less value than white men in organized industry but almost as valuable as the whites, when properly led, at the front."[36]

Millikan clung to his prejudices about race throughout his life, his views unchanged by the democratic movements sweeping the globe after World War II. "You yourself will surely agree with me," he wrote Henry Luce, publisher of *Life*, in 1946, "that the only countries in the world that have yet risen to the degree of education in which constitutional, representative governments—improperly called 'democracies'—can exist, are the Anglo-Saxon and Scandinavian countries, Holland and Switzerland." Millikan doubted whether France should be included in this prestigious company. "But the rest of the world is and must be handled by something that approaches dictatorship in the present state of the world's development."[37]

Back home, Millikan regarded the enfranchisement of African Americans to be as dangerous and ill-advised as the end of British rule in India.[38] Visiting Mississippi in 1951, he was alarmed to find that "more than half of the population in this state is made up of negroes—a very serious situation. For it means that under universal suffrage they could *control* the state now, an unthinkable disaster in view of the sort of people they now are. This is one vital reason," he told his wife, "why the race problem should be left to the states and their local communities and kept out of national politics."[39] Perhaps Millikan's opposition to racial equality left its mark on Caltech's resistance to recruiting African American students and faculty.[40]

Greta Millikan shared her husband's angst about racial equality. A few years earlier she had raised her "feeble voice" at a meeting of the Pasadena Red Cross board to oppose a "crusading member," who had been "raising the roof to get a negro on the board.... A negro to represent negroes or any other minority group I opposed," she noted in her diary. "Thru persistent nagging, the above mentioned member succeeded in getting the board enlarged by one and then nominated her pet negro. We do face a real problem with negro communities replacing Japs."[41]

On the "Japanese Problem" during World War II, Millikan took a more complicated, but ultimately opportunistic position. In 1942, he spoke out against "hysterical" proposals to put all Japanese Americans in "concentration camps." To do this, he told Pasadena's Chamber of Commerce, would disrupt the production of food and generate "resentment because of unfair treatment of loyal American citizens."[42] The following year he joined the Pacific Coast Committee on American Principles and Fair Play, organized by Berkeley's President Robert Sproul to "defend the liberties of law-abiding persons of Oriental ancestry." But once the government made the decision to "relocate" Japanese residents on the basis of "military necessity," the Committee "dropped immediately the important questions it had been raising."[43]

In 1943, Millikan told counsel for an Assembly committee investigating the dangers of treason that he favored dispersal throughout the country of California's Japanese at the end of the war.[44] In 1944, in his introduction to a speech by the director of the War Relocation Authority at a crowded public event in Pasadena's Public Library, he emphasized that the Pacific Coast Committee was committed to preserving the Bill of Rights, not "coddling the Japanese."[45] After the war ended, Millikan did not hesitate to turn over to military intelligence the names and known addresses of all students of Japanese background who had studied at Caltech between 1929 and 1944.[46]

As to the Jewish Question, Robert Millikan was finely attuned to the prevailing anti-Semitism in academia prior to World War II. His personal distrust and dislike of Jews clashed with his self-interest in aggrandizing Caltech into a scientific powerhouse. In 1921, he hired Paul Epstein—"even though a Jew"—but turned down another physicist at the same time—"alas another Jew!!... We can't get more than about one Jew anyway!"[47] In 1929, Robert Oppenheimer, the son of German Jews, took up a joint appointment at Caltech and Berkeley.[48] And in the early 1930s, Millikan welcomed Albert Einstein as a visiting professor, despite his distaste for Einstein's pacifist politics, critique of capitalist exploitation of science, and outspoken support for "emancipation of the soul of the minority."[49] He regarded Einstein as a "child-like sort," who had been exploited by "the Charlie Chaplin type" and the "Upton Sinclair type."[50] By the 1930s, Jews were well represented in the doctoral programs of nationwide physics departments where, according to historian Daniel Kevles, "achievement was usually clear-cut, [and] talent and brilliance could make their way."[51] Millikan recruited Jewish physicists to Caltech, but he kept count and observed a quota.[52]

From 1933 to 1945, Millikan served on the governing board of the General Committee of the Emergency Committee in Aid of Displaced Foreign Scholars. He was kept well informed about the crisis facing Jewish intellectuals in Nazi-controlled countries, though not one of the six hundred and thirteen academic refugees seeking help in the United States ended up at Caltech.[53] Millikan shared the perverse reasoning of Ray Lyman Wilbur, Stanford's president, that making special allowances for Jewish intellectuals might only "increase anti-Semitism." After all, noted Wilbur in a letter to his fellow administrators a few months before war was declared, "we must recognize the fact that we cannot let any one nation adopt a policy by which it disgorges large numbers of its citizens on other nations."[54] Millikan remained politely supportive of the Emergency Committee, but did nothing to offer practical help. When its chairman Stephen Duggan wrote to him in 1942, asking for a personal favor in finding a temporary position for Herbert Levy, a German Jewish physicist, Millikan replied that Caltech "can do nothing further to aid him financially."[55]

In his capacity as chairman of the Huntington's board, the Library's reputation did not depend on hiring Jewish humanists. So, Jews were not hired on his watch at the Huntington and staff were expected to identify potential researchers who might be Jewish. "Hans Hecht is a noted Shakespearean scholar, formerly of Göttingen University," the Huntington's research director informed Millikan in 1935. "He is not a Jew."[56]

ANGLO-SAXON STATE

While Millikan was building up Caltech into a forward-looking university with close ties to the military-industrial complex and becoming a leading advocate of "a seamless continuum between the corporation, laboratory and classroom,"[57] under his leadership the Huntington remained a monument to the past. Overly cautious and imprudent investments—such as in German government bonds during the 1920s and again in 1930—created financial problems in the 1940s.[58] The board rarely delegated authority, made important decisions on the basis of personal relationships, and interfered in everyday operations and personnel matters, making it impossible for Huntington researchers to develop their own agenda.[59]

When a well-known intellectual, Robert Cleland, was hired as the first person on staff to be "thoroughly versed" in American history, it was made clear to him that a committee would oversee his work. "No member of the research staff at the Huntington Library," he was told, "is ever asked to assume responsibility for any general field."[60] The case of Robert Cleland illustrates how Millikan and other trustees recruited researchers who shared their cultural and racial politics. Cleland, one of the most influential California historians before World War II, taught for many years at Occidental College before being hired by the Huntington to develop its Western collections and shape the postwar future of California studies. Cleland, along with Phil Townsend Hanna, joined the Huntington's California Committee in 1941 when the Library initiated a campaign "to collect Californiana."[61] Widely read for his popular accounts of California history, Hanna helped to promote the view that the state's Indian populations were a "debased race, little advanced from the anthropoid ape." In Hanna's opinion, they were predestined to extinction because "within them was the ineradicable germ of disintegration." By contrast, noted Hanna, California owed its progress and productivity to the "noble lineage of Spain" and the Anglo-Saxon pioneers who introduced "a tonic constituent to the lethargic culture" of Mexico.[62]

Robert Cleland became a permanent member of the Huntington's staff in 1943, when the Library received a Rockefeller Foundation grant of $50,000 to develop a more systematic research agenda on topics relating to the Pacific Southwest. The following year, with Cleland bringing in an additional $21,000 from an anonymous donor, the Huntington began to shape the scholarly parameters of the history of California.[63] Central to Cleland's historiography was a racialized origins story. "By origin and tradition," Cleland had decided by the early 1930s, "California is essentially an Anglo-Saxon state."[64] He credited "the native aptitude of the Anglo-Saxon citizen for self-government" as the determining factor in bringing social stability to the Golden State.[65] He worried that California was at risk because "currents of foreign blood are emptying into the main stream." It would take all of California's "boldness and vigor," he observed, to confront "the most serious problem now faced by the United States, [which] is how to remain *American*."[66]

At the center of the "California Story" was a conception of race rooted in biological distinctions between the civilized and uncivilized. In defense of the virtues of white supremacy, California's leading public historians and academics created a racial typology that denied the state's complex hybridity and its legacy of conquest and terror. The construction of the racial integrity of Anglo Californians emphasized how fundamentally different they were from Indians, Mexicans, and Californios—typically portrayed as being incapable of or unwilling to make the desert bloom, the land reveal its gold, and the climate invigorate productivity—and from Asian immigrants, who were said to resist assimilation or threaten "Oriental domination of the land."[67]

Charles Goethe devoted a great deal of energy to elaborating this pyramid of racial traits. In Goethe's schema, "Nordic" was a "very definite scientific concept" that required constant use and defense. The term crystallized "that sense of scrupulous business honor of the Nordic race dating back to the time of the Crusades."[68] Unless countries such as the United States took measures to stop "a rotting hybridization" and preserve "the precious Nordic strain, " he warned, they would face the same decline as previous great empires experienced.[69] Goethe told the audience who came to hear his presidential address to the Eugenics Research Association in 1936 that the eugenics movement's progress was slow but steady. "We *are* moving toward the elimination of humanity's undesirables like Sambo, husband to Mandy, the 'washer-lady,' ... whose unfitness to propagate is most glaring."[70] Ten years later, he complained that "the hillbilly, the Sicilian of the slums, [and] the 'plantation negro' ... breed like rabbits."[71]

Cleland, like most contemporary historians, similarly articulated a polygenetic, racial typology in which upper class, Anglo Californians and the descendants of Spanish aristocracy represented the pinnacle of progress.[72] Chinese immigrants were to be distrusted because they "kept almost entirely to themselves, did not understand the white man, had no desire to associate with him, and refused to adopt his customs or manner of life."[73] By contrast, even though the "docility" of Mexican immigrants "invited injustice and exploitation," they made "excellent seasonal worker[s]. ...Many families returned year after year to the same ranches and occupied camp sites to which they were first assigned a generation before. Here in the evening the campfires spread their cheerful glow; laughter and music brought back memories of the California of the nostalgic and irrecoverable past; and life, for the moment at least, was simple, natural, and very sweet."[74] Mexicans differed from "shrewd, self-assertive, and aggressively ambitious" Japanese immigrants, whose imprisonment during World War II was justified as a "war measure" and as protection against "rowdyism and bloody reprisals springing out of the hysteria of war." Cleland, writing in 1947 from his research position at the Huntington, was glad that, "despite many individual exceptions, the disagreeable task was done with the idea of inflicting a minimum of injustice and unnecessary hardship."[75]

WHITE CITY

The entry of the United States into World War II in 1941 put an end to public expressions of mutual admiration between Nazi racial scientists and the majority of California eugenicists, but it did not stop support of policies of segregation, or the articulation and promotion of biologically based theories of social inequality.

During 1941 and 1942, Robert Millikan and other Huntington officials participated in a campaign to ensure that local property did not fall into the hands of "any person whose blood is not entirely of the White ... race." The Huntington

Land and Improvement Company and San Marino Civic Betterment Association worked with the Huntington's law firm—Gibson, Dunn, and Crutcher—to circulate a petition to restrict ownership of property in San Marino "exclusively by persons of the … Caucasian race."[76] The trustees were advised that the Huntington Library did not need to sign on to the proposal since its property could not be sold, according to terms of the original indenture. But, as Millikan instructed the board's secretary, "the situation is quite different with respect to the Huntington Land and Improvement Co."[77] The Civic Betterment Association—whose directors included representatives of Bank of America, Dean Witter, and Security–First National Bank—called upon property owners to "keep San Marino a 'white' city" and protect themselves against "non-caucasian encroachment." Change of ownership, a pamphlet warned, "can sprinkle our neighborhoods with people of any color and nationality!"[78]

Several members of the Huntington's board of trustees remained actively involved with the Human Betterment Foundation, the eugenics think tank in Pasadena, from its opening in 1929 until its closure in 1943, when Robert Millikan acquired its remaining assets for Caltech. Some Foundation members even remained in contact with their Nazi counterparts after 1943. At war's end, when Otmar Freiherr von Verschuer sought to ingratiate himself with occupation forces by disassociating himself from Josef Mengele, his protégé, Goethe and Paul Popenoe came to his defense.[79] Popenoe was glad to hear from him in July 1946, since he had been "very anxious about my colleagues in Germany…. I suppose sterilization has been discontinued in Germany?" he asked von Verschuer. Popenoe sent him a packet of food.[80] When Goethe heard directly from his German colleague in April 1948, he replied that he was "thrilled" to be in contact with him again.[81]

Charles Goethe kept faith with the Nazi eugenics program long after Popenoe and other colleagues reinvented themselves as experts on family planning and population control.[82] While others distanced themselves from eugenics, he stuck to his racial convictions. One of his last financial donations, made three months before his death, went to the Northern League, a white supremacist organization in the Netherlands working to build "cooperation between all the Nordic Peoples"—"the best, most intelligent and highest cultured Peoples of the world"—against "worthless peoples of Africa and Asia…. We would wish," wrote the League's Secretary to Goethe in April 1966, "that we had some more men like you among our members."[83] This was the same man described in a 1965 brochure, issued by my university, as "a man who has a profound love for God and man, a deep concern for human welfare, and a compelling desire to elevate mankind."[84]

Late in 1940, with American involvement in the world war on the horizon, the HBF's founder, Ezra Gosney, tried to privately distance the Foundation from Nazi policies. "We have little in this country to consider in *racial integrity*," he informed a colleague. "Germany is pushing that. We should stay clear of it lest we should be misunderstood."[85] In my search through the postwar publications, correspondence, and diaries of the HBF stalwarts, these three sentences of personal correspondence are the only evidence that might be generously construed as a critique of Nazi eugenics. Not one person associated with the Human Betterment Foundation or the Huntington Library issued a single public statement condemning the abuse of eugenics in Germany—not after the fall of the Nazi regime, not after the Nuremberg War Crimes Tribunal, not after the trials of doctors for war crimes, not after the collapse of ignorance.[86]

▣ Chapter 10 ▣

Loot

There is only one sort of discipline—PERFECT DISCIPLINE.
(General George S. Patton, Jr., 1944)

SEMITIC REVENGE

In July 1945, Patton was back in Europe, where he vented his rage on three enemies—Jews, communists, and the press, with Jews his favorite shorthand target. He was convinced that "Semitic" influences were at work to restrict fraternization between Americans and Germans. "All that sort of writing is done by Jews to get revenge. Actually the Germans are the only decent people left in Europe," he wrote Beatrice.[1] As he headed for a showdown with Eisenhower, Patton found it easy to recall and blame his old enemies, real and imagined. The press had betrayed him, just as he had feared and read about in *Mein Kampf.*[2] "They have utterly lost the Anglo-Saxon conception of justice."[3] He predicted, "unless we restore Germany we will insure that Communism takes America."[4]

Earlier in the year Patton had acquired a reputation as "The Liberator" in connection with his role in freeing concentration and prisoner-of-war camps from Nazi control. With Eisenhower, on April 12, 1945, he visited Ohrdruf-Nord, "one of the most appalling sights I have ever seen," he noted in his diary. He ordered his soldiers to visit the scene, "which I believe will teach our men to look out for the Germans." He also made local civilians witness the horrors. "The mayor of the town, together with his wife, when confronted with the spectacle, went home and hanged themselves."[5] At a press conference on April 13, Patton told the assembled media: "If any of you haven't visited the charnel house near here, you should go. It is the most horrible sight I have ever seen."

Patton also told the press to visit Buchenwald, "a similar camp only much worse." Here, the ex-prisoners "looked exactly like animated mummies and seemed to me on about the same level of intelligence."[6] When Eisenhower and Patton arrived for a tour, the survivors were too feeble to cheer. Patton, according to Eisenhower, refused to enter a room piled high with the naked bodies of dead men. "He said he would get sick if he did so."[7] Later, Patton ordered some fifteen hundred local citizens to parade through the camp so that they would have "first-hand knowledge of the infamy of their own government."[8]

This perception of Patton-as-liberator was reinforced in Margaret Bourke White's memorable book, published in 1946. It includes photographs of German civilians being forced to witness Buchenwald's mounds of corpses and emaciated survivors. "It was George Patton's idea," read the captions, "that Buchenwald's good German neighbors should visit it.... Fraulein, you who cannot bear to look, did you agree about the Jews? Will you tell your children the Führer was good at heart?"[9] These were Bourke White's words, which she put into Patton's mouth. The general himself did not express any public sympathy for Jewish survivors; he did not even acknowledge in April 1945 that Jews comprised a small but significant portion of the survivors in Germany. At that time, Patton referred to the concentration camps as "slave labor" prisons and its inhabitants as "political prisoners."[10]

In the aftermath of Patton's death, his erratic behavior and explosive racism were quickly erased and replaced by the stuff of myth. Senator Brian McMahon of Connecticut expressed a widely held view that the reason there were any survivors was "only because [generals] Eisenhower, Bradley and Patton got to Germany before they too were removed from concentration camps to the crematories."[11] Millions were grateful to Patton because he symbolized the end of a brutal war and the defeat of fascism. Stories about his role quickly took on fabulous proportions. A Polish survivor welcomed American troops serving under Patton: "You are the people of liberty. We? People? Still? Or again? Long live America. Long live the soldiers who liberated us to new life, to a future of beauty and joy."[12] At Dachau, a group of Hungarian Jews celebrated by learning the words to "God Bless America."[13] When prisoners held in Nazi camps heard that the Allies were close, they were said to chant: "Georgie Patton, come and get us! / Georgie Patton, set us free."[14]

Long after his death, this mythic image of Patton still comes in handy, especially in times of war when government officials relish parables of good versus evil.[15] According to a recent revisionist history, Patton is credited for his prescience in recognizing "the danger of an intrinsically evil Soviet Union, the need to save Eastern Europe from communism, and the desire for a strong postwar Germany." It was General Patton, argues historian Victor Hanson, who "restored the tradition of the great ideological democratic march." If he had led troops during Desert Storm, "Patton, of course, would have headed straight for the Iraqi capital and not left until the Republican Guard was annihilated and Saddam Hussein dead or in chains."[16]

The reality was very different from the public relations image. By the summer of 1945, Patton had little patience with democratic values. He hated Jews more than he hated Germans. In the aftermath of the war, he advocated quickly rebuilding and restoring Germany's power, and limiting Soviet influence in Europe. Patton was part of a political tendency, framed by Cold War sensibilities, that would prevail shortly after his death.[17] Instead of punishing postwar Germany, he wanted to see it "rebuilt as a buffer against the real danger, which is Bolshevism from Russia."[18] He worried that "military governments" would be exposed to "every sort of Jewish and Communistic attack from the press."[19]

Patton was reluctant to comply with President Truman's directive to Eisenhower, issued at the end of August, to improve conditions in the camps for Jews.[20] Truman's order was based on a State Department report, written by Earl Harrison. "Their present condition," wrote Harrison, "physical and mental, is far worse than that of other groups.... The first and plainest need of these people," he continued, "is a recognition of their actual status and by this I mean their status as Jews."[21] To Patton, the findings of "the brilliant Mr. Harrison" were more evidence that "the virus started by Morgenthau [Secretary of the Treasury] and Baruch [presidential adviser] of a Semitic revenge against all Germans is still working."[22]

The Jewish displaced persons (DPs) Patton saw in the camps were "lower than animals," who "never had any sense of decency or else they lost it all during their period of internment by the Germans. My personal opinion," he wrote his wife in September, "is that no people could have sunk to the level of degradation these have reached in the short space of four years."[23] He privately believed that "the result of [Truman's] policy will be that should the German people ever rise from the state of utter degradation to which they have now been reduced, there will be the greatest pogrom of the Jews in the history of the world."[24]

Patton had been well aware of the prominence of Jews in the Roosevelt administration, which was widely referred to as the "Jew Deal" by anti-Semites.[25] He considered writing to Henry Stimson, the Secretary of War, about the "pro-Jewish influence in the Military Government of Germany," but thought better of it the next day. Instead, he swapped anti-Semitic diatribes with a visiting priest.[26] He was "frankly opposed" to setting up war crimes tribunals—"it is not cricket and is semitic."[27] Suspicious about the arrival of a new adviser on political affairs, assigned to him by the State Department, Patton asked a colleague, "Does he belong to the chosen people?"[28]

The next day, Patton visited two Displaced Persons' camps with Eisenhower. He was impressed by the conditions—"extremely clean in all respects"—at the camp for Baltic DPs, but disgusted by "the greatest stinking bunch of humanity I have ever seen" at the Jewish camp. He attributed the chaos and disrepair to "these Jewish DP's, or at least a majority of them, [who] have no sense of human relationships." Patton "marveled that beings alleged to be made in the form of God can look the way they do or act the way they act." After the visit, he took a hot bath to wash away the smell of the camp before flying to a nearby chateau for two days of deer hunting.[29]

Patton was furious when he heard that General Louis Craig was under orders to evict twenty-two rich German families from their houses "in order to put the animals [Jews] in them." He told Craig to keep a close eye on the DPs and to move the Germans "with as much consideration as possible."[30] He was familiar with the "tribe of Judah from which the current sons of bitches are descended. However," he noted in his diary, "it is my personal opinion that this too is a lost tribe—lost to all decency."[31] He was convinced that "so far as the Jews are concerned, they do not want to be placed in comfortable buildings." The "non-Aryan press," he told his aide, was engaged in a vendetta against him.[32] In public, he tried to maintain a veneer of politeness. "I cannot understand who had the presumption to attribute to me anti-Semitic ideas which I certainly do not possess," he wrote Bernard Baruch at a time when he was convinced that Jews were engineering his downfall.[33]

Eisenhower had no choice but to remove Patton from his command after he lost his temper at an important press conference on September 22 and departed from official American positions authorized in the Potsdam Declaration. He spoke out against the "denazification program" and defended his decision to place Nazi supporters in the postwar government of Germany. "Do you want a lot of Communists?" he argued with a reporter.[34] Eisenhower lectured him for the last time on his "inability to keep my mouth shut" and transferred him to a desk job as commander of the Fifteenth Army, literally a paper organization responsible for compiling the history of the war. "We are writing a lot of stuff which no one will read," he told his wife.[35]

Patton blamed the "non-Aryan press" for plotting his demise.[36] "The noise against me," he wrote Beatrice, "is only the means by which the Jews and Communists are attempting and with good success to implement a further dismemberment of Germany."[37] Beatrice Patton was furious at "Eisenhower's cowardice towards the press. Crucified and thrown to the wolves," she wrote in her diary. "Not one voice raised in [George's] defense."[38] John O'Connell reported in the New York *Daily News* that a Jewish and communist cabal had made Patton into a scapegoat. The Cincinnati *Times-Star* said that his punishment "will probably delight those leftist commentators."[39] But it was too late to save Patton; he had become "almost recklessly indiscreet" and a political liability.[40] The assignment to the Fifteenth Army was clearly a stopgap measure until Eisenhower could decide what to do with his "problem child." Patton's death on December 21 from injuries suffered in a car accident conveniently lifted this difficult responsibility, and later fuelled conspiratorial rumors of assassination.[41] "He died at just the right time," observed Martin Blumenson, "while his triumphs in the war remained fresh, before he could destroy his reputation by absurd ravings."[42] With death came immediate political rehabilitation and sainthood. "In a single bound he regained his fame and surpassed it," concluded Blumenson. "How quickly after his fall from grace had his achievements been resurrected and acclaimed."[43]

EVIL CURIOSITIES

The Huntington now faced the problem of what to do about the Nuremberg Laws and other materials that Patton had temporarily deposited at the Library. If the board of trustees discussed the matter—which it very likely did—it left no written records of any conversations. On the rare occasions during the next fifty years that trustees and staff mentioned the Nuremberg Laws in correspondence or internal documents, the language was carefully confidential and vague: "these documents," "the papers," "a packet of papers," "certain documents." In June 1999, when Huntington officials announced to the surprise of everybody—except a handful of insiders—that they possessed the original copy of the Nuremberg Laws, hidden from history since Patton's visit on June 11, 1945, they fashioned a narrative that appeared to locate this revelation in a coherent and plausible context. Its main points can be summarized as follows:

In a public ceremony at the end of the war, Patton's troops presented him with the Nuremberg Laws, which they had captured after a skirmish with German troops. General Van Fleet then formally transmitted the documents to Patton. During his trip to California in 1945, Patton decided to give the Nuremberg Laws to the Huntington Library. At a meeting with Huntington officials on June 11, Patton asserted his ownership of a "document taken in Nuremberg.... [I]t is my property," Patton said.[44] "The close family friendship of the Huntingtons and the Pattons," read the Huntington's 1999 press release, "explains why General Patton gave these captured items to the Library in 1945."[45]

There were good reasons, the Huntington claimed in 1999, why the Library had not displayed the documents for fifty-four years. Perhaps nobody appreciated the historical significance of the Nuremberg Laws in the 1940s, speculated Robert Skotheim, the Huntington's president. "Probably Patton did not know that he had anything more than Hitler's signature and that the document was about Jews. The librarians then did what they do: keep stuff."[46] In addition, even if some members of the Huntington's board of trustees recognized their significance, the Nuremberg Laws were an anomaly in the Huntington's Anglo-American and literary collections. The Huntington, so went the rationale, preserved the Nuremberg Laws until presented with an opportunity for their exhibition at the Skirball Cultural Center.

"The Nuremberg Laws were never displayed at the Huntington," Skotheim explained at the June 28 press conference, "because they lay outside of its collecting and research areas." The document "in our vault [was] irrelevant to our work," he continued. "There was certainly no purpose at the Huntington except the purpose of preservation."[47] At the Huntington, I heard Skotheim say at the staff briefing on June 29, "we have no backup materials, no context. Here the Nuremberg Laws would only be evil curiosities." Other Huntington officials stayed on message, emphasizing that the Nuremberg Laws lacked "secondary or supportive source materials here."[48] They were "out of the scope of the Huntington," argued the chief curator of manuscripts. "There was nothing appropriate to do with them. They belong in a different context. Now at the Skirball they can be displayed in a proper context."[49]

The more that Huntington officials recounted this script to the press and public, the more real it must have seemed to its proponents. Unfortunately, though, the story about the documents' history, created by the Huntington's spokespersons in the summer of 1999, was as speculative and fanciful as was Patton's story in the summer of 1945 about how he had come into possession of the Nuremberg Laws. The Huntington's public announcement on June 26, 1999, was based on incomplete research, the withholding from the media of key documents, and at least the suspicion that its ownership of the Nuremberg Laws was tainted. If they had done more research on provenance, they would have told a different origins story.

DISCIPLINE IN PEACE

Near the war's end, U.S. military commanders were told to instill discipline in their troops in order to stop looting and fraternization. As early as 1943, the Joint Chiefs of Staff (JCS) had begun preparations for the postwar situation, but they did not anticipate the extent of the chaos, both on the ground and in military structures.[50] In the summer of 1944, the Supreme Headquarters of the Allied Expeditionary Force (SHAEF) developed a "Handbook for MG [Military Government] in Germany," which addressed issues of denazification and demilitarization at the end of the war. About the same time, the JCS crafted directive 1067, which instructed the occupying forces on how to implement the postwar policies.[51] Due to differences between the American and British governments over the final wording, eight versions of the directive were drafted between September 1944 and April 1945, when it was finally issued to General Eisenhower.[52]

One section of JCS 1067 directed Eisenhower to take control of all captured property, including archives and documents of the Nazi party, and to hold such property "pending a decision by the Control Council or higher authorities as to its eventual disposition." The army was ordered under JCS 1067 to dismantle "the laws purporting to establish the political structure of National Socialism and the basis of the Hitler regime and all laws, decrees and regulations which establish discriminations on grounds of race, nationality, creed or political opinions." Military commanders in Germany were instructed to "make special efforts to preserve from destruction and take under your control records, plans, books, documents, papers, files, and scientific, industrial and other information and data belonging to or controlled by" the German government and Nazi party.[53]

On June 1, General George S. Patton, Jr., sent out a "Letter of Instruction

No. 1" to his commanders in the Third Army, ordering them to "enforce discipline in peace" through the "inflexible enforcement of orders and regulations. Defects in discipline are not the fault of the individual soldier but of his officers." His instructions included such details as keeping shirts buttoned and obeying traffic regulations. While Patton was ordering his men not to "wander about like furtive pickpockets," he himself was busy collecting trophies to take home, exempting himself from his own order that "everything in the Army belongs to the United States."[54]

"An awful lot of war loot came home," says Hugh Cole, the Third Army's historian."[55] Officers who were in a position of authority or could get away from the front during World War II "really got the loot," recalls Don Johnson.[56] General Patton acquired more than most people, but the practice was widespread and informally sanctioned. Former President Herbert Hoover had his man in Germany at the end of the war looking for documents for his War Library archives at Stanford.[57] Even Rabbi Judah Nadich, Eisenhower's advisor on Jewish affairs, took home a couple of swords belonging to Joseph Goebbels.[58]

Patton had been amassing souvenirs of war since 1916, when he sent his father the silver mounted saddle and sword of Julio Cardenas, an officer in Pancho Villa's army, whom he had killed in Mexico.[59] In 1918, he gave his wife some cap ornaments taken from a dead German soldier in France.[60] During World War II, he sent home all kinds of memorabilia, including a Nazi flag "for the kids," German helmets, Nazi daggers, a Spanish canon, and a bronze bust of Hitler.[61] By the end of the war, he had collected enough military memorabilia to stock his personal museum in Massachusetts and give away the surplus as gifts.[62] As an amateur military historian, he also had a sharp and knowledgeable eye for books and documents. When he delivered the Nuremberg Laws to the Huntington on June 11, he made a point of informing Robert Millikan about their significance.[63]

PUBLIC PRESENTATION

There is no evidence, other than Patton's statement to the Huntington on June 11, 1945, that there was ever a "great public presentation" or that General Van Fleet "made the presentation" of the Nuremberg Laws to Patton. "As far I'm concerned the presentation to Patton was a figment of his imagination," observes Martin Dannenberg.[64] Most likely, he made up the story to assure the Huntington that he had a right to possess the documents. "I rather suspect," Don Johnson agreed with Dannenberg, "that Patton just grabbed on to the copy you discovered. Who would argue with him if he took it? He was a great student of History and would recognize this as having historical importance."[65]

If there had been such a presentation, Patton himself likely would have insisted on its documentation. He emphasized the importance of rituals "as a means of impressing our enemies, our allies, and our own troops."[66] He also demanded that important events be formally recorded so that there would be no acrimony or disputes based only on personal memory.[67] Yet, there is no record of any kind of ceremonial transmission of the Nuremberg Laws in Patton's daily diary, in his voluminous archives at the Library of Congress, or in the After Action Reports of III Corps. "Isn't that something," recalls a Third Army veteran, "old George grabbed this document for his own collection."[68]

Colonel Richard Stillman, who was a member of Patton's staff and has written several books about World War II, "has no information of a 90th Div. ceremony.... I cannot see how the 90th Div. could be involved. Patton was a raconteur."[69] This view is shared by Don Johnson, who was familiar with all the paperwork processed by Van Fleet's G-2. He, too, "never heard of any great public presentation by Van Fleet. There is no way the 90th could have been involved.... The more I think of Patton's story, the more I doubt it. The 90th Div was not a part of III Corps at this time and would have been attached to another Corps.... The tale doesn't make sense." Moreover, Patton was such a "publicity hound" that if there had been a "presentation," he would have made sure that there was media coverage of the event.[70]

As to the transmittal memo from Van Fleet to Patton, very likely Patton ordered the documentation and told Van Fleet "how he wanted it to be handled." More a personal memo than official correspondence, it lacked a security classification and no file copies were made.[71] "Ordinarily," recalls Don Johnson, G-2's "paper shuffler," a document "of this type would carry a 'confidential' or higher restriction which would require the recipient to sign for it and would insure careful handling by everyone.... So it appears that normal Army channels were disregarded. It is an interesting event, to say the least. But it clearly shows how an Army general could divert things to his own possession."[72] Historian Carlo D'Este is similarly "mystified" as to what possible role Van Fleet might have played. "In April 1945 (and later) he was commanding III Corps—which is a tactical/operational headquarters and surely not one through which such correspondence ... would have been sent."[73]

Clearly, Patton had no right to appropriate the Nuremberg Laws and he must have known that he was in violation of JCS 1067. Moreover, given his antipathy to the proposed war crimes tribunal—which he attributed to a "semitic" yearning for revenge—he was not motivated to forward incriminating documents to SHAEF in Paris.[74] Normally, Patton found it impossible to be discreet, and he must have been excited to get hold of the Nuremberg Laws and show the discovery off at the Huntington in front of George Washington's portrait. In June 1945, however, he was trying to avoid any kind of controversy that would get him in further trouble with Eisenhower.[75] "I think Patton lodged the item in the Huntington ... to avoid embarrassment and possible punishment for looting—the obvious source of this 'souvenir,'" suggests historian Paul Fussell.[76]

PROVENANCE

By the time of his visit to the Huntington, Patton had not yet made up his mind about what to do with the Nuremberg Laws. In his dictated statement, he asserts his ownership ("it is my property"), but does not transfer ownership to the Huntington. He did not leave any written instructions about how he intended to dispose of the Nuremberg Laws when he returned from Germany, but it is possible to discern his state of mind from what he said on June 11, comments he made about other documents, and from statements made by Huntington officials.

The only material that Patton clearly intended and articulated as a gift to the Huntington was the presentation copy of *Mein Kampf,* which, according to Patton, had been captured by the XX Corps near Weimar. Patton inscribed his name and dedication—"To the Huntington Library"—on the cover of *Mein Kampf* and dispatched it off to San Marino on April 15.[77] "This book may have historical value," he wrote, "and it is with this idea that I am sending it to the Library as a slight tribute to the memory of my father."[78] Receipt of this special edition of *Mein Kampf* was acknowledged by the Huntington's librarian, who wrote the general, "You may be sure that when it arrives we will have its bookplate marked [in memory of your father] and will display it as the gift of one who had an unusually large share in settling matters satisfactorily in the European theatre of operations."[79] Robert Millikan also thanked Patton for his "gift of special significance. In view of the war and of your own part in it, it makes it an historically exceedingly interesting addition to the Library's treasures."[80] Huntington officials sent out press releases announcing the prized acquisition and a month later put it on display, first for "Friends of the Library," and then for the general public.[81] On June 11, Millikan told his wife that he had "accepted for the Library the general's share of *Berchtesgaden* [Hitler's headquarters] loot—a huge de lux copy of *Mein Kampf.*"[82]

With respect to all the other items that Patton mailed to or left at the Huntington during 1945—including the Nuremberg Laws and supporting documentation—there was an understanding between the general and Huntington officials that ownership remained with Patton. "Nazi records" sent during the summer were intended to be "held in safe storage ... pending further instructions from you."[83] In September, the Huntington told Patton that it would be an honor to "act as a depository" for his "manuscript material on World War II."[84] The Huntington Library," Leslie Bliss wrote Patton in October, "is proud to act as depository for the material you have entrusted and are entrusting to it."[85]

After George Patton's death in December 1945, Beatrice Patton appointed herself the guardian of his official memory, continuing the role that she had always played in promoting and defending her husband's reputation.[86] A sophisticated, educated woman with contacts in the highest circles and public relations savvy, she was out and about during the war, instructing wives on how to keep their families together while their husbands and boyfriends were away.[87] She stood by her man through his bouts of out-of-control drinking that made him "giddy, mean, or maudlin in a flash"; and through his humiliating nine-year affair with her own half-niece, Jean Gordon, a close friend of their eldest daughter.[88]

Beatrice continually stoked Georgie's publicity machine during his lifetime, whether by accepting an invitation to tea at the White House or giving interviews to magazines. "The N. Y. Times tonight calls you the brilliant and mobile soldier, pretty good from them, but take my advice," she wrote Patton in 1943, "and have the [reporters] put out that the resistance was bitter or people may think otherwise."[89] After his death, Beatrice edited his memoir, *War As I Knew It*, and took charge of the decision about where his papers would be collected. She was torn between the Huntington—with its world-class reputation and association with George Patton, Sr., and the general's childhood—and the Library of Congress, which was more fitting for a national hero. Until Beatrice made a final decision, the family concentrated on knowing the location of Patton's important papers.

Not until 1951 was there any reference in Huntington documents to the Nuremberg Laws. At the January 17 meeting of the board of trustees, its assistant secretary, Robert Schad, reported that the Huntington had received a letter from Beatrice Patton "regarding a packet of papers turned over to the Huntington Library by General George S. Patton, Jr., in June, 1945." The general's sister also telephoned Schad about the same time "regarding certain documents which General Patton turned over to us during his visit to the Library in June, 1945."[90] Schad had prepared a response for the board, encouraging Mrs. Patton to deposit all of the general's memoirs and papers at the Huntington.[91] The board approved the letter, which was sent out the next day to Beatrice Patton, signed by the board's vice-chairman, William Munro, in Millikan's absence.

In this letter, the board informed Beatrice Patton that they had "preserved" the Nuremberg Laws at the Huntington since June 1945 without any publicity, in accordance with her husband's wishes. "They are not available for inspection by the public at the present time. All this has been reported to Miss Patton [the general's sister] by word of mouth."[92] The Huntington was eager not only to retain the Nuremberg Laws, but also to permanently acquire all of Patton's papers. Munro's letter, on behalf of the board, reminded Mrs. Patton that "the General also expressed the hope that at a later date certain of his papers might be deposited at the Library for safekeeping and for the benefit of posterity. The Trustees hope that, in view of the early and long association which General Patton had with Mr. Huntington and with the Library, this institution might be considered as the official depository." Munro noted that General Patton's papers would "be at home" with the Huntington's "already valuable collection of original papers of famous American patriots," including George Washington, Ulysses Grant, William Sherman, and Robert E. Lee. "If you are interested in placing these records with us, we would be glad to go over the details with you.... [T]here is ample endowment to preserve, for the people of the State, historical and valuable documents which the Trustees are willing to accept."

As further incentive, Munro informed Beatrice Patton that the general's papers would be safe in an "atomic bombproof storage structure incorporating a vault, two stories under ground, with walls of reinforced concrete ten feet thick."[93] The new structure, recently completed under the supervision of Caltech engineers, was reserved for "the institution's chief treasures among its paintings, manuscripts, and books."[94] The vault, about ten by twenty feet, contains "only the rarest and most important materials," curator Alan Jutzi told us on a guided tour in 1999. He pointed to an empty spot on one of the shelves, opposite the Jefferson and Lincoln letters, close to Shakespeare quartos, medieval manuscripts, and irreplaceable first editions. "That's where we kept the Nuremberg Laws."[95]

In March 1951, according to Robert Shad's minutes of a board meeting, Beatrice Patton replied that she was "favorably inclined" to deposit her husband's papers in the Huntington, but first she wanted to consult with her children. The board of trustees was pleased to hear the news.[96] But before making a final decision about where to locate her husband's papers, Beatrice Patton died suddenly in 1953.[97] The decision now rested with the Pattons' children, especially their eldest son, George S. Patton III, and eldest daughter, Ruth Ellen Patton Totten. In 1955, they chose the Library of Congress over the Huntington.[98]

A few years later, when the family decided to donate a second batch of papers to the Library of Congress, they emphasized the importance of maintaining the integrity of the collection. "This family," wrote Patton's son to the Library of Congress in 1963, "would not consider giving out anything but the *total* collection, not just the World War II material."[99] The following year, 1964, the Pattons turned over the remaining documents to the Library of Congress. Meanwhile, the Huntington retained possession of various documents that General Patton had deposited at the Library in 1945.

In 1969, the Pattons decided to honor their long association with the Huntington by donating as a gift all the family papers that were not intended for the Library of Congress. In a formal document, witnessed and signed, General Patton's daughter declared, "I, Ruth Patton Totten, do hereby give, to the Henry E. Huntington Library and Art Gallery, title to the collection of family papers commonly known as the Patton Papers. I specifically exclude from this gift the papers directly relating to my father, the late General George S. Patton, Jr.; these papers are in or destined for the Library of Congress."[100] Despite this specific, legal instruction, the Huntington continued to retain possession of several documents, including the Nuremberg Laws, that General Patton had deposited at the Library in 1945.

After the death of Nita Patton, General Patton's sister, on March 14, 1971, the Huntington renewed its efforts to acquire General Patton's papers.[101] Three members of the Huntington's staff visited her home in San Marino to take photographs and advise the heirs about any remaining documents and memorabilia.[102] The

Huntington was interested in collecting anything connected to the Patton family, even a double-barrel shotgun, valued at $15.[103] While sorting through boxes of documents from Anne Patton's house, a Huntington staff member found "some letters written by the General mainly to his father and sister."[104] Carey Bliss, the Huntington's curator of rare books, again tried to convince Ruth Patton Totten to donate the originals to the Huntington. "There are a few letters written by the General mainly to his father and sister. They relate to family matters and the business affairs of George S. Patton, Sr. and we would like very much to keep them in the collection here," wrote Bliss. "If you so desire, these few letters could be xeroxed and the xeroxed copies mailed to you or the Library of Congress."[105]

After consulting other members of the family, Mrs. Totten politely but firmly declined the Huntington's request. "I have talked to George about the three boxes of business letters and papers belonging to General Patton, and his personal letters to his father and sister," she wrote Bliss, "and we both feel that as the importance and value of a collection is in its completeness, these should be forwarded to me, after you have xeroxed what you want, and I will forward them to the Library of Congress to be with the other Patton Papers."[106]

The Huntington did not own any of the materials received from Patton in 1945, other than *Mein Kampf*, which he clearly identified as a gift to the Library. As much as it is possible to reconstruct his intentions, Patton very likely temporarily deposited the Nuremberg Laws at the Huntington "for sentimental and security reasons."[107] On four different occasions—in 1955, 1963, 1969, and 1973—the Patton family made it clear that all of General Patton's papers and documents inherited by his heirs should be maintained as one collection at the Library of Congress. Huntington officials apparently ignored their wishes in much the same way as General Patton ignored the directive to forward the Nuremberg Laws to the Supreme Headquarters of the Allied Expeditionary Force in Paris in 1945.

When Robert Skotheim, the Huntington's president, met with the media in the summer of 1999, he explained that the Library had not exhibited the Nuremberg Laws because they did "not fall within the subject areas of scholarly research or public display of our institution."[108] A search of the Huntington's records and annual reports, however, tells a different story.

The Huntington has always solicited and received gifts that expand its collections beyond its Anglo-American literary focus, especially trophy items or materials that are of historical or public interest, irrespective of their value to researchers. For example, in 1926, Edward Huntington authorized the purchase of the original Pizarro-La Gasca manuscripts, which documented the Spanish conquest of Peru in the sixteenth century.[109] A donation of French and Dutch cartoons was accepted in 1939.[110] After the war, the Huntington purchased a collection of one thousand lithographs by Honoré Daumier to add to its print collection.[111] In 1981, the Huntington investigated significant resources in a new area of research by becoming the repository for some three thousand master photographic negatives of the Dead Sea Scrolls. Beginning in 1980, the Huntington sent Robert Schlosser, its chief photographer, to Israel to photograph the Scrolls.[112] A more recent addition to the Huntington's collections is a rare first edition of Gregor Mendel's publication on genetics, *Versuche über Pflanzen-Hybriden*, first published in 1866.[113]

The Library, according to a 1944 guide for visitors, has had "frequent special exhibitions of literary and historical interest," many of which were unrelated to the Huntington's primary areas of research. [114] On Founder's Day in 1938, there was a special exhibit on "Mexico in the Sixteenth Century."[115] A bookplate belonging to Benito Mussolini was showcased in the Huntington's annual report of the same year.[116] In 1944, a letter written by Commodore Matthew C. Perry about U.S.-Japan relations was included in an exhibit on American naval history.[117] In 1945, Carey Bliss curated an exhibit on the history of the U.S. Army. "It is Americana of the best sort," reported the *Los Angeles Times*, "a display which reveals through the development of the Army the development of a powerful nation."[118] When the Huntington received Patton's gift of a special edition of *Mein Kampf*, officials sent out a press release to announce the event and put the book on public display.[119] In the 1950s, a collection of old armor was an attraction to visitors and in the early 1960s there was an exhibition of Daumier prints.[120]

The failure of the Huntington to accession or publicly acknowledge their possession of the Nuremberg Laws before 1999 was evidently unrelated to any purported irrelevance of the documents to the Huntington's research agenda or collections. On the contrary, the board of trustees had actively lobbied the Patton family in 1951 to permanently deposit at the Library not only the Nuremberg Laws, but also all of Patton's military papers and documents.[121] Even after the Patton family decided in 1955 to house the general's collection in the Library of Congress, the Huntington was eager to acquire Patton memorabilia.

A much more persuasive explanation in my view for the Huntington's long silence regarding the Nuremberg Laws can be found in the issue of title. If the documents were looted, then General Patton had no right to own them. If Patton's claim was lawful, then the Huntington should have honored his daughter's instruction in 1969 to transfer to the Library of Congress "the papers directly relating to my father."[122] The Huntington has an accessible copy of this bequest in its archives, filed under Patton family correspondence. It was not difficult to find.

The Huntington also possessed other materials in June 1999 that raised questions about the veracity of Patton's dramatic story and the issue of title: the memo by Frank Perls, written on April 28, 1945, which disputed Patton's account of how, where, and when the Nuremberg Laws were retrieved; and the 1951 letter in which Patton reportedly requested that the Nuremberg Laws "be preserved in the Huntington Library, but with no publicity about them." Moreover, the Library did not release an important internal memo, written in 1991, that raised concerns about "uncertainty over title."[123]

▣ Chapter 11 ▣

In Limbo

The past is everywhere.
(David Lowenthal, 1985)

QUIETLY IGNORED

For fifty-four years, from 1945 to 1999, the Huntington preserved the Nuremberg Laws in a basement vault reserved for its most precious items. They were not so much forgotten or abandoned as put on hold. They existed "in limbo, not assigned to any department or curator," says Alan Jutzi, chief curator of rare books since 1983. "They did not really belong to the Huntington because there was no official donation. They didn't go through a process of being accessioned. There was no paperwork. No one person was in charge of them. This is not true of any other important Huntington book or manuscript."[1] By the early 1980s, another leading member of the staff broke the silence and shared her suspicion that Patton had stolen the documents.

Each generation of Huntington officials knew about the presence and significance of the Nuremberg Laws, but the Library's records indicate that they did not take any initiative to do anything about them until the 1990s. Robert Schad—the assistant secretary to the board in 1945 and curator of rare books until his death in 1961—was well briefed on the issue. His son Jasper, who grew up in the area and did odd jobs at the Huntington during his teens in the 1940s, remembers his father showing him some of the documents that Patton had deposited at the Library.[2] Carey Bliss, who replaced Schad as curator of rare books in 1962, had been on the staff since 1945 and was involved in negotiations with the Patton family between 1971 and 1973. Martin Ridge, who was in charge of research between 1984 and 1998 (and acting director briefly in 1987 to 1988), knew about the Nuremberg Laws when he first came to the Huntington in the late 1970s.[3] He told friends and researchers about them. "It was certainly no secret," he recalled in 2000.[4] Berkeley historian Robert Middlekauff, who directed the Huntington from 1983 to 1987, remembers being taken down to the vault and shown the Nuremberg Laws when he first arrived. There were so many other priorities, mainly fiscal, he says, "I didn't give them a lot of thought."[5]

Alan Jutzi joined the staff in 1970 in the photography department and worked for a while under Carey Bliss. He says that he has been aware of the Huntington's copy of the Nuremberg Laws since about 1975, when he saw them in the inner vault.[6] In 1978, Mary Robertson became chief curator of rare manuscripts. "Some time later"—it could have been in 1979 or the early 1980s, she does not remember the exact year—the librarian Dan Woodward showed her the Nuremberg Laws in the vault. Robertson and Woodward were "hesitant to accession [the Nuremberg Laws] formally as part of our collections and open them up to research in the general way" because "they seem[ed] pretty clearly to be war loot, however exalted the source."[7] At that time, "they didn't loom large on my horizon," recalls Robertson. "Things sort of rested there," she says.[8]

Some ten years later, Mary Robertson again raised her concerns, this time in writing, with William Moffett, the new librarian hired in 1990. She informed him about the Huntington's possession of the Nuremberg Laws—"all extremely distasteful stuff"—and documents relating to the "provenance of the material." Robertson noted that "they have been in our vault since 1945, and have been quietly ignored for all of that time. A few of the staff know they are there, but I doubt the scholarly community does. I have never done the research to determine whether the text is widely known (surely it must be), or whether or not there are other signed copies. The scholarly value of the documents is limited if, as I think, the contents are already widely known; the main commercial value would lie in Hitler's signature related to such viciously anti-Semitic subject matter." Jutzi says that he also raised with William Moffett that the status of the Laws needed to be addressed, but "nothing happened."[9] Robertson informed Moffett that the question of legal title was problematic, "but it seems proper to me that at some time the materials should be made available to scholars. When you have time, perhaps we could talk about it."[10]

Apparently Moffett did not have time to talk about it because there was no response to Robertson's memo. Four and one-half years later, in 1996, she again raised the issue of the "pending problem" with his successor, David Zeidberg, director of the library and first Jewish administrator to be hired at the Huntington. Robertson attached her 1991 memo to Moffett, adding her concern about "a longstanding and unresolved issue concerning the proper disposition of a few Hitler manuscripts captured by Patton's 3rd Army and given by the general to the Huntington in 1945.... My own inclination is still that they should be brought out and made available to scholars; whether they should remain here at the Huntington or be turned over to some other institution is a decision you will want to be involved with."[11] Zeidberg went down to the inner vault to look at the Laws. "I knew they were signed by Hitler," he says. "It's not a common item on the market and I know about forgeries."[12]

Between 1996 and 1998, no action was taken and the documents remained in the vault. Zeidberg had other pressing priorities—grants to administer, personnel issues, and a staff of sixty to supervise. Meanwhile, the Huntington's president, Robert Skotheim, in the twilight of his career, began to consider ways of going public with the Nuremberg Laws. It would take eight years for Mary Robertson's 1991 memo to finally receive a response. Robert Skotheim's idea of loaning the Nuremberg Laws to another institution required considerable patience to put into practice. It took the Huntington a long time to shed its patrician past and respond to the new cultural dynamics of Los Angeles. Before exploring the details of how and why the decision was made, it is necessary to first understand the institutional changes that made it possible for the Huntington to make an unprecedented overture to a Jewish center on the Westside.

ECONOMICS OF CHANGE

Asked by fellow trustees for his assessment of the state of the institution in 1951, Herbert Hoover candidly observed that the Huntington had a reputation for its valuable collections, but "the Library remained a relatively undeveloped mine of source materials which needed a well-defined plan and vigorous direction for its realization."[13] The death of Robert Millikan in December 1953 had no immediate impact on the Huntington's governance or policies. The old guard continued to dominate the board of trustees, even as the region's monolithic power structure began to erode and the postwar world around San Marino rapidly changed.[14] By 1951, the Jewish population of Los Angeles had grown to three hundred thousand.[15] By 1960, the African American population in the region had more than doubled, to almost half a million.[16] Ten years later, Los Angeles County's Latino population, mostly of Mexican origin, would increase beyond one million.[17] Until the 1970s, however, the Huntington remained stagnant, largely due to Millikan's legacy.

William Munro, Millikan's confidante at Caltech, took over the chairmanship of the board of trustees in 1954. James Page, director of Union Oil and president of the California Bank, remained a trustee from 1945 until his death in 1962. Herbert Hoover remained on the board, but rarely attended meetings, until 1957, when he was replaced by Jonathan Lovelace, a Republican investment banker. The only new professional blood on the board during the 1950s was J. E. Wallace Sterling, who had academic experience as president of Stanford University before becoming a trustee in 1954. But Sterling was also an insider in the sense that he had served as director of the Huntington from 1947 to 1948, and had a longtime association with Caltech—as did Munro, Page, and Hoover.[18]

Millikan's racialized worldview also prevailed for many years. Elmo Conley, a partner in the law firm that had been active in the campaign to preserve racial covenants in San Marino, was recruited to the board in 1954. When he died in 1957, his replacement, Homer Crotty, also was a member of Gibson, Dunn, and Crutcher.[19] In 1957, another Republican lawyer, John O'Melveny, was recruited to the board from a law firm that had refused to hire Jewish associates from 1909 to 1956.[20] Unlike Caltech, which hired the occasional Jewish scientist, the Huntington observed the downtown ban. Between the 1920s and 1940s, Jews in the Los Angeles region had became pariahs in the "citadels of exclusiveness" they had helped to found.[21]

Even the social movements of the 1960s took another two decades to have any consequential impact on the Huntington's research program and organizational culture.[22] Homer Crotty, chairman of the board, was disturbed in the late 1960s by the "enormous turbulence in the collegiate and educational world" and vowed that the Huntington would remain committed "to preserve those values in which we believe."[23] Children were still being excluded from the art gallery, and visitors without shoes were turned away from the gardens.[24] The Huntington's ambience continued to evoke Edwardian Oxbridge, on which it was based. "Happily, much of the former stuffiness has disappeared from the Huntington," reported a 1972 guide to Southern California, but still it did not recommend visits by fidgety children.[25]

It was economics, not student revolts or politics, that finally forced changes upon an inbred system of cronyism. Thirty years after the Huntington opened to the public in 1928, it had its first operating budget deficit. For twenty-five of the thirty-five years from 1958 to 1993, the institution incurred annual operating budget deficits that had to be covered by reserve funds.[26] Crotty sounded the economic alarm in 1967 and, confronted with a long-term financial crisis, the trustees embarked on a development program in 1969.[27]

In January 1972, the Huntington's trustees established an eighteen-member Board of Overseers to guide the day-to-day administration of the Library's policies and projects. Overseers were recruited on the basis of their commitment to the Huntington's resources, their social contacts, and fundraising abilities. This was an important first step away from the paternalistic model established by Millikan and toward instilling an ethic of professionalism in the Huntington's governance. Although the five-man board of trustees retained "final authority over the institution as a whole," the overseers created a new bloc of power within the organization, and protected the staff's ability to develop programs without meddling interference from on high.[28] The following year, the Board of Overseers was organized into five committees (Library, Art Gallery, Gardens, Public Education, and Research) and plans were made to broaden outreach and develop public education programs.[29] During the next twenty years, the number of overseers increased to sixty and their role was consolidated as middle managers in the Huntington's bureaucracy.[30]

By the late 1970s, the attention to finances had paid off in the form of corporate sponsorship, which funded new building projects, expanded the endowment, and infused the Huntington's old money with more diverse and cosmopolitan sources of wealth: Atlantic Richfield donated one million dollars, and Bank of America $100,000. Between 1979 and 1982, the number of corporate sponsors grew from fourteen to twenty-one, including Union Oil, Chevron, Ahmanson Foundation, and Armand Hammer. By 1990, there were over one hundred corporate sponsors. "Energetic fund raising and tight management" in the mid-1980s, observes Robert Skotheim, made it possible to eliminate the annual deficit. The Huntington celebrated its seventy-fifth anniversary in 1995 with the highest surplus in its history—$560,000.[31] Ten years later, the Library's staff exceeded three hundred and seventy, it had an endowment of about $145 million, plus new buildings for the library and botanical education, and its assets doubled.[32]

PUBLIC FACE

Along with the Folger Library, the Newberry Library, and the Pierpont Morgan Library, the Huntington is one of a handful of independent, nonprofit, research libraries in the United States that is globally recognized for its collections and facilities. The Library has always specialized in primary source materials for researchers working on the histories of seventeenth and eighteenth-century Britain, Puritanism, Revolutionary and Civil War America, the nineteenth century, and the West and Southwest. The original mission of the Library had emphasized a commitment to the modernist project of intellectual history, in particular the role of Great Ideas and Great Men in the development of Anglo-American civilization. But as the Huntington began its economic transformation, it also opened its doors for the first time to new constituencies and new epistemological frameworks.

In the wake of the social movements of the 1960s, academia was a center of ferment and change. "Even unique institutions" such as the Huntington, conceded Robert Skotheim, "must respond to the changing world in which they exist."[33] Under the leadership of historian Robert Middlekauff, the Huntington's chief executive from 1984 to 1988, the Library raised nearly one million dollars in gifts and pledges, including $66,000 from the National Endowment for the Humanities, to support fellowships for graduate students and assistant professors. Skotheim credits this effort by Middlekauff as a key moment in the "democratization of the Huntington. Before him there were few women and no younger scholars here."[34] The Huntington's library, however, remained an exclusive institution, limited to less than two thousand researchers each year. "Even in its rejuvenated, opened-up state," the mission of the Huntington was still "traditional, in the sense of being collection-based, scholarly, and of interest to few in the population generally."[35]

Under Robert Skotheim's leadership as president (1988 to 2001), space was opened up for significant reforms, as the Huntington began to develop a "broader educational use to which our collections are put."[36] With a doctorate in history from the University of Wisconsin and a track record as a professor, administrator, and small college president, Skotheim was well suited to juggling and negotiating the needs of competing constituencies. His own intellectual orientation was not sympathetic to the post-1960s currents in feminist and radical history, but he understood that the Huntington's growth required systemic changes. He preferred historians who demonstrated a "detached scholarly quest for understanding the past" and kept their distance from "partisan polemics of yesterday or today."[37] Consequently, it was not difficult for him to genuinely reassure the Huntington's old guard that "nothing in today's multi-cultural society diminishes the importance of the history of Anglo-American political and civil liberties. Nothing in today's society reduced our curiosity to understand the meanings of being American.... Today's children," noted Skotheim in his address at the ceremony marking the Huntington's seventy-fifth anniversary in 1995, "will spearhead, as they mature in the next century, a renewed communal idealism celebrating American democratic aspirations. They will affirm that they are the legatees of the only historic national traditions on earth which assert human equality, irrespective of birth, race, or religion."[38]

Skotheim was comfortable with an institution that used a Norman Rockwell graphic to promote a fundraiser at which croquet was played on the lawn and Pimm's cups were served.[39] At the same time, he was seriously committed to propelling the Huntington out of its Edwardian past into the new realities of cultural power in Los Angeles. He was convinced that the Huntington was obliged to provide "greater access for diverse populations" and to open "doors ever wider to previously excluded audiences."[40] Under his presidency, age limits and term limits were established for the board of trustees. The policy established by Edward Huntington to forbid the loan of any of the Huntington's collections to other institutions was amended in 1992, when the trustees authorized the selective lending of objects from the Art Gallery.[41] In 1994, the Library was also given permission to selectively loan books and documents, with the exception of materials that had "intrinsic value" to the Huntington, such as the Gutenberg Bible or the Ellesmere Chaucer.[42]

Progressive intellectuals with ideas that had rarely been expressed to the Library's audiences before were given a forum to express controversial viewpoints.[43] As part of its efforts to widen the Huntington's popular appeal, a Contemporary Authors Series began in 1994–1995. In its first year, speakers included A. S. Byatt, Amy Tan, and Jane Smiley.[44] More significantly, Huntington's curators were given new opportunities to organize exhibits that were not simply testaments to the glorious past. Perhaps the best example of this shift was the impressive exhibit on "Land of Golden Dreams: California in the Gold Rush Decade, 1848–1858," curated by Peter Blodgett in 1999. Blodgett's perspective, which reflected current scholarship on California and the West, revealed how California before and after 1848 was part of the Mexican-American borderlands and how it was transformed by the rise of global markets. The exhibit, one critic noted, challenged "facile popular notions of the Gold Rush," by integrating the West into "the national narrative of racism and sectionalism."[45]

In November 1998, for the first time in the Huntington's history, all five trustees, forty-five of the sixty overseers, and the principal officers met to authorize changes in the Huntington's mission statement. The retreat was the result of months of staff meetings and internal discussions. Skotheim sought and achieved a statement that "recognizes the more recent 'public face' of the institution as well as the more traditional 'private face' of scholarly research." It reads as follows: "Building on Henry E. Huntington's legacy of renowned collections and gardens that enrich the visitor, The Huntington today encourages research and promotes education in the arts, humanities, and botanical sciences through the growth and preservation of its collections, through the development and support of a community of scholars, and through the display and interpretation of its extraordinary resources to the public."[46] It was in the context of this formal commitment to a more "public face" and a "community of scholars" that Skotheim considered how to disclose the Huntington's copy of the Nuremberg Laws and to make an overture to new cultural institutions in the Westside section of Los Angeles.

DÉTENTE

At the end of the twentieth century, Pasadena had opened up to tourism and the entertainment industry, becoming "one of Los Angeles' two popular outdoor, adult playgrounds."[47] San Marino, once a bastion of upper class, white supremacy, is now home to a sizable number of wealthy Chinese Americans, who own one-third of the expensive homes in the township and whose children comprise a majority in the local public schools.[48] In contrast to the Huntington's celebrated Japanese Gardens, which were conceived in 1912 by Edward Huntington as an "exotic pleasure garden" for his future wife and middle-class Anglo Protestants, the planned Chinese Garden, scheduled to open in 2005, represents the growing power in local affairs of San Marino's Chinese Club.[49]

Early in 1996, Robert Skotheim expressed an interest to Huntington's curators in putting on a small exhibit related to Jewish life and culture as an expression of support for the Skirball Cultural Center, which was due to open to the public in April.[50] He asked the Library's California specialist, Peter Blodgett, to search the Western American collections for materials that might be used in such an exhibit. In 1970, the Huntington had published the first comprehensive history of Jews in Los Angeles; a few years earlier, it had also published a study of the leading Jewish banker in Southern California.[51] The Huntington has significant holdings, Blodgett reported, on two influential Jews: the nineteenth-century banker Isaias Hellman and Adolph Sutro, a mining entrepreneur and mayor of San Francisco.[52] In 1997, Skotheim expressed his continuing interest in the issue by inviting Werner Gundersheimer, director of the Folger Shakespeare Library, to speak at the Huntington's Founder's Day lecture about his experiences in the United States as a Jewish refugee from nazism.[53]

During a visit to the Skirball Cultural Center soon after its opening in April 1996, Skotheim changed his mind about putting on an exhibit about California's Jews and decided instead to explore the possibility of donating or loaning the Nuremberg Laws to the Skirball.[54] "From the moment I met you and toured the Skirball," Skotheim later recalled in a note to Uri Herscher, the Skirball's president, "I vowed to place the Patton materials with you."[55] Other connections between the Huntington and Skirball helped to cement this rapprochement. Robert Erburu, the powerful chief executive of *Times Mirror*, was both chairman of the Huntington's board of trustees and a member of the Skirball's board of trustees.[56] Erburu had all the right qualifications and experience to make links between East and West: he was on the boards of the J. Paul Getty Trust and the National Gallery of Art, and was the all-time leading fundraiser for the Huntington.[57] Erburu told Skotheim that he would support his initiative regarding the Nuremberg Laws.

Another important go-between was Loren Rothschild, an investment counselor and rare book collector, who serves on the Skirball's board of trustees and is an influential member of the Library Committee of the Huntington's Board of Overseers. Skotheim asked Rothschild to sound out Uri Herscher on his receptivity to exhibiting the Nuremberg Laws at the Skirball. Herscher was more than open to this overture, given his interest in building ties with all kinds of cultural institutions. He had already recruited Skotheim to the Skirball's advisory committee on American values. "It is all about relationships," he says quite frankly.[58]

Once Skotheim received the green light for the project from Erburu and Herscher, he turned it over to David Zeidberg, the Huntington's library director, and Mary Robertson, curator of rare manuscripts. Zeidberg became the point man for getting Skotheim's idea approved by various committees within the Huntington and working out the contractual and security aspects of the proposal. Robertson was in charge of assuring that the documents were technically prepared for exhibit. According to Zeidberg, who had recently arrived at the Huntington after twelve years as head of UCLA's special collections, dealing with the Nuremberg Laws was low on his list of priorities.[59]

It took another three years to move the process forward. "It could have been vetoed at any step," recalls Skotheim, "bogged down in a number of places." The decision had to be approved by lawyers, curators, and manuscript specialists. "Before we took it to the trustees, we had to make sure that all the ducks were lined up." The slowness of his staff's response at times made Skotheim "apprehensive that perhaps it would not be as easy as I assumed." But reminded of the proposal when Uri Herscher visited the Huntington in September 1998 for a special viewing of a George Washington exhibit, Skotheim urged Zeidberg to move the project through the Huntington's cumbersome bureaucracy.[60]

The announcement on June 23, 1998, of the formation of President Clinton's Advisory Commission on Holocaust Assets in the United States may also have reminded Skotheim that the Huntington had in its vault an item that had been identified by a trusted member of his staff as "war loot." During the 1990s, the issue of artifacts looted during the Nazi era was increasingly in the public eye. The Clinton Commission published a lengthy report, focusing on the disposition of the assets of holocaust victims. "The Commission's effort," concluded its chairman, "has focused on moral restitution, which is accomplished by confronting the past honestly and internalizing its lessons."[61] The American Association of Museums (AAM) also investigated what had happened to European paintings and Judaica stolen or looted during the Nazi era. The AAM defined Judaica as "the material culture of the Jewish people," including ceremonial objects, historical artifacts, literature, and items that signify "momentous events." The association issued guidelines to its members regarding "The Unlawful Appropriation of Objects during the Nazi Era" and procedures for providing public information about "Objects Transferred in Europe during the Nazi Era."[62]

Whatever the reasons for the new urgency, six months after Herscher's visit, Skotheim was ready to offer him a proposal. On March 2, 1999, Uri Herscher again visited Skotheim at the Huntington. Accompanying him were two key members of his staff: Stanley Chyet, Herscher's former professor at the Hebrew Union College in Cincinnati, who went on to become his assistant and trusted adviser in Los Angeles; and Robert Kirschner, the program director who would be responsible for incorporating the Nuremberg materials into the Skirball's core exhibit.[63] When the group was assembled, Mary Robertson retrieved the Nuremberg Laws from the vault and Zeidberg showed everybody Patton's gift of *Mein Kampf*. It was a difficult moment for Herscher, for it reminded him of his "mournful family" and "the grandmothers I never knew. I felt that I was holding a death warrant in my hands." Excusing himself, he entered the bathroom and stood at the sink, washing his hands over and over again.[64]

At the March 2 meeting, Skotheim and Herscher shook hands on the transaction, with the proviso that the formal decision required approval of the Huntington's board. Skotheim and Zeidberg told the Skirball team that besides the Nuremberg Laws and *Mein Kampf*, they would also make available for display Patton's statement of provenance and the photograph of Patton handing over the Nuremberg Laws to Robert Millikan in 1945. It was clear to everyone at the meeting that this was a "package deal," that the statement and photograph were important to the Huntington because they cemented the important historical relationship between the Patton and Huntington families.[65] According to accounts of those present, Skotheim and Zeidberg gave no indication that the Huntington possessed contradictory evidence of provenance, and nobody brought up the topic of Patton's attitude toward Jews.[66]

"I will be very glad to accept the material for the Skirball Cultural Center on an indefinite loan basis," Herscher wrote the day after his visit to the Huntington. "The material is clearly of great and tragic importance for the history of the twentieth century. It is a revelation of the immense evil a political regime can embark upon and also, by the very fact of your considering the inclusion of the material in our collection, an ironic and decisive answer to that evil."[67] Skotheim, in turn, expressed his "deep satisfaction at being in a position wherein I could make this transfer of documents possible. There is no doubt that the Holocaust is the governing event of my generation. It defined my scholarly preoccupations, and shaped my view of the world. The Holocaust assaulted all of us, spiritually and intellectually, even though most of us were not attacked literally and physically."[68]

There was plenty of time to implement the agreement thoughtfully and carefully, since the Skirball would not be ready for the exhibit until December or the beginning of 2000. The center was planning to close down its main exhibit in September in order to retrofit the building. Also, Robert Kirschner, who was put in charge of the project for the Skirball, had to refigure the core exhibit to incorporate the Nuremberg Laws; moreover, they planned to ask Moshe Safdie, the architect who had created Yad Vashem, to design a special case for the Nuremberg Laws. Kirschner had about ten months—a sufficient amount of time to get everything ready.[69]

With December 1999 as the intended deadline to complete the transfer, David Zeidberg also had sufficient time to move the project through the Huntington's legal, technical, and political processes. But some time in May, Sharon Waxman, a Los Angeles-based reporter for the *Washington Post,* picked up a story at a Skirball luncheon that the Huntington Library would soon loan a special edition of *Mein Kampf* and some important Nazi documents to the Skirball. She began calling Catherine Babcock, the Huntington's director of communications, in an attempt to verify the rumor. Babcock tried to stall her, says Waxman, in return for an exclusive story at a later date.[70] "The story was leaked to the *Washington Post,*" says Zeidberg. "They kept hounding us."[71] Waxman's persistence, according to Skotheim and Zeidberg, forced the Huntington's hand. "We wanted the story written the right way," said Babcock, who had hoped the coverage would coincide with the display of the documents and that they would be made available to all the media at the same time. "When the *Washington Post* reporter threatened to break the story, we decided to move up the date."[72]

Huntington officials were worried less by premature publicity than, it seems, by Waxman's interest in why the Nuremberg Laws had languished for so long in their basement. Hoping to avoid this kind of scrutiny, they decided to move up the loan date to June.[73] What should have taken another seven months—completing the loan agreement, doing a title search, verifying provenance, investigating how previous boards of trustees had handled the Nuremberg Laws, getting the Laws appraised, preparing the documents for transfer, and building the display case— was compressed into a little over one month.[74] As a result, these tasks were hurried and others bypassed as the Huntington hunkered down to meet the extraordinary deadline of June 29.

In the rush, the Huntington's archivist quickly assembled a handful of internal documents relating to the Nuremberg Laws, but a full search of the Huntington's institutional records did not take place until the middle of September and was prompted by several requests for this information by Cecilia and me.[75] The Overseers' Library Committee was quickly convened and gave its approval on condition that the Huntington did not give up its ownership of the Nuremberg Laws. Some members of the committee wanted to make sure that the long-term association between the Huntington and Patton families was preserved.[76] The expert hired to assess the authenticity of the documents was given less than two weeks to prepare a report.[77] The small team assembled to work on the project on a need-to-know basis was told to keep the whole matter confidential and avoid any leaks. "I was asked to keep quiet," says one participant, "because the press was bothering the Huntington about the past, asking them where the stuff had been for so long." The Skirball cooperated with the speedup by agreeing to clear out a display of materials about Albert Einstein and to make the case available for the Nuremberg materials by the end of June.

The troubles started even before the display of the Nuremberg Laws formally opened to the public on June 29. Huntington and Skirball officials called a press conference for Monday, June 28, at which they planned to launch the exhibit, provide the media with background documents, and have experts on hand to answer reporters' questions. Catherine Babcock, the Huntington's director of communications, had been crafting a press release for two months and planning how the story would break.[78] The *Washington Post*, whose reporter thought that she had been promised an exclusive, refused to honor the June 28 embargo and "rushed the story into the paper" on Saturday, June 26.[79] To preempt the *Post* from having an exclusive, the Huntington sent out its press release on the same day.[80] It was too late to make the front page of the *New York Times*, but the *Los Angeles Times* reconfigured its layout to accommodate the Huntington.[81] Owing to the subsequent public relations fiasco, the Huntington produced its own video, which reported an uncompromisingly positive story, in order to reassure its board of trustees, corporate sponsors, and influential friends.[82]

Beyond what it perceived as a hostile and unsympathetic media, as well as growing discontent among its own staff about the atmosphere of secrecy and paranoia, the Huntington quickly had other problems on its hands.[83] On June 28, the day of the press conference, the Huntington received an e-mail from Gerhard Jochem, an archivist with Nuremberg's City Archives. He was "deeply concerned" about the Huntington's assertion of ownership of the Nuremberg Laws. Jochem claimed that the city of Nuremberg had in its possession the authentic, original Laws. "In our opinion the documents found there [at the Huntington] are drafts." In 1935, the night before the Reichstag met on September 15, Hitler ordered the Minister of the Interior to prepare four versions of the Laws (A to D). "It is most likely," wrote Jochem, "that the copy held by the Huntington Library is one of the versions A to C."[84] As it turned out, luckily for the Huntington, there were two originals of the final version of the Nuremberg Laws and, as Zeidberg informed Jochem after two weeks of technical research by the Library's senior photographer, "it appears now that we both have original copies of D."[85]

Huntington officials were not prepared for the media onslaught because they had no real idea about the provenance of the Nuremberg Laws. Cecilia O'Leary and I would need to undertake several months of research to get a complete picture of what had happened. The Huntington's internal records are off limits to research, unless the researcher is a vetted insider.[86] Our request to do research in these records was denied, and was apparently perceived by some administrators as potentially damaging to the Library's reputation. Overall, our efforts to get the Huntington to take ethical responsibility for its mishandling of the Nuremberg Laws and to make its processes more transparent were unsuccessful. After several weeks of bargaining, we were given access to records, but only to those that we specifically requested. Only our interviews with Huntington staff and research in other collections eventually enabled us to reconstruct what had happened to the Nuremberg Laws during the missing fifty-four years.

The three main questions that the Huntington was challenged to address concerned how Patton chose the Library as a depository; on what basis Patton asserted his ownership; and why the Nuremberg Laws had remained buried in the vault for fifty-four years. In June, Mary Robertson and David Zeidberg, who handled the Nuremberg project for the Library, had neither informed nor persuasive answers to these questions because the Huntington had not done adequate research on the topics. Robertson's concern was with assuring that the documents were technically prepared for display at the Skirball, while Zeidberg's preoccupation was with security issues, in particular ensuring that the Skirball could protect the documents from right-wing terrorists or a mentally disturbed visitor.[87] Moreover, the curator of rare books, who had detailed knowledge of the history of the Huntington's collection of Patton-related materials, had not been consulted.[88]

Known to the Huntington at least as early as April, but not made available to the media in June were: the memo written by Frank Perls on April 28, 1945, in which he described the discovery of the Nuremberg Laws in Eichstätt; the letter written by trustee William Munro in 1951, in which he summed up Patton's 1945 instructions to the Huntington; and Mary Robertson's 1991 memo, in which she raised her concern about the "uncertainty of title." There are several reasons that could explain why the Huntington withheld these documents from the media and public. First, there was a clear discrepancy between Patton's hyperbolic account and Perls's sober description of how the Third Army recovered the Nuremberg Laws. By withholding the Perls memo, the Huntington was not obliged to address Patton's veracity. Even after almost all the details in Patton's story had been proved to be untrue, the Huntington did not retract his statement, which was reported in the *New York Times* and *Washington Post* as evidence of provenance.[89] Moreover, when the Skirball unveiled its Nuremberg display to the public at the end of June, among the items prominently displayed was Patton's fanciful recollection posing as a statement of fact. By December, even Skotheim admitted that it was "a work of fiction."[90]

Second, Perls's memo mentioned that the bank vault in Eichstätt also contained the "jewels of the Count Stauffenberg family."[91] In 1945, Patton had told the Huntington that the vault contained only the Nuremberg Laws. "That was *all* that was in the vault," he informed Robert Millikan, a fabrication no doubt designed to protect the Huntington from any hint of impropriety.[92] Stauffenberg had been executed for his role in the plot to assassinate Hitler. Although Perls says that the 203d CIC detachment "did not open the sealed package" of jewels—an account later confirmed by Martin Dannenberg, who thought that they might have been booby-trapped—the reference alone alarmed people at the Huntington. When Mary Robertson read Perls's memo in 1991, she was alerted to "the 'Indiana Jones' side of all of this: mentioned in one of the provenance statements ... was a sealed packet of Stauffenberg family jewels ... which were transmitted along with the documents, but which are not mentioned in General Van Fleet's or Patton's statements. Who knows where they are now—except not at the Huntington."[93]

When they re-read Robertson's memo in 1999, Skotheim and Zeidberg no doubt worried that the issue of the jewels might be enough of an attractive red herring to encourage the media to sniff around for a scandal. With the recent formation of the Commission on Holocaust Assets, museums around the country were highly sensitive to any allegations of improper acquisitions. The possibility that Patton had helped himself to some valuable loot continued to worry the Huntington's president. "My greatest curiosity," Skotheim wrote Martin Dannenberg in August, some six weeks after the Skirball exhibit was opened, "concerns the Stauffenberg family jewels. Do you remember them being in the vault? Notice that Patton says nothing else was in the vault."[94] What Skotheim did not know until later in the year was that the jewels had been returned to the Stauffenberg family after the war.[95] Even then, Skotheim continued to obsess about the jewels in public talks about the Nuremberg Laws.[96]

Third, the Huntington was concerned about whether they rightfully owned the Nuremberg documents. Mary Robertson's 1991 memo pointedly referred to them as "war loot." Under pressure to loan the documents to the Skirball before the *Washington Post* broke the story, the Huntington apparently skipped a title search. Research in the library's internal documents would have revealed that Patton's daughter had informed the Huntington in 1969 that "papers directly relating to my father" belonged in the Library of Congress, not the Huntington.[97] In May 1999, the Huntington hired an expert in rare documents, who authenticated the Nuremberg Laws and signatures, but he was not asked to verify the Huntington's title, nor did he have time to locate any other original copies.[98]

The Huntington faced a problem: it had not accessioned the Nuremberg Laws in the previous fifty-four years and could not loan documents it did not own. Some time in June, without any investigation of provenance, the Huntington solved its dilemma by simply asserting its ownership "as a gift from General Patton," without first checking its own internal records, consulting with the National Archives about the question of title, or investigating whether other original copies of the documents existed in Germany.[99] In its public statements, the Huntington based its ownership claims on the fact that the Nuremberg Laws "were later given to the Huntington by the General...."[100] The press accepted as fact that Patton had "donated them to the institution."[101] Drawing upon information provided by the Huntington, the *New York Times* reported that Patton "presented [the Nuremberg Laws] as a gift—along with a confiscated limited edition of Hitler's *Mein Kampf*—to the Huntington Library in Pasadena."[102]

The Huntington had documentation of Patton's dubious claim that General Van Fleet "made the presentation to me. So it is my property." But, as Skotheim recognized in 1999, "there was no way to document that it really belonged to Patton."[103] Moreover, Huntington officials did not produce any evidence that Patton or his heirs intended to donate the Nuremberg Laws to them. Skotheim remained concerned that the Huntington's right to title was tainted. "Do you think Patton knew he was not supposed to keep the documents," Skotheim asked Dannenberg in August. "That would explain why he did not want publicity about them if, in fact, he did not want publicity."[104]

If the Huntington in June 1999 had done a complete job of vetting provenance and if the media had done a thorough investigation rather than simply hinting at scandal, it would have become clear that neither Patton nor the Huntington had a rightful claim to ownership. Skepticism about title is probably the main reason that the Huntington kept the Nuremberg Laws out of sight and mind for so long. Knowing that it was a valuable historical document, they kept it with their prized artifacts in the most secure vault. Not until the 1990s—long after the Holocaust became widely recognized—did it occur to Huntington officials that there might be public interest in an icon associated with one of the most important racial tragedies of the twentieth century. In the 1980s, the Huntington's research director thought of the Nuremberg Laws as one of "the many oddities" donated to the Library.[105] "We don't accession everything," explained the curator of rare manuscripts in 1999. "We also have a Babylonian clay tablet that records the sale of a cat."[106]

Robert Skotheim's generous decision to loan the Nuremberg Laws to the Skirball Cultural Center was influenced by the Huntington's need to make connection with the new centers of cultural power in Los Angeles, and to respond to the extraordinary growth of Jewish and Hollywood-based philanthropy. It perhaps crossed somebody's mind that a display of the Nuremberg Laws at the Huntington would have opened up a Pandora's box of troubles: questions about title, General

Patton's unsavory views about Jews, Edward Huntington's chauvinism, Robert Millikan's racism, and local gossip about the Huntington's reputation for anti-Semitism. In the 1990s, the Huntington had slowly and reluctantly accommodated itself to internal reforms of its governance and research programs, and opened its doors to a more diverse group of scholars and researchers. Yet evidently, it was not yet ready for the kind of introspection that would disturb its own origins story.

In contrast, as a new institution the Skirball Cultural Center was not haunted by skeletons in the closet or weighed down by tradition's thrall. For his part, Uri Herscher, the Skirball's president, did not want to get drawn into any controversy about ownership or what motivated the Huntington to keep the Nuremberg Laws off the books for so long. "I didn't ask for an explanation," he told the press. "I was more concerned that these documents be presided over by a Jewish institution."[107]

The Skirball had to worry about a different set of challenges: how to represent General Patton, the notorious anti-Semite and loyal son of the Huntington clan; whether to display the Nuremberg Laws as a shrine or as an integral component of its main exhibition; which narrative to choose in explaining the significance of the Nuremberg Laws for American Jews; and what history lessons to teach.

◙ Chapter 12 ◙

History Lessons

Stand too close to horror, and you get fixation, paralysis, engulfment; stand too far, and you get voyeurism or forgetting. Distance matters.

(Eva Hoffman, 2004)

STORY OF THE OBJECTS

When Cecilia and I visited the Skirball for the first time on July 2, 1999, the main attraction was the Nuremberg Laws. From the moment we arrived at the center, the greeter at the door and ticket-seller encouraged us to head straight for the new acquisition. We joined a steady flow of visitors, attracted by the widespread publicity, and followed a docent through the core exhibition until we arrived at a murky case, protected by an armed security guard, located next to the holocaust memorial. We were surprised to find a crowded, poorly lit display, with very little contextual information. At that time, we did not know that the Nuremberg materials had been prepared in a rush or that they were displayed in a case designed to house an Albert Einstein exhibit. The Skirball's program director, however, was well aware of the limitations: his staff had been given only weeks, not the anticipated months, to prepare for the public opening.[1]

In its debut, the Skirball's Nuremberg case consisted of materials loaned by the Huntington: the four pages of original Nuremberg Laws and the envelope in which they were found in Germany in 1945; the presentation edition of *Mein Kampf*; the photograph documenting delivery of the Nuremberg Laws to the Huntington on June 11, 1945; and Patton's statement of provenance, dictated at the Huntington on the same day.[2]

General Patton was a powerful presence in this original tableau, even competing with Hitler for viewers' attention: Patton's name is associated with the capture of the Nuremberg Laws, his statement frames the story of their capture, his signature, not Hitler's, is scrawled on the cover of *Mein Kampf*, and his image dominates the photograph. The single photograph in the original display was not only a visual attraction in a case of documents, but it also provided a narrative that tied the exhibit together. The Huntington made the photograph available to reporters, and the print media gave it a prominent place in their coverage.[3]

In the photograph, George Washington in military regalia looks down from his portrait, while the World War II general hands over the Nuremberg Laws—in an envelope embossed with Nazi insignia—to physicist Robert Millikan, chairman of Huntington's board of trustees. The image communicates continuity between General Washington and General Patton, known respectively as "the father" of the nation and "the liberator" of Europe, related by blood and a determination to defend the republic against the monarchy, and democracy against fascism. The photograph also speaks to the centrality of war in the American experience, the alliance between science and the military, and power sharing between civil and political authorities. There are also less heroic and more contradictory

12.1 R. Millikan and Gen. Patton: transfer of the Nuremberg Laws.

ways of reading this image, but in June 1999 the Huntington promoted it and the Skirball provisionally accepted it as a statement about the triumph of American values over totalitarianism.

Initially, at least, the Skirball tried to respect the Huntington's historical and ceremonial ties with Patton. Uri Herscher appreciated the Huntington's generosity and felt a genuine bond with Robert Skotheim's efforts to move the Huntington in new directions. In a press release issued on June 26, Herscher's diplomatic wording awkwardly credited Patton for helping the world to preserve memories of the holocaust. The general, said Herscher, "no doubt had something of the sort in mind."[4] And when the Nuremberg case was installed on June 25, 1999, and opened to the public on June 29, a text panel was faithful to the Huntington's version of a suitable past:

Early Nazi Documents Captured by U.S. Army

"In April 1945, American troops opened a locked vault in Eichstaett, Germany. Inside they found the original transcript, signed by Adolf Hitler, of the Nazi regime's 1935 Nuremberg Laws depriving Jews of German citizenship. This was the first crucial decree leading to the Holocaust. A month later, the typescript was presented to General George S. Patton, Jr., Commanding General of the Third Army.

Shortly before his untimely death, Patton donated the typescript to the library founded by his father's friend, Henry Huntington, in San Marino, California.

He also sent the library a rare presentation edition of Hitler's anti-Semitic, anti-democratic tract *Mein Kampf*, which had been captured near Weimar, Germany.

These documents remained unexhibited for over half a century. In June 1999, recognizing the historical context provided by the Skirball Cultural Center, the Huntington Library transferred the documents to the Skirball on indefinite loan, as a witness to the most tragic chapter of Jewish and world history."[5]

It was an emotional jolt to witness the Nuremberg Laws up close, but I was also derailed by the benign presence of General Patton. By this time, I knew that he had harbored an enormous loathing of Jews. I would have the same gut response a few years later when I drove by the Charles M. Goethe arboretum in Sacramento, aware that my university had chosen to honor a eugenicist who despised most of humanity. As it stood in the summer of 1999, the exhibit at the Skirball gave the impression that Patton-the-liberator, true to his nickname, had helped to rescue "democracy and democratic values" from fascism.[6] It was difficult to reconcile this persona with the General Patton who had blamed Jewish conspiracies for America's failure to take on the "Mongolian [Russian] savages," regarded Jewish survivors as a "sub-human species," and had sought to undermine de-Nazification policies, forcing Eisenhower to remove him from his command.[7]

During our first visit to the Skirball, Cecilia and I decided that simply to document the history of the exhibit was insufficient; we also had an ethical obligation to enter into a dialogue with Skirball officials about what we knew about Patton. We had tried, unsuccessfully, to get the Huntington to address its institutional amnesia and publicly acknowledge its dubious claim to title of the Nuremberg Laws. Our energy now focused on trying to knock Patton off the triumphant pedestal he occupied in the Skirball's Nuremberg case.

We raised our concerns with the Skirball's president at our first meeting on July 20, 1999. Uri Herscher was well aware of Patton's reputation for anti-Semitism, and was not surprised to hear about the general's more pervasive racism and Robert Millikan's similar bigotry. "Not the finest of America's sons," he observed about Patton after we summarized our research. A colleague had recently informed him that Patton's personal, annotated copy of Hitler's *My Struggle (Mein Kampf)* was up for auction at Christie's. "I'm going to make a hero of somebody like that?" asked Herscher rhetorically, pointing to the framed collage of family pictures and documents that testify to the loss of family members in the holocaust. Among Hitler's victims were Herscher's grandparents, aunts, uncles, and cousins that "it was never my privilege to know."[8]

Within the next six months, the Nuremberg case at the Skirball was changed five times.[9] Gradually, the Skirball reframed the exhibit and removed most of the prominent Patton materials. Herscher tried to do so without fanfare or publicity, allowing the Huntington to save some face in what had become a humiliating fiasco. In public speeches and conversations with visitors, he first distanced himself from Patton by emphasizing "the debt of gratitude we owe to the United States Armed Forces, whose courage and determination during World War II were so decisive to the liberation of Europe from Hitler's genocidal grip."[10] The photograph of Patton transferring the Nuremberg Laws to Robert Millikan was not to be interpreted "as a tribute to these gentlemen."[11]

The appearance of Martin Dannenberg on the scene provided a serendipitous opportunity to change the exhibit. Dannenberg's letter to the *Washington Post* appeared on July 19, 1999. He followed this up with a letter to the Skirball, in which he "set the record straight" about Patton's role in "the original discovery of this infamous document."[12] Our interviews with Martin Dannenberg—first by telephone on August 12 and 13, and then in person on October 3 at his home in Baltimore—verified and documented his claims about how the Nuremberg Laws had been retrieved at the end of the war. Dannenberg's narrative not only contested Patton's fanciful story, but also raised the likelihood that Patton had knowingly looted an important Nazi document. Cecilia and I quickly shared our findings with Uri Herscher, officials at the Huntington, and the *Washington Post's* Sharon Waxman.[13]

The Nuremberg case was dismantled on September 7, 1999, to accommodate the planned retrofitting of the building that housed "Visions and Values," the center's core exhibition that traces Jewish life "from antiquity to America." During the temporary closure, Herscher made the decision to remove Patton's story and change the text panel. Faced with evidence that completely discredited Patton's account of the provenance of the Nuremberg documents, the Skirball pulled his dictated statement from the display case and returned it to the Huntington on October 6, 1999. "As soon as we found out it was bogus, we changed the case," said the Skirball's senior curator.[14]

Herscher then invited Martin Dannenberg and members of his family to visit the Skirball on December 12 for a commemorative event celebrating the opening of the new Nuremberg case, designed by architect Moshe Safdie to complement the center's holocaust memorial. With hundreds in attendance—including officials from the Huntington and Marianne Perls, Frank's niece—Dannenberg gave a dignified, factually precise account of how he found the Nuremberg Laws.[15] "That scoundrel Patton sometimes stretched the truth," Dannenberg told the audience.[16] He also provided the Huntington with a photograph of himself taken in 1945: Dannenberg in military uniform, standing next to a Counter-Intelligence Corps jeep. This was Herscher's opportunity to replace the photograph of the anti-Semitic general with one of the Jewish master sergeant.

12.2 The Skirball's Nuremberg Laws case, designed by Moshe Safdie, December 1999.

12.3 Martin Dannenberg reunited on December 12, 1999, with the Nuremberg Laws that he retrieved on April 27, 1945.

Soon after Dannenberg's visit, the Skirball's docents were briefed on "Patton's antagonisms to Jews and other minorities. They share this fact with our visitors,"

Uri Herscher told me.[17] The center also changed a key caption in the display. The original Nuremberg exhibit, which opened on June 29, 1999, informed visitors that "the typescript was presented to General George S. Patton, Jr., Commanding General of the Third Army" and that "Patton donated the typescript to the library founded by his father's friend."[18] By 2000, the first sentence had been removed and the second one changed: "General George S. Patton, Jr., deposited the typescripts with the library founded by his father's friend, Henry Huntington, in San Marino, California."[19] In museum parlance, there is a world of difference between *donated* and *deposited.*

In the exhibition, as it now stands, visitors must search for signs of Patton's once-dominating presence. Gone are his familiar, larger-than-life photographic presence and his fabricated war story. What remains is his signature on *Mein Kampf*, which can be read ambiguously as the mark of a conqueror trumping his enemy or, for those in the know, as the sign of a secret admirer of fascist ideology.

OBJECTS OF THE STORY

Beyond managing the diplomatic and historical problems presented by the Patton materials, the Skirball faced another difficult issue: where to locate the Nuremberg materials physically and symbolically within the center's generally optimistic interpretation of Jewish history. The Skirball was not originally conceived as a place to tell stories. When leaders of the Cincinnati-based Hebrew Union College began to plan a new institution on the West Coast in the 1980s, they imagined a traditional museum that would house and display thousands of Jewish artifacts and memorabilia collected during the previous hundred years. But Uri Herscher, Stanley Chyet, and other like-minded reformers argued for a new kind of institution, one that would reflect the rise to power of mostly secular Jews in the political economy of Los Angeles. When the Huntington opened to the public in the 1920s, Los Angeles was a segregated city, with Jews barred from professional jobs downtown and ownership of homes in many neighborhoods, even as they found a niche within the emerging movie industry.[20] By the 1950s, their numbers rose to three hundred thousand in the Los Angeles area, and Jewish entrepreneurs dominated the construction and financing of suburban development, the building of shopping centers, and the development of retail supermarkets.[21]

By the time the Skirball Cultural Center opened in 1996, over half a million Jews were living in Los Angeles, the third-largest concentration of Jews in the world after New York and Tel Aviv.[22] With an annual operating budget of $10.2 million in 2001, the Skirball attracted two and one-half million visitors in its first five years, about the same number as the Huntington.[23] Unlike the Huntington, however, which is located in the suburban hinterlands, the Skirball is in the heart of Los Angeles, "where Sepulveda, Mulholland, and the 405 freeway come together," noted architect Moshe Safdie. "The Skirball is architecture for a city where buildings are experienced at sixty miles per hour."[24]

The Skirball shifted its emphasis away from the inward-looking orientation of many ethnic museums that are designed to strengthen and unify a people facing a hostile world, or a world that could quickly turn hostile. This type of institution typically focuses on preserving icons and relics, documenting past hardships, and instilling a shared cultural affinity. The Skirball similarly has a commitment to maintaining Jewish artifacts and customs, and serving the needs of Jewish communities in Los Angeles. But it also consciously breaks with an insular tradition that emphasizes the preservation of a unique Jewish identity in the face of cultural dissolution and assimilation. Instead, the Skirball's ethos is future-oriented and utopian, with a focus on affirmation and progress. "At a time when there is so much discord surrounding us," observed Safdie in 1996, "so much distrust that makes up our cities, when there is chaos in our built environment and a general pessimism about the idea of community, I hoped we could make a place that seeks serenity and calm."[25]

Uri Herscher envisioned a "new paradigm"—the Skirball as a "true meeting place" and "surrogate home for *everyone*." The best of Jewish qualities, he argues, are "human and humane" values. "This is a place that embraces the whole community, that invites people from all backgrounds to see themselves reflected in our particular story." Consequently, what is emphasized at the Skirball is not what makes Jews culturally, ethnically, and religiously unique and distinct from other groups, but what they have in common with other American immigrants and citizens, and what other ethnicities have in common with Jews. The Skirball is a place "where cultures connect."[26] The orientation is on "Jewish life," notes the *Los Angeles Business Journal*, "but the broad programming has made it a destination for everyone."[27]

The Skirball's core exhibition, "Visions and Values," presents the familiar epic journey by Jews from "Antiquity to America," but there is also an effort to represent Jewish diversity. "We weren't looking for an official version of Jewishness," observes Robert Kirschner, the Skirball's program director. "The exhibition reflects a real cross-section of the opinions and attitudes of the community, with all the dissonance that involves."[28] Moreover, the Skirball's cultural programming, which attracts more visitors than does its exhibitions, is eclectically multicultural, including concerts, plays, readings, and seminars that often are not directly linked to Jewish themes. A typical month in 2005 offered West African music, an experimental theater group from England, an African-American storyteller, and a talk by journalist Robert MacNeil.

The Skirball scrupulously tries to avoid the fetishization of artifacts and icons. The core exhibition "is not *about* objects. It *uses* objects, to tell a story," says Uri Herscher. "We should love objects, but we should love people more." The center presents its fine collection of museum-quality materials in a story-driven ambience. Undergirding the center's diverse programming is a finely tuned, consistent narrative that emphasizes not only how hospitable the United States has been to Jewish immigrants, but also the fundamental compatibility of Jewish and American values.[29] The core exhibition tells the story of Jews' "successful integration into present-day American life."[30] It includes "vignettes of representative figures"— such as union organizer Rose Schneiderman, businessman Levi Strauss, and physicist Albert Einstein—to illustrate the ability of Jews to find their place in the land of "struggle and opportunity."[31] The prevailing motif is not so much "Never Again" as "California Here We Come."

"Visions and Values" stays on message, emphasizing that "American and Jewish ideals are congruent, and they underscore the hopeful promise of American liberty."[32] An orientation video at the entrance to the exhibition reminds visitors of the "remarkable parallels between the principles of American democracy and the ideals that Jews have cherished." Red, white, and blue icons are displayed throughout the exhibition, reinforcing the connection. Moreover, the Skirball's bookstore has a large Americana section: books for children—such as *Stars and Stripes Forever*, *America the Beautiful*, *Children's Encyclopedia of American History*, and *The Poems of Abraham Lincoln*—a large magnetic American flag, a pen topped by a statue of liberty, and a kaleidoscope decorated with the American flag.

The Skirball recognizes that the quest for liberty and justice "has often been a struggle," but the stories told in the exhibition reveal very little about the significance and texture of these struggles.[33] The focus is on "the open society of the United States," not its closed doors and dead ends.[34] This new perspective reflects the favorable economic, political, and social conditions in which Jews found themselves during the last thirty years. Still, it is a significant strategic shift for an organization with roots in a Jewish activist tradition and a reputation for confronting injustice. In 1940, the Hebrew Union College's (HUC) president Julian Morgenstern helped to create the Jewish College in Exile in Cincinnati as a base for leading Jewish intellectuals who were forced to flee Nazi Germany. In 1956, a delegation from HUC to the South was arrested for its participation in the Montgomery bus boycott. And in 1972, the college graduated Sally Priesand, the first woman to be ordained as a rabbi in the United States.[35]

The founders of the Skirball share this politicized background. Uri Herscher experienced the "Jewish story" as a "mournful" experience, "full of loss," and was inspired by New Left activism when he came to the United States as an immigrant from Israel.[36] He received his B.A. from U.C. Berkeley in a radicalized sociology department during the tumultuous sixties, at about the same time as I was taking similar classes there.[37] Herscher's colleague, Stanley Chyet, also felt a responsibility to take stands on challenging issues, such as the need for reconciliation between Jews and Arabs. As Chyet wrote, "I love the doves / of Jerusalem / which sail and squabble / over the Temple Mount / and nest /

impartially / in the Western Wall / and the Dome of the Rock / the Yeshiva Porat Yosef / and the museum of Al-Aksa."[38]

Yet there are few signs of intra-Jewish squabbling in the Skirball's core exhibition. The Skirball teaches very little about the long, complex tradition of Jewish leftism in the United States—in the socialist and communist movements, in which Jews played a leading role; in the civil rights, feminist, gay-lesbian, and anti-war movements; in the liberal wing of the Democratic party—or its contributions to critiques of injustice and inequality. Perhaps the Skirball's departure from this activist tradition, rooted in opposition and confrontation, is a reflection of the collapse of the old and new Lefts, and of a Jewish base that is now composed of comfortable insiders.

If you study carefully at the Skirball, you can learn that "not all immigrants came willingly" to this country; that in the Republic's early years, Jews were denied basic rights and Africans suffered "systematic oppression"; and that the "acculturation process" could be "a very harsh reality for many."[39] But visitors will find little information about the history of anti-Semitism and racism in the United States, and almost nothing about the long trail of prejudice and discrimination in the Golden State. A token display on anti-Semitism, tucked away in a small enclave, is presented as "the legacy of historical antagonisms in Europe rather than as something completely indigenous."[40] Reproductions of late-nineteenth-century racial stereotypes in an English magazine convey the message that "*Puck* may have depicted Jews outrageously," but the texts quickly reassure us that "Jews were treated no more harshly than other ethnic groups."

This approach is consistent with recent developments in multicultural education, in particular a tendency to focus on the social and cultural contributions made by the victims of racism to the larger society. A celebratory emphasis on "strengths"—which has replaced the traditional stereotyping of backwardness, inferiority, and cultural deprivation—tends to minimize the tragic past in order to communicate an image of positive agency. Since the 1980s, attention to the state's tragic origins and bloody development in California textbooks has been meager, choosing instead to describe how "people from everywhere built California," with vignettes of Chinese railroad workers, Japanese farmers, Mexican agricultural workers, and so on through the cultural rainbow.[41]

With its concentration on good news and progress, the Skirball is not the place to find information or engagement concerning the history of antagonisms between Jews and other ethnic groups, especially African Americans, Asians, and Latinos, on the precarious state of race relations in Los Angeles, or on intra-Jewish prejudices and disagreements. So it comes as something of a surprise to find in the Skirball's memorial to the holocaust a modest critique of the timidity of Jewish organizations during World War II: "Had there been strong, concerted pressure from American Jewish leaders, the government might have tried to help the Jews of Europe. But that pressure never came."

This statement stands out incongruously in an exhibition that chooses to avoid texts or displays suggesting any kind of disunity among Jews. At the Skirball, you will not be exposed to Jews fighting each other over slavery during the Civil War or families torn apart over the Palestinian Question today. With volatile debates swept out of sight, the long-established tradition of disputation is erased from Jewish character: the Jew apparently no longer relishes a good argument. The exhibition concludes with a room devoted to "Jewish rebirth" in Israel, a parallel story to the Jewish freedom story in the United States. Here, Israel becomes, without debate or controversy, simply a "stable democracy" and a source of "pride and solidarity among Jews throughout the world."[42]

REFRAMING

In March 1999, after Robert Skotheim and Uri Herscher shook hands on their agreement, Skirball officials were excited that they had pulled off a coup by beating out seasoned competition for the Nuremberg Laws. Initially, however, they were not sure about how to frame and contextualize the new trophy. Some staff members worried that the inclusion of *Mein Kampf* might glorify nazism, and even attract right-wing fanatics eager to worship a relic of anti-Semitism. Others were concerned that the Nuremberg Laws would distract from the center's focus on the Jewish-American experience—that the objects would overwhelm the exhibition's storyline.[43]

The Skirball had previously faced this issue when a decision was needed on how to represent the holocaust. By the late 1980s, when the core exhibition was being planned, any new Jewish institution felt morally obliged to include some kind of holocaust memorial.[44] The national Holocaust Museum would open in Washington, D.C., in 1993, and every city with a sizable Jewish population subsequently commemorated the "paradigm of historical horror par excellence."[45] Yet unlike the national museum, which seeks to educate visitors about the holocaust's historical contexts, most Jewish museums and cultural centers represent memory of the holocaust as a "sacred mystery."[46] This approach typically emphasizes The Holocaust as specific only to the Jewish experience and as resistant to historical analysis. The problem with framing the holocaust in the mystical imagery of catastrophe and rebirth is that the viewer is encouraged to abandon critical intelligence and the application of political lessons to today's tragedies.[47]

In New York's Jewish Museum, for example, the holocaust is commemorated in a small, chapel-like side room off the permanent exhibit. There is one case of concentration camp items—uniform, spoon, and artwork—and a case of rescued objects, including a silver Torah crown that was made in Nuremberg early in eighteenth century. It is a modest display of objects and there is no effort to make sense of the holocaust. A text panel on the wall describes "the Shoah" as a "rupture in Jewish history.... The enormity of these crimes defies comprehension." The museum's shop, however, responds to people's hunger for explanation and interpretation: there are five shelves of books on the holocaust, compared to four shelves on religion, one and one-half shelves on Israel, and one shelf on American Jewry.[48]

The Skirball's holocaust display followed a similar course, opting for respectful imagery and an emphasis on memorial over interpretative story. There are no photographs of corpses or emaciated survivors, no displays of abandoned shoes or gold teeth, no grinning Nazis. Instead of bloody horrors, six large dignified portraits of fully endowed people who died in the camps represent the holocaust's victims. "These are not atrocity photos," says Kirschner.[49] At the end of the portrait gallery is a "quiet cylindrical space" that contains a stone pedestal holding a single candle flame, drawing visitors "into a memory space and place for reflection."[50]

Soon after the Huntington's loan was confirmed in the spring of 1999, the Skirball decided to locate the Nuremberg case next to its holocaust gallery. But, unlike the holocaust memorial, Herscher and his staff wanted to integrate the new materials into the core exhibition, to use the objects to "tell a story."[51] This was a difficult challenge because it would be traumatic for visitors to stop and look at Hitler's signature on a document that they perceive as signing their ancestors' death warrant; unnerving to look at an obscenely huge and kitschy, vanity edition of *Mein Kampf*; and for those who remember World War II, disturbing to see Patton's egomaniacal signature on the cover of Hitler's bible of the master race. Yet the Skirball was determined to assure that the Nuremberg case was more than a "display of horror."[52]

I returned to the Skirball early in 2005 to see how they had resolved these dilemmas. Having weathered several permutations, and purged the Patton-Millikan photograph and Patton's memoir, the Nuremberg case now displays the Laws, the envelope in which they were kept since the 1930s, *Mein Kampf*, and a photograph of Master Sergeant Martin Dannenberg standing next to his jeep. The triangle-shaped case, specially designed by Moshe Safdie, is somber black and is juxtaposed with the cone-like form of the adjacent holocaust memorial. Perhaps it symbolizes a wedge being inserted into the smooth flow of Jewish history.[53] The totemic power of the objects in the Nuremberg case

12.4 Master Sergeant Dannenberg replaces General Patton.

still provokes horror and awe. "This always gives me goose-bumps," says a docent leading a tour. "It tells of our demise," she says, pausing. "But here we are."

The Nuremberg exhibition is more than a wrenching emotional experience. Now it tells a story, an Americanized story, and teaches history lessons.[54] "Do you know what is the best revenge for the Holocaust?" asked Uri Herscher in 1996. "It's to rebuild our lives and make sure that the story that was once lived with such vibrancy will have a chance to be retold decades and centuries after Hitler."[55] The acquisition of the Nuremberg Laws enabled the Skirball to contrast "Hitler's genocidal grip" with "a reasoned system of democratic thought and process, as in the United States."[56] The "poison of Nazism," says Uri Herscher, "did *not* have the final word. Democracy and its values have prevailed."[57]

Playing continually on a monitor next to the Nuremberg case is a three-minute video that reinforces the message in the texts. First we see images of Nazi mobs and hear how the Nuremberg Laws "paved the way to the Holocaust." Then we see the Allies invading Germany in 1945, troops blowing up a huge swastika in Nuremberg, Eisenhower leading an American delegation into a concentration camp, and American troops marching through the streets. "Tyranny did not prevail," concludes the video as an image of the U.S. flag waves in the background. "Democracy endures."

The Skirball has effectively integrated the Nuremberg materials into its triumphal perspective on American democracy and its utopian celebration of an inclusive, multicultural California, where "cultures connect." But it has done so at a price. The problem, as W. G. Sebald sardonically observes, is that "whenever one is imagining a bright future, the next disaster is just around the corner."[58] The Skirball is located in one of the most racially divided and economically stratified regions in the United States, a place where "social polarization has increased almost as rapidly as population."[59] Generally, Los Angeles is a metropolis in which cultures disconnect. For me, the soothing reassurance about democracy's triumph grates not only against the magical power of a Nazi relic, but also against the segregated worlds of privilege and inequality that constitute Southern California.

MINING THE PAST

When Cecilia and I interviewed Robert Skotheim, the Huntington's president in 1999, he insisted that the Library was not an appropriate place to exhibit the Nuremberg Laws. "The Skirball is a history teacher making a contribution," he explained. "There are no historical lessons here."[60] His position was based on the assumption that an artifact so closely associated with anti-Semitism and the holocaust deserves to be located within a Jewish center as a matter of historical context and historical justice. He has a good point: it may be symbolically appropriate for the Nuremberg Laws to be displayed now at the Skirball. At the same time, though, there are valuable history lessons to be extricated from the Huntington's past.

Perhaps the Huntington's board of trustees had this in mind in 2001 when, following the media brouhaha over the Nuremberg Laws and the retirement of Robert Skotheim, it took the unprecedented step of hiring as its new president Steven Koblik, a Jew with expertise on the holocaust.[61] With an undergraduate degree from Berkeley—in history and Scandinavian studies in 1963, the year I arrived there for graduate school—and a doctorate in European History from Northwestern, Koblik was president of liberal Reed College in Portland from 1992 until his appointment at the Huntington. Koblik has written about anti-Semitism in Sweden during the Nazi era. "I have always identified enthusiastically as a Jew," says Koblik, "but dealing with the Holocaust reinforced this identification."[62] His book calls attention to how the "the silence of the democratic world played its part" in enabling the Nazi regime to slaughter millions.[63] Now, the Huntington has an opportunity to open up its own past to the light, to understand how its own silence was complicit in social injustice.

First, there are legal-ethical issues regarding the mishandling of the Nuremberg Laws. The evidence leads me to conclude the following: Patton looted the documents, and the Huntington did not raise this possibility in its public pronouncements. Nor did the Huntington act upon the request made by the general's heirs to transfer all his personal papers to the Library of Congress. Moreover, when the decision was made in 1999 to exhibit the Nuremberg Laws at the Skirball, the Huntington skipped a serious investigation of provenance. Much of its energy was consumed by public relations and controlling potential damage to its reputation. At the launching of the loan to the Skirball, the Huntington did not release documents that at least would have raised questions about Patton's veracity.

Guidelines issued by the American Association of Museums regarding unlawful appropriations during the Nazi era do not exactly fit the Huntington's copy of the Nuremberg Laws. The Laws were not looted or stolen from holocaust victims. There are no heirs seeking financial remuneration, no litigants pressing a claim, and no state or municipality is seeking the return of a sacred object of national significance. Also, the AAM makes no specific recommendations regarding looted manuscripts and documents.[64]

Nevertheless, the spirit of the AAM's guidelines is applicable: the Huntington's copy of the Nuremberg Laws marks a "momentous" event in the history of Jews and, if available, would be sought after by museums that focus on Jewish history. The document is extremely rare and commercially valuable. Moreover, it was looted, not from victims of the holocaust, but from the Nazis and the U.S. Army. The "stewardship of collections," notes the AAM, "entails the highest public trust and carries with it the presumption of rightful ownership, permanence, care, documentation, accessibility, and responsible disposal."[65] Museums have a public responsibility to ensure that they are the rightful owners of their collections and that there is full documentation of provenance. This is especially the case with the Huntington Library, whose public obligations are recognized in the California Constitution.

Legal ownership is not easily determined. If Patton had forwarded the Nuremberg Laws as ordered, the Allies probably would have used them as a propaganda exhibit at the Nuremberg War Crimes Tribunal before turning them over to the National Archives. After the war, the U.S. Army returned many documents and objects to the new German government, but materials considered historically significant or politically inflammatory—such as Hitler's personal paintings or the photographs taken by his personal photographer, Heinrich Hoffman—were retained by the U.S. government, unavailable to the public for many years.[66] Very likely, the Nuremberg Laws would have ended up at the National Archives.

In the absence of claims of ownership—from the U.S. or German governments, or the heirs of General Patton, or even Martin Dannenberg—the Huntington's possession of the Nuremberg Laws prevails for the moment. Dannenberg is "glad that the documents are now in a place where they will be seen by an understanding public." Yet the Huntington and Skirball should consider his diplomatic recommendation: "I am sure other museums will want to borrow them in the future and I hope, because of their importance and what they represent, that they can be temporarily loaned to other responsible institutions."[67]

Beyond the legal-ethical issues involving provenance loom more complicated matters of public history. There is much important material to be excavated at the Huntington. Its handling of the Nuremberg Laws teaches a great deal about how the Library's founding fathers shaped the boundaries and parameters of its collections and exhibitions; the role of race and gender in the recruitment of staff and scholars, the development of a research agenda, and the shaping of organizational culture; and how ideas have practical consequences, whether through legitimating eugenics policies in Nazi Germany and the United States, or reinforcing legacies of exclusion through racial discrimination and segregation.

The Huntington's loan of the Nuremberg Laws to the Skirball served several purposes: it was an act of generosity to a new cultural center; an effort to bridge the cultural divide between east and west Los Angeles; and a desire to broaden the Huntington's fundraising opportunities. Intentionally or not, the loan also diverted attention from its own history. As the Huntington moves toward diversifying its public programs and reaching out to new constituencies, it would benefit from a full and honest reckoning with the past. A possible model is the Maryland Historical Society, which invited artist Fred Wilson to mine its archives and mount an exhibit in Baltimore between 1992 and 1993. Wilson was given full access to collections, as well as the authority to determine contents and labeling of the cases.[68]

The result was a challenging and disturbing exhibition that exposed the history of racism in Maryland; demonstrated the ways in which museums selectively confer status on the basis of cultural and class hierarchies; and explored the collusion and participation of museums in the history of racial repression.[69] Wilson, notes historian Ira Berlin, "turns the traditional historical museum against itself."[70]

A mining of the Huntington's collections might involve releasing to the public and researchers all materials associated with the provenance of the Nuremberg Laws, in compliance with AAM's recommendation that important acquisitions be made "available for further research, examination, and public review and accountability."[71] As the Huntington's new president has observed, "the study of history depends upon documents."[72] In addition, the Huntington has the opportunity to explore the historical threads that link the holocaust with the homeland, and to make its own institutional amnesia a topic of inquiry. This could be accomplished by opening up internal records to scholars and researchers; engaging the Huntington's staff in an examination and discussion of past practices and policies; and inviting curators from outside the Library to mount exhibitions that address the Huntington's role in shaping California's historiography and iconography.

🔲 Chapter 13 🔲

Past and Present

History is what gives a place meaning.

(Rebecca Solnit, 2004)

IN THE EYES OF OTHERS

"I felt I had to make the sculpture," replied George Segal when he was asked about his motivation for constructing *The Holocaust*. His multi-figured installation of sprawling life-size bodies, cast in whitened bronze, was erected in San Francisco's Lincoln Park in 1984. "I decided I had to go for my own emotional jugular," explained the artist.[1] My experience with the Nuremberg project has been a similarly compelling process. What started in the summer of 1999 as a short-term exercise in historical detective work became a five-year exploration of amnesia and origins stories, my own included. Why did I take it so personally?

When I left England in 1963, aged twenty-one, I left behind an identity in which being a Jew was an important component. As a child I was exposed to my immigrant grandparents' direct experience of pogroms, flight, and uneasy settlement in a new land. They did not want to go back to the worlds they had left behind, not even in their imaginations. I remember their silences. I cannot recall even one conversation with my paternal grandparents about their experiences in Poland. And when my maternal grandmother Edith talked about her youth in late-nineteenth-century Romania, she evoked an idyllic world of bountiful wheat fields, not the ominous anti-Semitism that drove out her family.

The only part of her past in Romania that she would discuss with me in detail involved the food that filled her groaning table in the northwest seaside resort of Southport. She was an extraordinarily talented chef, but put nothing on paper since she could barely write her own name. It took years before she was willing to pass on her culinary expertise to me, her firstborn grandson. On trips back to England, I made a point of asking her for recipes.[2] She resisted for a long time because it offended her sense of gender propriety. But she was also a seasoned pragmatist who knew when it was time to concede: after her only son left his wife for another man, she abandoned her visceral homophobia.

175

Edith's instructions were a theatrical performance, delivered with animated facial gestures and punctuated by arguments over timing and ingredients with my mother, who was usually present. She resisted giving exact amounts. A dish that my mother Eileen pretentiously called *Haricots Verts à la Romanian* involved cooking green beans in the oven—the longer the better. It begins dramatically, with white flour and pepper fried in a dry skillet until smoking brown. "How much?" I would ask timidly. "A handful of flour, lots of pepper," she would shout as she did when talking to foreigners or minor bureaucrats. "Salt, you didn't mention salt," I'd point out. She would throw up her hands in mock disgust and look away. "Of course salt. Always a little salt." As she spoke, I would take notes and encourage her digressions because I was just as interested in the historical context of, say, borscht with boiled potatoes, as I was in how to stop the soup from curdling.

My parents raised me in the 1940s in much the same way as Käte and Hugo Perls raised their children in the 1920s: standing tall, assimilated for success. I was the first person in my extended family to go to university, and the first to go on to graduate school. But Monty and Eileen also passed on to me, mostly in subtle ways, a sense of alert attentiveness to the possibility that the good life could quickly unravel. "Ve British much stick together," joked my dad, who spoke respectable middle-class English. It was a joke with an edge. The erosion of organized British anti-Semitism happened during my lifetime, so I remained aware that I was an outsider even as I mingled with insiders, and that I needed to stay on my toes.

Despite all the cultural capital I accumulated in my youth—visits to museums and art galleries, Shakespeare in Stratford, avant-garde theater in London, vacations "on the Continent" long before the *hoi polloi* crossed the English Channel, and exposure to the arts high and low—I felt uneasy at the university, self-conscious about my identity as an interloper from the provinces. Oxford is only about one hundred and fifty miles away from Manchester, but in 1960 it was on a different planet. I was a northerner with a detectable regional accent, and a secular Jew from a nouveau riche family with leftist politics. I was surrounded by people who spoke plummy English, had gone to private schools, came from old money, were nominally Protestants, and voted Conservative. Close friends, sports, jazz, and beat literature imported from San Francisco got me through the experience, but the three years in Oxford were not the best years of my life.

This all changed in 1963, when I moved to the United States. Graduate schools there had expressed little interest in my academic abilities, but paid close attention to my apparent pedigree. It was enough that I had been an undergraduate at Oxford and that I had a solid name like Platt, evoking the breeding of landed gentry and old-school ties. What to W. E. B. Du Bois was "the arrogance of the Englishman amuck"—the sense that "whiteness is the ownership of the earth forever and amen"—was an attractive quality to university administrators in the United States, who did everything possible in the 1950s and 1960s to drain people like me out of Europe's brain pool.[3] "Nobody gives you your identity, you have to reinvent yourself every day," observed a transplanted, Jewish, Polish-born writer confronting "the blessings and the terrors of multiplicity" that await most immigrants to the United States.[4] Yet, there was a ready-made identity waiting for me to slip into: I was admitted to Berkeley largely on the preferential basis of appearing to be a white, educated, generically British intellectual, still something of a rarity at West Coast universities in the 1960s.

I was received as an Oxonian, a representative of a cultured civilization, which was a new identity for me. Unlike Käte Perls, I had no trouble getting my visa and later my green card. I did not even have to consider getting into the country illegally or worry about finding work under the table. I arrived in the United States protected by the Johnson-Reed Act of 1924, which until 1965 gave preferences to immigrants from Western Europe. I was given the red carpet treatment, with fellowships and teaching assistantships that, together with money from my parents, enabled me to get through graduate school in three years and be debt-free when I completed my doctorate in 1966.

I was not expected to make "a life in a new language," as did Eva Hoffman when she arrived from Poland.[5] Nobody told me to "stop talking that burwburwbuburugubu," as a New York teacher chastised Piri Thomas for talking Puerto Rican Spanish to a friend in class. "You must speak English," she told the New York-born writer, "you're in America now."[6] Nobody had to tame my "wild tongue," as they tried to tame Gloria Anzaldúa's, who had her knuckles rapped with a sharp ruler when a teacher caught her speaking Spanish during recess in Texas. Unlike Chicano students at Pan American University, I was not required to take two speech classes. "Their purpose," Anzaldúa recalled, was "to get rid of our accents."[7]

It was a surprise to me to be treated as British in the United States. My parents had brought me up with a healthy skepticism of nationalism. They were leftist children of immigrants who were neither surprised nor offended when I refused to stand for "God Save the Queen." In England, I relished thumbing my nose at John Bull, Rudyard Kipling, and other symbols of "little Englandism."[8] Yet, once in the United States, without even trying I could easily pass as the quintessential Brit. When I told people that I was Jewish, they were often surprised to hear that Jews lived in England. My national identity, constructed from cultural elements that were foreign to me, now trumped my ethnic identity.

As the grandson of barely literate East European immigrants, with a hybrid accent clearly identifiable as regional to anybody south of the midlands in England, I arrived on the West Coast in 1963 with what was perceived as the Queen's English, which I was encouraged to carefully preserve and keep well polished, like good silver. My voice, despite its shaky provenance, was an asset that entitled me to be taken seriously; and in the highly competitive, middle-class world of academia, every edge makes a difference, as it did in my career. After graduate school, I moved up the ivory tower with rapid success: first a fellowship at the University of Chicago, and then, in 1968, a full-time position in Berkeley back in the criminology department where I received my doctorate. The following year, my first book, a muckraking critique of juvenile justice, was published.[9] At the age of twenty-seven, I had made it into the privileged ranks of academia—just as Käte and Hugo Perls had made it in the art world of Berlin in the 1920s, as my father and Martin Dannenberg had made it in business in postwar Manchester and Baltimore, and as Frank Perls had made it selling Picassos and Matisses to the Hollywood set. All that remained was to stay on top and keep my balance.

In the 1970s in the United States, anti-Semitism was the last thing on my mind. The part of me that was Jewish was no longer a barrier to upward mobility, certainly not to a university career in the social sciences. In the 1930s, Jews made up forty percent of the workers in garment factories and faced quotas in academia.[10] Some forty years later, it was other ethnic groups that were trying to batter through the walls of discrimination, while Jews had joined the establishment and now helped to keep the doors shut. Jews comprised approximately one-quarter of undergraduates at Yale, Harvard, Princeton, and Columbia; they made up one-fifth of the faculty at elite universities and one-quarter in the Ivy League.[11] Being a Jew during my adult life was a matter of personal choice and cultural familiarity rather than a master status externally imposed. I was no longer "obliged," as Sartre put it at the end of World War II, to feel myself "perpetually Jewish in the eyes of others."[12]

My Jewish identity would only flare to the surface, like a volcanic eruption, during discussions about the Israel-Palestine Question. A few years ago, my sister Sue and her husband Yossi visited us from Israel. My longtime friend Mark, who is Jewish, invited us to his home for a Thanksgiving meal with his family, including his mother Millie. I asked Mark beforehand if there were any topics to be avoided. "Israel, of course," he replied. "Of course," I concurred. Cecilia, too, suggested that I avoid the subject. "I know," I replied irritably. And Sue, I later found out, had taken Yossi aside and told him in English and Hebrew, "No political arguments with my brother." If Lydia had not insisted on serving a pitcher of cosmopolitans—"yummy," murmured my brother-in-law in Arabic, discovering their unanticipated pleasures for the first time—we might have made it through the meal on pleasant chitchat.

It was my activism more than my politics, and certainly not my Jewishness, that got me in so much trouble that even my acquired British pedigree could not save me. Berkeley's chancellor was not pleased when I campaigned with the local Black Panthers for community control of the police; and the University of California Regents were even less impressed when I was arrested at a People's Park demonstration. Not surprisingly, in 1976 my career took a sharp dive when I was denied tenure at Berkeley and found myself, with many others, blacklisted for practicing what I preached. Once you choose to bite the hands that pull you up the ladder, it does not take long before you are back on the ground floor. Still, my credentials were good enough to land a job in the California State University system, where I have been fortunate to teach for the last twenty-five years.

My leftist politics in the 1970s—rooted firmly, so I thought at the time, in Marxism, internationalism, and the New Left—did not require a renunciation or denial of being a Jew because so many comrades were Jewish. My inspirational models were the white students, more than half of whom were Jewish, who went to the South for the Freedom Summer in 1964.[13] I came of political age at a time when we were convinced that human beings are not fixed by our biology, genes, or ancestral origins; that we have the capacity to shed our pasts and grow new skins. I did not consider it a transgression of racial etiquette, for example, to write a biography of E. Franklin Frazier, an African American intellectual who grew up in the segregated United States, his life as the working-class grandson of slaves so different from my own privileged background.[14] When I went on a speaking tour of universities to discuss the book, white audiences invariably wanted to know what motivated me, a white guy, to write about "black issues," whereas African American audiences wondered how I could expect to get "inside the black experience." I felt then, and still do, that the "issues" belong to us all, and that as members of a single human race we share profound commonalities. It is the socially created differences, not the bodies we are born into, that make us perpetually different in the eyes of others.

Until the summer of 1999, I had no occasion to delve into my Jewish identity. My cultural-identity makeover as an immigrant to the United States and my self-selected political identity within the Left did not oblige me to live in a world that, to paraphrase Sartre, took me only or primarily as a Jew. I was propelled into the past by a serendipitous conjuncture: the Huntington's Edwardian atmosphere—so reminiscent of my experience as an outside insider at Oxford in the early 1960s—and the revelation of an icon associated with a historical moment when "the Jew" was under attack and "in full war."[15]

PUBLIC HISTORY

When writer-to-be Primo Levi survived the concentration camps, his first instinct was to "get rid of everything"—raze the buildings and ovens until there was nothing left to remind the world of nazism. Later, he changed his mind. "These are not mistakes to efface," he realized.[16] It is a difficult decision to remember a catastrophe such as the holocaust, not only because it provokes the recollection of tormented pain and suffering, but also because it involves difficult choices about the content and form of remembrance. And once the process begins, it is not something easily controlled or put in a secure place. The Huntington's decision to excavate the Nuremberg Laws from its vault opens up its own past to scrutiny, just as the Skirball's decision to display the Nuremberg Laws opens up debates about nazism as historical aberration or business as usual.

The decision to remember, whether made personally or socially, is a selective process and an "ongoing activity."[17] There is no such thing as a neutral act of commemoration. All memory is partial, my own included. The past never rests in peace: it is always in motion, subject to revision and reinterpretation, dogmatized into eternal truths or splintered into a thousand fragments. "Every act of recognition," observes geographer David Lowenthal, "alters what survives. We can use the past fruitfully only when we realize that to inherit is also to transform."[18]

Not surprisingly, states and governments have a tendency either to bury any past that interferes with glorious stories of national origins and development, or to reinvent a past that is suitably heroic and inspirational.[19] Too often, museums and cultural centers—with their increasing reliance on corporate sponsorship— reproduce this approach by reducing historical controversies to sentimental pabulum. For example, visitors to the recently opened National Underground Railroad museum in Cincinnati can pick up a poster that proclaims "Never Lose Your Thirst for Freedom" and is illustrated by a flickering candle in a Coca Cola bottle. Too often, and especially in the case of holocaust-related memorials, the tendency is to smooth over history's rough edges, to privilege "piety and consensus" over critical thinking, to "foreclose discussion rather than to free and encourage it."[20]

Facing their own identity crisis, private museums typically are opting for spectacular architecture and blockbuster exhibitions, rather than searching for ways to become sites of public debate and democratic engagement.[21] In this era of fiscal crisis and cutbacks in government support for cultural projects, there is pressure on public institutions to settle for a safe middle ground and to avoid controversy.[22] Yet, more than ever, we need our cultural institutions to address the complexity of our interdependent world and to expose the tectonic fissures that run deep in our society. And we need them to encourage us to make unexpected connections and think unlikely thoughts, as well as provoke debates even within ourselves.

We could begin here in California by exploring the contradiction between the promises of the Golden Land and its long trail of sorrows. It was in Alta California, after all, that genocidal policies reduced the population of indigenous peoples from an estimated three hundred thousand in 1769 to fifteen thousand in the 1900s.[23] It was the pioneer stock of good Californians who helped to invent the Indian reservation, which combined elements of the penal colony and the concentration camp. It was California's regime that led the way in perfecting the pogrom against Chinese immigrants, a model for future ethnic cleansers.[24] And it was here that laws were passed to justify Aryan supremacy and enforce the ghettoization of Latino, Asian, Jewish, and African American residents.[25] "Are we standing on a mountain of death," asked Sebald when he visited the site of the Battle of Waterloo. "Is that our ultimate vantage point? Does one really have the much-vaunted historical overview from such a position?"[26] The same questions apply here on our own "shadowed ground."[27]

Imagine, for example, an exhibition on the Nuremberg Laws that is designed to engage its audience critically by raising questions about similarities and differences between German and American racial policies. Besides materials that celebrate the defeat of fascism and the triumph of democracy, we might include a copy of a Pasadena pamphlet—published during the heyday of nazism—that warned property-owners of the dangers of "non-caucasian encroachment." There could be examples of mutually flattering correspondence between "racial scientists" in Germany and eugenicists in Southern California. Below the photograph of General Patton and Robert Millikan, perhaps there could be selections from Patton's diary in which he denounces Jews as "lower than animals," and from Millikan's letters in which he makes fun of "coons" and opposes voting rights for African Americans. These juxtaposed images are intended to shake up linear conceptions of progress, as well as alert us to dangers closer to home. Such an exhibition would not be "out of context" at the Huntington or "belong" only to a Jewish cultural center, but would be the substance of a *public* history.

My preference is for museums, memorials, cultural centers, and other public institutions that get us to think of history as an argument rather than a received truth; that encourage us to grapple with the past as a process of disorientation and reorientation rather than a neatly packaged, sanitized parable.[28] This is not, I admit, an easy task. It is disturbing to open up the settled past—whether unexamined dimensions of my own Jewish identity, the Huntington's selective memory and reluctance to confront institutional legacies, my university's adulation of a Nazi-loving eugenicist, or the Skirball's unquestioning celebration of American values. But it is more disturbing to leave the past comfortably shrouded in amnesia.

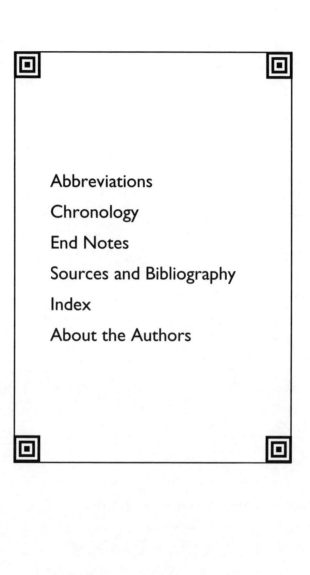

Abbreviations

Chronology

End Notes

Sources and Bibliography

Index

About the Authors

Abbreviations

AAM	American Association of Museums
BLA	Bernhard Lösener Affidavit
CCS	Combined Chiefs of Staff
CIC	Counter-Intelligence Corps
CMGC	Charles M. Goethe Collection
CSUS	California State University, Sacramento
DP	Displaced Person
ERC	Emergency Rescue Committee
ERCR	Emergency Rescue Committee Records
ERO	Eugenics Record Office
ERP	Eleanor Roosevelt Papers
ESC	Eugenie Söderberg Collection
ESGP	Ezra S. Gosney Papers
FPP	Frank Perls Papers
G-2	Military Intelligence Division of U.S. Army Ground Staff
G-5	Civil Affairs and Military Government Division
HBF	Human Betterment Foundation
HHPL	Herbert Hoover Presidential Library
HL	Huntington Library
HLA	Huntington Library Archives
HLC	Harry Laughlin Collection
HPC	Hugo Perls Collection
HUC	Hebrew Union College
IMT	International Military Tribunal
JCS	Joint Chiefs of Staff
LOC	Library of Congress
MC	Robert Andrews Millikan Collection
MDP	Martin Dannenberg Papers
MG	Military Government
MGS	Manchester Grammar School
MI	Military Intelligence
MII	Military Intelligence Interpreter
MPP	Marianne Perls Papers
NARA	National Archives and Records Administration
NSDAP	National Socialist German Workers' (Nazi) Party
SAC	Special Agent-in-Charge
SCCA	Skirball Cultural Center Archives
SHAEF	Supreme Headquarters, Allied Expeditionary Force
SS	*Schutzstaffel* (Protection Squad)

Chronology

1850   Birth of Henry Edwards (Edward) Huntington.

1875   Hebrew Union College founded in Cincinnati.

Birth of Charles M. Goethe.

1900   Six thousand Jews live in Nuremberg.

1903   Edward Huntington buys property in Pasadena for future Library.

George S. Patton, Sr., appointed general manager of Huntington Land and Improvement Company.

1904   George S. Patton, Jr., admitted to West Point.

1910   Marriage of Hugo Perls and Käte Kolker.

Birth of Franz (Frank) Perls.

1912   George S. Patton, Jr., visits Nuremberg as tourist.

1913   Incorporation of San Marino.

1915   Birth of Martin Dannenberg.

1919   Huntington Library incorporated, first board of trustees appointed.

Karl Liebknecht murdered in Germany.

1921   Robert Millikan becomes chairman of Executive Council, California Institute of Technology.

1923   Robert Millikan awarded Nobel Prize in Physics.

1924   Death of Arabella (Belle) Huntington.

1925   Robert Millikan joins Huntington's board of trustees.

George S. Patton, Sr., becomes chairman of Huntington's board of trustees.

Huntington Library opens to the public.

1927   Max Ferrand hired as Huntington's first director.

Death of Edward Huntington.

First Nazi party rally held in Nuremberg in August.

1929   Ezra S. Gosney establishes the Human Betterment Foundation (HBF) in Pasadena, hires Paul Popenoe as director.

Huntington trustees Henry Robinson and William Munro become charter members of board of HBF.

HBF publishes *Sterilization for Human Betterment*.

1930   Huntington's tax-exempt status recognized in the Constitution of California.

Sterilization for Human Betterment is published in Germany.

1931   Hugo and Käte Perls move to Paris.

1933   Charles M. Goethe establishes Eugenics Society of Northern California in Sacramento.

Nine thousand Jews live in Nuremberg.

Adolf Hitler is appointed chancellor of Germany on January 30.

Frank Perls moves to Paris in March.

The Nazi party comes to power in Germany on March 23.

The Nazi party organizes a one-day boycott of Jewish-owned businesses on April 1.

The Nazi government enacts the Law for the Prevention of Genetically Diseased Offspring (Sterilization Law) on July 14.

1934   The Sterilization Law takes effect in Germany on January 1.

George S. Patton, Jr., underlines and annotates his copy of Adolf Hitler's *My Battle*, the first American edition of *Mein Kampf*, on March 15.

The American Public Health Association hosts an exhibition on Nazi eugenics at its annual conference in Pasadena in September.

Fourth Nazi party rally is held in Nuremberg in September.

1935   "Reich Party Congress of Freedom" opens in Nuremberg on September 10.

Hitler identifies "Jewish Marxism" as one of the main enemies of the Nazi state on September 11.

Nuremberg Laws (including the Flag, Citizenship, and Blood Laws) proposed by Hitler and ratified by the Reichstag during the Nazi party rally in Nuremberg on September 15.

Nazi Marital Health Law prohibits marriage between "superior" and "inferior" German citizens on October 18.

Original copy of the Nuremberg Laws is given to mayor of Nuremberg in tribute to the "City of the Reich Party Rallies" on December 20.

1936   Charles M. Goethe is appointed president of the Eugenics Research Association.

Harry Laughlin, director of Eugenics Record Office in Long Island, receives honorary doctorate from University of Heidelberg.

1937   Robert Millikan joins the board of Human Betterment Foundation.

Frank Perls arrives in New York in October.

1938   Robert Millikan becomes chairman of Huntington's board of trustees.

Jews attacked in Germany during *Reichskristallnacht*, November 9–10.

1939 SS *St. Louis*, carrying Jewish refugees, refused entry in Cuba in May.

Hitler authorizes "mercy killings" of five thousand physically disabled children in September.

1940 First use of gas chambers in Germany to murder physically and mentally disabled adults.

Frank Perls opens a gallery in Los Angeles in April.

Käte Perls imprisoned in Gurs concentration camp in May.

Käte Perls is released from Gurs in June.

Emergency Rescue Committee is established in New York during the summer.

Käte Perls imprisoned in Hotel Bompard, Marseille.

Eleanor Roosevelt asks State Department to investigate Käte Perls's situation in December.

1941 Jews in Germany required to wear *Jude* sign in public.

Käte Perls released from Bompard.

1942 Closure of Human Betterment Foundation, assets transferred to California Institute of Technology.

Frank Perls inducted into U.S. Army on October 1.

Käte Perls arrives in Cuba.

Leo Katzenberger, prosecuted under the Blood Law for extramarital sexual relations with Aryan woman, is executed in Munich on June 3.

1943 Frank Perls becomes American citizen in April.

Patton reprimanded for slapping shell-shocked soldiers in August.

Nuremberg Laws deposited in a bank in Eichstätt for safekeeping during war in October.

1944 Supreme Headquarters Allied Expeditionary Force created in Paris as joint British-American command in Europe on January 17.

Frank Perls lands in France with military intelligence team on June 13.

Käte Perls arrives in New York, *ca.* August.

Martin Dannenberg ships out for Europe with Counter-Intelligence Corps (CIC) in August.

1945 Allies bomb Nuremberg in January.

Frank Perls assigned as translator to Martin Dannenberg's CIC team.

General Patton sends deluxe edition of *Mein Kampf* to Huntington on April 15.

April 20: Hitler's birthday and the day the Allies capture Nuremberg.

203d Detachment of Army's Counter-Intelligence Corps (including Martin Dannenberg and Frank Perls) retrieves Nuremberg Laws in Eichstätt on April 27.

Joint Chiefs of Staff issues directive 1067, ordering the Commander-in-Chief of U.S. Forces to take control of "all archives, monuments and museums of Nazi inception" on April 29.

Germany surrenders; end of World War II in Europe. Patton put in command of Bavaria on May 9.

Sixty-five Jews remain in Nuremberg.

Patton claims original copy of Nuremberg Laws presented to him by General Van Fleet on May 27.

Mein Kampf exhibited to public at Huntington on June 5.

Patton greeted in Los Angeles with parades and huge crowds on June 9.

Patton visits the Huntington, deposits Nuremberg Laws for safekeeping on June 11.

Death of Käte Perls on August 24.

Eisenhower orders Patton to comply with de-Nazification policies on September 11.

Eisenhower removes Patton from command of the Third Army, and assigns him to Fifteenth Army on October 6.

International Military (War Crimes) Tribunal is convened in Nuremberg in November.

Patton dies from injuries received in a car accident on December 21.

1951   United Nations acknowledges crimes of "genocide."

Huntington officials place Nuremberg Laws in new bombproof vault in August.

1953   Sudden death of Beatrice Patton from aortic aneurysm on September 30.

Death of Robert Millikan on December 19.

1955   Patton family donates General Patton's papers to the Library of Congress.

Charles M. Goethe is awarded honorary degree by California State University, Sacramento.

1965   California State University, Sacramento, celebrates Charles M. Goethe's 90th birthday in March.

1966   Death of Charles M. Goethe.

1969   On November 28, Ruth Patton Totten, General Patton's daughter, donates

Patton family papers to Huntington, but excludes General Patton's papers.

1970 George C. Scott plays the general in *Patton*.

1971 *Patton* wins seven Oscars.

1972 Publication of first volume of *The Patton Papers, 1885–1940*, edited by Martin Blumenson.

Skirball Museum opens in Los Angeles.

1973 Yad Vashem Holocaust History Museum opens in Israel.

1974 Publication of the second volume of *The Patton Papers, 1940–1945*, edited by Martin Blumenson.

1975 Death of Frank Perls in February.

1978 NBC airs mini-series, "Holocaust."

1979 Rabbi Uri Herscher becomes executive vice-president of Hebrew Union College in Los Angeles.

1988 Robert Skotheim is appointed president of the Huntington.

1991 Huntington's curator of manuscripts identifies the Nuremberg Laws as "war loot" on September 11.

1993 Release of Steven Spielberg's *Schindler's List*.

Museum of Tolerance opens in Los Angeles in February.

President Clinton and twenty-three heads of state attend the opening of the U.S. Holocaust Museum in Washington, D.C., in April.

1996 Skirball Cultural Center opens to the public in Los Angeles. Uri Herscher is appointed Skirball's president on April 21.

1997 J. Paul Getty Museum opens in Los Angeles in December.

1998 President Clinton and Congress establish the Presidential Advisory Commission on Holocaust Assets in the United States on June 23.

1999 On behalf of Skirball Cultural Center, Uri Herscher accepts the Nuremberg Laws and other materials on indefinite loan from Huntington on March 3.

Presidential Advisory Commission on Holocaust Assets in the United States holds its first meeting on March 16.

Huntington accessions its copy of the Nuremberg Laws in June.

The Huntington announces the loan of the Nuremberg Laws to Skirball Cultural Center on June 26.

Exhibit of the Nuremberg Laws opens at Skirball Cultural Center on June 29.

Skirball removes Patton's account of provenance from the Nuremberg Laws case in September.

Martin Dannenberg visits and speaks at Skirball Cultural Center on December 12.

2000   Skirball changes the Nuremberg Laws display case, substituting a photograph of Martin Dannenberg for the photograph of Patton and Millikan, *ca*. January.

Presidential Advisory Commission on Holocaust Assets in the United States releases its final report, *Plunder and Restitution,* on December 15.

2001   Robert Skotheim retires as president of the Huntington, succeeded by Steven Koblik, president of Reed College.

End Notes

🔲 Chapter 1: Origins Stories

1.   Its current official name is The Huntington Library, Art Collections, and Botanical Gardens.

2.   Huntington Library and Art Gallery, *Annual Report 1946–1947*, p. 1. The Huntington Library or Huntington Library and Art Gallery are hereafter cited as HL. The Huntington's annual reports are available in the Huntington's library.

3.   Rick Lyman, "What's Doing in Pasadena," *New York Times*, December 9, 2001, Travel, p. 15.

4.   Robert Clark, "Research Shangri-La," *Westways*, January 1943, pp. 22–23; George Ellery Hale, "The Future Development of The Huntington Library and Art Gallery," October 14, 1925. A copy of this manuscript is in the Robert Andrews Millikan Collection, California Institute of Technology, box 12, folder 8. The collection is hereafter cited as MC.

5.   Susan Green (editor), *The Huntington Library: Treasures from Ten Centuries* (London: Scala Publishers, 2004), p. 17.

6.   General information about the Huntington comes from a public relations packet provided by the Huntington's Communications Department, especially "About the Huntington" and "Huntington Fact Sheet," January 1999.

7.   "'Invented tradition' is taken to mean a set of practices, normally governed by overtly or tacitly accepted rules and of a ritual or symbolic nature, which seek to inculcate certain values and norms of behaviour by repetition, which automatically implies continuity with the past." Eric Hobsbawm and Terence Ranger (editors), *The Invention of Tradition* (Cambridge: Cambridge University Press, 1983), p. 1.

8.   Josiah Royce, *California from Conquest in 1846 to the Second Vigilance Committee in San Francisco: A Study of American Character* (Boston: Houghton Mifflin, 1886), p. 222.

9.   Joan Didion, *Where I Was From* (New York: Alfred A. Knopf, 2003), p. 71.

10.   Cecilia E. O'Leary, *To Die For: The Paradox of American Patriotism* (Princeton: Princeton University Press, 1999).

11.   We explore this dilemma in Tony Platt and Cecilia O'Leary, "Patriot Acts," *Social Justice,* vol. 30, no. 1 (2003), pp. 5–21.

12.   W. G. Sebald, "An Attempt at Restitution," *The New Yorker*, December 20–27, 2004, p. 112.

13.   Elaine Dutka, "Hitler Papers, Held Since '45 by Huntington, to Go on Display," *Los Angeles Times*, June 26, 1999, p. 1.

14.   The Huntington Library, "Rare Photographic Archive of Dead Sea Scrolls at Huntington Library Will Be Open to All Scholars," press release, September 22, 1991, Huntington Library Archives (hereafter cited as HLA).

15.   See, for example, coverage of the Huntington's seventy-fifth anniversary, acknowledged in HL, *Annual Report 1994–1997*, p. 29; or a visit to the Huntington by Sweden's Crown Princess Victoria, *The Huntington Calendar*, January–February 2002.

16.   I am using the English spelling of the city, Nuremberg, rather than Nürnberg or Nuernberg, except when quoting from primary sources.

17.   Huntington Library and Skirball Cultural Center, "Huntington Library to Loan Original Nuremberg Laws Signed by Hitler to the Skirball Cultural Center," joint press release, June 26, 1999.

18.   The imagery is attributed to the astronomer George Ellery Hale, a close adviser of Huntington. See James Thorpe, *Henry Edwards Huntington: A Biography* (Berkeley: University of California Press, 1994), p. 390; Ray Allen Billington, "The Genesis of the Research Institution," *The Huntington Library Quarterly*, vol. 22, no. 4 (August 1969), p. 352.

19.   Thorpe, pp. 19–20. The other three entrepreneurs were Leland Stanford, Mark Hopkins, and Charles Crocker.

20.   Green, p. 15.

21.   The Huntington produced a short video for its board of trustees and influential contacts to show how widely the announcement was reported. *Nuremberg Laws Loan to the Skirball*, news clip compilation (Huntington Library: Sandpail Productions, 1999).

22.   Sharon Waxman, "Hidden History of the Nazi Laws, *Washington Post*, June 26, 1999, p. 1; Elaine Dutka, "Hitler Papers, Held Since '45 by Huntington, to Go on Display," *Los Angeles Times*, June 26, 1999, p. 1, CNN, "Jewish Educational Center to Display Original Nuremberg Papers," *CNN.com*, June 27, 1999; Neil Mackay, "Found: Hitler's Blueprint for the Holocaust," *The Sunday Herald*, June 27, 1999; *Agence France Presse*, "Nuremberg Laws to Go on Public Display for the First Time," *Agence France Press*, June 26, 1999; Sharon Waxman, "A Key Nazi Document Surfaces," *International Herald Tribune*, June 28, 1999, p. 2; Bernard Weinraub, "Signed Nuremberg Laws to Go on View," *New York Times*, June 26, 1999, p. B12; Word for Word, "On Display in Los Angeles: Legal Foreshadowing of Nazi Horror," *New York Times*, July 4, 1999, Week in Review, p. 7; "Weekend All Things Considered," National Public Radio, June 27, 1999; "Sunday Today," National Broadcasting Company, June 27, 1999.

23.   Saul Friedländer, *Nazi Germany and the Jews: The Years of Persecution, 1933–1939* (New York: HarperCollins, 1997), p. 142.

24.   For a detailed account of the passage of the Nuremberg Laws, see Ian Kershaw, *Hitler, 1889–1936: Hubris* (New York: W. W. Norton, 1999), pp. 568–573.

25.   See William L. Shirer, *The Rise and Fall of the Third Reich: A History of Nazi Germany* (New York: Simon and Schuster, 1960).

26.   Kershaw, p. 570.

27.   Adolf Hitler, *Mein Kampf*, translated by Ralph Mannheim (Boston: Houghton Mifflin, 1999), p. 300.

28.   Kershaw, pp. 474–475; Shirer, p. 233.

29.   Raul Hilberg, *The Destruction of the European Jews* (New York: Holmes and Meier, 1985), vol. 3, p. 1044.

30.   Translation by *New York Times*, July 4, 1999, Week in Review, p. 7.

31.   Quoted in Dutka, p. 1.

32.   Interview with Saul Friedländer, July 1, 1999.

33.   Hitler's memo (September 1, 1939) appeared in the exhibition on *Deadly Medicine: Creating the Master Race* at the United States Holocaust Memorial Museum in 2005. It is reproduced in the book about the exhibition—Dieter Kuntz and Susan Bachrach

(editors), *Deadly Medicine: Creating the Master Race* (Washington, D.C.: United States Holocaust Memorial Museum, 2004), p. 133.

34.   Mackay; CNN; American Library Association, "Huntington Loans Nuremberg Documents to Jewish Cultural Center," *AL Online*, July 5, 1999; Tom Tugend, "In Their Rightful Place," *The Jewish Journal of Greater Los Angeles*, July 2, 1999, p. 8.

35.   Lorraine Glennon (editor-in-chief), *The 20th Century: An Illustrated History of Our Lives and Times* (North Dighton, Mass.: JG Press, 2000), p. 252. See, also, "Nuremberg Laws," *Encyclopaedia Judaica* (New York: Macmillan, 1971), vol. 12, p. 1282.

36.   Michael Berenbaum (ed.), *Witness to the Holocaust* (New York: HarperCollins, 1997), p. 24. This view derives from Hilberg, vol. 1, p. 27: "A destruction process is a series of administrative measures that must be aimed at a definite group."

37.   Quoted in Huntington-Skirball joint press release, June 26, 1999.

38.   Eric Chaim Klein, "Appraisal of the Huntington's Copy of the Nuremberg Laws," memorandum, no date (*ca.* June 1999). Copy made available to the author.

39.   Michael Berenbaum estimates the value at $2.5 million. Personal communication from Michael Berenbaum, August 10, 1999.

40.   Interview with Eric Chaim Klein, August 3, 1999.

41.   Quoted in Daniel B. Wood, "Some Dark Words of History Come to Light," *Christian Science Monitor*, July 1, 1999.

42.   Skotheim's remarks at a briefing of Huntington staff and researchers on "The Huntington's Loan to the Skirball Cultural Center of Hitler Materials Given to the Library in 1945 by General Patton," June 29, 1999; interview with Robert Skotheim, July 19, 1999.

43.   "Nuremberg Laws Loaned to the Skirball Cultural Center," HL, *Huntington Calendar*, September–October, 1999, p. 2.

44.   Huntington briefing, June 29, 1999.

45.   Retrieved from *www.skirball.com*, November 25, 2004.

46.   Interview with Michael Berenbaum, July 21, 1999.

47.   Huntington-Skirball joint press release, June 26, 1999.

48.   Waxman, "Hidden History of the Nazi Laws."

49.   Waxman, "A Key Nazi Document Surfaces."

50.   Wood, "Some Dark Words of History Come to Light."

51.   Anne-Marie O'Connor, "Jewish Museum to Display Hitler's Nuremberg Laws," *Los Angeles Times*, June 29, 1999, p. B3.

52.   Letter from Maurice Axelrad to *Washington Post*, July 17, 1999, p. 18.

53.   Waxman, "Hidden History of the Nazi Laws."

54.   Quoted in ibid., p. 9.

55.   Maura Kelly, "Revisions and a Revelation," *www.slate.msn.com*, June 26, 1999.

56.   Associated Press, "Original Text of Nuremberg Laws to Be Exhibited for First Time," June 27, 1999.

57.   Wood, "Some Dark Words of History Come to Light."

58.   Author's notes from Huntington staff briefing, June 29, 1999; interview with Saul Friedländer, July 2, 1999.

59.   Quoted in Dutka, "Hitler Papers," p. 19.

60.   Wood, "Some Dark Words of History Come to Light."

61.   Author's field notes, July 2, 1999.

62. Quoted in Dutka, "Hitler Papers," p. 19.

63. Quoted in Tugend, "In Their Rightful Place," p. 8.

64. Interview with David Zeidberg, July 13, 1999.

65. "Weekend All Things Considered," National Public Radio, June 27, 1999, transcript.

66. "Sunday Today," NBC Television, June 27, 1999, transcript.

67. Interview with Saul Friedländer, July 2, 1999.

68. Dutka, "Hitler Papers, Held Since '45 by Huntington, to Go on Display."

69. Quoted in Huntington-Skirball joint press release, June 26, 1999.

70. From transcript of "Sunday Today," NBC, June 27, 1999.

71. "Statement Dictated by General George S. Patton, Jr. Regarding Document Taken in Nuremberg," June 11, 1945, HLA.

72. By "Emman," Patton meant Max Amann, whose mansion Patton occupied after the war ended. Patton exaggerated Amann's importance in the Nazi hierarchy, but he had been a close confidante of Hitler from the earliest days of the Nazi party. He made his fortune from publishing *Mein Kampf* and served as Hitler's "press baron." See letter from Patton to Frederick Ayer, May 24, 1945, in Martin Blumenson, *The Patton Papers, 1940–1945* (New York: Da Capo Press, 1996), p. 718; Kershaw, pp. 91, 241.

73. General Patton claimed that he was related to George Washington through his grandmother, Susan Thornton Glassell Patton. He was also related through his great-great-grandfather to Hugh Mercer, who fought with Washington and died in the War of Independence. See Martin Blumenson, *The Patton Papers, 1885–1940* (Boston: Houghton Mifflin, 1972), pp. 23–24, 51, 190.

74. "Statement Dictated by General George S. Patton, Jr. Regarding Document Taken in Nuremberg," June 11, 1945, HLA.

75. This position was equivalent to president at other universities.

76. Judith R. Goodstein, *Millikan's School: A History of the California Institute of Technology* (New York: W.W. Norton, 1991), pp. 58–59; Carey McWilliams, *California: The Great Exception*, originally published in 1949 (Berkeley: University of California Press, 1998), pp. 260–261.

77. Daniel J. Kevles, *The Physicists: The History of a Scientific Community in Modern America* (Cambridge: Harvard University Press, 1997), pp. 155–156. Millikan's oil drop experiment (1910–1913) was identified at the end of the twentieth century by the Museum of Science and Industry in Chicago as one of the most enduring scientific innovations of the previous century. Kari Haskell, "The Present as Past: A 2099 Retrospective," *New York Times*, December 26, 1999, Week in Review, p. 5.

78. Goodstein, p. 105.

79. Quoted in William M. Kramer, *A Lone Traveler: Einstein in California* (Los Angeles: Skirball Cultural Center, 2004), pp. 10, 15.

80. Martin Blumenson, *Patton: The Man Behind the Legend, 1885–1945* (New York: Berkley Books, 1987), p. 9.

81. "Bright Stars," *Sunset*, August 1919, p. 45.

82. Margaret Bourke White, *"Dear Fatherland, Rest Quietly": A Report on the Collapse of Hitler's "Thousand Years"* (New York: Simon and Schuster, 1946), p. 22. The photographs appear after p. 6.

83. Quoted in Huntington-Skirball joint press release, June 26, 1999.

84. Quoted in Thorpe, p. 165.

85. Ibid., pp. 200–201; see, also, Blumenson, *The Patton Papers, 1885–1940*, p. 147.

86. Ibid., pp. 402, 505.

87. Letter from Henry Huntington to Senator Bard, February 1904, ibid., pp. 80–81.

88. See, for example, Georgie's letters to his father on July 31, 1904; October 30, 1904; November 12, 1904; and January 16, 1905. See, also, his memoir, "My Father," 1927, ibid., pp. 94, 101–102, 103, 109–110, 136.

89. Letter from George S. Patton, Jr., to President, Huntington Library, April 15, 1945, HLA.

90. Interview with Robert Patton, September 10, 1999. "He's like a saint in this town," a librarian from the San Marino Public Library told me, March 26, 2001.

91. Interview with David Zeidberg, July 13, 1999.

92. Interview with Robert Skotheim, July 19, 1999.

93. Letter from Robert Skotheim to Uri Herscher, March 5, 1999, Skirball Cultural Center Archives (hereafter cited as SCCA).

94. Author's notes from briefing of Huntington staff and researchers, June 29, 1999.

95. Staff briefing and interview with Robert Skotheim, July 19, 1999.

96. Letter from David Zeidberg to Gerhard Jochem, July 15, 1999, HLA.

97. Interview with David Zeidberg, July 13, 1999.

98. Waxman, "Hidden History," p. 9.

99. Tugend, "In Their Rightful Place," p. 27. For similar imagery, see also Waxman, "Hidden History."

100. Letter from Robert Skotheim to Uri Herscher, March 5, 1999, SCCA.

101. Huntington staff briefing, June 29, 1999.

102. Quoted in Dutka, "Hitler Papers," p. 1.

103. Vivian M. Patraka, *Spectacular Suffering: Theatre, Fascism, and the Holocaust* (Bloomington: Indiana University Press, 1999), p. 115.

104. On the display of slave shackles and whipping posts in an exhibit, see Lisa G. Corrin (ed.), *Mining the Museum: An Installation by Fred Wilson* (New York: The New Press, 1994). On lynching postcards, see James Allen, Hilton Als, John Lewis, and Leon F. Litwack, *Without Sanctuary: Lynching Photography in America* (Santa Fe: Twin Palms Publishers, 2004). For reporting on the lynching exhibit in New York, see Roberta Smith, "An Ugly Legacy Lives On, Its Glare Unsoftened by Age," *New York Times*, January 13, 2000, pp. B1, 8; and Somini Sengupta, "Historic Images of Hate, In a Compelling Display," *New York Times*, January 24, 2000, p. 23.

105. From author's interviews and field notes, June 29, 1999; July 12, 1999.

106. Interview with Mary Robertson and David Zeidberg, October 8, 1999.

107. The quote comes from Pat Barker's novel, *Another World* (New York: Farrar, Strauss and Giroux, 1998), p. 75.

▣ Chapter 2: Present Absences

1. Max Ferber, one of four men exiled from Germany, is profiled in W. G. Sebald, *The Emigrants* (London: Harvill Press, 1996), pp. 191, 225.

2. Ibid., p. 192.

3. Albert M. Hyamson, *The Sephardim of England: A History of the Spanish and Portuguese Jewish Community, 1492–1951* (London: Methuen & Company, 1951).

4. V. D. Lipman, *Social History of the Jews in England, 1850–1950* (London: Watts & Co., 1954), p. 103. See, also, Bill Williams, *The Making of Manchester Jewry, 1740–1875* (Manchester: Manchester University Press, 1976); Lloyd P. Gartner, *The Jewish Immigrant in England, 1870–1914* (London: Simon Publications, 1960); and Ian Taylor, Karen Evans, and Penny Fraser, *A Tale of Two Cities: Global Change, Local Feeling and Everyday Life in the North of England* (London: Routledge, 1996).

5. In 1954, there were thirty-one thousand Jews in the Manchester area. See Lipman, pp. 102–103, 171.

6. The previous generation of German Jewish immigrants controlled "the top of the social pyramid" as merchants, bankers, and professionals. Ibid., p. 27.

7. The trial of mostly Jewish physicians accused of the "Doctors' Plot" in 1953 was the beginning of the end of his admiration for Soviet-style communism.

8. Sebald, *The Emigrants*, p. 21.

9. Eva Hoffman, *After Such Knowledge: Memory, History, and the Legacy of the Holocaust* (New York: PublicAffairs, 2004), pp. 34, 85.

10. Zygmunt Bauman, *Modernity and the Holocaust* (Ithaca: Cornell University Press, 2000), p. 17. The first edition was published in 1989.

11. Neil A. Lewis, "Genocide, as Defined Since 1951 by a U.N. Treaty," *New York Times*, March 31, 1999, p. 11.

12. A brief discussion of the etymology of "holocaust" can be found in *The American Heritage College Dictionary* (Boston: Houghton Mifflin, 1997), third edition, pp. 648–649. See, also, a useful analysis of the changing cultural meanings of "the holocaust" in Jeffrey C. Alexander, "On the Social Construction of Moral Universals," in Jeffrey C. Alexander, Ron Eyerman, Bernhard Giesen, Neil J. Smelser, and Piotr Sztompka, *Cultural Trauma and Collective Identity* (Berkeley: University of California Press, 2004), pp. 196–263.

13. For a detailed account of this process and its results, see Edward T. Linenthal, *Preserving Memory: The Struggle to Create America's Holocaust Museum* (New York: Viking, 1995).

14. See, for example, Daniel J. Goldhagen, *Hitler's Willing Executioners: Ordinary Germans and the Holocaust* (New York: Knopf, 1996); Christopher Browning, *Ordinary Men: Reserve Police Battalion 101 and the Final Solution in Poland* (New York: HarperCollins, 1992).

15. Phillip Lopate, "Resistance to the Holocaust," in David Rosenberg (ed.), *Testimony: Contemporary Writers Make the Holocaust Personal* (New York: Times Books, 1989), p. 289. See, also, Michael Mann, "The Dark Side of Democracy: The Modern Tradition of Ethnic and Political Cleansing," *New Left Review* 235 (May/June 1999), pp. 18–45; and Bauman, *Modernity and the Holocaust*.

16. Hoffman, p. 104. See, also, Bernhard Giesen, "The Trauma of Perpetrators: The Holocaust as the Traumatic Reference of German National Identity," in Alexander et al., pp. 112–154.

17. Giesen, p. 140.

18. On the proliferation and varieties of holocaust memorials, see James E. Young (editor), *The Art of Memory: Holocaust Memorials in History* (New York: The Jewish Museum, 1994).

19. Thomas J. Peters and Robert H. Waterman, Jr., *In Search of Excellence: Lessons from America's Best-Run Companies* (New York: Warner Books, 1984), p. 180. Despite the book's title, Platt Clothiers Ltd. was an English company, based in Manchester.

20. Hasia Diner, *The Jews of the United States, 1654 to 2000* (Berkeley: University of California Press, 2004), pp. 206–207.

21. See, generally, Paul Fryer, *Staying Power: The History of Black People in England* (London: Pluto Press, 1984); and Kathleen Paul, *Whitewashing Britain: Race and Citizenship in the Postwar Era* (Ithaca: Cornell University Press, 1997).

22. An estimated three thousand Jews fought on the side of the Confederacy. See Diner, p. 155.

23. Lopate, p. 293.

24. Tony Kushner, *Homebody/Kabul* (New York: Theatre Communication Group, 2002), p. 147.

25. On the limits of this kind of ethnic reductionism, see Stuart Hall. "New Ethnicities," *ICA (Institute of Contemporary Arts) Documents* 7 (1988), pp. 27–30.

26. Personal communication from Howard Zinn, January 21, 2001.

27. Joseph Roth, "The Auto-da-Fé of the Mind" (1933), in Joseph Roth, *What I Saw: Reports from Berlin, 1920–1933*, translated by Michael Hofmann (New York: W. W. Norton, 2004), p. 209.

28. Bauman, p. 232. See, also, Bauman's afterword (pp. 222–250) to the 2000 edition of his book, "The Duty to Remember—But What?"

29. On December 9, 1945, Patton's car, in which he was a passenger, was in an accident in Bad Nauheim, Germany. Patton hit his head and injured his spinal cord. He died from his injuries on December 21, 1945. See Blumenson, *The Patton Papers, 1940–1945*, pp. 817–835.

30. On Patton's mystical belief in reincarnation, see Carlo D'Este, *Patton: A Genius for War* (New York: HarperPerennial, 1995), pp. 320–328.

31. Ibid., p. 811.

32. U.S. Army, *Patton, Old Blood and Guts: A Biography of the Controversial WWII General* (U. S. Army: Army Pictorial Center, n.d.).

33. Home Box Office, *Patton: The Man Behind the Myth*, narrated by Hal Holbrook (1980).

34. Sarah Brash (ed.), *The American Story: World War II* (Richmond: Time-Life, 1997), p. 99.

35. Alden Hatch, *George Patton: General in Spurs* (New York: Modern Library, 1950), p. 15. By 1973, the eleventh hardback edition of this book was in print.

36. Charles Peifer, Jr., *Soldier of Destiny: A Biography of George Patton* (Minneapolis: Dillion Press, 1989), pp. 7, 117. In this genre, see also John Devaney, *The True Story of Gen. George S. Patton, USA* (New York: Julian Messner, 1982); and William Bancroft Mellor, *General Patton: The Last Cavalier* (New York: Putnam Publishing Group, 1971).

37. Porter B. Williamson, *I Remember General Patton's Principles* (Tucson: Management and Systems Consultants, 1979).

38. See, for example, Edgar F. Puryear, Jr., *American Generalship—Character Is Everything: The Art of Command* (Novato, California: Presidio Press, 2000).

39. Alan Axelrod, *Patton on Leadership: Strategic Lessons for Corporate Warfare*

(Paramus, N.J.: Prentice Hall, 1999). The ad for the book, with its preface by New York Yankees' owner George Steinbrenner, appeared in the *New York Times*, October 31, 1999.

40. A plaque at the Patton family plot in the San Gabriel cemetery, a few miles from the Huntington Library, reads: In Memoriam Gen. George S. Patton, Jr. "The Liberator." See, also, Bourke White, pp. 38–39.

41. Francis Russell, "Pistol Packin' Patton," *National Review*, July 28, 1970, p. 798.

42. During the war, Colonel Frank Murphy was General George C. Marshall's executive officer. See D'Este, p. 750.

43. Marion Armstrong, "Tragic Tyrant," *Christian Century*, April 10, 1970, p. 455.

44. Rex Reed, "Rex Reed at the Movies," *Holiday*, April 1970, p. 25.

45. For a discussion of this insight, see Robert Brent Toplin, *History by Hollywood: The Use and Abuse of the American Past* (Urbana: University of Illinois Press, 1996). See, also, "Patton: Lust for Glory," *Sight and Sound*, Summer 1970; "Patton," *Film Quarterly*, Summer 1970; and Vincent Canby, "Patton," *New York Times*, February 3, 1970, p. 128.

46. Quoted in "Old Blood and Guts," *Time*, February 9, 1970, p. 78. A few years later, Scott continued to defend Patton as "a man of honor, dignity, and so forth." See *Playboy* interview, "George C. Scott," *Playboy*, December 1980, p. 101.

47. Hugh Sidey, "Anybody See Patton?" *Life*, June 19, 1970, p. 28.

48. Interview with Hugh Cole, August 30, 1999.

49. Patton diary entry, October 1, 1945, in Blumenson, *The Patton Papers, 1940–1945*, pp. 787–788.

50. Letter from George to Beatrice, September 14, 1945; letter from George to Beatrice, August 31, 1945. See Blumenson, *The Patton Papers, 1940–1945*, pp. 750, 744.

51. Interview with Martin Blumenson, August 30, 1999.

52. Martin Blumenson, *Patton: The Man Behind the Legend, 1885–1945* (New York: William Morrow, 1985), pp. 288, 302.

53. Ladislas Farago, *The Last Days of Patton* (New York: McGraw-Hill, 1981), pp. 100, 101.

54. Interview with Carlo D'Este, February 21, 2000. See, also, D'Este, pp. 753–754.

55. Letter from George Patton to Beatrice, September 14, 1945; Patton diary entry, October 2, 1945. See Blumenson, *The Patton Papers, 1940–1945*, pp. 750, 790.

56. Interview with Rabbi Judah Nadich, July 29, 1999. See, also, Judah Nadich, *Eisenhower and the Jews* (New York: Twayne Publishers, 1953).

57. David Max Eichhorn quoted in Louis Barrish (editor), *Rabbis in Uniform: The Story of the American Jewish Military Chaplain* (New York: Jonathan David, 1962), p. 279. According to Eichhorn, Patton would not allow a Jewish chaplain to be assigned to the staff at his headquarters.

58. Fred Ayer, Jr., *Before the Colors Fade: Portrait of a Soldier, George S. Patton, Jr.* (Boston: Houghton Mifflin, 1964), p. 209.

59. Interview with Hasia Diner, July 1, 1999.

60. Interview with Rabbi Abraham Cooper, March 14, 2000.

61. Interview with Michael Berenbaum, July 21, 1999.

62. Herscher, quoted in Huntington-Skirball joint press release, June 26, 1999.

63. Interview with Uri Herscher, July 20, 1999.

64. "Statement Dictated by General George S. Patton, Jr.," June 11, 1945, HLA.

65. Blumenson, *The Patton Papers, 1940–1945*, p. 721.

66. See, for example, "Generals Will Make Southland Tour Today," *Los Angeles Times*, June 10, 1945; "Patton Worships in Church Where He Was Baptized," *Los Angeles Times*, June 11, 1945.

67. Personal communication from Fred Bauman, Manuscript Division, Library of Congress, July 6, 1999. The George S. Patton, Jr. collection contains more than 26,000 items.

68. Interview with Greg Bradsher, August 10, 1999.

69. Waxman, "Hidden History of the Nazi Laws."

70. Martin Dannenberg, "The Discovery at Eischstatt," *Washington Post*, July 17, 1999, p. 18.

71. Interview with Martin Dannenberg, August 12, 1999. See, also, letter from Martin Dannenberg to Uri Herscher, president of the Skirball Cultural Center, Los Angeles, August 5, 1999, Martin Dannenberg Personal Papers (hereafter cited as MDP).

72. Interview, October 8, 1999.

73. Author's interviews and field notes, June–July 1999.

74. "Genocide differs from other murders in having a *category* for its object," observes Zygmunt Bauman, p. 227. On the contemporary elasticity of Jewish identity, see Diner, p. 358.

75. Skirball Cultural Center, "An Interview with Moshe Safdie," unpublished transcript, February 1996, SCCA. Safdie has designed many important buildings in Israel, including the Yad Vashem memorial in 2005 — replacing the old Holocaust History Museum, which was opened in 1973 by the Holocaust Martyrs' and Heroes' Remembrance Authority. See Steven Erlanger, "Israel Dares to Recast a Story Set in Stone," *New York Times*, February 13, 2005, p. 16.

76. Skirball Cultural Center, "'In Thrall to Hope': A Conversation with Dr. Uri D. Herscher," unpublished transcript, February 1996, SCCA.

77. Diner, pp. 121–122.

78. Information is based on interviews with Uri Herscher (July 20, 1999; August 16, 1999; October 8, 1999; February 16, 2001) and on a public relations packet provided by the Skirball Cultural Center.

79. "In: Skirball Center, Out: Getty Center," *Los Angeles Business Journal*, December 31, 2001–January 6, 2002.

80. Suzanne Muchnic, "You Don't Have to Be Jewish…," *Los Angeles Times*, September 7, 2003, p. E65. See, also, Naomi Pfefferman, "Skirball at Five," *The Jewish Journal of Greater Los Angeles*, April 13, 2001, pp. 40–41.

81. Skirball, "'In Thrall to Hope.'"

82. Peggy Park Bernal, *The Huntington* (San Marino: Huntington Library, 1992), p. 7; Skirball, "'In Thrall to Hope.'"

83. Muchnic, p. E65.

84. For a description of the Skirball's core exhibit, see Grace Cohen Grossman (editor), *New Beginnings: The Skirball Museum Collections and Inaugural Exhibition* (Berkeley: University of California Press, 1996).

85. The reference to "present absences" comes from Eugene Ionesco's production notes to his play, *The Chairs*, translated by Martin Crimp (London: Faber and Faber, 1997), p. 59.

▣ Chapter 3: Tall Like Germans

1. "Frank Perls Dies; Coast Art Dealer," *New York Times*, February 10, 1975.

2. This account of Frank (née Franz) Perls and his family is based in part on personal papers owned by his niece, Marianne Perls. This private collection is hereafter cited as MPP.

3. Personal communication from Martin Dannenberg, February 12, 2005. On the status of Jews in the United States prior to World War II, see Ronald Takaki, *A Different Mirror: A History of Multicultural America* (Boston: Little, Brown & Company, 1993), pp. 277–310; Diner, pp. 205–258. A wooden sign from the early twentieth century that reads "Gentiles Only" is on display in the permanent exhibit of the Jewish Museum in New York. From the author's notes, February 27, 2005.

4. Unless otherwise noted, the following profile of the Perls family is based on Frank Perls, "An Attempt to Introduce," unpublished manuscript, November 6, 1973, 46 pp., MPP. I have attempted to cross-reference and verify all names, places, and dates mentioned in this memoir.

5. Kathleen Paul, *Whitewashing Britain: Race and Citizenship in the Postwar Era* (Ithaca: Cornell University Press, 1997), p. 66. Even as persecution of Jews increased during the first five years of the Nazi government, England only allowed 11,000 Jewish refugees to enter the country.

6. According to the church certificate, Franz Perls was baptized as a Lutheran, November 29, 1910, MPP.

7. Perls, "An Attempt to Introduce," pp. 1–6; Certificate of Naturalization, April 13, 1943, issued to Frank Perls in San Luis Obispo, MPP.

8. Quoted in "Little Man, Big Doings," *Time*, September 23, 1935, p. 22. The attack on "degenerate art" (*entartete Kunst*), launched in 1937, involved the confiscation and destruction of some twenty thousand works.

9. Bauman, p. 31.

10. Hilberg, vol. 1, pp. 55, 169.

11. Ibid., pp. 69–80, 159–166.

12. Ibid., pp. 73–74.

13. Henry Friedlander, "From 'Euthanasia' to the 'Final Solution,'" in Dieter Kuntz and Susan Bachrach (editors), *Deadly Medicine: Creating the Master Race* (Washington, D.C.: United States Holocaust Memorial Museum, 2004), pp. 155–183. It is estimated that in 1935 some seven hundred and fifty thousand individuals were *Mischlinge* or mixed German-Jewish origins. See Benoit Massin, "The 'Science of Race,'" in *Deadly Medicine,* p. 120.

14. The following profile is based on research in the Hugo Perls Collection, AR6400, Leo Baeck Institute, New York. The collection is hereafter cited as HPC.

15. Hugo Perls, untitled, undated memoir in German, 249 pages, HPC, Memoir Microfilm Project, reel 20, box 9, folder 953. Translations of the memoir are by John Englander and Eva Englander, Leo Baeck Institute. Hereafter cited as Hugo Perls memoir.

16. Letter of reference from Bryn Hovde, president of the New School for Social Research, to Dr. C. R. Morey, American Embassy in Rome, March 8, 1948, HPC 6/16. See, also, Hugo Perls, "Curriculum Vitae," *ca.* 1948, HPC 6/20.

17. Roth, p. 217.

18. Frank Perls, "Encounters with Picasso," catalogue produced for exhibition, "Picasso: 45 Selected Graphics from 1904 to 1968," Frank Perls Gallery, Los Angeles, October–November, 1971, MPP.

19. Hilberg, vol. 1, p. 158.

20. Hugo Perls memoir, p. 235.

21. Frank Perls, "An Attempt to Introduce," pp. 5–6.

22. Hugo Perls, "The German Inheritance from Hegel to Hitler," unpublished manuscript, *ca.* 1965, HPC 6/2, p. 23.

23. Frank Perls, "An Attempt to Introduce," p. 10.

24. Hugo Perls memoir, p. 82.

25. Frank Perls, "An Attempt to Introduce," p. 13.

26. Hugo Perls memoir, p. 82.

27. Hugo Perls, "The German Inheritance," p. 12.

28. George S. Patton, Jr., "Federal Troops in Domestic Disturbances," unpublished lecture notes, November 1932, in Blumenson, *The Patton Papers, 1885–1940,* p. 898.

29. Frank Perls, "An Attempt to Introduce," p. 13.

30. Ibid., p. 9.

31. Ernst Toller, "Corpses in the Wood" (1916). "Ernst Toller," *www.spartacus. schoolnet.co.uk/FWWtoller.htm*, retrieved March 4, 2005.

32. Frank Perls, "An Attempt to Introduce," p. 18.

33. Toller left Germany in 1933, eventually reaching the United States. There he committed suicide in 1939 after his sister and brother were deported to a concentration camp. News of his death apparently accelerated the death of writer Joseph Roth in Paris on May 27, 1939. See "About the Author" in Roth, pp. 225–226.

34. Frank Perls, "An Attempt to Introduce," pp. 12, 23.

35. Robert S. Wistrich, *Who's Who in Nazi Germany* (London: Routledge, 1995), pp. 222–223. When he was released from Spandau in 1966, von Schirach published a memoir condemning nazism.

36. This information comes from transcripts sent from German universities to Frank Perls in Los Angeles in June 1949, available in the Frank Perls Papers, Smithsonian Archives of American Art, Washington, D.C. The collection is hereafter cited as FPP.

37. Frank Perls, "An Attempt to Introduce," p. 12.

38. Hugo Perls, "Curriculum Vitae."

39. Kershaw, pp. 463–464.

40. Frank Perls, "An Attempt to Introduce," p. 20.

41. Frank Perls, "Personal History Statement," January 18, 1945, FPP.

42. The original sketch, "par Picasso pour Perls," September 9, 1955, is owned by Marianne Perls. In a letter to his father (November 16, 1955), Frank mentioned the drawing by Picasso and that he had been hired to act in the movie. The letter can be found in the Eugenie Söderberg Collection, Special Collections and University Archives, Stony Brook University, New York. The collection is hereafter cited as ESC.

43. Hugo Perls, "Curriculum Vitae."

44. Hugo Perls, "The German Inheritance," p. 20.

45. Copies of newspaper stories carried in November–December 1937 (including the *New York Times*, November 7, 1937) are in FPP. The source of the first quote is unidentified.

46.   This information is based on an affidavit written by Frank Perls, "To Whom It May Concern," *ca.* December 1940, in the Eleanor Roosevelt Papers, Franklin D. Roosevelt Library, Hyde Park, New York. The collection is hereafter cited as ERP.

47.   Information on the Gurs camp is from the United States Holocaust Memorial Museum, "Holocaust Encyclopedia," *www.ushmm.org* (retrieved February, 2005).

48.   See, for example, letter from Lester States, Chase National Bank, to Klaus Perls, August 27, 1940; and R. S. Wareham, National City Bank of New York, to Klaus Perls, September 30, 1940, ERP.

49.   Frank's request is documented in an entry, dated July 6, 1940, in the Name Card Index 1940–1944, State Department Central Decimal File, National Archives and Records Administration (NARA). Information provided by Daniel Rooney, archivist, Civilian Records, NARA, April 6, 2005.

50.   Letter from Klaus Perls to Mildred Adams, Emergency Rescue Committee, September 23, 1940, Emergency Rescue Committee Records, 1936–1957 (GER-032), German and Jewish Intellectual Émigré Collection, M. E. Grenander Department of Special Collections and Archives, University at Albany, State University of New York. The collection is hereafter cited as ERCR.

51.   Anita Kassof, "Varian Fry and the Emergency Rescue Committee," United States Holocaust Memorial Museum," *www.ushmm.org*, retrieved February 12, 2005.

52.   Letter from Klaus Perls to Mildred Adams, September 23, 1940, ERCR.

53.   Andy Marino, *A Quiet American: The Secret War of Varian Fry* (New York: St. Martin's Press, 1999), p. 152.

54.   Letter from Klaus Perls to George Warren, October 3, 1940, ERCR.

55.   Klaus Perls, "Biographical Sketch of Mrs. Käte Perls," October 26, 1940, ERCR.

56.   Letter from Klaus Perls to Mildred Adams, October 21, 1940, ERCR.

57.   This anecdote appears in Frank Perls, "An Attempt to Introduce," p. 14.

58.   Letter from Walter Huston to Mrs. Roosevelt, December 15, 1940, ERP.

59.   Frank Perls, "To Whom It May Concern," *ca.* December 1940.

60.   Letter from Mrs. Roosevelt's secretary to Mr. Huston, December 20, 1940, ERP.

61.   Letter from Mrs. Roosevelt's secretary to Sumner Welles, December 20, 1940, ERP.

62.   See, generally, Michael Berenbaum, "Holocaust"; Hasia Diner, "Jews"; and Carl Joseph Bon Tempo, "Refugees," in Maurine H. Beasley, Holly C. Shulman, and Henry R. Beasley (editors), *The Eleanor Roosevelt Encyclopedia* (Westport, Connecticut: Greenwood Press, 2000), pp. 239–241, 281–284, 431–435.

63.   Public Broadcasting System (American Experience), "Breckinridge Long (1881–1958)," *www.pbsorg/wgbh/amex*, retrieved March 5, 2005. See, also, Diner, "Jews," p. 283, and Tempo, p. 433.

64.   Allida Black and June Hopkins (editors), "Sumner Welles," *Teaching Eleanor Roosevelt* (2003), *www.nps.gov/elro/glossary/welles-sumner.htm*, retrieved March 5, 2005.

65.   Letter from Sumner Welles to Eleanor Roosevelt, December 30, 1940, ERP.

66.   Letter from Walter Huston to Mrs. Roosevelt, January 8, 1941, ERP.

67.   According to State Department records, Frank Perls wrote to Eleanor Roosevelt

on December 20, 1940, asking for her help in getting a visa for Käte Perls. Information is from the Name Card Index 1940–1944, State Department Decimal File, NARA. Information provided by Sally Kuisel, archivist, Civilian Records, NARA, March 24, 2005.

68. "Re Mrs. Käte Perls," February 20, 1941; letter from Lotta Loeb to Klaus Perls, February 21, 1941, ERCR.

69. According to State Department records, a visa was issued to Hugo Perls on November 24, 1941.

70. Letter from Dr. Arieh Tartakower, World Jewish Congress, to Hugo Perls, February 18, 1942, HPC 6/18. In this letter, the Congress bills Hugo Perls for costs associated with sending cables to the Department of State regarding "visa case of Hugo and Käte Perls."

71. Takaki, pp. 373–377.

▣ Chapter 4: Human Betterment

1. C. M. Goethe, "P.G." [Pan-Germanism], unpublished memo (*ca.* 1934), sent to Harry Laughlin, director of the Eugenics Research Office in Cold Spring Harbor, Long Island, N.Y. Truman State, Harry Laughlin Collection, C. M. Goethe Correspondence D-2–4: 3. This collection is hereafter cited as HLC.

2. See, for example, George L. Mosse, *Nazi Culture: Intellectual, Cultural and Social Life in the Third Reich* (New York: Schocken Books, 1981), especially chapter 3, "The Foundation: Racism."

3. For the influence of American eugenics on German sterilization policies, see Stefan Kühl, *The Nazi Connection: Eugenics, American Racism, and German National Socialism* (New York: Oxford University Press, 1994); for more recent research on this issue, see Edwin Black, *War Against the Weak: Eugenics and America's Campaign to Create a Master Race* (New York: Four Walls Eight Windows, 2003). Black's book focuses primarily on the eugenics movement on the East Coast.

4. Quoted in Daniel J. Kevles, *In the Name of Eugenics: Genetics and the Uses of Human Heredity* (Cambridge: Harvard University Press, 1995), p. xiii.

5. Sheila Faith Weiss, "German Eugenics, 1890–1933," in *Deadly Medicine*, p. 15.

6. See, for example, Richard Hofstadter, *Social Darwinism in the United States* (Boston: Beacon Press, 1965).

7. Laura Briggs, *Reproducing Empire: Race, Sex, Science, and U.S. Imperialism in Puerto Rico* (Berkeley: University of California Press, 2002), p. 99.

8. Gunnar Broberg and Nils Roll-Hansen (editors), *Eugenics and the Welfare State: Sterilization Policy in Denmark, Sweden, Norway, and Finland* (East Lansing: Michigan State University Press, 1996); Nancy Leys Stepan, *"The Hour of Eugenics": Race, Gender, and Nation in Latin America* (Ithaca: Cornell University Press, 1991); Daniel J. Kevles, "International Eugenics," in *Deadly Medicine*, pp. 41–59.

9. The literature on the American eugenics movement is considerable. See, in particular, Mark Haller, *Eugenics: Hereditarian Attitudes in American Thought* (New Brunswick: Rutgers University Press, 1963); Daniel J. Kevles, *In the Name of Eugenics* (1995); Elof Axel Carlson, *The Unfit: A History of a Bad Idea* (Cold Spring Harbor, Long Island, N.Y: Cold Spring Harbor Laboratory Press, 2001); Wendy Kline, *Building a Better Race: Gender, Sexuality, and Eugenics from the Turn of the Century to the Baby Boom*

(Berkeley: University of California Press, 2001); Nancy Ordover, *American Eugenics: Race, Queer Anatomy, and the Science of Nationalism* (Minneapolis: University of Minnesota Press, 2003); Edwin Black, *War Against the Weak*; and Alexandra Minna Stern, *Eugenic Nation: Faults and Frontiers of Better Breeding in Modern America* (Berkeley: University of California Press, 2005).

10. Paul Popenoe and Roswell Hill Johnson, *Applied Eugenics* (New York: Macmillan, 1926), p. 301.

11. Letter from Harry Laughlin to Carl Schneider (August 11, 1936), quoted in Black, p. 312.

12. The following analysis of the Human Betterment Foundation is based on research in the E. S. Gosney Papers and Records of the Human Betterment Foundation, California Institute of Technology, Pasadena, California. The collection is hereafter cited as ESGP.

13. "The Human Betterment Foundation," *Eugenics,* vol. 1, no. 1 (January 1929), p. 18.

14. Popenoe did not have a graduate degree in biology, but presented himself to the public as a biologist. See Kenneth M. Ludmerer, *Genetics and American Society: A Historical Appraisal* (Baltimore: Johns Hopkins University Press, 1972), p. 148.

15. David A. Valone, "Eugenic Science in California: The Papers of E. S. Gosney and the Human Betterment Foundation," introduction to ESGP.

16. "Caltech May Get Foundation Fund," *Los Angeles Times*, November 21, 1943.

17. "This organization is not designed to take up original scientific research, but rather to investigate the results and possibilities for human betterment by a safe, conservative application of the discoveries made by scientists, and to give this information to the public." Paul Popenoe and E. S. Gosney, *Twenty-Eight Years of Sterilization in California* (Pasadena: Human Betterment Foundation, 1938), p. 40.

18. Paul Popenoe, "Eugenics, Sterilization, Democracy" (*ca.* 1933), ESGP 1.6.

19. On Linden's position within the Interior Ministry under Wilhelm Frick, see Hilberg, vol. 1, p. 66; on Gütt's career, see Wistrich, p. 93. On Nazi recognition of the HBF's publications, see Kühl, pp. 42–50.

20. Susan Bachrach, "Introduction," in *Deadly Medicine*, p. 9.

21. Gisela Bock, "Nazi Sterilization and Reproductive Policies," in *Deadly Medicine*, p. 87.

22. Claudia Koonz, *The Nazi Conscience* (Cambridge: Belknap Press, 2003), p. 3.

23. Roth, p. 209.

24. "Address by Reichminister for the Interior Dr. Frick Before the First Meeting of the Expert Council for Population and Race Politics," Berlin, June 28, 1933. An English translation of this speech was printed in Germany and sent to the Human Betterment Foundation. A copy of the speech is in ESGP 22.1.

25. See, generally, Robert N. Proctor, *Racial Hygiene: Medicine Under the Nazis* (Cambridge: Harvard University Press, 1988), pp. 95–117.

26. "Commentary on German Sterilization Law," July 28, 1933, translated by George Dock, HBF Board Member, ESGP 21.7.

27. Kühl, p. 43.

28. Letter from George Dock to E. S. Gosney, January 31, 1934, ESGP 21.7.

29. Popenoe, "Eugenics, Sterilization, Democracy."

30. Quoted in Kühl, p. 58, and Black, p. 277. The letter from Goethe to Gosney is reproduced in the HBF's annual report, February 12, 1936.

31. Carlson, p. 215. The number typically used is between sixty and sixty-five thousand. Ordover (p. 134) estimates that seventy thousand people "are known to have been sterilized" between 1907 and 1945. Untold thousands of women were also sterilized without their informed consent after World War II. By the 1980s, an estimated one-third of Puerto Rican women of childbearing age was sterilized, many as a result of coercion and trickery by social work and public health agencies. See Briggs, p. 143.

32. Black, p. 398.

33. Paul Popenoe, "The German Sterilization Law," *Journal of Heredity,* vol. 25, no. 7 (July 1934), p. 257.

34. Goethe, "P.G." [Pan-Germanism].

35. Quoted by Bock, p. 62.

36. Ibid., pp. 61–71.

37. C. M. Goethe, *Eugenic Pamphlet* no. 12 (no date), quoted in May Second Committee, "Sacramento State's Own Doctor Strangelove," April 1965, Charles M. Goethe Collection 85: D9, University Archives, California State University, Sacramento. The Goethe Collection is hereafter cited as CMGC.

38. Kevles, *Deadly Medicine,* p. 55.

39. Bock, p. 62.

40. Ibid., pp. 79–80.

41. Michael Burleigh, "Nazi 'Euthanasia' Programs," in *Deadly Medicine*, p. 131; Bock, pp. 79–80.

42. The article was published without the photograph in the *Journal of Heredity* (July 1934), pp. 257–260. The original article, with a space for Hitler's photograph, is in the ESGP 21.7.

43. Popenoe, "The German Sterilization Law," pp. 257, 259, 260.

44. On Gütt's ideas and rise to power, see Kershaw, p. 487; and Jeremy Noakes, "Nazism and Eugenics: The Background of the Nazi Sterilization Law of 14 July 1933," in R. J. Bullen, H. Pogge von Strandmann, and A. B. Polonsky (editors), *Ideas into Politics: Aspects of European History, 1880–1950* (London: Croom Helm, 1984), pp. 75–94.

45. Popenoe, "The German Sterilization Law," p. 260.

46. Wistrich, p. 269.

47. Ibid., pp. 91–92.

48. Letter from Paul Popenoe to geneticist L.C. Dunn (January 22, 1934), quoted in Ludmerer, p. 118.

49. Letter from Popenoe to von Verschuer, July 16, 1936, quoted in Black, p. 342.

50. Official Program of the Sixty-Third Annual Meeting of the American Public Health Association, Pasadena, September 3–6, 1934, p. 31.

51. "Nazis Issue Rules of Choices of Wife," *New York Times*, August 25, 1934, p. 15; "Dr. Gebhard Is Honored," *New York Times*, August 25, 1934, p. 15.

52. "Health Data Exhibited," *Pasadena Star-News*, September 4, 1934, part II, p. 9.

53. Kevles, *In the Name of Eugenics*, p. 118.

54. "Asks Negro Sterilization: Germany Strikes at Children Left Behind by French Colonials," *New York Times*, February 8, 1934, p. 4. See, also, Friedländer, pp. 207–208.

55. Dr. K. Burchardi, "Why Hitler Says: 'Sterilize the Unfit!'" *Los Angeles Times*, August 11, 1935, Sunday Magazine p. 25.

56. Proctor, pp. 112–114.

57. "The Race Law of the Third Reich, Speech of Reich Minister Dr. Frick," February 15, 1934, ESGP 22.2. This English translation was found in the HBF's files.

58. This profile of Goethe is based on research in CMGC. I also draw upon the research and advice of Alexandra Stern, author of *Eugenic Nation.*

59. C. M. Goethe, "Patriotism and Racial Standards," *Eugenical News,* vol. 21, no. 4 (July–August, 1936), p. 66.

60. Biographical details of Goethe's life are taken from Andrew Schauer, *Charles Matthias Goethe, 1875–1966,* unpublished report, 1976, CMGC.

61. Letter from Guy West to Harold Severaid, March 24, 1965, Severaid Collection, University Archives, California State University, Sacramento; George S. Craft, Jr., *California State University, Sacramento: The First Forty Years, 1947–1987* (Sacramento: CSUS Foundation, 1987), p. 132.

62. Personal communication from Alexandra Stern.

63. Documentation for both Goethe groves—the one dedicated for his wife in 1948 and the one dedicated to him in 1976—is in a binder titled "Save-the-Redwoods League Dedicated Groves" (undated, unpublished), provided by Ranger Brent Critch, Prairie Redwood Creek Visitors Center, January 10, 2003. According to Alexandra Stern, Goethe was a principal actor in the naming of three memorial groves—the Jedediah Smith Grove, the Lizzie H. Glide and Mary Glide Goethe Grove, and Drury Brothers Grove. He also was involved in the founding of several other redwoods groves, including the Madison Grant Forest and Elk Refuge.

64. Telegram from Lyndon Johnson to Goethe, March 27, 1965; letter from Earl Warren to Goethe, March 28, 1965; letter from Stuart Udall to Goethe, March 3, 1965; letter from Edmund Brown to Goethe, no date. CMGC 85: 1.

65. Letter from Goethe to Harry Laughlin, March 15, 1926, HLC C-4–1: 2.

66. Letter from Goethe to S. W. Ward, February 26, 1926, HLC C-4–1: 2.

67. Goethe, undated newsletter from Florence, Italy, *ca.* June 1926. HLC C-4–1: 2.

68. Carey McWilliams, "Racism on the West Coast," *New Republic* no. 110 (May 29, 1944), pp. 732–733; and *New Republic* no. 110 (June 12, 1944), pp. 784–786.

69. Letter from Goethe to the editor of *Daily News,* South Africa, July 19, 1954, quoted in Schauer, p. 147.

70. Haller, p. 182.

71. I presented my research findings on the university's collusive relationship with C. M. Goethe in a public address in February 2004. My report—*What's in a Name? Charles M. Goethe, American Eugenics, and Sacramento State University,* February 2004, is available in the library at California State University, Sacramento. See, also, Tony Platt, "Curious Historical Bedfellows: Sac State and Its Racist Benefactor," *Sacramento Bee,* February 29, 2004, p. E3.

72. See letter from Nixon to Goethe, September 11, 1951, unfiled materials, CMGC.

73. Letter from Strom Thurmond to Goethe, March 11, 1957, CMGC 85F3: 12.

74. Griffin sent Goethe a copy of a notorious 1957 photograph, taken at the Highlander Folk School gathering in Tennessee, that purported to show the influence of communists on the Civil Rights movement. The photograph, which includes Martin Luther King and Rosa Parks, is annotated on the back with names and communist affiliations. See

unfiled materials, CMGC. See, also, Thomas Bledsoe, *Or We'll All Hang Separately: The Highlander Idea* (Boston: Beacon Press, 1969), pp. 84–99.

75. See, Stern, *Eugenic Nation*, pp. 134–149.

76. Schauer, p. 125.

77. On Goethe's role in American eugenics, see Stern, *Eugenic Nation*, chapters 4 and 6; and Alexandra Minna Stern, "Buildings, Boundaries, and Blood: Medicalization and Nation-Building on the U.S.-Mexico Border, 1910–1930," *Hispanic American Historical Review,* vol. 79, no. 1 (1999), pp. 41–81. See, also, my unpublished report, *What's in a Name?*

78. C. M. Goethe diary entry, August 5, 1902, quoted in Schauer, p. 204.

79. In 1912, 1925, 1929, and 1934. Goethe's passports are in CMGC 85F7.

80. Diary entry, May 20, 1934. Goethe's travel diaries are in CMGC 85F7.

81. Diary entries, June 8, 1934. On Hitler's vegetarianism, see Kershaw, pp. 261–262, 343, 345.

82. Diary entries, June 9, June 10, July 11, July 19, 1934.

83. Diary entry, June 9, 1934.

84. Diary entry, June 11, 1934.

85. Diary entry, July 19, 1939.

86. Diary entry, July 11, 1939. Leon Blum, born in Paris in April 1872, resigned in June 1937, and became prime minister again in March 1938 until his government fell one month later. He was later imprisoned by the Nazis from February 1942 until the end of World War II in 1945. He died in 1950.

87. Due to Blum's "characteristic Jewish clannishness," Goethe observed, his government had "favored Hebrews as against Arabs consistently [in Algeria and Morocco]. As a result all Islam became inflamed." Diary entries, July 10 and July 11, 1939.

88. Black (p. 379) calls Goethe a "Nazi agitator."

89. Goethe, Immigration Study Commission newsletter, October 29, 1928. HLC C-4–1: 2.

90. C. M. Goethe, "P.G." [Pan-Germanism].

91. C. M. Goethe newsletter, untitled (January 12, 1935). HLC D-2–4: 3.

92. Goethe, "P.G." [Pan-Germanism].

93. Letter from C. M. Goethe to Ellsworth Huntington, September 26, 1935, CMGC, unfiled materials. Ellsworth Huntington is not related to the San Marino Huntingtons.

94. C. M. Goethe, "Patriotism and Racial Standards," *Eugenical News* (July–August 1936), vol. 21, no. 4, pp. 65–69.

95. Diary entry, April 15, 1936.

96. Kühl, p. 30.

97. C. M. Goethe, *Seeking to Serve* (Sacramento: Keystone Printing Company, 1949), p. 142.

98. Letter from C. M. Goethe to James G. Eddy, October 27, 1937, HLC D-2–4: 3.

99. According to Edwin Black (pp. 338–340), von Vershuer played a leading role in integrating eugenics into "the normal course of studies of medical students." Hitler, observed von Verschuer, was "the first statesman to recognize hereditary biology and race hygiene." By the late 1930s, von Verschuer was arguing that "our position on the race question has its foundation in genetics" and that "the complete racial separation between Germans and Jews is therefore an absolute necessity."

100. Letter from Goethe to von Verschuer, April 15, 1937, quoted in Black, p. 343.
101. Letter from Goethe to von Verschuer, December 23, 1937, quoted in Black, p. 343.
102. Letter from Goethe to von Verschuer, February 26, 1938, quoted in Black, p. 344.
103. Letter from Goethe to von Verschuer, November 22, 1938, quoted in Black, p. 344. *Kristallnacht* took place on November 9–10. See Friedländer, p. 270.
104. Paul Popenoe, "The Nation's Greatest Asset," April 1936, ESGP 1.6.
105. Frick, "The Race Law of the Third Reich."
106. Popenoe, "Eugenics, Sterilization, Democracy" (*ca.* 1933), ESGP 1.6.
107. Ibid.; Frick, "The Race Law of the Third Reich" (1934).
108. Bock, p. 81.
109. Burleigh, pp. 127–153; Bachrach, p. 10.
110. The quotes are from Frick, "The Race Law of the Third Reich."
111. Bock, p. 81.

🔲 Chapter 5: Blood and Honor

1. E-mail from Gerhard Jochem to the Huntington Library, June 28, 1999.
2. W. G. Sebald, "A Natural History of Destruction," *New Yorker*, November 4, 2002, p. 66.
3. W. G. Sebald, *After Nature,* translated by Michael Hamburger (New York: Random House, 2002), p. 86.
4. George S. Patton, Jr., *War As I Knew It* (Boston: Houghton Mifflin, 1947), p. 313.
5. Diary entry, April 27, 1945, in Blumenson, *The Patton Papers, 1940–1945*, p. 693.
6. Patton visited Nuremberg after participating in the 1912 Olympic Games in Stockholm. In a memoir written in 1927, he remembered that his wife and father "used to eat donkey meat sausages and drink beer in little restaurants." Blumenson, *The Patton Papers, 1885–1940*, p. 233.
7. "Nuremberg," *Encyclopaedia Judaica*, vol. 12, pp. 1274–1279.
8. Gerhard Jochem, "Leaving Nuremberg," Yizkor Book Project, July 16, 2001, *www.jewishgen.org/yizkor/Nuremberg*, retrieved June 11, 2004. The aim of this Web site is "to join again fragments of a precious artifact, the German-Jewish history in Nuremberg."
9. Rothschild's account of his visit was published in the *San Diego Union*, July 9, 1873. It is reproduced in Jochem, "Leaving Nuremberg."
10. On the distribution of Jews in German cities, see Hilberg, vol. 1, p. 158.
11. Ludwig C. Berlin, "Dr. Walter Berlin, Nuremberg," June 21, 2004, *www.rijo-research.de*, retrieved February 20, 2005. This Web site, edited by Susanne Rieger and Gerhard Jochem, is dedicated to restoring the history of Jews in Nuremberg.
12. Information about the Katzenberger family comes from *www.geocities.com/Heartland/Pointe/6230*, retrieved February 24, 2005.
13. Herbert Kolb, "Bernhard Kolb, Nuremberg," June 21, 2004, *www.rijo-research.de*, retrieved February 20, 2005.
14. The International Military Tribunal (IMT) convened in Nuremberg from November 20, 1945, to October 1, 1946. The USA, USSR, Great Britain, and France administered the IMT. The Soviet Union wanted the trials to be held in Berlin, but agreed

to Nuremberg if IMT headquarters were established in Berlin. See Higher Superior Court of Nuremberg, "International Military Tribunal: The Nuremberg War-Crimes Trial (1945–1946)," *www.justiz.bayern.de/olgn*, retrieved February 10, 2005.

15. Shirer, p. 90.

16. Kershaw, p. 179.

17. Paul Gilroy, *Against Race: Imagining Political Culture Beyond the Color Line* (Cambridge: Harvard University Press, 2000), p. 147. See, also, Kershaw, p. 310.

18. Shirer, p. 90.

19. Kershaw, pp. 483–484. However, streets and squares in every town were named after Hitler.

20. Ibid., p. 526.

21. Quoted in Shirer, p. 230.

22. Max Domarus, *Hitler: Speeches and Proclamations, 1932–1945*, vol. 2, translated by Chris Wilcox and Mary Fran Gilbert (Wauconda, Ill.: Bolchazy-Carducci, 1992), p. 689.

23. Kershaw, p. 566.

24. Domarus, p. 702.

25. Shirer, p. 274.

26. For examples of these interpretations, see Gilroy, *Against Race,* especially chapter 4, "Hitler Wore Khakis: Icons, Propaganda, and Aesthetic Politics"; Kershaw, *Hitler*; Hilberg, *The Destruction of the European Jews;* and Bauman, *Modernity and the Holocaust.*

27. Hilberg, vol. 1, p. 55.

28. Bock, p. 71.

29. Henry Friedlander, pp. 155, 156.

30. Kershaw, p. 559.

31. This was not the case, though, in Streicher's Franconia, where a vicious pogrom was carried out against local Jews in the spring of 1934. Ibid., p. 559.

32. Ibid., pp. 559–560.

33. According to a Gestapo report, cited ibid. p. 561.

34. Ibid.

35. Hilberg, vol. 1, pp. 36, 38.

36. Kershaw, p. 563.

37. Ibid., pp. 563–564.

38. Shirer, p. 233.

39. Kershaw, pp. 566–567.

40. Domarus, p. 687.

41. Ibid., pp. 692–693.

42. The following account of passage of the Nuremberg Laws is based on an affidavit given by Dr. Bernhard Lösener to the Office of Chief of Counsel for War Crimes, U.S. War Department, February 24, 1948. This document is in the Collection of World War II War Crimes Records, RG 238, National Archives and Records Administration (NARA), Washington, D.C. The Bernhard Lösener affidavit is hereafter cited as BLA.

43. On the chain of command in the Ministry of the Interior, see Hilberg, vol. 1, p. 66.

44. In his 1947–1948 testimony to investigators from the War Crimes Tribunal,

Lösener claimed that he tried without success to exempt "half Jews" from the Nuremberg Laws. Hitler crossed out a sentence that Lösener wrote into the legislation with Stuckart's approval: "These laws are applicable to full Jews only." Lösener was transferred to a position in the Reich Administrative Court in March 1943, where he remained until he was arrested and detained by the Gestapo in November 1944 on the grounds that he had hidden people accused of an attempt on Hitler's life. He was in prison when the Russians entered Berlin. BLA.

45.   Hilberg, vol. 1, p. 70. The quotations cited by Hilberg come from a letter written in 1942 by Wilhelm Stuckart.

46.   Ibid., vol. 1, pp. 71, 178.

47.   Kershaw, p. 569.

48.   Hitler's speech to the Reichstag is reproduced in Domarus, pp. 703–706.

49.   Hitler singled out an incident in New York in which dockworkers tore down a swastika from a German steamer.

50.   Domarus, pp. 705–706.

51.   Ibid., p. 707.

52.   Ibid., p. 708.

53.   Personal communication from Gerhard Jochem, September 10, 1999.

54.   Peter Novick, *The Holocaust in American Life* (Boston: Houghton Mifflin, 1999), pp. 20–21. For a view that takes issue with Novick, whose interpretation I share, see Lipstadt's argument that press coverage in the United States was uneven and tended to minimize the pervasiveness of anti-Semitism in Germany. Deborah E. Lipstadt, *Beyond Belief: The American Press and the Coming of the Holocaust, 1933–1945* (New York: The Free Press, 1986), pp. 57–62.

55.   Otto D. Tolischus, "Reich Adopts Swastika as Nation's Official Flag; Hitler's Reply to 'Insult,'" *New York Times*, September 16, 1935, p. 1. A subhead to the story notes "Anti-Jewish Laws Passed"; in a long story, the *Times* reproduced wording of the laws and Hitler's speech to the Reichstag.

56.   Associated Press, "Hitler Accuses Lithuanians of Torturing Nazis," *Sacramento Bee,* September 16, 1935, p. 1.

57.   "Little Man, Big Doings," *Time*, September 23, 1935, p. 23. As a result of the Blood Law, thousands of German women gave up jobs in Jewish households and in Jewish-owned hotels and guesthouses. See Hilberg, vol. 1, p. 159.

58.   I draw upon Gilroy (p. 152) for this interpretation.

59.   Quoted by Kershaw, p. 573.

60.   Henry Friedlander, pp. 158–159; Hilberg, vol. 1, p. 80.

61.   Bauman, p. 105.

62.   Kershaw, p. 569. See, also, Shirer, p. 233; and Presidential Advisory Commission on Holocaust Assets in the United States, *Plunder and Restitution: The U.S. and Holocaust Victims' Assets* (Washington, D.C.: U.S. Government Printing Office, 2000), Staff Report, p. 15.

63.   Ludwig Berlin, "Dr. Walter Berlin." This view of the police chief is also reported in the *Encyclopaedia Judaica,* vol. 12, p. 1279: "Dr. Benno Martin, head of police, rescued many Jews from death and alleviated the suffering of others."

64.   "Nuremberg," *Encyclopedia Judaica*, ibid.

65. Jochem, "Leaving Nuremberg."

66. "Nuremberg," *Encyclopedia Judaica.*

67. Albert Kimmelstiel, quoted in Jochem, "Leaving Nuremberg."

68. Herbert Kolb, "Bernhard Kolb, Nuremberg."

69. At *www.geocities.com/Heartland/Pointe/6230.*

70. Hilberg, vol. 1, pp. 163–165.

71. At *www.geocities.com/Heartland/Pointe/6230.*

72. The police chief's role—"Dr. Benno Martin wanted to carry out the deportation as inconspicuously as possible and so he chose a site away from the city that was easy to guard"—is described in *www.nuernberg.de/tourismus* and in Ludwig Berlin, "Dr. Walter Berlin, Nuremberg." On the fate of Jews in Nuremberg, see Gerhard Jochem, "Leaving Nuremberg."

73. Roth, p. 208.

74. Hugo Perls, "The German Inheritance," p. 25.

75. The following analysis is based on unfiled, unprocessed documents that General Patton delivered to the Huntington Library on June 11, 1945. Translated for the author by Eva Ackerman. Letter from Lammers to Alfred Rosenberg, Führer's Representative for the Supervision of the General Intellectual and Ideological Education of the NSDAP, August 9, 1937, HLA. The Nuremberg Laws were probably sent to Nuremberg on December 20, 1935, according to documentation on an envelope accompanying the Laws.

76. According to the mayor's handwritten notes, August 11, 1937, on a letter from Lammers to the mayor, August 9, 1937, HLA.

77. Letter from Lammers to Rosenberg, March 18, 1937, HLA.

78. Rosenberg's letter, dated April 5, 1937, is referenced in a letter from Lammers to Rosenberg, April 8, 1937, HLA.

79. Letter from Rosenberg to Lammers, July 29, 1937, HLA.

80. According to Ian Kershaw (p. 533), "Hans Heinrich Lammers, the head of the Reich Chancellery, and sole link between the ministers and the Führer, naturally attained considerable influence over the way legislation (or other business of ministers) was presented to Hitler."

81. Letter from Lammers to Rosenberg, March 18, 1937, HLA.

82. Given Hitler's propensity to intervene in the minutiae of government, it is possible that Lammers did get his approval of this policy. On Hitler's "personalized style of rule," see Kershaw, p. 533.

83. Letter from Lammers to Rosenberg, April 8, 1937. Lammers reiterated the policy in a letter to Rosenberg's chief of staff on August 9, 1937, HLA.

84. Personal communication from Gerhard Jochem, Nuremberg City Archives, May 26, 2000.

85. Benno Martin was chief of the Nuremberg-Fürth police department until he was promoted to head of the police and SS in military district XIII. Personal communication from Gerhard Jochem, July 21, 2001. This account is based on interviews with Martin Dannenberg and a memo by Frank Perls, "Nuernberg Laws," April 28, 1945, HLA.

86. According to documentation on an envelope left at the Huntington by General Patton in 1945, the Laws were deposited "by order of Director A and Director B" on October 9, 1943, HLA.

▣ Chapter 6: Hitler's Signature

1. The following account of Jews in Cuba relies on Boris Sapir, *The Jewish Community of Cuba: Settlement and Growth*, translated by Simon Wolin (New York: The Jewish Teachers' Seminary and People's University, 1948); "Cuba," *Encyclopaedia Judaica*, vol. 12, pp. 1146–1151; and Donna Katzin, "The Jews of Cuba," *The Nation* (May 25, 1974), pp. 658–660.

2. Sapir, p. 28.

3. Ibid., p. 51.

4. Ibid., p. 57.

5. Ibid.; *Encyclopaedia Judaica*, p. 1148.

6. Letter from Elise Flatow to Hugo Perls, August 6, 1944, HPC 6/18. Apparently, several German Jews who had been incarcerated in Gurs found their way to Cuba. On the role of a German Jewish activist who helped people find escape routes, see Douglas Martin, "Lisa Fittko, 95; Helped Rescue Many Who Fled the Nazis," *New York Times*, March 21, 2005, p. 16.

7. Sapir, pp. 26–30.

8. Letter from Elise Flatow to Hugo Perls, August 6, 1944, HPC 6/18.

9. According to State Department records, Käte was a passenger on the ship *Nyasa* (possibly *Nyassa*) on January 31, 1942. It is possible that she arrived first in the United States, was denied entry, and then went to Cuba. State Department Central Decimal File 1940–1944, NARA. See, also, letter from Käte to Hugo, April 28, 1942, HPC 6/18.

10. Over several months, Hugo sent Käte close to $1,000. Hugo kept receipts and later accounted for the money after her death. See various receipts and letter from Hugo Perls to Milton Annis (October 21, 1945), HPC 6/18.

11. David Kratz, "The Iconoclastic Eye of Klaus Perls," *M Magazine*, December 1987, p. 124.

12. Letters from Käte to Hugo, July 14 and December 12, 1942, HPC 6/18.

13. Letter from Käte to Hugo, April 28, 1942, ibid.

14. Letters from Käte to Hugo, April 14 and April 28, 1942, ibid.

15. Letter from Elise to Hugo, April 19, 1942, ibid.

16. Michael Berenbaum, "Holocaust," p. 240.

17. Personal communication from Marianne Perls, April 20, 2005.

18. Personal communication from Marianne Perls; Käte's location is mentioned in Frank Perls's application for promotion, "Personal History Statement" (January 18, 1945), FPP. See, also, "Perls, Kate," announcement of death, *New York Times* (August 25, 1945), p. 19.

19. Klaus Perls, now in his 90s, turned his gallery into a very successful business. See Kratz, pp. 122–128. Hugo and Käte's youngest son, Thomas, came to the United States in 1939. He earned a Ph.D. in physics at Yale and worked for NASA and Lockheed. Personal communication from Marianne Perls, March 17, 2005.

20. Interview with Billy Wilder (September 30, 1999). I brought Wilder together with Frank's niece, Marianne Perls, for lunch (October 7, 1999), but he was very ill and frustrated by his poor memory.

21. Frank Perls, "Sunset Boulev*art*," unpublished manuscript (*ca.* 1973), MPP.

22. His obituary—"Frank Perls Dies; Coast Art Dealer"— appeared in the *New York Times*, February 10, 1975.

23. Letter from Frank Perls to Francis Biddle, August 28, 1942, FPP.

24. Frank Perls's application for an exemption from the Wartime Civil Control Administration, September 11, 1942, and supporting documents are in FPP.

25. Letter from Frank Perls to Attorney General Francis Biddle. August 28, 1942, FPP.

26. Letters from Frank Perls to Francis Biddle, August 28 and September 10, 1942; Frank Perls, "Minutes of Telephone Call," September 14, 1942; Frank Perls, "Application for Exemption from Curfew," September 11, 1942; letter from Lt. Col. William A. Boekel to Frank Perls, September 15, 1942, FPP.

27. Letter from U.S. Attorney Leo Silverstein to Frank Perls, October 1, 1942, FPP.

28. Letter from Frank Perls to "Dear Sir," February 4, 1943, FPP.

29. Frank Perls, "An Attempt to Introduce," MPP; see, also, Frank Perls, "Personal History Statement," January 18, 1945, FPP.

30. The Ground Staff of the army was organized into six sections. Some of these sections were designated "G" for "Ground." Thus, G-1 was Personnel, and G-2 Military Intelligence. Personal communication from Martin Dannenberg, March 21, 2005.

31. Blumenson, *The Patton Papers, 1940–1945*, p. 410.

32. Handwritten log of MII Team No. 421, April 15–June 20, 1944, FPP.

33. Letter from Elise Flatow to Hugo Perls, August 6, 1944, HPC 6/18.

34. Frank Perls, "At Attempt to Introduce," pp. 39–40.

35. Major General L. S. Hobbs, "Citation," September 24, 1944, FPP.

36. "Guts and Gaffe," *Newsweek,* May 8, 1944, p. 26. For details of the "Knutsford incident," see Blumenson, *The Patton Papers, 1940–1945*, pp. 439–453.

37. Ayer, p. 115.

38. Quoted in D'Este, p. 818.

39. Letter from General Eisenhower to General Marshall, April 15, 1945, in Blumenson, *The Patton Papers, 1940–1945*, p. 676.

40. Letter from George Patton, Sr., to "My Dear Son," February 20, 1919, in Blumenson, *The Patton Papers, 1885–1940*, p. 686.

41. George S. Patton, diary entry, February 5, 1943, in Blumenson, *The Patton Papers, 1940–1945*, p. 169.

42. John Field, "Patton of the Armored Force," *Life*, November 30, 1942, pp. 113–121.

43. For examples of his "war face" and how he created it as part of his public persona, see *Patton: The Man Behind the Myth*, Home Box Office documentary, 1980.

44. *Washington Sunday Star*, December 15, 1940, in Martin Blumenson, *The Patton Papers, 1940–1945*, p. 17.

45. Field, pp. 113–121.

46. Oscar W. Koch, *G2: Intelligence for Patton* (Philadelphia: Whitmore Publishing Co., 1971), p. 72.

47. *Life*, July 7, 1941; Field, pp. 113–121; *Newsweek* and *Time*, July 26, 1943; *Newsweek*, August 28, 1944; *Time*, April 9, 1945.

48. Ted Shane, "These Are the Generals—Patton," *The Saturday Evening Post*, February 6, 1943, p. 19; Frederick C. Painton, "Old Man of Battle," *Reader's Digest*,

September 1943, pp. 8–12; George Creel, "Patton at the Pay-Off," *Collier's*, January 13, 1945. For a transcript of a typical radio portrait, see Blumenson, *The Patton Papers, 1940–1945*, p. 178.

49.   Diary entry, July 2, 1943, in Blumenson, *The Patton Papers, 1940–1945*, p. 270.

50.   George S. Patton, Jr., "God of Battles," *Women's Home Companion*, November, 1943, p. 19; G. S. Patton, Jr., "Fear," *Cosmopolitan*, May 1945, p. 37; "Patton's Prayer," *Newsweek*, January 29, 1945, p. 76. See, also, Carmine A. Prioli, *Lines of Fire: The Poems of General George S. Patton, Jr.* (Lewiston, N.Y.: Edwin Mellen Press, 1991), p. xv.

51.   On the details of the "slapping incident," see Blumenson, *The Patton Papers, 1940–1945*, pp. 326–342.

52.   Eisenhower's reprimand is in a letter to Patton, August 17, 1943; letter from Eisenhower to Marshall, August 24, 1943. Both letters are in Blumenson, ibid., pp. 329, 337–338.

53.   Patton diary entry, April 27, 1944, ibid., p. 444.

54.   By early 1945, the public had "begun to misremember" the slapping incident. See *Time*, April 9, 1945, p. 34.

55.   Frank Perls, "An Attempt to Introduce," pp. 39–40.

56.   The following account of American military operations in the Nuremberg area is based on III Corps Histories and Historical Reports (1944–1946), Research Group 338, NARA, Washington, D.C. Hereafter cited as RG 338.

57.   General James A. Van Fleet took over III Corps in March 1945. A graduate in 1915 of West Point and classmate of Eisenhower, he was a military commander in the Patton mold. After World War II, Truman put him in charge of the anti-Communist military mission in Greece. In 1951, he headed the Eighth Army in Korea. George Forty, *The Armies of George S. Patton* (New York: Sterling, 1998), pp. 88–89.

58.   After Action Reports, "The Phantom Swings South," p. 32, RG 338, box 1.

59.   Ibid., p. 33.

60.   "I don't see what the [German] fools are fighting for," Patton told the press. Blumenson, *The Patton Papers, 1940–1945*, pp. 693–694.

61.   Unless otherwise noted, the account of the discovery of the Nuremberg Laws in Eichstätt is based on interviews with Martin Dannenberg.

62.   CIC evolved from the Military Intelligence Service's Counter-Intelligence Branch. Presidential Advisory Commission on Holocaust Assets in the United States, Staff Report, p. 218.

63.   SHAEF was created on January 17, 1944, as a joint British-American command for military operations in Europe. It was dissolved on July 11, 1945. Ibid., p. 221.

64.   "Interviewing Agent's Comments" attached to "Personal History Statement," January 18, 1945, FPP.

65.   See letter from David Speer to Major Ryser, January 12, 1945; David Speer, "Commendation of Master Sergeant Frank R. Perls," February 6, 1945; Harry Lindauer, "Appointment as Second Lieutenant," February 20, 1945; Frank Perls, "Personal History Statement," January 18, 1945, FPP.

66.   Information about Martin Dannenberg is based on interviews by Cecilia O'Leary, August 12–13, 1999; October 3, 1999; December 11–12, 1999; and July 11, 2001; and personal communications with the author.

67. Captain John Orend, "Transfer of Enlisted Man," January 5, 1945; Lindauer, "Appointment as Second Lieutenant," February 20, 1945, FPP.

68. Letter from Frank Perls to George and Hélène Biddle, January 18, 1945, MPP.

69. "Interviewing Agent's Comments," attached to Frank Perls's "Personal History Statement," January 18, 1945, FPP.

70. For example, a story about the discovery of the Nuremberg Laws in a French magazine was titled "Le Parchemin de Franck Perls."

71. Undated references to and articles by Frank Perls—"Somewhere in France," "Nazis Put in Own Torture Cells," "Visitor in Paris Reports Art Life Little Changed by War"—are in MPP.

72. Dannenberg and his wife "now live in one of the more notorious of these neighborhoods, Guilford." Personal communication from Martin Dannenberg, July 20, 2001.

73. Personal communication from Martin Dannenberg, March 13, 2005.

74. Rauch and the major are identified as "Director A and Director B" on the envelope in which the Nuremberg Laws were deposited in the bank on October 9, 1943, HLA.

75. Shortly after the discovery, Dannenberg documented the event on the back of the two photographs: "MED—Perls in vault of bank at Eichstätt and Nurnberg Laws found there. Apr. 27, 1945." "Nurnberg Laws found in Eichstätt." Frank Perls and General Patton used other dates to mark the discovery of the Nuremberg Laws, but Dannenberg's documentation of April 27, 1945, is the most persuasive.

76. See Shirer, pp. 1044–1069, for an account of the plot and execution.

77. Letter from Frank Perls to Captain Speer, June 15, 1945, FPP.

▣ Chapter 7: Patton's Trophy

1. Joseph Driscoll, "Nuernberg Set of Racial Laws in U.S. Hands," *New York Herald Tribune*, May 1, 1945. The printed version of the story differs from the copy given to Dannenberg in that Dannenberg's name is absent and Frank Perls is made the hero of the discovery. The *Tribune* article was provided by Marianne Perls, MPP; the typewritten copy by Martin Dannenberg, MDP.

2. Letter from Sally to Tommy Perls, May 1, 1945, MPP.

3. Untitled, monthly newsletter, May 1945, circulated by Rabbi Abraham Shusterman to his congregation in Baltimore, MDP.

4. Martin Dannenberg, "Talk to Har Sinai Congregation," October 1945, MDP.

5. Letter from Frank Perls to George and Helène Biddle, June 24, 1945, MPP.

6. Letter from Frank Perls to Captain Speer, June 15, 1945, FPP.

7. Driscoll, "Nuernberg Set of Racial Laws in U.S. Hands." *New York Herald Tribune*, May 1, 1945.

8. "Le Parchemin de Franck Perls," *Images du Monde* 19 (May 15, 1945), MPP.

9. "The Nuremberg Laws Against Jews," *The Times*, May 1, 1945.

10. Memo from Frank Perls to G-2, III Corps, April 28, 1945, HLA.

11. In these final days of the war, III Corps headquarters moved every few days. From April 26 to 29, it was located in Beilngries. Letter from Don Johnson to Martin Dannenberg, September 19, 1999, MDP.

12. Forty, p. 122.

13. Letter from Don Johnson to Martin Dannenberg, September 15, 1999. Dannenberg confirms that Horner "dismissed it [the discovery] as a minor matter." Letter from Martin Dannenberg to Don Johnson, June 29, 1999, MDP.

14. According to George Forty (p. 231), Patton's headquarters were based in Erlangen from April 22 to May 2, when they moved to Regensburg. Dannenberg is "fairly confident" that he delivered the Nuremberg Laws to Patton's headquarters two or three days after the discovery in Eichstätt, but he does not remember the town in which Lucky Forward was located. During the last weeks of the war, the location of Patton's headquarters constantly changed.

15. Personal communication from Martin Dannenberg, March 13, 2005.

16. Letter from Frank Perls to Captain Speer, June 15, 1945, FPP.

17. Memo "To Whom It May Concern," from Captain Clyde Nissen, June 15, 1945, FPP.

18. Memo from Frank Perls to Commanding General, July 19, 1945, FPP.

19. Letter from Cornelis Goinga to Sgt. Perls, February 22, 1945, FPP.

20. Letter from Frank Perls to Captain Cornelis Goinga, August 6, 1945, FPP.

21. Certificate of Honorable Discharge, September 19, 1945, FPP.

22. On Patton's postwar role, see Blumenson, *The Patton Papers, 1940–1945*, pp. 705–729.

23. Farago, p. 226.

24. Quoted in Blumenson, *The Patton Papers, 1940–1945*, p. 707.

25. Letter from Patton to Beatrice, May 13, 1945, ibid., p. 712.

26. Letter from Eisenhower to General Marshall, April 15, 1945, ibid., p. 689.

27. Ibid., p. 700.

28. Memo from McCarthy to Marshall, June 12, 1945, quoted in D'Este, p. 750.

29. Tom Cameron, "Los Angeles Conquered by Charm of Warriors," *Los Angeles Times,* June 10, 1945; Walter Cochrane, "Millions Cheer Generals Along Parade Route," *Los Angeles Times*, June 10, 1945.

30. Cameron, ibid.

31. Robert Patton, *The Pattons: A Personal History* (New York: Crown Publishers, 1994), pp. 105, 117, 196.

32. Ray Zeman, "Thousands Hail Heroes; Generals' Deeds Reborn in Coliseum Pageantry," *Los Angeles Times,* June 10, 1945.

33. Tom Cameron, "Suburbs Cheer Patton, Doolittle," *Los Angeles Times*, June 11, 1945.

34. Walter Cochrane, "Patton Explains 3rd's Tactics in Europe War," *Los Angeles Times*, June 12, 1945. On criticisms of Patton, see "Gen. Patton Criticized for Language in Public," *Los Angeles Times*, June 18, 1945; and "His Pastor Says Patton May Think War Certain," *Los Angeles Times*, July 16, 1945.

35. Letter from Robert Millikan to General Patton, June 7, 1945. A copy of this letter is in MC 13.3.

36. Greta B. Millikan, "Notes 1945," MC 83.5.

37. Ibid.

38. Letter from G. S. Patton, Jr., to President, Huntington Library, April 15, 1945, HLA. A copy of the letter is also available in the George S. Patton Papers, Manuscript Division, Library of Congress.

39. Interview with Robert Skotheim, July 19, 1999.

40. Quoted in Blumenson, *The Patton Papers, 1940–1945*, p. 795.

41. Phone interview with Hugh Cole, August 30, 1999.

42. Memorandum from Joseph Stein to Colonel H. M. Forde, May 19, 1945. The memo and the "Golden Book of Aviation"—a tribute "to those men who distinguish themselves by heroic and fearless deeds in the execution of their service in the Luftwaffe"— are in HLA.

43. "Statement Dictated by General George S. Patton, Jr."

44. Frank Mason was a former Hearst executive and assistant to the Secretary of the Navy. On Frank Mason's correspondence with Hoover about Patton's demotion in September–October 1945, see Frank E. Mason Papers, Herbert Hoover Presidential Library.

45. As a charter member of the Human Betterment Foundation in Pasadena, Robert Millikan was kept informed of Nazi sterilization policies.

46. Letter and public statement from Herbert Hoover to Samuel McCrea Cavert, Federal Council of Churches, November 13, 1938, Herbert Hoover Presidential Library, Post-Presidential Subject, "Jews." Hereafter cited as HHPL.

47. Untitled statement ("There is a possible plan ...") published in *New York World Telegram*, November 19, 1945. Ibid., Post-Presidential Subject, "Jewish-Zionist Correspondence."

48. Goodstein, pp. 97–98; Stephen Duggan and Betty Drury, *The Rescue of Science and Learning: The Story of the Emergency Committee in Aid of Displaced Foreign Scholars* (New York: Macmillan, 1948).

49. United Press, "Patton Talks with Truman, Says He's Just 'One-Gun Man,'" *Los Angeles Times*, June 14, 1945.

50. Letter from Leslie Bliss to General Patton, July 31, 1945, HLA. The three volumes of "Nazi records" were a Luftwaffe memorial book for officers, signed by Hermann Göring; a presentation book for Hitler, documenting gains in industrial production in Cologne, dated January 30, 1943; and a presentation book of black and white photographs, commemorating Hitler's visit to Cologne. On August 18, in a letter to Bliss, Patton said that the helmets were "intended ... for my private museum in Hamilton, Massachusetts" and should be turned over to his sister. As of August 2001, the three volumes were still in storage at the Huntington and had not been accessioned or evaluated by experts.

51. Letter from Patton to Bliss, August 18, 1945, HLA.

52. Letter from Bliss to Patton, September 10, 1945, HLA.

53. Letter from Patton to Bliss, September 11, 1945, HLA. Bliss noted on Patton's letter that the *After Action Reports* had been "Rec'd & placed in Stack Storage." As of August 2001, the Huntington had no official record of these documents and could not find them.

54. Letter from Bliss to Patton, October 31, 1945, HLA. As of August 2001, the Huntington has no official record of the manuscript and documents, and cannot find them.

55. Interview with Hugh Cole, August 30, 1999.

56. Letter from William Munro to Mrs. Patton, January 18, 1951, HLA.

57. Letter from Bernice Miller, secretary to Hoover, to Millikan, June 28, 1945, Herbert Hoover Library, Post-Presidential Individual File, "Millikan."

58. Hoover and Millikan maintained a friendly and politically sympathetic

relationship over many years. "If you are coming east soon the President will be very glad to have you come and spend some time at the White House with him," Hoover's secretary cabled Millikan in 1929. For examples of correspondence between Millikan and Hoover, see MC 40.13.

59. Edwin Hubble, the astronomer, was absent from the meeting.

60. Minutes of Trustees Meeting, July 9, 1945, MC 13.4.

61. Greta B. Millikan, "Notes 1945," MC 83.5.

62. HL, *Eighteenth Annual Report, 1944–1945*, p. 9.

63. This euphemism for the Nuremberg Laws is used in letter from William Munro to Mrs. Patton, January 18, 1951, HLA.

▣ Chapter 8: Outpost of Civilization

1. Interviews with Jasper Schad and Anthony Bliss, May 26, 2000. Their fathers and, in Anthony's case, grandfather were long-time employees of the Huntington.

2. The term was used by Max Farrand, the Huntington's first director of research, in a memorandum, "To Mr. Huntington and Trustees of the Henry E. Huntington Library and Art Gallery," January 1927, MC 12.8. This formulation of the trustees, notes the Huntington's recently retired president, "was not without Western, as well as American, chauvinism." Robert A. Skotheim, "Report of the President," HL, *The Huntington Annual Report, 1991–1994*, p. 1.

3. John S. Hittell, *The Commerce and Industries of the Pacific Coast of North America* (San Francisco: A. L. Bancroft & Co., 1882), "Preface," p. 61.

4. Carey McWilliams, *Southern California: An Island on the Land*, originally published 1946 (Santa Barbara: Peregrine Smith, 1973), p. 48.

5. Mike Davis, *City of Quartz: Excavating the Future in Los Angeles* (London: Verso, 1990), p. 102.

6. William Deverell, *Whitewashed Adobe: The Rise of Los Angeles and the Remaking of Its Mexican Past* (Berkeley: University of California Press, 2004), p. 7 and chapter 5. A decade later, some fifty thousand Mexicans were "repatriated" during the Depression. See, also, George J. Sánchez, *Becoming Mexican American: Ethnicity, Culture, and Identity in Chicano Los Angeles, 1900–1945* (New York: Oxford University Press, 1993), p. 106.

7. Davis, p. 116; Max Vorspan and Lloyd P. Gartner, *History of the Jews of Los Angeles* (San Marino, California: The Huntington Library, 1970), p. 206.

8. Thorpe, pp. 1–2.

9. Ibid., pp. 19–20.

10. Oscar Lewis, *The Big Four: The Story of Huntington, Stanford, Hopkins, and Crocker, and of the Building of the Central Pacific* (New York: Alfred A. Knopf, 1938), p. 267.

11. Thorpe, pp. 156–157.

12. Lewis, pp. 267–268.

13. Thorpe, p. 173.

14. Lewis, p. 268; Thorpe, pp. 294–305, 307–308.

15. Lewis, p. 269. See, also, Thorpe, p. 390; Billington, p. 352.

16. Billington, p. 366.

17. Green, p. 9.

18. Thorpe, pp. 403, 512–515.

19. Peggy Park Bernal, *The Huntington* (Ojai, Calif.: Legacy Communications, 1992).

20. Lewis, pp. 269, 270. See, also, Thorpe, pp. 434–464.

21. Thorpe, pp. 388–389.

22. Davis, p. 113.

23. Thorpe, pp. 391–395.

24. Ibid., pp. 291–292.

25. Ibid., pp. 200–201.

26. HL, *First Annual Report, October 3, 1928*, available in California State Archives, Sacramento, California, "Huntington 1928–1980." See, also, Thorpe, p. 392. The Huntington's tax exempt status was later incorporated into the Constitution of California, Article IX, Section 15, on November 4, 1930, after a public ballot favored by over two-thirds of the electorate. State of California, *Statement of Vote at General Election Held on November 4, 1930* (Sacramento: California State Printing Office, 1930). The constitutional amendment was proposed to the California Senate by C. C. Baker, seventeenth district (Contra Costa), and Frank C. Weller, thirty-sixth district (San Bernardino), in recognition of the Huntington's contribution to the "public welfare" as a "free public library and art gallery, museum, and park." State of California, *Proposed Amendments to the Constitution* (Sacramento: California State Printing Office, 1930).

27. Thorpe, p. 511.

28. Kyle Palmer, "Huntington's Gift Praised," *Los Angeles Times*, May 12, 1923, p. 2; Thorpe, p. 510.

29. Fred Hogue, "Huntington's Monument Unmatched in World," *Los Angeles Times*, May 29, 1927, p. 3.

30. "Library Trust Board Formed," *Los Angeles Times*, April 9, 1922.

31. "Trust Indenture: Henry E. Huntington Library and Art Gallery," August 30, 1919, MC 12.8.

32. Thorpe, pp. 392, 505.

33. Tony Bennett, "The Exhibitionary Complex," in Nicholas B. Dirks, Geoff Eley, and Sherry B. Ortner (editors), *Culture/Power/History: A Reader in Contemporary Social Theory* (Princeton: Princeton University Press, 1994), pp. 123–154.

34. Lawrence W. Levine, *Highbrow/Lowbrow: The Emergence of Cultural Hierarchy in America* (Cambridge: Harvard University Press, 1988), p. 252.

35. Letter from George Ellery Hale to George S. Patton, August 22, 1925, MC 12.8.

36. On an insider's view of the Pattons, see, generally, Robert H. Patton, *The Pattons: A Personal History of an American Family*.

37. Ibid., pp. 72–73, 125.

38. Hon. George S. Patton, "Why Women Should Not Be Given the Vote," *The West Coast Magazine*, September 1911, reprinted as a pamphlet, Rare Book no. 374655, HL.

39. Robert Millikan, "Some Exceptional Opportunities in Southern California," unpublished speech, April 11, 1924, MC 27.9.

40. Edward Huntington approved Hale's proposal on October 14, 1925. The board of trustees revised the trust indenture on February 8, 1926. Billington, pp. 358–359.

41. George E. Hale, "The Future Development of the Huntington Library and Art Gallery," October 14, 1925, MC 12.8.

42. Max Farrand, "To Mr. Huntington and Trustees of the Henry E. Huntington Library and Art Gallery," January 1927, MC 12.8.

43. Hale, "The Future Development."

44. Similarly, a relatively minor decision to charge an admissions fee to the gardens and exhibits required permission from the California attorney general in 1996. HL, *Annual Report, 1994–1997*, p. 24.

45. Interview with Anthony Bliss, May 26, 2000. According to a restriction imposed by Edward Huntington, the Library was required to remain "without any circulation or withdrawal privileges." HL, *First Annual Report, 1927–1928*, p. 11. This policy was not amended until 1992, when the Huntington's trustees authorized the selective lending of objects from the Art Gallery to other institutions. The Library implemented a similar policy in 1994. Personal communication from David Zeidberg, August 7, 2001.

46. Davis, p. 101.

47. McWilliams, *Southern California*, pp. 92, 293.

48. Letter from Robert Millikan to Max Millikan, December 10, 1947, MC 13.8.

49. In 1991, the by-laws were amended to limit each trustee to a term of three years and five consecutive terms. A trustee could only serve until he or she was 72 years old. In 1996, the age limit was raised to 75. Personal communication from Catherine Babcock, July 16, 2001.

50. The first and most recent chief administrators were employed for fourteen and thirteen years respectively. Louis Booker Wright joined the permanent research staff in 1932 and remained until 1948, when he resigned to become director of the Folger Shakespeare Library in Washington, D.C. Edwin Gay, a core member of the Huntington's Research Group, was associated with the Library for ten years, a relatively short tenure for Huntington staffers. The most recent president, Steven Koblik, assumed office on September 4, 2001. Martin Ridge served briefly as Acting Director, 1987–1988. HL, *Annual Report 1945–1946*, p. 1. HL, *Annual Report 1947–1948*, p. 1.

51. Interview with Anthony Bliss, May 26, 2000.

52. HL, *Annual Report, 1982–1983*, p. 7.

53. HL, *Annual Report, 1961–1962*, p. 1.

54. HL, *Annual Report, 1950–1951*, pp. 1–2; *Annual Report, 1965–1966*, p. 1.

55. Lewis Lapham, "Cloak and Gown," *Los Angeles Times Book Review*, April 9, 2000, pp. 1–3.

56. For example, James Page, director of Union Oil and president of the California Bank; Philip Hawley, board of directors of Atlantic Richfield; Louis Lundborg, vice-president, Bank of America; Thomas McDaniel, president of Southern California Edison; Ed Shannon, CEO of Santa Fe International; Jesse Tapp, vice-president, Bank of America; Lawrence Tollenaere, CEO of Ameron; and Robert Wycoff, president of Atlantic Richfield.

57. Namely, Herbert Hoover, Lee DuBridge, Robert Millikan, William French Smith, Marion Jorgensen's husband Earle Jorgensen, and Ruth (and husband Ed) Shannon.

58. Namely, William Dunn, Elmo Conley, Homer Crotty, William French Smith, and Robert Erburu. U.S. Solicitor General Theodore Olson (2001–2004) is a partner in the same firm.

59. For example, George Ellery Hale was very influential in organizing the National Research Council in 1917; Robert Millikan built Caltech's close ties to business and government, especially during World War II; Henry Pritchett was president of the Carnegie Foundation; and Wallace Sterling was president of Stanford University.

60. At the time of their appointment, the three women—Marion Jorgensen, Nancy Munger, and Ruth Shannon—were married to powerful and influential men: Earle Jorgensen, a director of Northrop and Reagan adviser; Charles Munger, vice-chairman of Berkshire Hathaway, described by *Fortune* as Warren Buffett's alter ego; and oil executive Ed Shannon. In 1990, the Shannons donated over one million dollars to the Center for the Performing Arts at Whittier College. See "Earle Jorgensen, Wealthy Reagan Confidant, Dies," *Los Angeles Times*, August 13, 1999; Carol J. Loomis, "The Inside Story of Warren Buffett," *Fortune*, April 11, 1988, pp. 26–34; Mary Lou Loper, "A Leading Lady in the Performing Arts Voluntarism," *Los Angeles Times*, November 1, 1990.

61. Marylyn Warren was appointed chief development officer in 1989, followed by Alison Sowden as chief financial officer in 1990. David S. Zeidberg was appointed director of the Library in 1996.

62. Interview with Carlo D'Este, February 21, 2000; D'Este, pp. 753–754. A recent history repeats the claim that Patton's anti-Semitism was triggered by exhaustion, noting that his overall record was in fact anti-racist. There is no evidence that Patton was "either prejudicial or bigoted." Victor Davis Hanson, *The Soul of Battle: From Ancient Times to the Present Day, How Three Great Liberators Vanquished Tyranny* (New York: The Free Press, 1999), pp. 280–281, 285, 446. For a rare exception to this view in the contemporary historical literature, see Lou Potter, *Liberators: Fighting on Two Fronts in World War II* (New York: Harcourt Brace Jovanovich, 1992).

63. Blumenson, *The Patton Papers, 1885–1940*, pp. 6–8; *The Patton Papers, 1940–1945*, pp. 6, 760, 857.

64. *Los Angeles Times*, July 22, 1945. When Patton's name was floated as a possible Republican candidate for Congress, he issued a statement that all his life he had "stayed completely out of politics." *Los Angeles Times*, October 11; October 12, 1945. On the racist and anti-Semitic views of Congressman John Rankin of Mississippi, one of Patton's strongest supporters, see Leonard Dinnerstein, *Anti-Semitism in America* (New York: Oxford University Press, 1994), p. 136.

65. See, generally, C. Wright Mills, *The Power Elite* (New York: Oxford University Press, 1956), chapter 9.

66. "Intervention in this country [Mexico] would be the most futile thing in the world," he wrote his father in 1916. "We must take it or leave it. If we leave it ruine [*sic*] total and complete will follow." Letter from Patton to father, April 28, 1916, in Blumenson, *The Patton Papers, 1885–1940*, p. 329. To his father-in-law he reported on "the utter degredation [*sic*] of the inhabitants.... One must be a fool in deed to think that people half savage and wholly ignorant will ever form a republic. It is a joke." Letter from Patton to Frederick Ayer, June 27, 1916, ibid., p. 344.

67. Robert Patton, p. 225.

68. Letter from Patton to Caroline Trask, May 14, 1942, in Blumenson, *The Patton Papers: 1940–1945*, p. 69.

69. Ibid., p. 159.

70. Blumenson, *The Patton Papers, 1885–1940*, p. 47.

71.   On Patton's life as "the richest officer in the army and also the most ostentatious," see his grandson's memoir, Robert Patton, pp. 142–143.

72.   Blumenson, *The Patton Papers, 1940–1945*, pp. 60–61.

73.   Edward T. Linenthal, *Changing Images of the Warrior Hero in America: A History of Popular Symbolism* (New York: The Edwin Mellen Press, 1982), p. 4.

74.   On Patton's identification with the Confederacy, see Ashley Halsey, "Ancestral Gray Cloud over Patton," *American History Illustrated*, March 1984, pp. 42–48.

75.   According to his nephew, Patton was "completely consistent in the expression of his convictions." Ayer, p. 225.

76.   Letter from Georgie to father, December 30, 1916, in Blumenson, *The Patton Papers, 1885–1940*, p. 368.

77.   Letter from Georgie to father, September 28, 1916, ibid., p. 351.

78.   Winfield Hogaboom, "George S. Patton, Jr., Soldier, Diplomat, Poet," *Los Angeles Graphic*, June 23, 1917, p. 5. This can be found in George S. Patton Scrapbook, vol. 4, Rare Book # 426913, HL.

79.   Patton lecture, "The Secret of Victory," March 26, 1926, in Blumenson, *The Patton Papers, 1885–1940*, p. 796.

80.   Patton, unpublished account, July 1932, ibid., pp. 894–896.

81.   Patton, "Federal Troops in Domestic Disturbances," November 1932, ibid., pp. 898, 900.

82.   This information is from a 1999 Christie's New York catalogue in which Patton's personal copy of Hitler's *My Battle* (1933, first American edition) was offered for sale at an estimated $15,000 to $20,000. Patton signed his copy "G S Patton Jr March 15, 1934." Patton's underlining and annotations appear on seven pages of the book.

83.   Ayer, p. 114.

84.   Patton diary entry, October 1, 1918, in Blumenson, *The Patton Papers, 1885–1940*, p. 621.

85.   Robert Patton, p. 277.

86.   He made exceptions for upper-class rulers of other "races," such as the Berber Pasha of Marrakech who invited him to a boar hunt in 1943. Patton appreciated his "hereditary qualities of leadership" and his sense of superiority, which "is so inbred that he does not have to show it." Ibid., pp. 123, 124.

87.   Ibid., pp. 72, 76, 77, 80, 90, 99.

88.   Letter from Beatrice to Aunt Nannie, July 1, 1915, in Blumenson, *The Patton Papers, 1885–1940*, pp. 291–292.

89.   Robert Patton, pp. 200, 217–218.

90.   General Pershing was referred to as "Nigger Jack"—later, more politely, as "Black Jack"—as a result of serving with the all-black Tenth Cavalry Regiment in Montana. See D'Este, p. 157.

91.   Robert Patton, p. 144. See, also, Vernon L. Williams, *Lieutenant Patton and the American Army in the Mexican Punitive Expedition, 1915–1916* (Austin: Presidial Press, 1983).

92.   Letter from Patton to Beatrice, October 20, 1915, in Blumenson, *The Patton Papers, 1885–1940*, p. 298.

93.   Letter from Patton to Aunt Nannie, November 1, 1915, ibid., p. 304.

94.   Letter from Patton to Beatrice, May 17, 1916, ibid., p. 336.

95. Robert Patton, p. 127.

96. Ibid., p. 125. Patton's sister later became a Rooseveltian liberal, whose politics differed greatly from her brother's. But she also remained one of Georgie's strongest supporters and defenders.

97. Ibid., p. 129.

98. Patton, "My Father as I Knew Him and of Him from Memory and Legand [*sic*]," 1927, in Blumenson, *The Patton Papers, 1885–1940*, p. 26.

99. Robert Patton, pp. 127–128.

100. Ibid., pp. 220, 228.

101. Letter from Patton to Beatrice, June 26, 1943, in Blumenson, *The Patton Papers, 1940–1945*, p. 268.

102. George S. Patton, *War As I Knew It* (Boston: Houghton Mifflin, 1947), p. 160.

103. Patton, "Notes on the Arab," January 1943, in Blumenson, *The Patton Papers, 1940–1945*, p. 146. "It may well be that this donkey pace, which he has emulated for two thousand years, has reduced his mental reaction to a similar tempo…. [H]e is, in his filth and poverty, contented and perhaps happy." Ibid., p. 147.

104. Letter from Patton to Beatrice, December, 1942, ibid., p. 139.

105. Robert Patton, p. 259; letter from Patton to Beatrice, July 21, 1945, in Blumenson, *The Patton Papers, 1940–1945*, p. 731.

106. Letter from Beatrice to Patton, January 23, 1943, in Blumenson, *The Patton Papers, 1940–1945*, p. 159.

107. Ibid., p. 760.

108. See, generally, Ayer, *Before the Colors Fade*.

109. Patton to Fred Ayer, May 5, 1943, in Blumenson, *The Patton Papers, 1940–1945*. p. 242.

▣ Chapter 9: White Man's Burden

1. James Allen, "Afterword," in Allen, Als, Lewis, and Litwack, p. 204.

2. Leo Frank was pardoned in 1985. The photographs of Frank are numbered 34 and 35 in *Without Sanctuary*. For Allen's soulful commentary, see pp. 177–178.

3. Goethe, "Patriotism and Racial Standards," pp. 67, 68.

4. "Jewish Physicians in Berlin," *Eugenical News* 19 (1934), p. 126.

5. HL, *Twenty-Seventh Annual Report, 1953–1954*, pp. 2–3.

6. Robert Millikan, "The New Opportunity in Science," *Science,* September 26, 1919, p. 294.

7. Kevles, *The Physicists*, p. 244.

8. Ibid., 374–389.

9. Letter from Goethe to Ellsworth Huntington, September 26, 1935. CMGC, unfiled materials.

10. The term is used in a letter from Archer Huntington to Herbert Hoover, December 1, 1944, MC 13.2.

11. Letter from Millikan to A. R. Olpin, May 19, 1943, MC 14.13. A few years later, Millikan informed Henry Luce that the country has "certainly been moving back rapidly toward totalitarianism—which inevitably lands in dictatorship." Letter from Millikan to Luce, March 18, 1946, MC 41.13.

12. Millikan, "The New Opportunity in Science," p. 285.

13. Quoted in Kevles, *The Physicists*, p. 289.

14. Quoted in Goodstein, p. 245.

15. Ibid., p. 259.

16. Letter from L. R. Groves to Millikan, December 20, 1945, MC 28.8.

17. See, for example, "Millikan Urges World Police Force for Preserving Peace," *Los Angeles Times*, October 16, 1942; "U.N. Best Hope, Millikan Says," *Los Angeles Times*, January 30, 1951.

18. Millikan's views were quoted in a letter from Remsen Bird, president of Occidental College, to Thomas Mann, April 11, 1938, MC 37.19.

19. Letter from Millikan to Ned Dearborn, March 25, 1941, MC 37.4.

20. Letter from Lee Matthews to Millikan, August 4, 1948; letter from Millikan to Matthews, August 5, 1948, MC 37.10.

21. Millikan, *Science and the New Civilization*, p. 11.

22. "Millikan Raps New Deal," *Los Angeles Times*, October 7, 1936.

23. See, for example, "Students Hear Millikan Rap Thursday Pension Plan," *Los Angeles Times*, September 27, 1938; "Millikan Tells School Views," *Los Angeles Times*, May 7, 1938.

24. On April 2, 1943, Millikan joined Madame Chiang Kai-shek at a reception at the Ambassador Hotel in Los Angeles, MC 89.5.

25. "Sen. Knowland and Millikan to Aid Nixon Drive," *Los Angeles Times*, September 10, 1950.

26. Letter from Millikan to Norman Angell, May 14, 1945, MC12.6.

27. Popenoe and Johnson, pp. 361–362, 374–389.

28. Robert H. Kargon, *The Rise of Robert Millikan: Portrait of a Life in American Science* (Ithaca: Cornell University Press, 1982), p. 77.

29. Robert Millikan, "The Practical Value of Pure Science," *Science,* January 4, 1924, p. 10.

30. Letter from Millikan to Greta Millikan and his sons, December 31, 1925, MC 50.7.

31. Letter from Millikan to Greta Millikan, August 21, 1926, ibid.

32. Letter from Millikan to Greta Millikan, August 30, 1926, ibid.

33. Popenoe and Johnson, pp. 284–285.

34. Ibid., pp. 285, 289, 292–297.

35. Ibid., p. 301.

36. Ibid., p. 319.

37. Letter from Millikan to Henry Luce, March 18, 1946, MC 41.13.

38. "Everything constructive that is being done [in India] is due to the British," he wrote Henry Luce, February 20, 1946, ibid.

39. Letter from Millikan to Greta Millikan, November 17, 1951, MC 50: 12b.

40. As of April 2000, of Caltech's nine hundred undergraduates, only eleven were black. Only two out of two hundred and eighty faculty members were black. In the 1999 to 2000 academic year, no African Americans enrolled in the freshman class. Leo Reisberg, "A Top University Wonders Why It Has No Black Freshmen," *Chronicle of Higher Education*, April 28, 2000, pp. 52–55.

41. Greta B. Millikan, "Notes," April 1945, MC 83.5.

42. Letter from Millikan to Pasadena Chamber of Commerce, February 4, 1942, MC 26.12.

43. Rob Wagner, "Los Angeles—Powerhouse of Race-Baiting," *Script*, July 15, 1944. This document is in the Pacific Citizen Archives, Series 6, Sub-series 5, Japanese American National Museum, Los Angeles.

44. "V.F.W. Leader Testifies Before Assembly Group," *Los Angeles Times*, December 10, 1943. The Pacific Coast Committee took the position that "the swarming of persons of one race in a Ghetto or a Little Mexico or Tokyo … is a profound social and political error and a potent breeder of social and political ills." Wagner, "Los Angeles—Powerhouse of Race-Baiting."

45. "Pasadena Hears W.R.A. Director Defend Policies," *Los Angeles Times*, September 30, 1944.

46. Millikan received the request from Alan Waterman, U.S. Office of Scientific Research and Development, on August 14 and replied on August 23, 1945. MC 29.4.

47. Letter from Robert Millikan to George Ellery Hale, July 16, 1921. George Ellery Hale Collection 29.21–22, California Institute of Technology.

48. Kevles, *The Physicists*, pp. 216–217.

49. Whereas Millikan was an uncritical supporter of the scientific establishment, Einstein warned students at Caltech (in a speech on January 30, 1930) that "science has enslaved men to machines; men who work long, wearisome hours mostly without joy in their labor and with the continual fear of losing their pitiful income." See Otto Nathan and Heinz Norden (editors), *Einstein on Peace* (New York: Simon and Schuster, 1960), p. 122. On Einstein's views about racial inequality, see Kramer, pp. 32–33.

50. Letter from Millikan to Major General Amos Fries, March 8, 1932, MC 24.8.

51. Kevles, *The Physicists*, p. 279.

52. Interview with Judith Goodstein, July 7, 1999.

53. See, generally, Duggan and Drury.

54. Letter from Ray Lyman Wilbur, president of Stanford, to James B. Conant, president of Harvard, copied to Millikan, December 27, 1938, MC 32.7.

55. Even though Millikan had given his name as a reference for Levy in 1939, he now told Duggan that "I have no personal knowledge of him." Letter from Stephen Duggan to Robert Millikan, December 7, 1942; letter from Millikan to Duggan, December 17, 1942, MC 35.7.

56. Letter from Max Ferrand to Robert Millikan, MC 12.12.

57. Davis, p. 57. Of the sixty-five scientists nationwide awarded the Medal of Merit for their work with the Office of Scientific Research and Development during the war, nine were based at Caltech. McWilliams, *California: The Great Exception*, p. 250.

58. See, for example, Price, Waterhouse & Co.'s "Report and Financial Statements," Huntington Library, June 30, 1944, MC 13.2.

59. For example, when an opening occurred on the Huntington's finance committee, Millikan maneuvered behind the scenes to get his candidate appointed. See letter from Robert Millikan to Edwin Hubble, July 19, 1943, MC 12.17.

60. Letter from William Munro to Robert Cleland, July 10, 1942, MC 12.16.

61. HL, *Annual Report 1941–1942*, p. 12.

62. Phil T. Hanna, *California Through Four Centuries: A Handbook of Memorable Historical Dates* (New York: Farrar & Rinehart, 1935), pp. vii, viii, 95. As editor of

Westways, a widely read publication of the Automobile Club of Southern California, Hanna dropped Carey McWilliams's regular column from the magazine after McWilliams's radical critique of agricultural working conditions—*Factories in the Fields*—was published in 1939. See Carey McWilliams's introduction to the second edition of *Southern California: An Island on the Land* (Santa Barbara: Peregrine Smith, 1973), p. xvii.

63. HL, *Annual Report 1943–1944*, p. 1; *Annual Report 1944–1945*, p. 3.

64. Robert Cleland, *A History of California: The American Period* (New York: Macmillan, 1930), p. 466.

65. See Cleland's introduction to Hero Eugene Rensch and Ethel Grace Rensch, *Historical Spots in California* (Stanford: Stanford University Press, 1932), vol. 2, p. xxvi.

66. Cleland, *A History of California*, pp. 466, 467.

67. The phrase is from a popular high school textbook of the 1930s, A. A. Gray, *History of California from 1542* (Boston: D. C. Heath, 1934), p. 605.

68. Goethe, Immigration Study Commission newsletter, October 29, 1928, HLC C-4–1: 2; Goethe, *Seeking to Serve* (Sacramento: Keystone Printing Company, 1949), p. 185; Goethe, "Patriotism and Racial Standards," p. 67.

69. Letter from Goethe to Editor, *Tribune*, Winnipeg, May 7, 1928. HLC C-4–1: 2.

70. Goethe, "Patriotism and Racial Standards," p. 65.

71. C. M. Goethe, *War Profits and Better Babies* (Sacramento: The Keystone Press, 1946), p. 19.

72. For similar views, see Rockwell Hunt, *New California the Golden* (Sacramento: California State Department of Education, 1937).

73. Cleland, *A History of California*, p. 416.

74. Robert Glass Cleland, *California in Our Time, 1900–1940 (*New York: Alfred A. Knopf, 1947), pp. 252–253. Migrants from Oklahoma, on the other hand, were characterized as "genuine Americans, mostly of Anglo-Saxon forebears." Ibid., p. 263.

75. Ibid., pp. 243, 251.

76. Letter from E. H. Conley to San Marino Civil Betterment Association, October 16, 1941. Attached to the letter is a copy of the proposed restrictive covenant, dated March 15, 1941, MC 12.16.

77. Letter from Millikan to Charles Culver, February 20, 1942, ibid.

78. San Marino Civic Betterment Association, "San Marino Property Owners!" pamphlet, 1942, ibid.

79. Owing to his relationship with Mengele—assigned to Auschwitz in 1943 to carry out his medical experiments—von Verschuer was investigated for war crimes but never prosecuted. With the support of his American colleagues, in 1950 von Verschuer joined, and later became dean of, the Institute of Human Genetics at the University of Münster. He died in a car accident in 1969. Black, pp. 344–366, 376, 379–380.

80. Letter from Popenoe to von Verschuer, July 25, 1946, quoted in Black, p. 377.

81. Letter from Goethe to von Verschuer, April 16, 1948, quoted in Black, p. 379.

82. By the time of the Human Betterment Foundation's dissolution, Paul Popenoe, its executive director, shifted his attention to the American Institute of Family Relations in Los Angeles. The Institute was based on programs that had been set up in Germany in the 1920s to identify and train compatible individuals for marriage. With Popenoe as its director, the Institute promoted traditional gender roles and railed against the pathology of homosexuality. Goethe was an enthusiastic supporter of the Institute and one of its

main patrons. By 1962, the Institute had a staff of seventy, with seven branches in the Los Angeles area. On the resurrection of eugenics in the form of family counseling, see Kline, pp. 141–145, 153–154, 161. According to Schauer (p. 200), the American Institute of Family Relations initially received close to $80,000 from Goethe's estate, perhaps over $100,000 by the time of the final disbursement.

83. Letter from J. Kruls to Goethe, April 9, 1966, CMGC 85C: 14.

84. Rodger Bishton, "Charles M. Goethe: The Man and His Life, A Biographical Sketch," March 28, 1965. Author's personal copy.

85. Letter from Gosney to Mr. Reid, September 9, 1940, ESGP 1.2.

86. There is no evidence, as suggested by David Valone in his wishful introduction to Caltech's collection of the Gosney Papers, that Gosney issued a "condemnation of German eugenic theory." See Valone, "Eugenic Science in California," p. viii, ESGP.

▣ Chapter 10: Loot

1. Letters from Patton to Beatrice, August 27 and 31, 1945, in Blumenson, *The Patton Papers, 1940–1945*, pp. 743, 744. See, also, Patton's diary entry for September 22, ibid., p. 766.

2. In his personal copy of *Mein Kampf*, Patton noted in the margin the pages in which Hitler criticized the press. As Robert Patton notes (p. 282), "Georgie had virtually total recall of anything he read."

3. Patton diary entry, September 22, 1945, in Blumenson, *The Patton Papers, 1940–1945*, p. 766.

4. Letter from Patton to Beatrice, September 22, 1945, ibid., p. 767.

5. Patton diary entry, April 11, 1945, ibid., pp. 683–684.

6. Ibid., pp. 685, 686.

7. Letter from Eisenhower to Marshall, April 15, 1945, ibid., p. 688.

8. Patton, *War As I Knew It*, pp. 298–299.

9. The photographs and captions appear in Bourke White, between pages 38 and 39.

10. It was not until the summer that Patton began to comment on Jewish Displaced Persons in the camps. See Blumenson, *The Patton Papers, 1940–1945*, pp. 683–688. Even in his war memoir, published posthumously in 1947, there are no references to Jews, only to a "horror camp" or "slave camp." See Patton, *War As I Knew It,* pp. 294, 298, 299.

11. Quoted in Novick, p. 73.

12. Gerda Weissman, "Letter from a Polish Survivor," May 15, 1945, in Barish pp. 111, 113.

13. David Max Eichhorn, "Dachau," in Barish, p. 69.

14. Hatch, p. 14.

15. Edward T. Linenthal, "Nostalgia for Clarity: The Memory of Patton," *Studies in Popular Culture* 5 (1982), p. 77.

16. Hanson, pp. 285, 304, 411, 412. For a similar perspective, see Willamson Murray and Allan R. Millett, *A War to Be Won: Fighting the Second World War* (Cambridge: Harvard University Press, 2000).

17. When Secretary of the Treasury Henry Morgenthau proposed the permanent deindustrialization of Germany, Secretary of War Henry Stimson privately called the plan

"semitism gone wild for vengeance." Cited in Novick, p. 91. For details of the right-wing ideologues that fuelled and shared Patton's views, see Farago, chapters 14 and 15.

18. Patton diary entry, September 29, 1945, in Blumenson, *The Patton Papers, 1940–1945*, p. 784.

19. Patton letter to Beatrice, October 1, 1945, ibid., p. 787.

20. Patton diary entry, August 29, 1945, in Blumenson, *The Patton Papers, 1940–1945*, p. 743.

21. Excerpts from Earl G. Harrison's report and President Harry Truman's directive to General Eisenhower are reprinted in Berenbaum, pp. 311–322.

22. Patton diary entry, September 15, 1945, in Blumenson, *The Patton Papers, 1940–1945*, p. 751.

23. Patton diary entry, September 15, 1945; and letter to Beatrice, September 21, 1945, ibid., pp. 751, 759.

24. Patton diary entry, October 1, 1945, ibid., pp. 787–789.

25. Diner, p. 237.

26. Patton diary entries, August 31 and September 1, 1945, in Blumenson, *The Patton Papers, 1940–1945*, pp. 744–745.

27. Patton letter to Beatrice, September 14, 1945, ibid., p. 750.

28. Patton letter to Keith Merrill, September 16, 1945, ibid., p. 752.

29. Patton diary entries, September 17, September 18, September 19, 1945, ibid., pp. 753–757.

30. Patton diary entry, September 21, 1945, ibid., p. 759.

31. Patton diary entry, October 2, 1945, ibid., p. 790.

32. Letter from Patton to Charles Codman, October 4, 1945, ibid., p. 791.

33. Patton letter to Baruch, December 3, 1945, ibid., p. 805.

34. Raymond Daniel, "Patton Belittles Denazification; Holds Rebuilding More Important," *New York Times*, September 23, 1945, p. 26.

35. Patton diary entry, September 29, 1945; letter from Patton to Beatrice, October 10, 1945, in Blumenson, *The Patton Papers, 1940–1945*, pp. 782, 796.

36. Letter from Patton to Charles Codman, October 4, 1945, ibid., p. 791.

37. Letter from Patton to Beatrice, September 29, 1945, ibid., p. 786.

38. Quoted in Robert Patton, p. 279.

39. Blumenson, *The Patton Papers, 1940–1945*, pp. 790, 791.

40. Farago, p. 170.

41. Ibid., p. 297.

42. Blumenson, *Patton: The Man Behind the Legend*, p. 302.

43. Blumenson, *The Patton Papers, 1940–1945*, p. 836.

44. "Statement Dictated by General George S. Patton, Jr.," June 11, 1945, HLA.

45. Joint Press Release, "Huntington Library to Loan…," June 26, 1999, HLA.

46. Interview with Robert Skotheim, July 19, 1999.

47. The Huntington, "Nuremberg Laws Loan to Skirball" (video, 1999).

48. Interview with David Zeidberg, July 13, 1999.

49. Interview with Mary Robertson, July 15, 1999. For similar comments about the lack of "an appropriate context at the Huntington," see librarian David Zeidberg, quoted in Sharon Waxman's *Washington Post* article, June 26, 1999, p. 9.

50. In 1943, the U.S. Army created a command element known as the Civil Affairs

and Military Government Division (G-5). Attached to the Supreme Headquarters Allied Expeditionary Force (SHAEF), G-5 was assigned to organize a military government in occupied territories and to ensure political and financial control of looted assets. See Presidential Advisory Commission on Holocaust Assets in the United States, Staff Report, pp. 23–24.

51.　The JCS was created as a result of a decision made during the Anglo-American military staff conference in 1941 and 1942 in Washington, D.C., to establish the Combined Chiefs of Staff (CCS). The JCS was the U.S. representative to the CCS. It became the principal agency for coordination between the army and navy. Ibid., p. 219.

52.　Ibid., p. 29.

53.　Joint Chiefs of Staff, Directive to Commander in Chief of U.S. Forces of Occupation Regarding the Military Government of Germany, April 29, 1945. This document is available in the Records of the U.S. Joint Chiefs of Staff, Record Group 218, Box 108, National Archives and Records Administration, Washington, D.C. Information on JCS 1067 was provided by Greg Bradsher, Director, Holocaust-era Assets Records Project, NARA.

54.　G. S. Patton, Jr., "Letter of Instruction No. 1," June 1, 1945, Records of United States Army Commands (1942–), Record Group 338, III Corps, Box 1, NARA.

55.　Interview with Hugh Cole, August 30, 1999.

56.　Letter from Don Johnson to Martin Dannenberg, September 19, 1999, MDP.

57.　At the end of the war, Hoover had several people in Germany "ferreting out collections of papers reflecting historical developments during the Nazi period and getting their owners to donate them to the Hoover Institution on War, Revolution and Peace." Personal communication from Dale Mayer, Principal Archivist for References Services, HHPL, March 17, 2000.

58.　Interview with Judah Nadich, July 29, 1999.

59.　Blumenson, *The Patton Papers, 1885–1940*, p. 331.

60.　Ibid., p. 597.

61.　Blumenson, *The Patton Papers, 1940–1945*, pp. 380, 679, 774; Ayer, p. 92.

62.　Much of this material later ended up in the Patton Museum, run by the army. Interview with Charles Lemons, curator, Patton Museum, Fort Knox, Kentucky, August 6, 1999. The Patton Museum is one of the most popular U.S. Army museums in the country, attracting some three hundred and sixty thousand visitors annually.

63.　"Statement Dictated by General George S. Patton, Jr."

64.　Letter from Martin Dannenberg to Don Johnson, September 22, 1999, MDP.

65.　Letter from Don Johnson to Martin Dannenberg, September 15, 1999, MDP.

66.　Patton, "Letter of Instruction No. 1," June 1, 1945.

67.　Forty, p. 114.

68.　Letter from Don Johnson to Martin Dannenberg, July 13, 1999, MDP.

69.　Letter from Richard Stillman to Martin Dannenberg, August 25, 1999, MDP.

70.　Letters from Don Johnson to Martin Dannenberg, September 15 and September 19, 1999, MDP.

71.　According to Don Johnson (in his letter of September 15, 1999, to Martin Dannenberg), "the Third Corps code was always used on official correspondence. Its absence [in Van Fleet's transmittal letter] is interesting and to me denotes the equivalent of a personal memo to Gen. Patton, not anything through Army channels."

72. Letter from Don Johnson to Martin Dannenberg, November 22, 1999, MDP.

73. Personal communication from Carlo D'Este, February 22, 2000.

74. By June 8, the U.S., French, and British governments had reached an agreement on how to proceed with a war crimes tribunal. Letter from Patton to Beatrice, September 14, 1945, Blumenson, *The Patton Papers, 1940–1945*, p. 750.

75. Interview with Hugh Cole, August 30, 1999.

76. Personal communication from Paul Fussell, May 18, 2000.

77. According Alan Jutzi, the Huntington's curator of rare books, this is the only book in the Huntington's vast collection that is signed on its front cover.

78. Letter from G. S. Patton, Jr., to President, Huntington Library, April 15, 1945, HLA. A copy of the letter is also available in the George S. Patton Papers, Manuscript Division, LC.

79. Letter from Leslie Bliss to General Patton, May 3, 1945, HLA.

80. Letter from Millikan to Patton, June 7, 1945, MC 13.3.

81. *Mein Kampf* was first exhibited on Friends' Day, June 4, and then to the public on June 5. For publicity surrounding the acquisition and exhibit, see "Library Receives Book from Patton," *Los Angeles Times*, May 6, 1945; "*Mein Kampf*, Gift from Patton, Arrives at Huntington Library," *San Marino Tribune*, June 7, 1945.

82. Greta B. Millikan, "Notes 1945," MC 83.5.

83. Letter from Leslie Bliss to General Patton, July 31, 1945, HLA.

84. Letter from Bliss to Patton, September 10, 1945, HLA.

85. Letter from Bliss to Patton, October 31, 1945, HLA.

86. According to Patton's biographer, "it might be said that Patton was, as man and legend, to a large degree, the creation of his wife." Blumenson, *The Patton Papers, 1885–1940*, p. 13.

87. Robert Patton, p. 261.

88. After Patton's death in 1945, Beatrice confronted Jean Gordon about the affair. Shortly afterwards, Jean Gordon committed suicide. The pathological side of the Patton family's private lives—including the general's troubled relationship with his alcoholic daughter, Bea, who died of a heart attack at the age of forty-one—is largely ignored by military historians. See Robert Patton, pp. ix, 228, 233–235, 288–289.

89. Letter from Beatrice to Patton, July 30, 1943, in Blumenson, *The Patton Papers, 1940–1945*, p. 308.

90. Letter from William B. Munro to Mrs. Patton, January 18, 1951, HLA.

91. Minutes of Trustees Meeting, January 17, 1951, HLA. According to Dan Lewis, the Huntington's Institutional Archivist, this is the only mention in trustees' minutes of Patton's visit. Personal communication from Dan Lewis, July 20, 1999. As to the query from Mrs. Patton that prompted this response, "this letter does not exist in our files," said David Zeidberg in a personal communication to the author, September 22, 1999.

92. Letter from William Munro to Mrs. Patton, January 18, 1951, HLA.

93. Ibid.

94. Minutes of Special Meeting of the Huntington Board of Trustees, August 6, 1951, HHPL, Post-Presidential Subject File, "Huntington Library."

95. Interview with Alan Jutzi, July 15, 1999.

96. The correspondence is reported in the minutes of the Board of Trustees' meeting, March 28, 1951, HLA. According to Huntington librarian, David Zeidberg, this

correspondence "does not exist in our files." Personal communication from David Zeidberg to author, September 22, 1999.

97. On Beatrice's death from an aneurysm, see D'Este, pp. 807–808.

98. The papers of General Patton were given to the Library of Congress in 1955. Additional papers were donated in 1964. The total collection comprises over twenty-six thousand items. "George S. Patton: A Register of his Papers in the Library of Congress," Manuscript Division, Library of Congress, 1998.

99. Letter from Lieutenant Colonel George S. Patton to head of the Manuscript Division, Library of Congress, June 17, 1963. Information provided to the author by Fred Bauman, Library of Congress, May 30, 2000.

100. This untitled document ("I, Ruth Patton Totten, do hereby give …"), dated November 28, 1969, is in HLA. Alan Jutzi, Huntington Curator of Rare Books, made a copy available to the author, August 10, 1999.

101. "Patton Sister Anne Dies in San Marino," *Star News*, March 15, 1971.

102. Carey Bliss, "Visit to the Home of Anne Patton," April 19, 1971, memorandum, HLA.

103. Letter from Doris Hughes (trust officer for Nita Patton's estate) to Carey Bliss, March 23, 1972.

104. "Information for letter to Mrs. Totten" (*ca.* November 30, 1972), memorandum, HLA.

105. Letter from Carey S. Bliss to Ruth Patton Totten, November 30, 1972, HLA.

106. Letter from Ruth Ellen Patton Totten to Carey Bliss, January 2, 1973, HLA.

107. Interview with Joanne Patton, General Patton's daughter-in-law, August 13, 1999.

108. Skotheim quoted in joint press release, June 26, 1999.

109. "Rare Manuscripts Bought," *Los Angeles Times*, February 12, 1926.

110. HL, *Annual Report 1938–1939*, p. 9.

111. HL, *Annual Report 1946–1947*, p. 11.

112. Elizabeth Hay Bechtel, founder of the Ancient Biblical Manuscript Center in Claremont, California, financed the project. In September 1991, the Huntington made its photographic archive of the Scrolls accessible to scholars. The Huntington Library, "Rare Photographic Archive of Dead Sea Scrolls at Huntington Library Will Be Open to All Scholars," press release, September 22, 1991, HLA. See, also, HL, *Annual Report 1991– 94*, p. 3.

113. HL, *Huntington Calendar*, March–April 2001, p. 4.

114. The Huntington, "Visitors' Guide to the Exhibitions of the Henry E. Huntington Library and Art Gallery," 1944. Author's personal collection.

115. HL, *Annual Report 1937–1938*, p. 19.

116. Ibid., p. 21.

117. "Library Exhibits Japs' Duplicity Back in '53," *Los Angeles Times*, February 1, 1944.

118. "Army Exhibit Displayed," *Los Angeles Times*, January 21, 1945; "History of U.S. Army Depicted at Library," *Los Angeles Times*, March 18, 1945.

119. "Library Receives Gift from Patton," *Los Angeles Times*, June 10, 1945; "General Patton Presents Library with Captured Book, 'Mein Kampf,'" *San Marino Tribune*, May 10, 1945; "Mein Kampf, Gift from Patton Arrives at Huntington Library," *San Marino*

Tribune, June 7, 1945. The Huntington's failure in 1999 to research provenance led to the inaccurate statement that "the Huntington did not exhibit *Mein Kampf* and the Laws because (as isolated horrors) they lay outside its areas of concentration and expertise." *Huntington Calendar*, September/October 1999.

120.   John A. Crow, *California as a Place to Live* (New York: Charles Scribner's Sons, 1953), p. 79. The Huntington, *Annual Report 1961–1962*, p. 3.

121.   Letter from William Munro to Beatrice Patton, January 18, 1951, HLA.

122.   Untitled document, signed by Ruth Patton Totten, November 28, 1969, HLA.

123.   Memo from Mary Robertson, curator of rare manuscripts, to Bill Moffett, Huntington librarian, September 11, 1991, HLA.

▣ Chapter 11: In Limbo

1.   Interview with Alan Jutzi, July 12, 1999.

2.   Interview with Jasper Schad, May 26, 2000.

3.   Ridge, at that time a professor of history at Indiana University, was a Visiting Fellow at the Huntington in 1977 and 1978. He joined the Huntington's research team as a specialist in American history in 1978. See HL, *Annual Report 1977–1978*, p. 57; *Annual Report 1978–1979*, p. 46.

4.   Personal communication from Martin Ridge, May 18 and May 19, 2000.

5.   Interviews with Robert Middlekauff, July 6, 1999; August 30, 1999.

6.   Interview with Alan Jutzi, July 12, 1999.

7.   Memo from Mary Robertson to Bill Moffett, September 11, 1991, HLA.

8.   Interview with Mary Robertson, July 15, 1999.

9.   Interview with Alan Jutzi, July 12, 1999.

10.   Memo from Mary Robertson to Bill Moffett, September 11, 1991, HLA.

11.   Memo from Mary Robertson to David Zeidberg, "Pending Problem — Nazi Mss. Here," March 1, 1996, HLA.

12.   Interview with David Zeidberg, July 13, 1999.

13.   Millikan defended the Huntington's research record. Minutes of Special Meeting of Board of Trustees, Huntington Library, August 6, 1951, HHPL, Post-Presidential Subject File, Huntington Library and Art Gallery.

14.   On the dispersion of the city's political power, see Davis, p. 105.

15.   Diner, p. 283.

16.   Vorspan and Gartner, p. 225.

17.   Rodolfo Acuña, *Occupied America: A History of Chicanos* (New York: Harper & Row, 1988), p. 319.

18.   Sterling, like Munro, had taught history and government at Caltech. Hoover also served on Caltech's board of trustees. Page was chairman of the Caltech board from 1943 to 1954.

19.   With the exception of the years 1926 to 1953, this law firm always had a representative on the board of trustees from 1919 to 2001. William French Smith, Reagan's first attorney general, was a member from 1971 to 1990. Robert Erburu, who became chief executive of Times Mirror, was on the board from 1991 to 2001.

20.   All major downtown law firms enforced the same anti-Semitic policy during this period. See Davis, p. 146.

21. Vorspan and Gartner, p. 205.

22. "Even the august Huntington Library was affected by the 1960s," recalled Robert Skotheim in 1999, but democratization of the institution did not begin until much later. Skotheim, "Outline for Talk."

23. HL, *Annual Report 1968–1969*, pp. 7–8.

24. Skotheim, "An Invitation to the Huntington's 100th Anniversary."

25. Nancy Meyer, *Where to Take Guests in Southern California* (Los Angeles: Ward Ritchie Press, 1972), p. 78.

26. Skotheim, "Outline for Talk."

27. HL, *Annual Report 1966–1967*, p. 7; *Annual Report 1969–1970*, p. 7.

28. HL, *Annual Report 1971–1972*, pp. 10, 71–72.

29. HL, *Annual Report, 1972–1973*, pp. 28–30.

30. HL, *Annual Report 1991–1994*, p. 61.

31. HL, *Annual Report 1979–1980*, p. 11; *Annual Report 1981–1982*, p. 10; *Annual Report, 1994–1997*, p. 23; *Annual Report 1988–1989*, p. 7.

32. HL, *Annual Report 2003*; personal communication from Lisa Blackburn, February 9, 2005.

33. HL, *Annual Report 1990–1991*, p. 3.

34. HL, *Annual Report 1991–1994*, p. 2. Interview with Robert Skotheim, July 19, 1999.

35. Skotheim, "Outline for Talk," p. 8.

36. Ibid. Until 1991, the top administrative officer at the Huntington was known as director. The title was then changed to president.

37. Robert Allen Skotheim, *Totalitarianism and American Social Thought* (New York: Holt, Rinehart and Winston, 1971), p. 123.

38. Skotheim, "An Invitation to the Huntington's 100th Anniversary," pp. 8, 10.

39. The event took place on June 13, 1999.

40. HL, *Annual Report 1994–1997*, p. 1.

41. According to a restriction imposed by Edward Huntington, the Library was required to remain "without any circulation or withdrawal privileges." HL, *First Annual Report, 1927–1928*, p. 11.

42. David Zeidberg, "History of Lending for Exhibition from the Library Division," August 7, 2000, HLA.

43. For example, Skotheim invited progressive historian Gary Nash, UCLA professor of history, to give the Founder's Day lecture on March 1, 1999. He also brought in speakers on women's issues and encouraged the formation of a women studies seminar. Historian Anne Firor Scott spoke on Southern women at the Founder's Day lecture, March 2, 1998. HL, *The Huntington Calendar*, March–April 1998 and March–April 1999.

44. HL, *Annual Report 1994–1997*, p. 30.

45. Peter Blodgett, *Land of Golden Dreams: California in the Gold Rush Decade, 1848–1858* (San Marino: The Huntington, 1999); Andrew C. Isenberg, "The California Gold Rush, the West, and the Nation," *Reviews in American History* vol. 29, no. 1 (March 2001), pp. 62–71.

46. Robert Skotheim, "A Report on Trustee/Overseer Retreat," HL, *The Huntington Calendar*, January–February 1999, p. 1.

47. The second is Santa Monica. Tim Goodman, "Los Angeles Is Just a Factory Town," *San Francisco Chronicle*, January 28, 2001, Datebook p. 44.

48. Skotheim, "Outline for Talk."

49. The reference to the Japanese Gardens is from The Huntington, "Historic Anecdotes," public relations handout, no date, HLA. The Chinese Garden, funded in its first phase with a $10 million bequest, will be on a twelve-acre site. See HL, *The Huntington Calendar*, January–February 2002, pp. 4–5. See, also, interview with Jin Chen, designer of the Chinese Garden in Huntington Library, *The Huntington Calendar*, March–April 2003, pp. 4–5.

50. Memo from Mary Robertson to David Zeidberg, March 1, 1996, HLA.

51. Vorspan and Gartner, *History of the Jews of Los Angeles* (1970); Robert Glass Cleland and Frank P. Putnam, *Isaias W. Hellman and the Farmers and Merchants Bank* (San Marino: Huntington Library, 1965).

52. Personal communication from Peter Blodgett, November 3, 1999.

53. The Founder's Day lecture is an important public event at the Huntington. Gundersheimer spoke on February 24, 1997. HL, *Huntington Calendar*, January–February 1997.

54. The following account of the Huntington's decision to loan the Nuremberg Laws to the Skirball is based on interviews with Robert Skotheim, July 19, 1999; David Zeidberg, July 13, 1999; Alan Jutzi, July 12, 1999; Mary Robertson, July 15, 1999; David Zeidberg and Mary Robertson, October 8, 1999; and Uri Herscher, July 20, 1999, and August 16, 1999.

55. Letter from Robert Skotheim to Uri Herscher, March 5, 1999, SCCA.

56. Erburu was with Gibson, Dunn, and Crutcher (the law firm long associated with Huntington family interests) before joining Times Mirror in 1961 as its general counsel. He became chief executive and chairman of Times Mirror in 1986, retiring in January 1996.

57. Erburu retired from the Huntington in June 2001 after twenty years on the board and ten years as its chair. HL, *The Huntington Calendar*, May–June 2001, p. 4. See, also, James Bates, "Mark Willes to Head Times Mirror Media: Chairman Robert Erburu to Retire," *Los Angeles Times*, May 2, 1995, p. 1.

58. Herscher quoted in Tugend, p. 27. The account of the developing relationship between Skirball and the Huntington is based on interviews with Robert Skotheim (July 19, 1999), Uri Herscher (July 20, 1999 and August 16, 1999), and Loren Rothschild (July 20, 1999).

59. Interview with David Zeidberg, July 13, 1999.

60. Interview with Robert Skotheim, July 19, 1999.

61. Remarks of Edgar M. Bronfman, January 16, 2001, in a press release announcing publication of *Plunder and Restitution: The U.S. and Holocaust Victims' Assets; Findings and Recommendations of the Presidential Advisory Commission on Holocaust Assets in the United States and Staff Report*, December 2000.

62. American Association of Museums, "Guidelines Concerning the Unlawful Appropriation of Objects During the Nazi Era," issued in November 1999 and amended April 2001; American Association of Museums, "AAM Recommended Procedures for Providing Information to the Public about Objects Transferred in Europe during the Nazi Era," issued May 4, 2001.

63. On the role of Stanley F. Chyet (1931 to 2002) at the Skirball, see Uri D.

Herscher, "President's Message," *Oasis,* vol. 6, no. 1 (Summer–Fall 2003), pp. 3–5. *Oasis* is the Skirball's in-house magazine.

64. Tugend, pp. 8, 27.

65. Interview with Robert Kirschner, January 20, 2005.

66. Skotheim, Zeidberg, Robertson, and Kirschner told me that they were not aware of Patton's anti-Semitism at the time. Herscher was aware, and I did not interview Chyet. Interviews with Robert Kirschner and Grace Cohen Grossman, January 20, 2005; with Uri Herscher, July 20, 1999; with Robert Skotheim, July 19, 1999; and with Mary Robertson and David Zeidberg, October 8, 1999.

67. Letter from Uri Herscher to Robert Skotheim, March 3, 1999, SCCA.

68. Letter from Robert Skotheim to Uri Herscher, March 5, 1999, SCCA.

69. Interviews with Robert Kirschner and Grace Cohen Grossman, January 20, 2005.

70. Personal communication from Sharon Waxman, August 16, 2001.

71. Interview with David Zeidberg, July 13, 1999.

72. Interview with Catherine Babcock, July 1, 1999.

73. Interview with David Zeidberg, July 13, 1999.

74. By contrast, when a librarian at the Connecticut Historical Society, looking through artifacts in a storage area, accidentally discovered a flag that had been in Abraham Lincoln's theater box on the night of his assassination in 1865, the Society did three years of "exhaustive research" before announcing its discovery to the press and public. Paul Zielbauer, "Found in Clutter, a Relic of Lincoln's Death," *New York Times*, July 5, 2001, p. 1.

75. This search, which took the Huntington's archivist one week to complete, was done between September 5 and September 22 at the request of Platt and O'Leary. Interviews with Dan Lewis, July 7 and July 14, 1999; letter to the author from David Zeidberg, September 22, 1999.

76. Interview with David Zeidberg, July 13, 1999.

77. Interview with Eric Klein, August 3, 1999.

78. Huntington briefing of staff and researchers, June 29, 1999.

79. Personal communication from Sharon Waxman, August 16, 2001; interview with Catherine Babcock, July 1, 1999.

80. "Huntington Library to Loan Original Nuremberg Laws Signed by Hitler to the Skirball Cultural Center," Huntington-Skirball joint press release, June 26, 1999.

81. Huntington briefing, June 29, 1999.

82. HL, *Nuremberg Laws Loan to the Skirball* (video, 1999).

83. Author's field notes, June 28 to July 13, 1999.

84. Personal communication from Gerhard Jochem to Huntington, June 28, 1999.

85. Letter from David Zeidberg to Gerhard Jochem, July 15, 1999. Unknown to the Huntington at that time, the second original set of Nuremberg Laws was exhibited in May 1995 by a Jewish congregation, Neuen Israelitische Friedhof, in Nuremberg. Information provided by Gerhard Jochem, Nuremberg City Archives, August 31, 1999, and June 28, 2001.

86. James Thorpe, director of the Huntington from 1966 to 1983, was given access for his biography of Henry Edwards Huntington.

87. Zeidberg's security concerns were warranted. A white supremacist, who went on a shooting rampage in Los Angeles on August 10, told police that the Skirball had been one

of his targets, but its high security discouraged him. Stacy Finz, "Race a Factor in Slaying of Mail Carrier," *San Francisco Chronicle*, August 13, 1999.

88.   Interview with Alan Jutzi, July 12, 1999.

89.   Patton's statement was reprinted in full without comment in the *New York Times*, July 4, 1999, Week in Review, p. 7. Sharon Waxman also relied on Patton's statement in her *Washington Post* article, June 26, 1999.

90.   Personal written communication from Robert Skotheim to Marianne Perls, December 16, 1999, MPP.

91.   Frank Perls, "Nuernberg Laws," memorandum, April 28, 1945, HLA.

92.   "Statement Dictated by General George S. Patton, Jr. Regarding Document Taken in Nuremberg," June 11, 1945, HLA. Emphasis in original.

93.   Memorandum from Mary Robertson to Bill Moffett, September 11, 1991, HLA.

94.   Letter from Robert Skotheim to Martin Dannenberg, August 16, 1999, MDP.

95.   Personal communication from Gerhard Jochem, September 10, 1999.

96.   See, for example, Robert Skotheim, "Where Are the Stauffenberg Family Jewels?" This talk was given to the California Club in Los Angeles, December 16, 1999.

97.   This untitled document ("I, Ruth Patton Totten, do hereby give ..."), dated November 28, 1969, is in HLA.

98.   Interviews with Eric Kline, August 3, August 7, August 13, 1999.

99.   "The Huntington considers itself the legal owner of these documents. They were accessioned as a gift from General Patton before they were loaned for exhibition at the Skirball Cultural Center." Personal communication from David Zeidberg, August 24, 1999.

100.   Joint press release, June 26, 1999.

101.   Dutka, p. 18.

102.   Kuntz, p. 7.

103.   Interview with Robert Skotheim, July 19, 1999.

104.   Letter from Skotheim to Dannenberg, August 16, 1999, MDPP.

105.   Personal communication from Martin Ridge, May 19, 2000.

106.   Interview with Mary Robertson, July 15, 1999.

107.   Quoted in O'Connor, p. B3.

▣ Chapter 12: History Lessons

1.   Interview with Robert Kirschner, July 27, 1999.

2.   In addition, the Huntington also provided an original photocopy of the Nuremberg Laws, retrieved in Eichstätt in 1945, to be used in rotation with the originals.

3.   See, for example, Dutka, 1999; Kuntz, 1999.

4.   Quoted in joint Skirball-Huntington press release, June 26, 1999.

5.   From author's notes, July 2, 1999.

6.   The phrase appeared in a text panel in the original exhibit.

7.   Quoted in Blumenson, *The Patton Papers, 1940–1945*, pp. 731, 787.

8.   Interview with Uri Herscher, July 20, 1999.

9.   Patton's statement was removed, the text panel was changed, a new display case was installed, the Patton-Millikan photograph was removed, and Dannenberg's photograph was added. The chronology of changes in the Nuremberg Laws case was provided by

Grace Cohen Grossman, the Skirball's senior curator, in an interview, January 20, 2005, and by personal communication, February 8, 2005.

10.　This "Message from the President" appeared next to the Nuremberg case at the Skirball. Herscher makes a point of thanking "our Armed Forces," not Patton.

11.　Letter from Uri Herscher to author, April 17, 2000.

12.　Letter from Dannenberg to Herscher, August 5, 1999, MDP.

13.　We sent memoranda to Uri Herscher on August 2, 1999; to David Zeidberg, Mary Robertson, and Robert Skotheim, on October 6, 1999; and to Uri Herscher on November 1, 1999. Sharon Waxman's article, based on our research, was published as "Judgment at Pasadena," *Washington Post*, March 16, 2000.

14.　Interview with Grace Cohen Grossman, January 20, 2005.

15.　"Discovering the Nuremberg Documents: An Eyewitness Account," Martin Dannenberg in conversation with Uri Herscher, December 12, 1999, Skirball Cultural Center. In his introduction to the event, Herscher publicly credited the authors for the research that corrected Patton's account.

16.　Author's notes, December 12, 1999.

17.　Letter from Uri Herscher to author, May 2, 2000.

18.　"Prelude to Catastrophe. Early Nazi Documents Captured by U.S. Army," caption for Nuremberg Laws case, Skirball Cultural Center, June 29, 1999.

19.　Text label of Nuremberg Laws exhibition, September 7, 2000.

20.　Davis, p. 119; Diner, p. 208.

21.　Diner, p. 235; Vorspan and Gartner, p. 235.

22.　Diner, p. 283.

23.　By 2004, the annual budget was $11.8 million and the Skirball employed one hundred and twenty-five full-time employees. Information provided by Pat Burdette, January 11, 2002, and Mia Cariño, April 1, 2005.

24.　Skirball Cultural Center, "An Interview with Moshe Safdie," February 1996.

25.　Ibid., p. 7.

26.　Skirball, "'In Thrall to Hope,'" 1996.

27.　"In: Skirball Center, Out: Getty Center," *Los Angeles Business Journal*, December 31, 2001–January 6, 2002.

28.　Quoted in Skirball Cultural Center, "A Walk Through *Visions and Values: Jewish Life from Antiquity to America*," press release, 1996, SCCA.

29.　"'In Thrall to Hope,'" pp. 1, 2, 4.

30.　Skirball Cultural Center, "Skirball Cultural Center Celebrates the Jewish Experience in America," press release, 1996.

31.　Grace Cohen Grossman and Robert Kirschner, *Visions and Values: Jewish Life from Antiquity to America* (Los Angeles: Skirball Cultural Center, 1996), p. 26.

32.　Grace Cohen Grossman, "Project Americana: Collecting Memories and Exploring the American Jewish Experience," in Grace Cohen Grossman (editor), *The Skirball Museum Collections and Inaugural Exhibition* (Berkeley: University of California Press, 1996), p. 93.

33.　The quote comes from the script of the Orientation Video to the core exhibition, no date, SCCA.

34.　Grossman and Kirschner, p. 5.

35.　Diner, pp. 243–244, 268, 351–352.

36. "'In Thrall to Hope,'" p. 2.
37. Herscher received his undergraduate sociology degree in June 1964 when I was in my second year of graduate study in the school of criminology.
38. Stanley F. Chyet, "I Love the Doves," *Oasis,* vol. 6, no. 1 (Summer–Fall, 2003), p. 5.
39. Grossman and Kirschner, pp. 23, 24; Grossman, p. 100.
40. Robert Kirschner quoted in "A Walk Through *Visions and Values.*"
41. I explore this development in "Desegregating Multiculturalism: Problems in the Theory and Pedagogy of Diversity Education," *Social Justice,* vol. 29, no. 4 (2002), pp. 41–46.
42. Text label in the Skirball's Israel gallery; Grossman, p. 186.
43. Interview with Robert Kirschner, January 20, 2005; field notes from conversations with curators and docents, July 2, 1999.
44. Interview with Grace Cohen Grossman, January 20, 2005. On the variety of holocaust memorials, see James E. Young (editor), *The Art of Memory.*
45. Hoffman, p. 170.
46. Linenthal, p. 122. Linenthal's book, *Preserving Memory*, provides a detailed account of how the President's Commission on the Victims of the Holocaust battled over the museum's memorializing and educational functions.
47. For critiques of the sentimentalization of holocaust memorials, see Arno J. Mayer, "Memory and History: On the Poverty of Remembering and Forgetting the Judeocide," *Radical History Review* 56 (1993), pp. 5–20; and Ian Buruma, "The Joys and Perils of Victimhood," *New York Review of Books*, April 8, 1999, pp. 4–9.
48. Author's research notes, February 27, 2005.
49. Quoted in "A Walk Through *Visions and Values.*"
50. Grossman and Kirschner, p. 28.
51. Interview with Robert Kirschner, January 20, 2005.
52. The phrase comes from Linenthal's (p. 135) discussion of the national Holocaust Museum.
53. Interview with Robert Kirschner, January 20, 2005.
54. On the Americanization of holocaust memorials, see Linenthal, pp. 255–272.
55. "'In Thrall to Hope,'" p. 3.
56. The first quote is from a text label, "A Message from the President of the Skirball Cultural Center." The second quote is in "Nuremberg Case Spotlight Talk," a two-page memo of talking points, April 29, 2003, Skirball Docent Program, SCCA.
57. Text label, "Message from the President of the Skirball Cultural Center."
58. W. G. Sebald, *The Rings of Saturn* (New York: New Directions Books, 1999), p. 226.
59. Davis, p. 7. This is especially true of the public school system, which has become hyper-segregated as a result of white flight to the suburbs and the growth of private schools. See Richard Lee Colvin, "School Segregation Is Growing, Report Finds," *Los Angeles Times*, June 12, 1999.
60. Interview with Robert Skotheim, July 19, 1999.
61. The Huntington, "New President Appointed at The Huntington," press release, January 3, 2001.
62. Tom Tugend, "Huntington Bound," *The Jewish Journal of Greater Los Angeles*, March 9, 2001, p. 15.

63. Steven Koblik, *The Stones Cry Out: Sweden's Response to the Persecution of the Jews, 1933–1945* (New York: Holocaust Library, 1988), p. 165.

64. Personal communication from Helen Wechsler, International and Ethics Programs, American Association of Museums, February 25, 2002.

65. American Association of Museums, "Code of Ethics for Museums," issued November 1993, updated February 2001.

66. Some two and one-half million photographs, including images of Hitler, are now accessible to the public at the National Archives. Hitler's paintings are preserved at the U.S. Army's Center of Military History. William H. Honan, "Court Considers Ownership of Seized Hitler Paintings," *New York Times*, May 8, 2001, p. B1.

67. Personal communication from Martin Dannenberg, December 26, 1999.

68. Lisa G. Corrin (editor), *Mining the Museum: An Installation by Fred Wilson* (New York: The New Press, 1994). The term "mining" is intended to convey both a process of excavation and ownership.

69. Lisa G. Corrin, "Mining the Museum: Artists Look at Museums, Museums Look at Themselves," ibid., pp. 1–22.

70. Ira Berlin, "Mining the Museum and the Rethinking of Maryland's History," ibid., p. 35.

71. American Association of Museums, "Guidelines Concerning the Unlawful Appropriation of Objects During the Nazi Era," issued November 1999, amended April 2001.

72. Koblik, p. 167.

▣ Chapter 13: Past and Present

1. Matthew Baigell, "George Segal's Holocaust Memorial: An Interview with the Artist," in James E. Young (editor), pp. 83–87.

2. I write about these recipes in a memoir, "To Die For," *Exquisite Corpse* 58 (July 1996), pp. 7–9.

3. W. E. B. Du Bois, *Darkwater* (1920), reprinted in David R. Roediger (editor), *Black on White: Black Writers on What It Means to Be White* (New York: Schocken Books, 1998), p. 185.

4. Eva Hoffman, *Lost in Translation: A Life in a New Language* (New York: Penguin Books, 1990), p. 160.

5. Ibid.

6. Humberto Cintron, "An Interview with Piri Thomas," *Forkroads*, Fall 1995, p. 47.

7. Gloria Anzaldúa, "How to Tame a Wild Tongue," *Borderlands/La Frontera: The New Mestiza* (San Francisco: Aunt Lute Books, 1999), p. 54.

8. On the panoply of cultural traits associated with British national character, see Raphael Samuel (editor), *Patriotism: The Making and Unmaking of British National Identity* (London: Routledge, 1989).

9. Anthony M. Platt, *The Child Savers: The Invention of Delinquency* (Chicago: University of Chicago Press, 1969).

10. Diner, p. 231.

11. Edward S. Shapiro, "The Friendly University: Jews in Academia Since World War II," *Judaism: A Quarterly Journal of Jewish Life and Thought*, June 22, 1997.

12. Jean-Paul Sartre, *Anti-Semite and Jew,* originally published in 1946 (New York: Grove Press, 1962), p. 76.

13. Takaki, p. 406.

14. Anthony M. Platt, *E. Franklin Frazier Reconsidered* (New Brunswick: Rutgers University Press, 1991).

15. Sartre, pp. 67, 150.

16. Primo Levi, "Revisiting the Camps," in Young, *The Art of Memory,* p. 185.

17. Young, p. 36.

18. David Lowenthal, *The Past Is a Foreign Country* (Cambridge: Cambridge University Press, 1985), p. 412.

19. Stanley Cohen, *States of Denial: Knowing About Atrocities and Suffering* (Cambridge: Polity, 2001).

20. Mayer, p. 7.

21. Michael Kimmelman, "Museums in a Quandary: Where Are the Ideals?" *New York Times,* August 26, 2001, Arts, p. 1; Michael Kimmelman, "Out of Minimalism, Monuments to Memory," *New York Times,* January 13, 2002, Arts, pp. 1, 37.

22. See, for example, controversies surrounding the Smithsonian's "The West as America" and Enola Gay exhibitions. William H. Truettner (editor), *The West as America: Reinterpreting Images of the Frontier* (Washington, D.C.: Smithsonian Books, 1991); and Philip Nobile (editor), *Judgment at the Smithsonian* (New York: Marlow & Co., 1995). More generally, see Ivan Karp and Steven D. Lavine, *The Poetics and Politics of Museum Display* (Washington, D.C.: Smithsonian Institution Press, 1991). For an example of an exhibition in Oakland, California, that tackles a controversial issue, see Marcia A. Eymann and Charles Wollenberg (editors), *What's Going On? California and the Vietnam Era* (Berkeley: University of California Press, 2004).

23. Albert L. Hurtado, *Indian Survival on the California Frontier* (New Haven: Yale University Press, 1988).

24. The Chinese population in California went from more than seventy-five thousand in 1880 to about forty-five thousand in 1900, from over nine percent of the population in 1860 to about three percent forty years later. Sucheng Chan, *This Bitter-Sweet Soil: The Chinese in California Agriculture, 1860–1910* (Berkeley: University of California Press, 1986), pp. 48–49.

25. Tomás Almaguer, *Racial Fault Lines: The Historical Origins of White Supremacy in California* (Berkeley: University of California Press, 1994).

26. Sebald, *The Rings of Saturn,* p. 125.

27. Kenneth E. Foote, *Shadowed Ground: America's Landscapes of Violence and Tragedy* (Austin: University of Texas Press, 1997).

28. Raphael Samuel, *Theatres of Memory: Past and Present in Contemporary Culture* (London: Verso, 1994); Patricia N. Limerick, "Disorientation and Reorientation: The American Landscape Discovered from the American West," in David Thelen and Frederick E. Hoxie (editors), *Discovering America: Essays on the Search for an Identity* (Urbana: University of Illinois Press, 1994).

Sources and Bibliography

Interviews

Catherine Babcock, July 1, 1999

Fred Bauman, July 6, 1999

Michael Berenbaum, July 21, 1999

Peter Blodgett, July 29, 1999

Martin Blumenson, August 30, 1999

Greg Bradsher, August 10, 1999; August 19, 1999

Lonnie Bunch, September 29, 1999

Hugh Cole, August 30, 1999

Martin Dannenberg, August 12–13, 1999; October 3, 1999; December 11–12, 1999; July 11, 2001

Carlo D'Este, February 21, 2000

Hasia Diner, July 1, 1999

Saul Friedländer, July 2, 1999

Judith Goodstein, July 6, 1999

Grace Cohen Grossman, January 20, 2005

Uri Herscher, July 20, 1999; August 16, 1999; October 8, 1999; February 16, 2001

Alan Jutzi, July 12, 1999; July 15, 1999; July 29, 1999

Ava Kahn, November 5, 1999

Robert Kirschner, July 27, 1999; January 20, 2005

Eric Klein, August 3, 1999; August 7, 1999; August 13, 1999

Charles Lemons, August 6, 1999

Maria Lepowsky, July 10–14, 1999

Dan Lewis, July 7, 1999

Dale Mayer, August 4, 1999

Robert Middlekauff, August 12, 1999; August 30, 1999

Judah Nadich, July 29, 1999

Joanne Patton, August 13, 1999

Robert Patton, September 10, 1999

Klaus Perls, August 12, 1999

Marianne Perls, August 13, 1999; October 7, 1999; January 21, 2005

Roy Ritchie, July 28, 1999

Mary Robertson, July 15, 1999; October 8, 1999

Loren Rothschild, July 20, 1999

Robert Skotheim, July 19, 1999
Steve Wasserman, June 30, 1999
Billy Wilder, September 30, 1999; October 7, 1999
David Zeidberg, July 13, 1999; October 8, 1999

Archives and Manuscript Collections

Albany, New York

> State University of New York at Albany, M. E. Grenander Department of Special Collections, German and Jewish Intellectual Émigré Collection, Emergency Rescue Committee Records, 1936–1957.

Baltimore

> Martin Dannenberg Personal Papers (private collection).

Hyde Park, New York

> Franklin D. Roosevelt Library, Eleanor Roosevelt Papers.

Kirksville, Missouri

> Truman State University, Special Collections, Papers of Harry H. Laughlin.

Los Angeles

> Japanese American National Museum, Pacific Citizen Archives.
> Los Angeles Times Library, Los Angeles Times, 1919–1945.
> Marianne Perls Papers (private collection).
> Skirball Cultural Center, Institutional Archives.

New York City

> Leo Baeck Institute, Hugo Perls Collection.

Pasadena, California

> California Institute of Technology, Robert Andrews Millikan Collection.
> California Institute of Technology, E. S. Gosney Papers and Records of the Human Betterment Foundation.
> California Institute of Technology, George Ellery Hale Collection.

Sacramento, California

> California State University, University Archives, Charles M. Goethe Collection and Harold Severaid Collection.
> Foundation of California State University, C. M. Goethe Permanent Records.

San Marino, California

> The Huntington Library and Art Gallery, Patton Family Papers.

The Huntington Library and Art Gallery, Institutional Archives.
The Huntington Library and Art Gallery, Annual Reports.
The Huntington Library and Art Gallery, Calendar.

Stony Brook, New York

Stony Brook University, Special Collections and University Archives, Eugenie Söderberg Collection.

Washington, D.C.

Library of Congress, Manuscript Division, George S. Patton, Jr. Papers.

National Archives and Records Administration, Military Records Section, WWII Operations Reports, WWII War Crimes Records, and State Department Central Decimal File.

Smithsonian Archives of American Art, Frank Perls Papers.

West Branch, Iowa

Herbert Hoover Presidential Library.

Books

Acuña, Rodolfo. *Occupied America: A History of Chicanos*. New York: Harper and Row, 1988.
Allen, James; Als, Hilton; Lewis, John; and Litwack, Leon F. *Without Sanctuary: Lynching Photography in America*. Santa Fe: Twin Palms, 2004.
Almaguer, Tomás. *Racial Fault Lines: The Historical Origins of White Supremacy in California*. Berkeley: University of California Press, 1994.
Anzaldúa, Gloria. *Borderlands/La Frontera: The New Mestiza*. San Francisco: Aunt Lute Books, 1999.
Axelrod, Alan. *Patton on Leadership: Strategic Lessons for Corporate Warfare*. Paramus, N.J.: Prentice Hall, 1999.
Ayer, Fred, Jr. *Before the Colors Fade: Portrait of a Soldier, George S. Patton, Jr.* Boston: Houghton Mifflin, 1964.
Barker, Pat. *Another World*. New York: Farrar, Strauss and Giroux, 1998.
Bauman, Zygmunt. *Modernity and the Holocaust*. Ithaca: Cornell University Press, 2000.
Bernal, Peggy Park. *The Huntington*. San Marino: Huntington Library, 1992.
Black, Edwin. *War Against the Weak: Eugenics and America's Campaign to Create a Master Race*. New York: Four Walls Eight Windows, 2003.
Bledsoe, Thomas. *Or We'll All Hang Separately: The Highlander Idea*. Boston: Beacon Press, 1969.
Blodgett, Peter. *Land of Golden Dreams: California in the Gold Rush Decade, 1848–1858*. San Marino, California: The Huntington, 1999.
Blumenson, Martin. *The Patton Papers, 1885–1940*. Boston: Houghton Mifflin, 1972.
Blumenson, Martin. *The Patton Papers, 1940–1945*. 1974. New York: Da Capo Press, 1996.
Blumenson, Martin. *Patton: The Man Behind the Legend, 1885–1945*. New York: William Morrow, 1985.

Briggs, Laura. *Reproducing Empire: Race, Sex, Science, and U.S. Imperialism in Puerto Rico.* Berkeley: University of California Press, 2002.

Browning, Christopher. *Ordinary Men: Reserve Police Battalion 101 and the Final Solution in Poland.* New York: HarperCollins, 1992.

Carlson, Elof Axel. *The Unfit: A History of a Bad Idea.* Cold Spring Harbor, New York: Cold Spring Harbor Laboratory Press, 2001.

Chan, Sucheng. *This Bitter-Sweet Soil: The Chinese in California Agriculture, 1860–1910.* Berkeley: University of California Press, 1986.

Cleland, Robert. *A History of California: The American Period.* New York: Macmillan, 1930.

Cleland, Robert. *California in Our Time (1900–1940).* New York: Alfred A. Knopf, 1947.

Cleland, Robert, and Putnam, Frank P. *Isaias W. Hellman and the Farmers and Merchants Bank.* San Marino, California: Huntington Library, 1965.

Cohen, Stan. *States of Denial: Knowing About Atrocities and Suffering.* Cambridge: Polity, 2001.

Crow, John A. *California as a Place to Live.* New York: Charles Scribner's, 1953.

Davis, Mike. *City of Quartz: Excavating the Future in Los Angeles.* London: Verso, 1990.

D'Este, Carlo. *Patton: A Genius for War.* New York: HarperPerrenial, 1995.

Devaney, John. *The True Story of Gen. George S. Patton, USA.* New York: Julian Messner, 1982.

Deverell, William. *Whitewashed Adobe: The Rise of Los Angeles and the Remaking of Its Mexican Past.* Berkeley: University of California Press.

Didion, Joan. *Where I Was From.* New York: Alfred A. Knopf, 2003.

Diner, Hasia. *The Jews of the United States, 1654 to 2000.* Berkeley: University of California Press, 2004.

Dinnerstein, Leonard. *Anti-Semitism in America.* New York: Oxford University Press, 1994.

Domarus, Max. *Hitler: Speeches and Proclamations, 1932–1945.* Translated by Chris Wilcox and Mary Fran Gilbert. Wauconda, Ill.: Bolchazy-Carducci, 1992.

Duggan, Stephen, and Drury, Betty. *The Rescue of Science and Learning: The Story of the Emergency Committee in Aid of Displaced Foreign Scholars.* New York: Macmillan, 1948.

Farago, Ladislas. *The Last Days of Patton.* New York: McGraw-Hill, 1981.

Foote, Kenneth E. *Shadowed Ground: America's Landscapes of Violence and Tragedy.* Austin: University of Texas Press, 1997.

Forty, George. *The Armies of George S. Patton.* New York: Sterling, 1998.

Friedländer, Saul. *Nazi Germany and the Jews: The Years of Persecution, 1933–1939.* New York: HarperCollins, 1997.

Fryer, Paul. *Staying Power: The History of Black People in England.* London: Pluto Press, 1984.

Gartner, Lloyd P. *The Jewish Immigrant in England, 1870–1914.* London: Simon Publications, 1960.

Gilroy, Paul. *After Race: Imagining Political Culture Beyond the Color Line.* Cambridge: Harvard University Press, 2000.

Goethe, Charles M. *Seeking to Serve*. Sacramento: Keystone Printing, 1949.

Goethe, Charles M. *War Profits and Better Babies*. Sacramento: Keystone Press, 1946.

Goldhagen, Daniel J. *Hitler's Willing Executioners: Ordinary Germans and the Holocaust*. New York: Knopf, 1996.

Goodstein, Judith R. *Millikan's School: A History of the California Institute of Technology*. New York: W. W. Norton, 1991.

Gray, A. A. *History of California from 1542*. Boston: D. C. Heath, 1934.

Green, Susan, ed. *The Huntington Library: Treasures from Ten Centuries*. London: Scala Publishers, 2004.

Grossman, Grace Cohen, and Kirschner, Robert. *Visions and Values: Jewish Life from Antiquity to America*. Los Angeles: Skirball Cultural Center, 1996.

Haller, Mark. *Eugenics: Hereditarian Attitudes in American Thought*. New Brunswick: Rutgers University Press, 1963.

Hanna, Phil T. *California Through Four Centuries: A Handbook of Memorable Dates*. New York: Farrar & Rinehart, 1935.

Hanson, Victor Davis. *The Soul of Battle: From Ancient Times to the Present Day, How Three Great Liberators Vanquished Tyranny*. New York: The Free Press, 1999.

Hatch, Alden. *George Patton: General in Spurs*. New York: Modern Library, 1950.

Hilberg, Raul. *The Destruction of the European Jews*. New York: Holmes and Meier, 1985.

Hitler, Adolf. *Mein Kampf*. German publication, 1925. Translated by Ralph Mannheim. Boston: Houghton Mifflin, 1999.

Hittell, John S. *The Commerce and Industries of the Pacific Coast of North America*. San Francisco: A. L. Bancroft & Co., 1882.

Hobsbawm, Eric, and Ranger, Terence, eds. *The Invention of Tradition*. Cambridge: Cambridge University Press, 1983.

Hoffman, Eva. *After Such Knowledge: Memory, History, and the Legacy of the Holocaust*. New York: PublicAffairs, 2004.

Hoffman, Eva. *Lost in Translation: A Life in a New Language*. New York: Penguin, 1990.

Hofstadter, Richard. *Social Darwinism in the United States*. Boston: Beacon Press, 1965.

Hunt, Rockwell. *New California the Golden*. Sacramento: California State Department of Education, 1937.

Hurtado, Albert L. *Indian Survival on the California Frontier*. New Haven: Yale University Press, 1988.

Hyamson, Albert M. *The Sephardim of England: A History of the Spanish and Portuguese Jewish Community, 1492–1951*. London: Methuen, 1951.

Ionesco, Eugene. *The Chairs*. Translated by Martin Crimp. London: Faber and Faber, 1997.

Kargon, Robert H. *The Rise of Robert Millikan: Portrait of a Life in American Science*. Ithaca: Cornell University Press, 1982.

Karp, Ivan, and Lavine, Steven D. *The Poetics and Politics of Museum Display*. Washington, D.C.: Smithsonian Institution Press, 1991.

Kershaw, Ian. *Hitler, 1889–1936: Hubris*. New York: W. W. Norton, 1999.

Kevles, Daniel J. *The Physicists: The History of a Scientific Community in Modern America*. Cambridge: Harvard University Press, 1997.

Kevles, Daniel J. *In the Name of Eugenics: Genetics and the Uses of Human Heredity.* Cambridge: Harvard University Press, 1995.

Kline, Wendy. *Building a Better Race: Gender, Sexuality, and Eugenics from the Turn of the Century to the Baby Boom.* Berkeley: University of California Press, 2001.

Koblik, Steven. *The Stones Cry Out: Sweden's Response to the Persecution of the Jews, 1933–1945.* New York: Holocaust Library, 1988.

Koch, Oscar W. *Intelligence for Patton.* Philadelphia: Whitmore Publishing, 1971.

Koonz, Claudia. *The Nazi Conscience.* Cambridge: The Belknap Press, 2003.

Kramer, William M. *A Lone Traveler: Einstein in California.* Los Angeles: Skirball Cultural Center, 2004.

Kühl, Stefan. *The Nazi Connection: Eugenics, American Racism, and German National Socialism.* New York: Oxford University Press, 1994.

Kushner, Tony. *Homebody/Kabul.* New York: Theatre Communication Group, 2002.

Levine, Lawrence W. *Highbrow/Lowbrow: The Emergence of Cultural Hierarchy in America.* Cambridge: Harvard University Press, 1988.

Lewis, Oscar. *The Big Four: The Story of Huntington, Stanford, Hopkins, and Crocker, and of the Building of the Central Pacific.* New York: Alfred A. Knopf, 1938.

Linenthal, Edward T. *Changing Images of the Warrior Hero in America: A History of Popular Symbolism.* New York: Edwin Mellen Press, 1982.

Linenthal, Edward T. *Preserving Memory: The Struggle to Create America's Holocaust Museum.* New York: Viking, 1995.

Lipman, V. D. *Social History of the Jews in England, 1850–1950.* London: Watts, 1954.

Lipstadt, Deborah E. *Beyond Belief: The American Press and the Coming of the Holocaust, 1933–1945.* New York: The Free Press, 1986.

Lowenthal, David. *The Past Is a Foreign Country.* Cambridge: Cambridge University Press, 1985.

Ludmerer, Kenneth M. *Genetics and American Society: A Historical Appraisal.* Baltimore: Johns Hopkins University Press, 1972.

Marino, Andy. *A Quiet American: The Secret War of Varian Fry.* New York: St. Martin's Press, 1999.

McWilliams, Carey. *California: The Great Exception.* 1949. Berkeley: University of California Press, 1998.

McWilliams, Carey. *Southern California: An Island on the Land.* 1946. Santa Barbara: Peregrine Smith, 1973.

Mellor, William Bancroft. *General Patton: The Last Cavalier.* New York: Putnam, 1971.

Meyer, Nancy. *Where to Take Guests in Southern California.* Los Angeles: Ward Ritchie Press, 1972.

Millett, Allan R. *A War to Be Won: Fighting the Second World War.* Cambridge: Harvard University Press, 2000.

Millikan, Robert A. *The Autobiography of Robert A. Millikan.* New York: Prentice Hall, 1950.

Millikan, Robert A. *Science and the New Civilization.* New York: Charles Scribner's, 1930.

Mills, C. Wright. *The Power Elite.* New York: Oxford University Press, 1956.

Mosse, George L. *Nazi Culture: Intellectual, Cultural and Social Life in the Third Reich.* New York: Schocken Books, 1981.

Nadich, Judah. *Eisenhower and the Jews*. New York: Twayne Publishers, 1953.

Novick, Peter. *The Holocaust in American Life*. Boston: Houghton Mifflin, 1999.

O'Leary, Cecilia E. *To Die For: The Paradox of American Patriotism*. Princeton: Princeton University Press, 1999.

Ordover, Nancy. *American Eugenics: Race, Queer Anatomy, and the Science of Nationalism*. Minneapolis: University of Minnesota Press, 2003.

Patraka, Vivian M. *Spectacular Suffering: Theatre, Fascism, and the Holocaust*. Bloomington: Indiana University Press, 1999.

Patton, George S., Jr. *War As I Knew It*. Boston: Houghton Mifflin, 1947.

Patton, Robert H. *The Pattons: A Personal History of an American Family*. New York: Crown Publishers, 1994.

Paul, Kathleen. *Whitewashing Britain: Race and Citizenship in the Postwar Era*. Ithaca: Cornell University Press, 1997.

Peifer, Charles, Jr. *Soldier of Destiny: A Biography of George Patton*. Minneapolis: Dillion Press, 1989.

Peters, Thomas J., and Waterman, Robert H. *In Search of Excellence: Lessons from America's Best-Run Companies*. New York: Warner Books, 1984.

Platt, Anthony M. *E. Franklin Frazier Reconsidered*. New Brunswick: Rutgers University Press, 1991.

Platt, Anthony M. *The Child Savers: The Invention of Delinquency*. Chicago: University of Chicago Press, 1969.

Popenoe, Paul, and Gosney, Ezra S. *Twenty-Eight Years of Sterilization in California*. Pasadena: Human Betterment Foundation, 1938.

Popenoe, Paul and Roswell Hill Johnson. *Applied Eugenics*. New York: Macmillan, 1926.

Potter, Lou. *Liberators: Fighting on Two Fronts in World War II*. New York: Harcourt Brace Jovanovich, 1992.

Presidential Advisory Commission on Holocaust Assets in the United States. *Plunder and Restitution: The U.S. and Holocaust Victims' Assets*. Washington, D.C.: U.S. Government Printing Office, 2000.

Prioli, Carmen A. *Lines of Fire: The Poems of General George S. Patton, Jr.* Lewiston, N.Y.: Edwin Mellen Press, 1991.

Proctor, Robert N. *Racial Hygiene: Medicine Under the Nazis*. Cambridge: Harvard University Press, 1988.

Puryear, Edgar F., Jr. *American Generalship—Character Is Everything: The Art of Command*. Novato, Calif.: Presidio Press, 2000.

Rensch, Hero Eugene, and Rensch, Ethel Grace. *Historical Spots in California*, vol. 1. Stanford: Stanford University Press, 1932.

Roth, Joseph. *What I Saw: Reports from Berlin, 1920–1933*. Translated by Michael Hoffman. New York: W. W. Norton, 2004.

Royce, Josiah. *California from Conquest in 1846 to the Second Vigilance Committee in San Francisco: A Study of American Character*. Boston: Houghton Mifflin, 1886.

Samuel, Raphael. *Theatres of Memory: Past and Present in Contemporary Culture*. London: Verso, 1994.

Sánchez, George J. *Becoming Mexican American: Ethnicity, Culture, and Identity in Chicano Los Angeles, 1900–1945*. New York: Oxford University Press, 1993.

Sapir, Boris. *The Jewish Community of Cuba: Settlement and Growth*. Translated by Simon Wolin. New York: The Jewish Teachers' Seminary and People's University, 1948.

Sartre, Jean-Paul. *Anti-Semite and Jew*. 1946. New York: Grove Press, 1962.

Schlink, Bernhard. *The Reader*. 1995. New York: Pantheon Books, 1997.

Sebald, W. G. *After Nature*. Translated by Michael Hamburger. New York: Random House, 2002.

Sebald, W. G. *The Emigrants*. 1993. Translated by Michael Hulse. London: Harvill Press, 1996.

Sebald, W. G. *The Rings of Saturn*. 1998. Translated by Michael Hulse. London: New Directions Books, 1999.

Shirer, William L. *The Rise and Fall of the Third Reich: A History of Nazi Germany*. New York: Simon and Schuster, 1960.

Skotheim, Robert. *Totalitarianism and American Social Thought*. New York: Holt, Rinehart and Winston, 1971.

Stepan, Nany Leys. *"The Hour of Eugenics": Race, Gender, and Nation in Latin America*. Ithaca: Cornell University Press, 1991.

Stern, Alexandra Minna. *Eugenic Nation: Faults and Frontiers of Better Breeding in Modern America*. Berkeley: University of California Press, 2005.

Takaki, Ronald. *A Different Mirror: A History of Multicultural America*. Boston: Little, Brown, 1993.

Taylor, Ian; Evans, Karen; and Fraser, Penny. *A Tale of Two Cities: Global Change, Local Feeling and Everyday Life in the North of England*. London: Routledge, 1996.

Thorpe, James. *Henry Edwards Huntington: A Biography*. Berkeley: University of California Press, 1994.

Toplin, Robert Brent. *History by Hollywood: The Use and Abuse of the American Past*. Urbana: University of Illinois Press, 1996.

Trombley, Stephen. *The Right to Reproduce: A History of Coercive Sterilization*. London: Weidenfeld and Nicolson, 1988.

Vorspan, Max and Lloyd P. Gartner. *History of the Jews of Los Angeles*. San Marino, California: The Huntington Library, 1970.

White, Margaret Bourke. *"Dear Fatherland, Rest Quietly": A Report on the Collapse of Hitler's "Thousand Years."* New York: Simon and Schuster, 1946.

Williams, Bill. *The Making of Manchester Jewry, 1740–1875*. Manchester: Manchester University Press, 1976.

Williams, Vernon L. *Lieutenant Patton and the American Army in the Mexican Punitive Expedition, 1915–1916*. Austin: Presidial Press, 1983.

Williamson, Porter B. *I Remember General Patton's Principles*. Tucson: Management and Systems Consultants, 1979.

Wistrich, Robert S. *Who's Who in Nazi Germany*. London: Routledge, 1995.

Wyatt, David. *Five Fires: Race, Catastrophe, and the Shaping of California*. New York: Oxford University Press, 1997.

Anthologies

Alexander, Jeffrey C. "On the Social Construction of Moral Universals." In *Cultural Traumas and Collective Identity*, edited by Jeffrey C. Alexander, Ron Eyerman,

Bernhard Giesen, Neil J. Smelser, and Piotr Sztompka. Berkeley: University of California Press, 2004.

Barish, Louis, ed. *Rabbis in Uniform: The Story of the American Jewish Military Chaplain.* New York: Jonathan David, 1962.

Bennett, Tony. "The Exhibitionary Complex." In *Culture/Power/History: A Reader in Contemporary Social Theory,* edited by Nicholas B. Dirks, Geoff Eley, and Sherry B. Ortner. Princeton: Princeton University Press, 1994.

Berenbaum, Michael, ed. *Witness to the Holocaust.* New York: HarperCollins, 1997.

Berenbaum, Michael. "Holocaust." In *The Eleanor Roosevelt Encyclopedia*, edited by Maurine H. Beasley, Holly C. Shulman, and Henry R. Beasley. Westport, Connecticut: Greenwood Press, 2000, pp. 239–241.

Brash, Sarah, ed. *The American Story: World War II.* Richmond: Time-Life, 1997.

Broberg, Gunnar, and Roll-Hansen, Nils, eds. *Eugenics and the Welfare State: Sterilization Policy in Denmark, Sweden, Norway, and Finland.* East Lansing: Michigan State University, 1996.

Burleigh, Michael. "Nazi 'Euthanasia' Programs." In Kuntz and Bachrach, *Deadly Medicine*, pp. 127–153.

Corrin, Lisa, ed. *Mining the Museum: An Installation by Fred Wilson.* New York: The New Press, 1994.

Craft, George S., Jr., ed. *California State University, Sacramento: The First Forty Years, 1947–1987.* Sacramento: CSUS Foundation, 1987.

Diner, Hasia. "Jews." In *The Eleanor Roosevelt Encyclopedia*, edited by Maurine H. Beasley, Holly C. Shulman, and Henry R. Beasley. Westport, Conn.: Greenwood Press, 2000, pp. 281–284.

DuBois, W. E. B. "Darkwater." In *Black on White: Black Writers on What It Means to Be White*, edited by David R. Roediger. New York: Schocken Books, 1998.

Eymann, Marcia A., and Wollenberg, Charles, eds. *What's Going On? California and the Vietnam Era.* Berkeley: University of California Press, 2004.

Friedlander, Henry. "From 'Euthanasia' to the 'Final Solution.'" In Kuntz and Bachrach, *Deadly Medicine*, pp. 155–183.

Giesen, Bernhard. "The Trauma of Perpetrators: The Holocaust as the Traumatic Reference of German National Identity." In *Cultural Trauma and Collective Identity*, edited by Jeffrey C. Alexander et al., pp. 112–154.

Glennon, Lorraine, editor-in-chief. *The 20th Century: An Illustrated History of Our Lives and Times.* North Dighton, Mass.: JG Press, 2000.

Grossman, Grace Cohen, ed. *New Beginnings: The Skirball Museum Collections and Inaugural Exhibition.* Berkeley: University of California Press, 1996.

Grossman, Grace Cohen. "Project Americana: Collecting Memories and Exploring the American Jewish Experience." In *The Skirball Museum Collections and Inaugural Exhibition*, edited by Grace Cohen Grossman. Berkeley: University of California Press, 1996.

Kevles, Daniel J. "International Eugenics." In Kuntz and Bachrach, *Deadly Medicine*, pp. 141–59.

Kuntz, Dieter, and Bachrach, Susan, eds. *Deadly Medicine: Creating the Master Race.* Washington, D.C.: United States Holocaust Memorial Museum, 2004.

Limerick, Patricia N. "Disorientation and Reorientation: The American Landscape Discovered from the American West." In *Discovering America: Essays on the Search for an Identity*, edited by David Thelen and Frederick E. Hoxie. Urbana: University of Illinois Press, 1994.

Lopate, Phillip. "Resistance to the Holocaust." In *Testimony: Contemporary Writers Make the Holocaust Personal*, edited by David Rosenberg. New York: Times Books, 1989.

Nathan, Otto, and Norden, Heinz, eds. *Einstein on Peace*. New York: Simon and Schuster, 1960.

Noakes, Jeremy. "Nazism and Eugenics: The Background of the Nazi Sterilization Law of 14 July 1933." In *Ideas into Politics: Aspects of European History, 1880–1950*, edited by R. J. Bullen, H. Pogge von Strandmann, and A. B. Polonsky. London: Croom Helm, 1984, pp. 75–94.

Nobile, Philip, ed. *Judgment at the Smithsonian*. New York: Marlow, 1995.

Samuel, Raphael, ed. *Patriotism: The Making and Unmaking of British National Identity*. London: Routledge, 1989.

Tempo, Carl Joseph Bon. "Refugees." In *The Eleanor Roosevelt Encyclopedia*, edited by Maurine H. Beasley, Holly C. Shulman, and Henry R. Beasley. Westport, Conn.: Greenwood Press, 2000, pp. 431–435.

Truettner, William H., ed. *The West as America: Reinterpreting Images of the Frontier*. Washington, D.C.: Smithsonian Books, 1991.

Weiss, Sheila Faith. "German Eugenics, 1890–1933." In Kuntz and Bachrach, *Deadly Medicine*, pp. 15–39.

Young, James E., ed. *The Art of Memory: Holocaust Memorials in History*. New York: The Jewish Museum, 1994.

Journals

Billington, Ray Allen. "The Genesis of the Research Institution." *The Huntington Library Quarterly*, vol. 22, no. 4 (August 1969): 351–372.

Davies, Godfrey. "The Huntington Library as a Research Center, 1925–1927." *The Huntington Library Quarterly*, vol. 11, no. 3 (May 1948): 293–306.

Eugenics. "The Human Betterment Foundation." *Eugenics* 1 (January 1929): 18.

Eugenical News. "Jewish Physicians in Berlin." *Eugenical News* 19 (1934): 126.

Goethe, Charles M. "Patriotism and Racial Standards." *Eugenical News*, vol. 21, no. 4 (July–August 1936): 65–69.

Hall, Stuart. "New Ethnicities." *ICA Documents* no. 7, Institute of Contemporary Arts [London], 1988: 27–31.

Isenberg, Andrew C. "The California Gold Rush, The West, and The Nation." *Reviews in American History* vol. 29, no. 1 (March 2001): 62–71.

Linenthal, Edward T. "Nostalgia for Clarity: The Memory of Patton." *Studies in Popular Culture* 5 (1982), pp. 72–79.

Mann, Michael. "The Dark Side of Democracy: The Modern Tradition of Ethnic and Political Cleansing." *New Left Review* 235 (May–June 1999): 18–45.

Mayer, Arno J. "Memory and History: On the Poverty of Remembering and Forgetting the Judeocide." *Radical History Review* 56 (1993): 5–20.

Millikan, Robert. "The New Opportunity in Science." *Science* 26 (September 1919): 285–297.
Millikan, Robert. "The Practical Value of Pure Science." *Science* 4 (January 1924): 7–10.
Platt, Tony. "Desegregating Multiculturalism: Problems in the Theory and Pedagogy of Diversity Education." *Social Justice,* vol. 29, no. 4 (2002): 41–46.
Platt, Tony. "To Die For." *Exquisite Corpse* 58 (July 1996): 7–9.
Platt, Tony, and O'Leary, Cecilia. "Patriot Acts." *Social Justice,* vol. 30, no. 1 (2003): 5–21.
Popenoe, Paul. "The German Sterilization Law." *Journal of Heredity* vol. 25, no. 7 (July 1934): 257–260.
Shapiro, Edward S. "The Friendly University: Jews in Academia Since World War II." *Judaism: A Quarterly Journal of Jewish Life and Thought* (22 June 1997).
Stern, Alexandra Minna. "Buildings, Boundaries, and Blood: Medicalization and Nation-Building on the U.S.-Mexico Border, 1910–1930." *Hispanic American Historical Review* vol. 79, no. 1 (1999): 41–81.

Newspapers and Magazines

Agence France Presse. "Nuremberg Laws to Go on Display for the First Time." *Agence France Presse,* 26 June 1999.
Armstrong, Marion. "Tragic Tyrant." *Christian Century,* 10 April 1970, p. 455.
Associated Press. "Hitler Accuses Lithuanians of Torturing Nazis." *Sacramento Bee* 16 September 1935, p. 1.
Associated Press. "Original Text of Nuremberg Laws to Be Exhibited for First Time." *Associated Press,* 27 June 1999.
Bates, James. "Mark Willes to Head Times Mirror Media: Chairman Robert Erburu to Retire." *Los Angeles Times,* 2 May 1995.
Burchardi, Dr. K. "Why Hitler Says: 'Sterilize the Unfit!'" *Los Angeles Times,* 11 August 1935.
Buruma, Ian. "The Joys and Perils of Victimhood." *New York Review of Books,* 8 April 1999, pp. 4–9.
Cameron, Tom. "Los Angeles Conquered by Charm of Warriors." *Los Angeles Times,* 10 June 1945.
Cameron, Tom. "Suburbs Cheer Patton, Doolittle." *Los Angeles Times,* 11 June 1945.
Canby, Vincent. "Patton." *New York Times,* 3 February 1970, p. 128.
Cintron, Humberto. "An Interview with Piri Thomas." *Forkroads,* Fall 1995.
Clark, Robert. "Research Shangri-La." *Westways,* January 1943, pp. 22–23.
Cochrane, Walter. "Patton Explains 3rd's Tactics in Europe War." *Los Angeles Times,* 12 June 1945.
Colvin, Richard Lee. "School Segregation Is Growing, Report Finds." *Los Angeles Times,* 12 June 1999.
Creel, George. "Patton at the Pay-Off." *Collier's,* 13 January 1945.
Daniel, Raymond. "Patton Belittles Denazification; Holds Rebuilding More Important." *New York Times,* 23 September 1945, p. 26.
Dannenberg, Martin. "The Discovery at Eischätt." Letter to *Washington Post,* 17 July 1999.

Driscoll, Joseph. "Nuernberg Set of Racial Laws in U.S. Hands." *New York Herald Tribune*, 1 May 1945.

Dutka, Elaine. "Hitler Papers Held Since '45 by Huntington to Go on Display." *Los Angeles Times*, 26 June 1999, p. 1.

Field, John. "Patton of the Armored Force." *Life*, 30 November 1942, pp. 113–121.

Film Quarterly. "Patton." *Film Quarterly*, Summer 1970.

Finz, Stacy. "Race a Factor in Slaying of Mail Carrier." *San Francisco Chronicle*, 13 August 1999, p. 1.

Goodman, Tim. "Los Angeles Is Just a Factory Town." *San Francisco Chronicle*, 28 January 2001, Datebook, p. 44.

Halsey, Ashley. "Ancestral Gray Cloud over Patton." *American History Illustrated*, March 1984, pp. 42–48.

Haskell, Kari. "The Present as Past: A 2099 Retrospective." *New York Times*, 26 December 1999, Week in Review, p. 5.

Hoffman, Eva. "The Uses of Hell." *The New York Review of Books,* 9 March 2000.

Hogaboom, Winfield. "George S. Patton, Jr. Soldier, Diplomat, Poet." *Los Angeles Graphic*, 23 June 1917, p. 5.

Hogue, Fred. "Huntington's Monument Unmatched in World." *Los Angeles Times*, 29 May 1927.

Honan, William H. "Court Considers Ownership of Seized Hitler Paintings." *New York Times*, 8 May 2001, p. B1.

Images du Monde. "Le Parchemin de Franck Perls," *Images du Monde*, 15 May 1945.

Katzin, Donna. "The Jews of Cuba." *The Nation*, 25 May 1974, pp. 658–660.

Kimmelman, Michael. "Museums in a Quandary: Where Are the Ideals?" *New York Times*, 26 August 2001, Arts, p. 1.

Kimmelman, Michael. "Out of Minimalism: Monuments to Memory." *New York Times*, 13 January 2002, Arts, p. 1.

Kuntz, Tom. "On Display in Los Angeles: Legal Foreshadowing of Nazi Horror." *New York Times*, 4 July 1999.

Lapham, Lewis. "Cloak and Gown." *Los Angeles Times Book Review*, 9 April 2000.

Lewis, Neil A. "Genocide, as Defined Since 1951 by a U.N. Treaty." *New York Times* 31 March 1999, p. 11.

Loomis, Carol J. "The Inside Story of Warren Buffett." *Fortune,* 11 April 1988, pp. 26–34.

Loper, Mary Lou. "A Leading Lady in the Performing Arts Voluntarism." *Los Angeles Times*, 1 November 1990.

Los Angeles Business Journal. "In: Skirball Center, Out: Getty Center." 31 December 2001 to 6 January 2002.

Los Angeles Times. "Army Exhibit Displayed." 21 January 1945.

Los Angeles Times. "Caltech May Get Foundation Fund." 21 November 1943.

Los Angeles Times. "Earle Jorgensen, Wealthy Reagan Confidant, Dies." 13 August 1999.

Los Angeles Times. "Generals Will Make Southland Tour Today." 10 June 1945.

Los Angeles Times. "Gen. Patton Criticized for Language in Public." 18 June 1945.

Los Angeles Times. "Gen. Patton Urged for Cabinet Post." 22 July 1945.

Los Angeles Times. "His Pastor Says Patton May Think War Certain." 16 July 1945.

Los Angeles Times. "History of U.S. Army Depicted at Library." 18 March 1945.

Los Angeles Times. "Library Exhibits Japs' Duplicity Back in '53." 1 February 1944.

Los Angeles Times. "Library Receives Book from Patton." 6 May 1945.

Los Angeles Times. "Library Trust Board Formed." 9 April 1922.

Los Angeles Times. "Millikan Raps New Deal." 7 October 1936.

Los Angeles Times. "Millikan Tells School Views." 7 May 1938.

Los Angeles Times. "Millikan Urges World Police Force for Preserving Peace." 16 October 1942.

Los Angeles Times. "Pasadena Hears W.R.A. Director Defend Policies." 30 September 1944.

Los Angeles Times. "Patton Talks with Truman, Says He's Just 'One-Gun Man.'" 14 June 1945.

Los Angeles Times. "Patton Worships in Church Where He Was Baptized." 11 June 1945.

Los Angeles Times. "Sen. Knowland and Millikan to Aid Nixon Drive." 10 September 1950.

Los Angeles Times. "Students Hear Millikan Rap Thursday Pension Plan." 27 September 1938.

Los Angeles Times. "U.N. Best Hope, Millikan Says." 30 January 1951.

Los Angeles Times. "V.F.W. Leader Testifies Before Assembly Group." 10 December 1943.

Lyman, Rick. "What's Doing in Pasadena." *New York Times*, 9 December 2001, Travel, p. 15.

Mackay, Neil. "Found: Hitler's Blueprint for the Holocaust." *The Sunday Herald*, 27 June 1999.

McWilliams, Carey. "Racism on the West Coast." *New Republic* 110 (29 May 1944), pp. 732–733; *New Republic* 110 (12 June 1944), pp. 784–786.

Muchnic, Suzanne. "You Don't Have to Be Jewish…" *Los Angeles Times,* 7 September 2003, p. E65.

New York Times. "Asks Negro Sterilization: Germany Strikes at Children Left Behind by French Colonials." 8 February 1934.

New York Times. "Dr. Gebhard Is Honored." 25 August 1934.

New York Times. "Frank Perls Dies; Coast Art Dealer." *New York Times,* 10 February 1975.

New York Times. "Nazis Issue Rules of Choices of Wife." 25 August 1934.

Newsweek. "Guts and Gaffe." 8 May 1944, p. 26.

Newsweek. "Patton's Prayer." 29 January 1945, p. 76.

O'Connor, Anne-Marie. "Jewish Museum to Display Hitler's Nuremberg Laws." *Los Angeles Times*, 29 June 1999, p. B3.

Painton, Frederick C. "Old Man of Battle." *Reader's Digest*, September 1943, pp. 8–12.

Palmer, Kyle. "Huntington's Gift Praised." *Los Angeles Times*, 12 May 1923, p. 2.

Pasadena Star-News. "Health Data Exhibited." *Pasadena Star-News,* 4 September 1934.

Patton, George S., Jr. "Fear." *Cosmopolitan*, May 1945, p. 37.

Patton, George S., Jr. "God of Battles." *Women's Home Companion*, November 1943, p. 19.

Playboy. "Interview with George C. Scott." *Playboy*, December 1980.

Reed, Rex. "Rex Reed at the Movies." *Holiday*, April 1970, p. 25.

Reisberg, Leo. "A Top University Wonders Why It Has No Black Freshmen." *Chronicle of Higher Education*, 28 April 2000, pp. 52–55.

Russell, Francis. "Pistol Packin' Patton." *National Review*, 28 July 1970, p. 798.

San Marino Tribune. "Mein Kampf, Gift from Patton, Arrives at Huntington Library." 7 June 1945.

Sebald, W. G. "An Attempt at Restitution." *The New Yorker*, 20–27 December 2004, pp. 110–114.

Sebald, W. G. "A Natural History of Destruction." *The New Yorker*, 4 November 2002, pp. 66–77.

Sengupta, Somini. "Historic Images of Hate, In a Compelling Display." *New York Times*, 24 January 2000, p. 23.

Shane, Ted. "These Are the Generals—Patton." *The Saturday Evening Post*, 6 February 1943, p. 19.

Sidey, Hugh. "Anybody See Patton?" *Life*, 19 June 1970, p. 28.

Sight and Sound. "Patton: Lust for Glory." Summer 1970.

Smith, Roberta. "An Ugly Legacy Lives On, Its Glare Unsoftened by Age." *New York Times* 13 January 2000, p. B1.

Solnit, Rebecca. "Check Out the Parking Lot." *London Review of Books*, 8 July 2004, pp. 32–33.

Star News. "Patton Sister Anne Dies in San Marino." 15 March 1971.

Sunset. "Bright Stars." August 1919, p. 45.

The Times. "The Nuremberg Laws Against Jews." 1 May 1945.

The Watchman. "Patton Urged as Candidate." *Los Angeles Times*, 11 October 1945.

Time. "Little Man, Big Doings." 23 September 1935, p. 22.

Time. "Old Blood and Guts." 9 February 1970, p. 78.

Tolischus, Otto D. "Reich Adopts Swastika as Nation's Official Flag: Hitler's Reply to 'Insult.'" *New York Times*, 16 September 1935, p. 1.

Tugend, Tom. "Huntington Bound." *The Jewish Journal of Greater Los Angeles*, 9 March 2001: 15–16.

Tugend, Tom. "In Their Rightful Place." *The Jewish Journal of Greater Los Angeles*, 2–8 July 1999.

Wagner, Rob. "Los Angeles—Powerhouse of Race-Baiting." *Script*, 15 July 1944.

Waxman, Sharon. "A Key Nazi Document Surfaces." *International Herald Tribune*, 28 June 1999, p. 2.

Waxman, Sharon. "Hidden History of the Nazi Laws: Nuremberg Document to Be Shown After 54 Years in Museum Vault." *Washington Post*, 26 June 1999, p. 1.

Waxman, Sharon. "Judgment at Pasadena," *Washington Post,* 16 March 2000.

Weinraub, Bernard. "Signed Nuremberg Laws to Go on View." *New York Times*, 26 June 1999, p. B12.

Wood, Daniel B. "Some Dark Words of History Come to Light." *Christian Science Monitor*, 1 July 1999.

Word for Word. "On Display in Los Angeles: Legal Foreshadowing of Nazi Horror." *New York Times*, 4 July 1999, Week in Review, p. 7.

Zeman, Ray. "Thousands Hail Heroes; Generals' Deeds Reborn in Coliseum Pageantry." *Los Angeles Times*, 10 June 1945.

Zielbauer, Paul. "Found in a Clutter, a Relic of Lincoln's Death." *New York Times*, 5 July 2001.

Web Sites

Black, Allida, and Hopkins, June (eds.), "Teaching Eleanor Roosevelt." *www.nps.gov/elro/glossary.htm*

Higher Superior Court of Nuremberg. *www.justiz.bayern.de/olgn*

Katzenberger. *www.geocities.com/Heartland/Pointe/6230*

Kelly, Maura. "Revisions and a Revelation." 26 June 1999, *www.slate.msn*

Nuremberg. *www.nuernberg.de/tourismus*

Public Broadcasting System. American Experience, *www.pbsorg/wgbh/amex*

Rieger, Susanne, and Jochem, Gerhard. Nuremberg. *www.rijo-research.de*

Skirball Cultural Center. *www.skirball.com*

Toller, Ernst. *www.spartacus.schoolnet.co.uk/FWWtoller.htm*

United States Holocaust Memorial Museum. *www.ushmm.org*

Yizkor Book Project. *www.jewishgen.org/yizkor/Nuremberg*

Index

NAME INDEX

Alfi, Sue, 26, 29, 178
Alfi, Yossi, 29, 30, 178
Allen, James, 121
Allison, Dave, 119
Amman, Max, 16–17
Anzaldúa, Gloria, 177
Ayer, Beatrice Banning, *see* Patton,
    Beatrice
Ayer, Frederick, 117
Ayer, Fred, Jr., 35, 120

Babcock, Catherine, 12, 23, 154, 155
Bard, Thomas R, 116
Barellet, Georges, 51
Baruch, Bernard, 135
Bauman, Zygmunt, 27, 32, 44, 80
Belloc, Hilaire, 28
Benjamin, Judah, 30
Benny, Jack, 102
Berenbaum, Michael, 11, 12, 13, 35
Berlin, Ira, 174
Berlin, Walter, 74, 81
Biddle, Francis, 87
Biddle, George, 87, 92, 99
Black, Edwin, 67
Bliss, Anthony, 114
Bliss, Carey, 115, 143, 144, 145, 146
Bliss, Leslie, 105–106, 115, 140
Blodgett, Peter, 150, 151
Blomberg, Werner von, 5–6, 79
Blum, Leon, 67
Blumenson, Martin,
    on Patton and Bonus Marchers, 118
    on Patton's anti-Semitism, 34, 116
    on Patton as celebrity, 19, 135
    on Patton's visit to Los Angeles, 36

Bock, Gisela, 76
Bradsher, Greg, 36
Brown, Edmund, 64
Burchardi, K., 62
Byatt, A. S., 150

Cardenas, Julio, 138
Carreño, Mario, 85
Chandler, Harry, 57
Chyet, Stanley, 153, 165, 167–168
Cleland, Robert, 122, 128–129
Cole, Hugh, 34, 103, 138
Conley, Elmo, 147
Cooper, Abraham, 35
Craig, Louis, 135
Crocker, Charles, 110
Crotty, Homer, 147–148

Daniels, Edith, 25, 28–29, 175–176
Daniels, Sam, 25
Dannenberg, Martin,
    as intelligence officer, 91–94
    growing up in Baltimore, 42–43, 92,
    94
    his letter to *Washington Post*, 36–37
    in Skirball exhibition, 170
    in U.S. Army, 36, 73, 91–94
    retrieval of Nuremberg Laws, 36–38,
    94–100
    views about Patton, 138
    visit to the Skirball, 163–164
Darrieux, Danielle, 48
Daumier, Honoré, 143
Davis, Bette, 102
D'Este, Carlo, 35, 139
Didion, Joan, 2

Diner, Hasia, 35
Dock, George, 59
Doolittle, Jimmy, 102
Douglas, Kirk, 48
Driscoll, Joseph, 98
Du Bois, W. E. B., 176
Duggan, Stephen, 127
Dukakis, Michael, 33
Dunn, William (Billy), 111, 112

Edwards, Jonathan, 110
Einstein, Albert, 19, 126–127, 155, 167
Eisenhower, Dwight D.,
    as portrayed during World War II, 19
    at end of the war, 137
    relationship with Patton, 90–91, 101,
    106, 135, 139
    visits concentration camps, 132, 134
Ellis, Havelock, 26
Emman, Max, *see* Amman, Max
Engels, Frederick, 26
Epstein, Paul, 126
Erburu, Robert, 115, 152

Farago, Ladislas, 101
Ferber, Max, 25
Ferrand, Max, 114
Flatow, Elise, 50, 85, 86
Fleming, Arthur, 19
Ford, Jack, 14
Fowler, William, 123
Frank, Leo, 121
Frazier, E. Franklin, 179
Frick, Wilhelm,
    as Hitler's Minister of Interior, 47
    role in enactment of Nuremberg Laws,
    6–9, 76–79
    role in enactment of Sterilization Law,
    59
    views about display of original
    Nuremberg Laws, 83
    views about race, 59, 62–63, 70–71

Friedlander, Henry, 76
Friedländer, Saul, 5, 11, 13, 14, 15, 23
Fussell, Paul, 139

Gainsborough, Thomas, 1
Galton, Francis, 56
Garland, Judy, 102
Gassol, Ventura, 85–86
Gebhard, Bruno, 61–62
Gersicoff, Leslie, 13
Gilroy, Paul, 109
Glide, Mary, 63
Goebbels, Joseph, 47, 75
Goethe, Charles M.,
    as eugenics leader, 55, 63–70, 121
    background of, 63
    honors received by, 63–64, 66
    racial views of, 55, 63–64, 121, 123,
    128–129, 130
    relationship to California State
    University, Sacramento, 55, 63–66
    relationship to Human Betterment
    Foundation, 57, 122
    views about Jews, 67, 70
    visits to Germany, 59, 67
    support of Nazi eugenics, 59–60,
    67–70, 130
Goethe, Henry, 65
Gordon, Jean, 141
Göring, Hermann, 6, 79, 104
Gosney, Ezra S., 57, 58, 59, 130–131
Grant, Ulysses, 141
Griffin, Marvin, 65
Gundersheimer, Werner, 151
Günther, Hans, 61
Gürtner, Franz, 8–9, 79
Gütt, Arthur, 58, 61

Hale, George Ellery, 111–114
Hammer, Armand, 149
Hanna, Phil Townsend, 128
Hanson, Victor, 133

Harrison, Earl, 134
Hatch, Alden, 33
Hecht, Hans, 127
Hellman, Isaias, 151
Hereford, Margaret, 119
Herscher, Uri,
    as president of Skirball Cultural
    Center, 4, 23
    relationship with the Huntington,
    152–154, 159
    role in exhibition of Nuremberg Laws,
    12, 14–15, 161–165
    views about General Patton, 22, 35–36,
    162–163
    vision of the Skirball Cultural Center,
    39–40, 165–169
Hertrich, William, 115
Hess, Rudolf, 8–9, 47, 79, 83
Hessen, Ludwig von, 47
Hilberg, Raul, 5, 72, 76, 77, 78
Hitler, Adolf,
    and Sterilization Law, 62, 68
    and World War II, 19
    as artist, 49
    as Nazi leader, 48, 59, 67–68, 74
    as vegetarian, 47, 67
    at 1935 Nuremberg Rally, 75–80
    author of *Mein Kampf*, 5, 38, 118
    authorizing "mercy killings," 71
    on degeneracy of modern art, 44
    on the Blood Law, 81–82
    on the Jewish Question, 78–79
    racial views, 29, 62
    role in enactment of Nuremberg Laws,
    3, 5–9, 11, 6–8, 75–80
Hittell, John, 109
Hoffman, Eva, 25, 27, 28, 160, 177
Hoffman, Heinrich, 173
Hoover, Herbert,
    and Millikan, 122–123
    and Patton, 117
    and Stanford War Library, 138

    as Huntington trustee, 106–108, 114,
    147
    expertise on Nazism, 104
Hoover, J. Edgar, 89, 114
Hopkins, Mark, 110
Horner, Bernard J., 92, 98, 100
Hubble, Edwin, 114
Huntington, Arabella (Belle), 4, 111, 112,
    114
Huntington, Archer, 112, 123
Huntington, Collis, 4, 110
Huntington, Henry Edwards (Edward),
    as founder of Huntington Library, 4,
    22, 109–115, 143, 151
    as supporter of California Institute of
    Technology, 19
    death of, 21, 111
    relationship with Arabella (Belle)
    Huntington, 4, 111
    relationship with Patton family, 19–21,
    104, 116
Huntington, Howard, 112
Huntington, Samuel, 110
Huston, Walter, 52–53

Jackson, Frederick, 112
Jackson, Stonewall, 113
Jochem, Gerhard, 79, 155–156
Johnson, Donald, 100, 138–139
Johnson, Lyndon, 64
Johnson, Roswell Hill, 57
Jordan, David Starr, 57
Jutzi, Alan, 115, 142, 145, 146

Katzenberger, David, 74, 81
Katzenberger, Lehmann (Leo), 74, 81–82,
    121
Katzenberger, Max, 74, 81–82
Kenyatta, Jomo, 29
Kershaw, Ian, 5, 74, 75, 76, 77
Kevles, Daniel, 62, 127
Kirschner, Robert, 153, 154, 166, 170

Klein, Eric, 11
Koblik, Steven, 172
Koch, Oscar, 90, 118
Kolb, Bernhard, 74, 81
Koonz, Claudia, 58
Kühl, Stefan, 59
Kushner, Tony, 30

Lammers, Hans Heinrich, 82–83
Lapham, Lewis, 115
Laughlin, Harry, 57, 68
Laval, Pierre, 86
Lee, Robert E., 113, 119, 141
LeRoy, Mervyn, 102
Levi, Primo, 179
Levine, Lawrence, 113
Levy, Herbert, 127
Lewis, Oscar, 111
Liebknecht, Karl, 46
Linden, Herbert, 58
Linenthal, Edward, 117
Leonard, Elmore, 40
Loewenberg, Peter, 11
Long, Breckinridge, 52–53, 86
Long, Leo, 89
Lopate, Phillip, 30
Lorre, Peter, 48
Lösener, Bernhard, 77–78
Lovelace, Jonathan, 147
Lowenthal, David, 145, 180
Luce, Henry, 125
Luxemburg, Rosa, 46
Lyden, Jacki, 14

MacNeil, Robert, 166
Mann, Thomas, 45, 123–124
Marino, Andy, 51
Marshall, George, 91, 101
Martin, Benno, 81–83
Mason, Frank, 104
Matthau, Walter, 32
McArthur, Douglas, 117
McCarthy, Frank, 33, 101–102
McMahon, Brian, 133

McWilliams, Carey, 110
Medicus, Franz, 77
Mendel, Gregor, 144
Mengele, Josef, 130
Middlekauff, Robert, 145, 149
Miller, Arthur, 40
Millikan, Greta, 102–103, 107, 126
Millikan, Robert A.,
    as head of California Institute of
    Technology, 18–19, 122
    as Nobel Prize winner, 19
    as trustee of Huntington, 19, 112–114,
    140, 147
    attitude toward Jews, 104, 116, 126–
    127
    in Skirball exhibition of Nuremberg
    Laws, 161
    involvement in eugenics movement, 55
    legacy at the Huntington, 147–148
    photographed with General Patton, 18
    political views, 122–124
    racial views, 70, 113, 124–126, 129–
    131
    relationship with Human Betterment
    Foundation, 57, 70
    role in acquisition of Nuremberg Laws,
    18, 36, 102–104, 106–108
    ties to military, 123
Minnelli, Vincente, 48
Miranda, Carmen, 102
Mitchell, Thomas, 52
Moffett, William, 146
Morgenstern, Julian, 167
Morgenthau, Henry, 86, 134
Munch, Edvard, 45
Munro, William, 57, 106–107, 114,
    141–142, 147
Mussolini, Benito, 144

Nadich, Judah, 138
Nixon, Richard, 34, 65, 124

O'Brien, Margaret, 102
O'Connell, John, 135

O'Leary, Cecilia E.,
    as fellow at the Huntington, 1–3
    as researcher, 36–39, 155–156
    meeting with Martin Dannenberg, 37,
    42
    visit to the Skirball, 160
O'Melveny, John, 147
Oppenheimer, Robert, 126

Page, James, 57–58, 107, 114, 147
Parks, Rosa, 65
Patton, Anne (Nita), 103, 142
Patton, Beatrice (Ayer), 103, 117, 119–
    120, 135, 140–142
Patton, George S., Jr.,
    as a child, 20
    as historian, 103
    as liberator, 33
    as military strategist, 32, 91
    as public celebrity, 19, 32–33, 90, 102
    as subject of movie, 33–34
    as subject of research, 33
    as young man, 20–21, 116–117
    attitude toward communism, 89–90
    attitude toward Jews, 34–36, 132–135,
    162
    claim to Nuremberg Laws, 4, 12–16,
    36–37, 99–100, 136–139
    gift of Mein Kampf to the Huntington,
    17, 21, 38, 103–105, 140
    in England preparing for D-Day, 88
    in Skirball exhibition of Nuremberg
    Laws, 32, 160–165
    incident with Frank Perls in France,
    88–89
    Knutsford incident, 89–91
    political views, 109, 115–118, 122
    racial views, 118–122
    role in post-World War II Germany,
    89–90, 101, 130–135
    slapping incident, 90
    views about repression in post-World
    War I Germany, 46

    visit to Los Angeles area in 1945, 36,
    102–103
    visit to the Huntington in 1945, 18,
    102–106
    war loot, 106, 137–138, 172–173
    war poetry, 84, 102, 117
    witnesses destruction of Nuremberg,
    72–73
Patton, George S., Sr., 19, 20, 90,
    as trustee of the Huntington, 112, 113
    death of, 21
    racial views of, 113, 117
    relationship with Edward Huntington,
    19–20
    views about son's impetuousness, 90
Patton, George S., III, 142–143
Patton, Georgie, see Patton, George S., Jr.
Patton, Robert, 21, 116
Peale, Charles, 18
Pechstein, Max, 45
Perls, Frank R. (Franz, Dada),
    as art dealer in United States, 86–87
    as enemy alien in United States, 87
    as immigrant to the United States, 50
    as military intelligence interpreter, 37,
    88–89
    as owner of Los Angeles gallery, 53
    assigned to 203d Counter-Intelligence-
    Corps, 92–93
    death, 42
    education, 48
    family background, 43, 45
    in exile in Paris, 48–49
    in U.S. Army, 87–89, 100–101
    incident with General Patton, 88–89
    photographed with Picasso, 49
    political views, 46
    role in retrieval of Nuremberg Laws,
    37–38, 94–100
    seeking visas for parents, 50–53, 85
Perls, Hugo,
    background and career in Weimar
    Germany, 43–45

in exile in Paris, 49
marriage to Eugenie Söderberg, 86
marriage to Käte Kolker, 45
on Nazi propaganda, 82
political beliefs, 45–46
seeking visas for family, 86
Perls, Käte (Kolker),
    attitude to Nazism, 47
    denied visa to the United States, 53–54
    family background in Germany, 43–44
    imprisoned in Gurs, 50
    imprisoned in Hotel Bompard, 51–53
    in Cuba, 84–86
    in exile in Paris, 49
    in the United States, 86
    marriage to Hugo Perls, 45
    on the run in France, 50–54
    political beliefs, 45–46
    relationship with Ventura Gassol,
        85–86
Perls, Klaus, 50–54
Perls, Marianne, 42, 163
Perry, Matthew C., 144
Pershing, Jack, 119
Pfundtner, Hans, 77
Phillips, James, 100
Picasso, Pablo, 45, 48, 49, 51, 85
Pickens, Maxwell (Easy), 37, 42, 94, 96
Platt, Annie, 25
Platt, Anthony M. (Tony),
    academic career, 178–179
    as fellow at the Huntington, 1–3, 31,
        38
    as graduate student in Berkeley, 177–
        178
    childhood and upbringing in England,
        25–29, 42, 89, 175–179
    experiences as a Jew, 25–31, 38–39,
        42, 72, 175–179
    views about Charles M. Goethe, 63–65
    views about General Patton, 33
    visits to the Skirball, 40–41, 160–162
Platt, Bernard, 25

Platt, Daniel, 29
Platt, Eileen, 26, 29, 176
Platt, Monty, 26–27, 29, 89, 176
Platt, Rebecca, 30
Platt, Stephen (Steve), 26, 29
Platt, Susan, see Alfi, Sue
Popenoe, Paul,
    as eugenics researcher, 58, 70
    as supporter of Nazi eugenics, 60–61,
        70, 130
    involvement with Human Betterment
        Foundation, 57, 70, 122
    political views, 123–124
    racial views, 125
Priesand, Sally, 167

Quinn, Anthony, 48

Rauch, Hans, 83, 94–96
Reagan, Ronald, 32
Reed, Rex, 33
Ridge, Martin, 145
Riefenstahl, Leni, 75
Robertson, Mary, 115, 146, 152–153,
    156–157
Robinson, Edward G., 102
Robinson, Henry, 57, 112
Rohe, Mies van der, 45
Roosevelt, Eleanor, 52–5, 86
Roosevelt, Franklin D., 86, 118
Roosevelt, Theodore, 124
Rosenberg, Alfred, 83
Roth, Joseph, 30, 31, 45, 58, 82
Rothschild, Abraham, 74
Rothschild, Loren, 152
Royce, Josiah, 2
Rubinstein, Artur, 44
Russell, Bertrand, 26

Safdie, Moshe, 39, 163, 166, 170
Sandburg, Carl, x
Sartre, Jean-Paul, 178, 179
Schacht, Hjalmar, 77
Schad, Jasper, 145

Schad, Robert O., 115, 141–142, 145
Schirach, Baldur von, 47
Schlink, Bernhard, x
Schlosser, Robert, 144
Schneiderman, Rose, 167
Scott, George C., 33–34, 102
Sebald, W. G.,
    on memory, x, 1, 98, 171, 180–181
    on World War II, 27, 72
Segal, George, 175
Selwyn, Henry, 27
Sherman, William, 131
Shirer, William, 75, 76
Shusterman, Abraham, 98
Skotheim, Robert,
    as president of Huntington Library, 4,
    12, 14, 22–23, 149–151
    loan of Nuremberg Laws to Skirball,
    147, 151–159
    views about General Patton, 19, 22
    views about Nuremberg Laws, 4,
    12–15, 103, 136–137, 143, 171
Smiley, Jane, 150
Söderberg, Eugenie, 86
Solnit, Rebecca, 175
Speer, Albert, 47
Speer, David, 92
Spielberg, Steven, 27
Sproul, Robert, 126
Stanford, Leland, 110
Stauffenberg, Claus Schenk Graf von, 96,
    157
Steiger, Rod, 43
Stein, Joseph, 103
Sterling, J. E. Wallace, 147
Stillman, Richard, 139
Stimson, Henry, 134
Strauss, Levi, 167
Streicher, Julius, 74, 76, 77, 81
Stuckart, Wilhelm, 77–78
Sutro, Adolph, 151

Tan, Amy, 150

Terman, Lewis, 57
Thomas, Piri, 27, 177
Thurmond, Strom, 65
Till, Emmett, 65
Toller, Ernst, 46–47
Totten, Ruth Ellen Patton, 119, 142, 143
Truman, Harry S., 101, 104, 134

Udall, Stewart, 64

Van der Rohe, Mies, 45
Van Fleet, James A.,
    and General Patton, 15, 36, 136, 138–
    139, 158
    and III Corps, 91
Van Gogh, Vincent, 48
Verschuer, Otmar Freiherr von, 61, 69–70,
    130

Wagner, Gerhard, 61, 77–78
Walter, Bruno, 45
Wardwell, H. P., 91, 100
Warren, Earl, 64
Washington, George, 18, 141
Waxman, Sharon, 13, 22, 36, 154, 163
Welles, Sumner, 53
Wendland, Charles W., 17
West, Guy, 63
West, Nathaniel, 38
Westinghouse, George, 124
White, Margaret Bourke, 19, 133
Wilbur, Ray Lyman, 127
Wilder, Billy, 48, 86–87
Wilson, Benjamin D. (Don Benito), 19,
    119
Wilson, Fred, 173–174
Wilson, Woodrow, 53, 117
Wise, Isaac Mayer, 39
Woodward, Daniel, 146

Zanuck, Darryl, 34
Zeidberg, David, 13–15, 22, 146–147,
    152–156
Zinn, Howard, 31

SUBJECT INDEX

Advisory Commission on Holocaust Assets in the United States, 152–153, 157
American Association of Museums, 153, 172–174
amnesia, *see* remembrance
anticommunism, 46, 89–90, 123–124, 135
anti-Semitism,
   and New Left, 30
   and the Huntington's reputation, 13, 38
   author's experiences with, 28–30
   in California, 110
   in Cuba, 84–85
   in England, 27–28
   in France, 50–54
   in Nazi Germany, 5, 47–48, 67, 75–82
   in United States, 28, 30, 86, 116
   in worldview of George S. Patton, Jr., 34–36, 132–135, 162
   in worldview of Robert A. Millikan, 126–127
apartheid, 29

Birth of a Nation, 119
Blood Law, *see* Nuremberg Laws

California,
   as hinterlands, 4
   ethnic cleansing in, 180
   genocidal policies in, 180
   ghettoes in, 180
   Gold Rush, 3, 150
   Indian Wars, 3
   narratives of, 2–3, 128, 180–181
   reservations in, 180
California Academy of Sciences, 64
California Institute of Technology,
   hosts Albert Einstein, 19, 126–127
   involvement in military-industrial complex, 123, 127
   relationship to Human Betterment Foundation, 57–58
   under Robert Millikan's leadership, 18–19
California State University, Sacramento, 55, 63–64, 66
Caltech, *see* California Institute of Technology
Camp Ritchie, 88
Civic Betterment Association, 130
Committee of Experts on Population and Racial Policy, *see* Nazi party
Commonwealth Club of California, 65
concentration camps,
   Auschwitz, 50
   Bompard, 51
   Buchenwald, 132–133
   Dachau, 48, 54
   Gurs, 50
Counter-Intelligence Corps, *see* Military Intelligence
Cuba, 84–86

Dead Sea Scrolls, 3, 143–144
Displaced Persons (DP's), 34, 134–135

Eichstätt, 36, 83, 91–98
Emergency Committee in Aid of Displaced Foreign Scholars, 127
Emergency Rescue Committee (ERC), 51–53
enemy aliens, 87
eugenic science, *see* eugenics
eugenics,
   in California, 57–70
   in Nazi Germany, 58–63
   in United States, 55–56
   promoted by Charles C. Goethe, 63–70
   promoted by Human Betterment Foundation, 57–70
   racial assumptions of, 56, 70–71
   various tendencies within, 56
Eugenics Record Office, 56–57

Eugenics Research Association, 63, 65, 69
Eugenics Society of Northern California, 65
exhibitions
    at the Huntington, 143–144, 150–151
    at the Skirball, 166–169
    of holocaust, 27–28
    of lynching, 23
    of *Mein Kampf*, 4, 17, 41, 170
    of Nuremberg Laws, 3–5, 82–83, 160–165, 169–171
    of slavery, 23

Golden Gate Park, San Francisco, 64

Hebrew Union College, 39
history, *see* public history
holocaust,
    author's memory of, 25
    first usage of term, 27
    historical interpretations of, 27–28
    memorialized, 27–28, 32, 103, 169
    survivors' silence about, 27
Human Betterment Foundation, *see* eugenics
Huntington Land and Improvement Company, 20, 129–130
Huntington Library,
    as company village, 109–115
    handling of Nuremberg Laws, 3–4, 14, 31, 103–108, 136–147, 152–159
    Henry Edwards (Edward) Huntington's vision of, 4, 110–115
    its lending policies, 150
    organizational culture, 109–115, 127–131
    origins and development of, 1–2, 110–115
    programs of, 3, 143–144
    racial worldview of, 122–129
    reform currents within, 147–151
    relationship with Patton family, 19–22, 140–143
    reputation for anti-Semitism, 38
    under Koblik presidency, 172
    under Skotheim presidency, 12, 149–154
    visited by General Patton, 102–103

Immigration Study Commission, 65
International Federation of Eugenic Organizations, 69
International Military Tribunal, *see* Nuremberg, War Crimes Tribunal

Jewish Museum, New York, 169–170
Jewish Question, *see* anti-Semitism
Jews, *see* Judaism and anti-Semitism
Joint Chiefs of Staff, 137
Judaism,
    and Christian converts, 43–44, 45–46
    and intermarriage, 28–29, 44
    author's relationship to, 25–31, 38, 40–41, 42–43, 175–179
    in academia, 178
    in Cuba, 84–86
    in England, 27, 175–176
    in France, 48–49
    in Nazi Germany, 43–54
    in New Left, 30
    in Nuremberg, 73–75, 80–82
    in United States, 42–43, 88, 110, 165, 176–179
    in Weimar Germany, 43–48

Kristallnacht, 67, 70, 81
Ku Klux Klan, 121

Law for the Prevention of Genetically Diseased Offspring (Sterilization Law), 59–62
Leo Baeck Institute, 43
Library of Congress, 142
loot, *see* war loot
Los Angeles, 102, 110–111, 151, 165, 171
lynching, 121

Manchester, England, 25–26
Manchester Grammar School, 28

media,
coverage of enactment of Nuremberg
Laws, 79
images of General Patton, 19, 32–34,
102, 133, 141
interest in Nuremberg Laws, 4–5,
12–15, 22–23, 98–99, 154–158
Mein Kampf,
and Jews, 5, 15–17, 21
displayed at the Skirball, 41, 153, 170
donated to the Huntington, 4, 140, 143
studied by Patton, 118
memory, *see* remembrance
"mercy killings," *see* Nazi party
Military Intelligence, *see* United States
Army
miscegenation, 125
museums,
and ethical responsibilities, 173–174
and Jewish history, 40, 166–170
as sites of controversy, 173–174, 181
as sites of progress, 112–113
as sites of sentimentality, 180

National Socialist German Workers party,
see Nazi party
Nazi party
and Marital Health Law, 76
and "mercy killings," 11, 71
and National Socialist German
Students' League, 47
anti-Semitic activism, 76–82
Committee of Experts on Population
and Racial Policy, 6, 59
rallies and propaganda, 74–82
rise to power, 47–48
views about "racial science," 55,
58–63
Nordic League, 130
Nuremberg,
as medieval city, 73
as repository of Nazi icons, 82–83
as site of enactment of Nuremberg

Laws, 72, 75–80
as site of Reich Party rallies, 74–75
as site of War Crimes Tribunal, 35, 74
bombed during World War II, 72–73,
91
Jewish residents of, 73–74, 81–82
Nuremberg Laws,
acquired by the Huntington, 3–4,
17–18, 103
as historical icon, 5, 11–12, 15, 23, 79
as Nazi icon, 82–83
as object of media attention, 4–5,
12–15, 22–23, 98–99, 154–158
bureaucratic implementation of, 44
commercial value of, 11
debates about purposes of, 5, 11, 76,
79–80
displayed at the Skirball, 15, 40–41,
160–165
Law for the Protection of German
Blood and Honor (Blood Law), 5,
9–11, 75–80
loaned to the Skirball, 12, 152–159
looted by General Patton, 4, 15–16,
104, 137–139
provenance of, 138–147
Reich Citizenship Law, 5, 7, 79–80
Reich Flag Law, 5–6, 77, 79–80
retrieved by U.S. Army, 36–38, 83,
91–97

origins stories, 2, 19, 109, 159

Pacific Coast Committee on American
Principles and Fair Play, 126
Palestine, 30
Pasadena, 21, 22, 55, 114, 151
Pasadena Music and Art Association, 111
patriotism, 3
Patton, 33–34
Perls Galleries, New York, 50, 86
Perls Gallery, Los Angeles, 53, 87
Prairie Creek Redwoods State Park, 64
Protocols of the Elders of Zion, 120

public history, 1, 173–174, 179–181
racial hygiene, *see* eugenics
racial science, *see* eugenics
racism,
    and anti-racism, 29, 178–179
    and Nordic internationalism, 63–70,
    130
    in England, 29
    in Germany, 60–61, 70
    in United States, 64–65, 70, 110, 113,
    116–131
refugees from nazism, 51–54
Reich Party Congress of Freedom, 75
Reichstag, 5, 48, 75
remembrance, 2, 32, 140, 162, 179–181

Sacramento State University, *see*
    California State University,
    Sacramento
San Marino
    as home of Patton family, 21, 113
    as site of the Huntington, 1, 13, 111–
    112, 114, 151
    as white city, 130
    visited by Patton, 102
Save-the-Redwoods League, 64
segregation, *see* racism
Skirball Cultural Center,
    and Americanization, 166–169
    architectural design, 39
    core exhibition in, 166–169
    holocaust memorial at, 169–170
    Nuremberg Laws exhibition at, 3–4,
    31–32, 40–41, 153–154, 160–165
    organizational culture of, 39–40
    origins and development of, 39–40,
    165, 167
    under Herscher's leadership, 39–40,
    165–169
    visited by the author, 40–41, 170–171
Smithsonian Art Archives, 43
Southern California, 19, 57, 102, 109–
    110, 113
Spartakist Rising, 46

sterilization, 56–63
Sterilization Law, *see* Law for the
    Prevention of Genetically Diseased
    Offspring
Supreme Headquarters Allied
    Expeditionary Force (SHAEF), 37,
    92, 100, 137, 139

The Huntington, *see* Huntington Library
The Huntington Library, Art Collections,
    and Botanical Gardens, *see*
    Huntington Library

United States Army
    Counter-Intelligence Corps, 36–37,
    91–97, 101
    during World War II, 87–91
    Military Intelligence, 88–89, 100–101
    role of General Patton in, 32–36,
    88–91, 120, 132–135, 137–139
    under Eisenhower's leadership, 19,
    90–91, 101, 132–135, 137–139
United States Holocaust Memorial
    Museum, 23, 169

Vichy regime, 50
Virginia Military Institute, 102, 116, 119

War Crimes Tribunal, *see* Nuremberg
war loot, 137–139
War Refugee Board, 86
West Point, 20, 116

Zeppelinfeld, 75
zionism, 26

About the Authors

Tony Platt is professor emeritus at California State University, Sacramento, where he has taught since 1977. Previously, he taught at U.C. Berkeley and the University of Chicago. His books include *The Child Savers: The Invention of Delinquency* (1969), *The Politics of Riot Commissions, 1917–1970* (1971), and *E. Franklin Frazier Reconsidered* (1991). His essays have appeared in the *Los Angeles Times*, *Monthly Review*, *Z Magazine*, *Souls*, and *Social Justice*. He is a founding member of the journal *Social Justice*.

Cecilia O'Leary received her Ph.D. from U.C. Berkeley and is now a professor of American History at California State University, Monterey Bay. Previously, she worked as a Landmarks Scholar and consultant at the National Museum of American History, Smithsonian Institution, Washington, D.C. She is the author of *To Die For: The Paradox of American Patriotism* (Princeton University Press, 1999) and a member of the editorial board of *Social Justice*, for which she edited a special issue on *New Pedagogies for Social Change*.